E. A. J. HONIGMANN, J. R. MULRYNE
R. L. SMALLWOOD and PETER CORBIN general editors

For over thirty years *The Revels Plays* have offered the most authoritative editions of Elizabethan and Jacobean plays by authors other than Shakespeare. The *Companion Library* provides a fuller background to the main series by publishing worthwhile dramatic and non-dramatic material that will be essential for the serious student of the period.

John Weever HONIGMANN
Rare Sir William Davenant EDMOND
Art made tongue-tied by authority CLARE
The Oldcastle controversy: Sir John Oldcastle, Part I,
and The Famous Victories of Henry V CORBIN, SEDGE
Brawl ridiculous: Swordfighting in Shakespeare's plays EDELMAN
Playhouse wills 1558–1642 HONIGMANN, BROCK
A textual companion to Doctor Faustus RASMUSSEN
Three Renaissance travel plays ed. PARR

All titles published in the USA by St. Martin's Press

Thomas Heywood

Three marriage plays

THE REVELS PLAYS COMPANION LIBRARY

Thomas Heywood
Three marriage plays

THE WISE-WOMAN OF HOGSDON
THE ENGLISH TRAVELLER
THE CAPTIVES

edited by Paul Merchant

Manchester University Press
Manchester and New York

distributed exclusively in the USA and Canada by St. Martin's Press

published by
MANCHESTER UNIVERSITY PRESS
Oxford Road, Manchester M13 9PL, UK
and Room 400, 175 Fifth Avenue
New York, NY 10010, USA

distributed exclusively in the USA and Canada
by ST. MARTIN'S PRESS, Inc.
175 Fifth Avenue, New York, NY 10010, USA

British Library Cataloguing-in-Publication data
A catalogue record for this book is available
from the British Library

Library of Congress Cataloging-in-Publication data
applied for

ISBN 0 7190 2221 5 *hardback*

Printed in Great Britain
by Biddles Ltd, Guildford and King's Lynn

CONTENTS

LIST OF ILLUSTRATIONS *page* vi

GENERAL EDITORS' PREFACE vii

PREFACE AND ACKNOWLEDGEMENTS viii

ABBREVIATIONS AND REFERENCES ix

INTRODUCTION

General 1

The Wise-woman of Hogsdon 5

The English Traveller 13

The Captives 19

Heywood in the twentieth century 26

A note on the texts 27

THE PLAYS

THE WISE-WOMAN OF HOGSDON 38

THE ENGLISH TRAVELLER 106

THE CAPTIVES OR THE LOST RECOVERED 187

Appendix: Authorial cuts in the *Captives* MS 266

LINEATION in Q *The Wise-woman of Hogsdon* and Q *The English Traveller* and MS *The Captives* 276

PRESS-CORRECTIONS in Q *The Wise-woman of Hogsdon* AND Q *The English Traveller* 279

ILLUSTRATIONS

Title page of the 1638 quarto of *The Wise-woman of Hogsdon* *page* 37

Title page of the 1633 quarto of *The English Traveller* 105

The first page of Heywood's manuscript of *The Captives* (BM MS Egerton 1994, fol. 52) 186

Reproduced by kind permission of the British Library

GENERAL EDITORS' PREFACE

Since the late 1950s the series known as the Revels Plays has provided for students of the English Renaissance drama carefully edited texts of the major Elizabethan and Jacobean plays. The series now includes some of the best known drama of the period and has continued to expand, both within its original field and, to a lesser extent, beyond it, to include some important plays from the earlier Tudor and from the Restoration periods. The Revels Plays Companion Library is intended to further this expansion and to allow for new developments.

The aim of the Companion Library is to provide students of the Elizabethan and Jacobean drama with a fuller sense of its background and context. The series includes volumes of a variety of kinds. Small collections of plays, by a single author or concerned with a single theme and edited in accordance with the principles of textual modernisation of the Revels Plays, offer a wider range of drama than the main series can include. Together with editions of masques, pageants, and the nondramatic work of Elizabethan and Jacobean playwrights, these volumes make it possible, within the overall Revels enterprise, to examine the achievement of the major dramatists from a broader perspective. Other volumes provide a fuller context for the plays of the period by offering new collections of documentary evidence on Elizabethan theatrical conditions and on the performance of plays during that period and later. A third aim of the series is to offer modern critical interpretation, in the form of collections of essays or of monographs, of the dramatic achievement of the English Renaissance.

So wide a range of material necessarily precludes the standard format and uniform general editorial control which is possible in the original series of Revels Plays. To a considerable extent, therefore, treatment and approach are determined by the needs and intentions of individual volume editors. Within this rather ampler area, however, we hope that the Companion Library maintains the standards of scholarship which have for so long characterised the Revels Plays, and that it offers a useful enlargement of the work of the series in preserving, illuminating, and celebrating the drama of Elizabethan and Jacobean England.

E. A. J. Honigmann
J. R. Mulryne
R. L. Smallwood
Peter Corbin

PREFACE AND ACKNOWLEDGEMENTS

In preparing this edition of Heywood plays for the Revels Plays Companion Library I was guided in the often difficult editorial choices of inclusion and exclusion by the first collection of plays in this series, *Three Jacobean Witchcraft Plays*, edited by Peter Corbin and Douglas Sedge. Like them, I have also benefited from the work of previous editors, especially Michael H. Leonard, whose edition of *The Wise-woman of Hogsdon* provided many useful suggestions which I have acknowledged in my commentary. For *The Captives*, I found the Malone Society transcript by Arthur Brown and R. E. Alton invaluable in the minefield of Heywood's extremely difficult manuscript, though I have naturally used the manuscript itself, in the original and in photographs, as my prime source, and have preferred my own reading to that of the transcript in a small number of cases. The preface to A. C. Judson's old-spelling edition of the same play was also useful, particularly in its discussion of sources.

I am indebted to my past colleagues at the University of Warwick, most frequently to Tony Howard, Peter Mack and Martin Wright, both for their responses to particular questions and for the discoveries, and often the exhilaration, of shared classes in Renaissance drama. More generally, I wish to thank the department for allowing me a leave of absence during the preparation of the text. In the same period, I received a British Academy award from their Small Grants Research Fund in the Humanities, which enabled me to study copies of the quartos in American libraries, and it is a particular pleasure to be able to acknowledge their help at last in the form of a completed volume. Of the many libraries where I was given friendly assistance, I should mention especially the Folger Library, where I was made most welcome for a month, and where part of the material of the Introduction was delivered at a noon-day colloquium.

Finally, among the many obligations incurred in a task of this kind, I am happy to acknowledge in particular the help of John Drakakis in pointing me towards the quarto of *The English Traveller* in the Scott Library at Abbotsford, and of Ernst Honigmann in his critical reading of my evidence for authorial miscopying in *The Captives*, together with his early advice on the choice of plays for this volume. Robert Smallwood, the pattern of perfection in a General Editor, has shown more patience than should be asked of anyone, and his many queries and suggestions have borne fruit throughout the edition. I was truly fortunate to have benefited from his keen eye, wide knowledge and close attention to detail.

My most personal thanks go to Eluned Brown for her support at many stages of the project, to my parents for their confidence that this task would some day be completed, and to my wife Grace for her encouragement when it seemed certain that it would not.

P.M.

ABBREVIATIONS AND REFERENCES

References to Shakespeare are to Alexander's *Complete Works* (1951), abbreviations of Shakespeare titles being taken from Onions. *OED* and Onions are the source of the majority of the glossarial notes. For identification of the many proverbs used in these plays, I have consulted Tilley (references in the form D250) and Dent (decimalised references in the form Q14.1). All books are published in London unless otherwise indicated.

EDITIONS

In the commentary and textual collation the following abbreviations identify the editions (in chronological order):

The Wise-woman of Hogsdon (*WWH*)

Q *The Wise-woman of Hogsdon*, 1638.

1672 MS notes in a Folger Library copy of *Q*, annotated as a prompt-book.

S *The Plays of Thomas Heywood* (edited reprint of *Q*), the Pearson reprint, ed. R. H. Shepherd, 6 vols, 1874.

Da MS notes in P. A. Daniel's copy of *S* in the Folger Library.

V *Thomas Heywood* (Mermaid edition), ed. A. W. Verity, 1888.

L *The Wise-woman of Hogsdon*, ed. Michael H. Leonard (Garland edition), 1980 (revision of Ph.D., University of Southern California, 1967).

The English Traveller (*ET*)

Q *The English Traveller*, 1633.

La *Specimens of English Dramatic Poets*, selections by Charles Lamb, 1808.

Di *The English Traveller*, in *Old English Plays*, vol. VI, ed. C. W. Dilke, 1818.

S as above.

Da as above.

V as above.

Hudson Robert J. Hudson, *A Critical Edition of Heywood's The English Traveller*, Ph.D., New York University, 1962.

The English Traveller is also available in a facsimile reprint (The English Experience, 606), New York, 1973.

The Captives (*Cap.*)

MS British Library MS Egerton 1994.

Bu *The Captives*, in *Old English Plays*, vol. IV, ed. A. H. Bullen, 1885.

J *The Captives*, ed. A. C. Judson, New Haven, 1921.

Br *The Captives*, Malone Society transcript, ed. Arthur Brown with R. E. Alton, 1953.

GENERAL

App. Appendix of passages cut by Heywood in *The Captives.*

Baines Barbara J. Baines, *Thomas Heywood*, Boston, 1984.

Bentley G. E. Bentley, *The Jacobean and Caroline Stage*, 7 vols, Oxford, 1941–68.

Brown Thomas Heywood, *The Captives* (Malone Society transcript), introduction.

Chambers E. K. Chambers, *The Elizabethan Stage*, 4 vols, Oxford, 1923.

Clark A. M. Clark, *Thomas Heywood, Playwright and Miscellanist*, Oxford, 1931.

Dent R. W. Dent, *Proverbial Language in English Drama excluding Shakespeare, 1495–1616*, Berkeley, 1984.

Dessen Alan C. Dessen, *Elizabethan Stage Conventions and Modern Interpreters*, Cambridge, 1984.

ELN *English Language Notes.*

Fleay F. G. Fleay, *A Biographical Chronicle of the English Drama 1559–1642*, 2 vols, 1891.

Greg W. W. Greg, *Dramatic Documents from the Elizabethan Playhouses*, Oxford, 1931.

Harbage Alfred Harbage, *Annals of English Drama 975–1700*, rev. S. Schoenbaum, 1964.

Henslowe R. A. Foakes and R. T. Rickert, *Henslowe's Diary*, Cambridge, 1961.

Herford & Simpson *Ben Jonson*, ed. C. H. Herford, Percy and Evelyn Simpson, 11 vols, Oxford 1925–52.

JEGP *Journal of English and Germanic Philology.*

Leonard (1967) and (1980) M. H. Leonard, *A Critical Edition of Thomas Heywood's 'The Wise Woman of Hogsdon'*, Ph.D., University of Southern California, 1967; revised edition, Garland Publishing, 1980.

Martin R. G. Martin, 'A critical study of *Gunaikeion*', *SP* 20 (April 1923), 160–83.

MLN *Modern Language Notes.*

MLR *Modern Language Review.*

Mostellaria (*Most.*) Plautus, *Mostellaria (The Haunted House)*, in Plautus, vol. III (Loeb), translated by Paul Nixon, 1924.

N & Q *Notes & Queries.*

Nungezer Edwin Nungezer, *A Dictionary of Actors*, New Haven, 1929.

OED *A New English Dictionary on Historical Principles.*

Onions C. T. Onions, *A Shakespeare Glossary*, Oxford, 1911.

Pantzer, *STC* Katharine T. Pantzer, *A Short-title Catalogue of Books Printed in England, Scotland and Ireland 1475–1640*, 3 vols, 1986–91.

Partridge Eric Partridge, *Shakespeare's Bawdy*, 1961.

Pearson The Pearson reprint, *The Plays of Thomas Heywood* (ed. R. H. Shepherd), 6 vols, 1874.

PQ *Philological Quarterly.*

RES *Review of English Studies.*

RORD *Research Opportunities in Renaissance Drama.*

Rudens (*Rud.*) Plautus, *Rudens (The Rope)*, in Plautus, vol. IV (Loeb), translated by Paul Nixon, 1932.

ShQ *Shakespeare Quarterly.*

ShS *Shakespeare Survey.*

SEL *Studies in English Literature.*

SP *Studies in Philology.*

Sugden E. H. Sugden, *A Topographical Dictionary to the Works of Shakespeare and his Fellow Dramatists*, Manchester, 1925.

ThN *Theatre Notebook.*

Thomas Keith Thomas, *Religion and the Decline of Magic*, 1971, repr. 1980.

Tilley M. P. Tilley, *A Dictionary of the Proverbs in England in the Sixteenth and Seventeenth Centuries*, Ann Arbor, 1950.

Texts by Heywood

Apology *An Apology for Actors*, 1612, with notes by J. W. Binns, New York, 1972.

Escapes *The Escapes of Jupiter*, ed. Henry D. Janzen (Malone Society Reprint), 1978.

1, 2 FMW *The Fair Maid of the West*, parts 1 and 2, ed. Robert K. Turner Jr, 1968.

Gun. *Gunaikeion, or Nine Books of Various History, Concerning Women*, 1624.

How a Man *How a Man May Choose a Good Wife from a Bad*, ed. A. E. H. Swaen, Bang, *Materialen*, 1912.

1, 2 IAge *The Iron Age*, parts 1 and 2, ed. Arlene W. Weiner, 1979.

WKK *A Woman Killed with Kindness*, ed. R. W. Van Fossen, 1961.

INTRODUCTION

GENERAL

While Heywood was by no means the only dramatist of his time interested in domestic themes, he explored the institution of marriage with unusual persistence,[1] and (as this volume's plays illustrate) found greater variety in the subject than is normally credited to him. By comparison with the conventional morality of conduct-book and pulpit, which presupposed a narrow range of duties in a wife, Heywood presents a wide range of married women of differing ages, characters and moral inclinations. *The Wise-woman of Hogsdon* (?1604), a comedy of intrigue, shows a young prodigal redeemed by a patient Griselda. *The English Traveller* (?1624), with its young wife, unfaithful both to her husband and to her childhood friend, provides a tragicomic reworking of *A Woman Killed with Kindness*. *The Captives* (1624) is a romance, its main plot the adventures and eventual marriages of two innocent girls, and its subplot the testing of a virtuous wife. To these strong women, who either defend their marriages or through independence strain them beyond the breaking-point, should be added the unmarried matchmaking Wise-woman of Hogsdon herself, irrepressible, dissident, opportunistic, the creator both of confusion and of harmony in her world. Peter Ure was perhaps right in his judgement that the term 'marriage play' is an impossibly broad category,[2] but, in the case of Heywood, marriage and its tensions provided the commonest motive for dramatic conflict, and a belief in what he called the 'exemplary' nature of women offered his usual means of resolution.

There was little disagreement between the numerous matrimonial conduct-books on the duties of a wife. The new middle-class values of thrift and temperance, modesty and respect for authority[3] were necessarily reflected in the microcosm of marriage, where the wife's domestic frugality, sweet temper and obedience were patterned after her husband's wisdom in business, his good name and his obedience to God and King. This notion of a family as a little monarchy is made explicit by the Cambridge Puritan William Perkins, who was lecturing at Emmanuel College possibly at the same time as Heywood's residence there in the early 1590s: 'A familie, is a naturall and simple society of certaine persons, having mutuall relation to one another, under the private government of one.'[4] Yet there was a tension already built into this very concept, as the Puritans were to find later in the public sphere. The citizen's wife was in reality a member of a corporation; the husband 'ought to make her a joynt Governour of the Familie with himselfe'.[5] In these circumstances, partnership also implied equality; Perkins himself described husband and wife as 'yokefellows'.[6]

Lawrence Stone has traced the evolution of the family from its characteristic type in the sixteenth century (called by Stone the 'Open Lineage Family') into other types of nuclear family predominating in the next century.[7] The Open Lineage Family 'was not an intimate association based on personal choice. Among the upper and middling ranks it was primarily a means of tying together two kinship groups, of obtaining collective economic advantages and securing useful political alliances.... For both men and women it was the price of economic survival, while for the latter it was the only career available.' Accordingly, houses of this earlier period had little privacy, 'which the rich lacked because of the architectural layout of their houses and the prying ubiquity of their servants, and the poor lacked because of confinement in a one- or two-room hovel'. The second family type, arising from a decline of local loyalties and a new allegiance to State and Church, was a more private but increasingly patriarchal nuclear family, where the husband and father could be 'a legalized petty tyrant within the home'. The third family to develop was 'organized around a principle of personal autonomy, and bound together by strong affective ties. Husbands and wives personally selected each other, rather than obeying parental wishes, and their prime motives were now long-term personal affection rather than economic or status advantage for the lineage as a whole.' At the same time, houses began to reflect the new intimacy: 'Internally, the house became more private... rooms became more specialized in function, as well as more numerous.'[8] The change from the dynastic marriage system to its more intimate, companionable form is placed considerably earlier by Alan Macfarlane, who sees the origins of the modern love marriage in the courtly love tradition and its Christian and Germanic predecessors.[9] For Macfarlane, England had already by the thirteenth century developed a distinctive concept of individual private property, and its corollary, personal liberty. Under such a system, marriage contracts without parental permission became possible. It was this debate about authority and equality in choosing a mate and in marriage itself, however early its origins, that was still a potent issue in 1624, when *The Captives* ends in something very like a pair of dynastic marriages, whereas *The Wise-woman of Hogsdon*, twenty years earlier, had been resolved in a series of love-matches.

In the early years of the seventeenth century, aspiring citizens were not only attempting to square their natural belief in liberty and equality of opportunity with their opposed, more orthodox instincts for order and authority. They were at the same time wrestling with the financial challenges of the new freedoms. On the one hand, a good match might be a means to augment or to secure a hard-won fortune. Honesty, the narrator of *The Passionate Morris Dance*, considering a 'troupe of lovers' in a house (not unlike the Wise-woman's) in Hogsdon, deplores this latest fashion: 'For men wil sooner match their daughters with my yong maister, a rich Coblers Sonne, though they be their heires, then with a Gentleman of a good house, being a yonger Brother. Heerby comes the decay of ancient gentilities, and this the making of upstart houses.'[10] A key example in Heywood is in the second scene of *1 The Fair Maid of the West*, where Spenser, a 'gentleman of fortunes, means, / And well revenu'd', gives the tavern wench Bess, a tanner's daughter, a hundred pounds for safe keeping, asking her what she will venture with him on the Island Voyage. Her reply is carefully worded: 'What I love best, my heart, for I could wish / I had been born to equal you in fortune / Or you so low to have been rank'd with me; / I could have then presum'd boldly to say/I love none but my Spenser.'[11] Her honesty and modesty make her a 'girl worth gold', courted by the Mayor of Fowey for his son, and a fitting eventual match for the well-born Spenser. In *Tell-Troth's New Year's Gift*, however, probably also by the courtly author of *The Passionate Morris Dance*, the disadvantages of such upward marriages are more obvious than the benefits: 'for either they marry their children in their infancy, when they are not able to know what love is, or else matche them with inequallity, joyning burning sommer with key-cold winter, their daughters of twentye yeares olde or under, to rich cormorants of threescore or upwards',[12] an analysis combining in a sentence two of the commonest problems discussed in the domestic drama: the miseries of enforced marriage and the unequal matching of January and May. Finally, while the male citizen of modest means could improve the family fortunes by marrying his daughter into money, or the impoverished nobleman might offer his title in marriage to a dowried woman of lower rank, the rich merchant's hopes might as easily be dashed by a love-match between his daughter and a prodigal. In the matter of social mobility, fortunes were as likely to sink as to rise. The citizen's worst fear was dramatised in *The Knight of the Burning Pestle*, when the prodigal Jasper wins the hand of Luce, the merchant's daughter. The citizen's response is succinct, and accurate: 'I do not like this.' The world of 1600 was one that had begun to be turned upside down, at the start of a surreptitious domestic revolution that was eventually to be as far-reaching as the political and industrial upheavals of the century.

Most importantly, it was not only within the home that women were achieving greater authority. The century from 1550 to 1650 saw a transformation in their social status, in part as a result of the Queen's high esteem, in part because of the enormous expansion in female literacy, but most as a direct result of the citizens' greater wealth and increased leisure. The new shops in the Exchange and elsewhere were filled with the clothes, perfumes and jewels of a suddenly extended empire, such as the gold chain which Chartley gives and takes back from Luce in *The Wise-woman of Hogsdon*, or in the same play the 'branched satin and wrought velvet' and the 'beaver for the city, and a black bag for the country'. As Chartley so freely promises, 'there are brave things to be bought in the city. Cheapside and the Exchange offer variety and rarity'. Perhaps the most influential form of entertainment for this rising class was the theatre, where wives could be seen in their new-bought jewels, attractive alike to gallants and to pickpockets, and could watch the performances of women as dynamic as Middleton's roaring girl Moll Frith, Shakespeare's strong-minded Katherine, known as the 'shrew', and his merry wives of Windsor, or Bess Bridges, Heywood's fair maid of the West, and his unnamed wise-woman of Hogsdon. These are characters drawn from the world of the audience, intelligent, resourceful women, capable of dominating a whole play. Nor was it necessarily true that the dramatists merely reflected current developments in society. It is at least as likely that they were important contributors to the debate on the changing status of women, and may well have initiated some terms of that argument. In the first scene of *The English Traveller* Mistress Wincott comments

> How, now, sister?
> This is a fashion that's but late come up,
> For maids to court their husbands.

The lines no doubt contain a general observation true enough to be amusing; yet they are at the same time an invitation to greater independence, or even boldness.[13] This degree of personal liberty shown in the 1620s by the modest (and significantly named) Prudentilla may indicate a wider spread of feminism since the turn of the century, when Shakespeare's Beatrice was clearly preaching sedition, however playfully, in her advice to Hero: 'It is my cousin's duty to make curtsy, and say "Father, as it please you." But yet for all that, cousin, let him be a handsome fellow, or else make another curtsy and say "Father, as it please me."'[14]

An important contribution to the cultural debate is represented by the striking cluster of plays on domestic themes around 1600. In addition to almost twenty known plays, the titles of well over two dozen lost plays can confidently be placed in this category.[15] The majority of the known and (to judge from their titles and other evidence) also of the lost plays fall into two main groups. On the dark side are found the 'homiletic tragedies',[16] of which the weakest are a form of lurid journalism, while the best are realistic contemporary morality plays that explore with shocking clarity two new character-types: the cruel and abusive husband, unfaithful, prodigal, often fatally violent, and the self-assertive wife who expresses her rebellion in adultery or by the murder of her husband. Examples of this genre are the anonymous *Arden of Faversham* (1592), Heywood's *1 and 2 Edward IV* (1592–9), the anonymous *A Warning for Fair Women* (1599) and *The Yorkshire Tragedy* (1608), Heywood's *A Woman Killed with Kindness* (1603) and Rowley, Dekker and Ford's

The Witch of Edmonton (1621). The height of the domestic blood tragedy was reached in *Othello* and *The Duchess of Malfi*, whose central characters in each case far transcend the popular types. Of this list, characteristically, the Heywood examples are the least sensational, erring more on the side of sentimentality. Marilyn Johnson has noted that in Heywood the prodigal men are generally forgiven, while the errant wives tend to die of shame.[17] Yet the effect is redemptive, rather than punitive: 'the wives are repentant, and forgiveness brings about a spiritual regeneration'. That is the resolution of *The English Traveller* also, this volume's example of the genre.

While this cluster of topical murder plays springs directly from contemporary social conditions, with no obvious antecedents in theatre,[18] the large group of domestic comedies of the same period are clearly a fusion of two older traditions: the intrigues of Roman and Italian comedy, and English prodigal son dramas.[19] The dominant figure in this group of plays is the 'patient wife', represented in Chettle, Dekker and Haughton's *Patient Grissel* (1600), *How a Man May Choose a Good Wife from a Bad* (1601–2), probably by Heywood,[20] the anonymous *London Prodigal* (1604) and *The Miseries of Enforced Marriage* (1606) by George Wilkins. Once again, Shakespeare's contributions to this genre (*Much Ado about Nothing*, *All's Well that Ends Well* and *The Winter's Tale*) are thoroughly original treatments of the basic theme, subtly suggesting in all three plots the 'wife killed with unkindness' motif of domestic tragedy. Despite the comic resolutions, these playwrights present at best a bitter-sweet portrait of marriage, in which the wronged wife must exert all her ingenuity to recover her rights.[21] Even *The Wise-woman of Hogsdon*, the breeziest of this group, has a persistently ironic edge. Taken together, the murder chronicles and the patient wife intrigues show clearly the perceived inequalities in marriage, and offer the first sketchy suggestions of a course towards emancipation, tentative steps on the path later taken by Ibsen, Strindberg, Wedekind and Brecht.

THE WISE-WOMAN OF HOGSDON

The Wise-woman of Hogsdon was published in 1638 'As it hath been sundry times Acted with great Applause', but this presumably authorial[22] statement is the only firm evidence for performance in the author's lifetime.[23] The play clearly belongs with the group of 'patient wife' dramas of 1600–05 discussed earlier, a dating reinforced by its references, noted by Fleay,[24] to the titles of a number of other plays, including *Mother Redcap* (1598), *The Devil and his Dam* (1600), *Cutting Dick* (1602), *Too Good to be True* (1602) and *A Woman Killed with Kindness* (1603), all performed by Heywood's fellows, the Admiral's and Worcester's Men.[25] *The Wise-woman* would also have been the latest of at least eight magician/witch plays in Henslowe's repertory, following after *Friar Bacon and Friar Bungay* (?1589, also a patient wife play), *Doctor Faustus* (?1592), *The Wise-man of West Chester*[26] (thirty-two performances between 1594 and 1597, the most popular play of the Admiral's Men), *The Witch of Islington* (1597), *Mother Redcap* (1598), *Friar Fox and Gill of Brentford* (1599) and *The Three Brothers* (1602), a tragedy requiring devils' suits, a witch's gown, and a coffin.[27] In an attempt to date the piece more precisely, Fleay identified *The Wise-woman of Hogsdon* with *How to Learn of a Woman to Woo*, a Heywood play performed at Court in December 1604. One must wonder if a play treating a white witch with such indulgence would have been popular with the new king, who had in the same year strengthened the penalties against such activities.[28] Yet the identification is not impossible, and there seems no reason to dispute the generally accepted date of 1604.[29]

The loss of the majority of the plays in the Henslowe list prevents us from seeing *The Wise-woman of Hogsdon* in its full popular context, but the two survivors, Greene's *Friar Bacon and Friar Bungay* and Marlowe's *Doctor Faustus*, suggest a specialised development of the Morality tradition, in which magic was seen as a form of psychic exploration. Natural magic (the term covering those sciences now known as mathematics, physics and chemistry) was a rigorous intellectual and experimental discipline that engaged some of the best minds in England. Sir Philip Sidney, his sister the Countess of Pembroke and Sir Edward Dyer all studied alchemy with John Dee, a magus consulted by Queen Elizabeth, and Sir Walter Raleigh and Thomas Hariot pursued chemical studies with the 'wizard' Earl of Northumberland.[30] A wide range of esoteric researches on the frontiers of science (in cabalistic number symbolism, optics, mechanics, astrology and magnetism as well as alchemy) suggested that the natural world was amenable to manipulation by the adept, and the future could be both predicted and, by the skilful practitioner, altered.[31] The Elizabethan magus and the Elizabethan dramatist were of the same trade: through art, both transformed the raw materials of nature.[32] Jonson expresses this idea in its purest form at the opening of his masque *Mercury Vindicated from the Alchemists at Court*:

> Soft, subtile fire, thou soule of art,
>   Now doe thy part
> On weaker Nature, that through age is lamed.[33]

Heywood translates this notion into theatre terms in *An Apology for Actors*: 'A description is only a shadow, received by the eare, but not perceived by the eye . . . but to see a souldier shap'd like a souldier, walke, speake, act like a souldier . . . so bewitching a thing is lively and well-spirited action, that it hath power to new-mold the harts of the spectators.'[34] In the context here of the word 'bewitching', terms like 'power' and even 'well-spirited' add an esoteric resonance to their literal meanings. The effects of this stage enchantment are ambiguous. On the one hand, the magic camera of Friar Bacon's prospective glass can be deadly, and he wisely abandons his craft; similarly Faustus is self-deceived by his own 'shows', offering too late to burn his books. Yet this theatre witchcraft had its redemptive side. If Greene's and Marlowe's magicians were at the back of Heywood's mind when fashioning his play, Lyly's Mother Bombie and Shakespeare's merry wives of Windsor were closer to hand. Mother Bombie (who is included in the Wise-woman's list of predecessors in II.i) provided a general model of a cunning-woman's manipulations in a well-plotted play of deception, and the particular device of disguised marriages. Her prophecies, the product more of sound psychology than of preternatural gifts, set her off from her equivalent in Plautus, the resourceful slave, whose skills are purely practical. Like her, Heywood's Wise-woman can anticipate the future, but by sound instinct rather than occult art. 'I think I can see as well into a millstone as another' is her ironic assessment. Keith Thomas put the matter succinctly: 'As her name reminds us, a *cunning* woman was simply a woman who knew more than other people.'[35] Yet she is at the same time conscious of the theatre in what she does ('Ha, ha, let me hold my sides and laugh. Here were even a plot to make a play on') and we may observe, though she makes no such claim, that her craft fashions harmony where there was little prospect of it. As the country Luce notes, only half in jest, 'This is no trade, but a mystery.' In turn, *The Merry Wives of Windsor* (where the intemperate Falstaff escapes disguised as a wise-woman, one of the play's sly jokes) may have suggested to Heywood the comic catechism of mangled Latin between Sir Boniface and Senser in IV.i, together with the device of the deliberate mismarriage. Yet its most important lesson may have been the greater mystery, that lust and jealousy can be tamed through humour, quick-wittedness and, in the final Windsor Forest scene, a hint of supernatural persuasion.

By bringing together the prodigal husband/patient wife traditions into the realm of magic, the dramatists had found a fresh metaphor for the precarious quality of personal relations. The practicalities of matchmaking, so firmly rooted in mundane considerations (parental approval, dowry-provision, the costs of setting up house and, in the case of most marriages, the imminent care of children) must always, at every level of society, have contrasted strongly with the Platonic ideals expressed in sonnets and prose romances. 'Witchcraft' in love poetry expresses danger with the delight, and in the romance tradition such enchantments as those of Circe, or the Green Knight's Lady, or Acrasia in the Bower of Bliss, were temptations to be resisted. The magical world expressed, among other things, the idea that love is both the maze with its Minotaur and the guiding thread. Chartley articulates the negative half of this proposition in II.i: 'Marriage is like Daedalus his labyrinth, and being once in, there's no finding the way out.' In *A Midsummer Night's Dream*, the Minotaur sleeps with the Queen, and the lovers are led into the maze and out again. In a later marriage play,[36] benign necromancy is needed to reunite Hermione with her husband, who recognises immediately how this moment can be both mysterious and domestic: 'If this be magic, let it be an art / Lawful as eating.' It is obvious that dramatists enjoyed both elements of the magician's art: its imposture, which as fellow professionals they understood perfectly, and its redemptive power, also a part of their craft, in which wonder and scepticism sat side by side. The King's Men expressed the two halves of the debate when they kept *The Tempest* and *The Alchemist* in their repertory simultaneously, and played them in the same season at Court in 1612.[37]

In *The Wise-woman of Hogsdon* these tensions and ironies are active throughout, though in a characteristically muted form. Its settings, for example, have the casual everyday familiarity that we expect from Heywood, in the opening tavern scene of dice-playing, or Luce minding the shop 'at work upon a laced handkerchief', or Tabor and Sir Boniface entering from dinner 'with a trencher, with broken meat and a napkin'.[38] The most fully realised setting is the Wise-woman's house in the northern suburbs, its walls hung with portraits of available girls, and with a secret chamber alongside the door, where the Wise-woman can listen as her assistant gleans personal details from her clients. It is a large and thriving establishment, 'with a midwife or two belonging to the house, and one Sir Boniface, a deacon, that makes a shift to christen the infants', and it is precisely located, next door to Mother Redcap's Tavern. This famous inn, with its own distinctive ale (see Commentary at II.i.90–1), stood on Camden High Street at the junction of Camden Road and Kentish Town Road until 1820, when it was replaced by the present handsome coaching-inn, called The Olde Mother Redcap until its change of name to The World's End in 1985.[39] Apparently Heywood transferred the Wise-woman and her place of resort from Hoxton to Kentish Town, conflating her character with Mother Redcap's—unless, as seems possible, Mother Redcap and her tavern were from the start Heywood's inspiration, and the 'Hogsdon' title supplied only to avoid conflict with Munday and Drayton's *Mother Redcap*, already in the repertoire.

Such clearly localised settings, peopled from all strata of contemporary life, with an intrigue plot involving layers of disguise and deception (see Commentary, headnotes to I.i, III.i, III.iii, IV.i, V.vi), would suggest a city comedy of the Jonson/Middleton type. Such an impression is supported by the play's vigorously colloquial language, with over eighty proverbial phrases, and by the racy opening scene of dice-play. The story, an amusing London jest of a cozener cozened, would be at home in any of the coney-catching pamphlets.[40] This is T. S. Eliot's view of the play: 'he succeeds with something not too far below Jonson to be comparable to that master's work; the wise woman herself, and her scenes with her clientele, are capitally done, and earn for Heywood the title of "realist" if any part of his work can.'[41] Seen in this light, as a city comedy, there would be satire in the scepticism about the Wise-woman, as revealed through her admitted deceptions of her clients, in Chartley's and Boister's abuse of her, and in the country Luce's analysis at III.i.44 'Believe me, this is a cunning woman, neither hath she her name for nothing, who out of her ignorance can fool so many that think themselves wise.' Yet Heywood's natural bent is not towards pure satire, as the ambivalent quality of the last quotation illustrates, and the play could as easily be read[42] as a modified Morality, presenting the Prodigal in danger with the opening parable of dice-play, following his descent into vice, and in the final discovery scene apparently removing one by one all his supports. In these terms, *The Wise-woman of Hogsdon* is a conscious or unconscious refashioning of *Everyman* as high comedy with a redemptive twist, and the Wise-woman will resemble both Luxuria, the Prodigal's misleader, and Fortuna, his nemesis.

Equally, the play can be viewed (as we have seen, following the example of *Mother Bombie*) as a domestication of classical comedy, with the Wise-woman as a variant of the Plautine witty slave, faintly coloured by the procuress-witch of Renaissance belief.[43] Yet these views, all of which catch at different aspects of the piece, leave unexplained its lightness of tone and rapid movement. Michael H. Leonard describes this quality judiciously: 'The play stands at one side of the mainstream of witch drama . . . a mingling of citizen satire and romantic comedy in which the seamier side of London is presented with actions and characters which are worthy, even ideal.'[44] Neil Carson in a similar vein contrasts the 'theatre of enchantment or illusion' of Dekker and Heywood with the 'theatre of estrangement' in the more rational and satiric work of Webster and Middleton for the boy companies.[45] For all its satire, Morality features and classicism, the play's overriding impression, with its resourceful heroine Luce in boy's clothes (calling herself, perhaps significantly, Jack) and its trials, mock-combats, and farcical word-play, is of pantomime, in which the Wise-woman combines, however improbably, the roles of Dame and of Fairy Godmother, both comic fraud and magician.

This play, then, joins the earlier witch-plays in presenting a mélange of realistic and romantic elements, of scepticism and fantasy. Commenting on the play's 'perfectly patterned' weaving of composite influences, Barbara J. Baines notes that 'instead of attempting to conceal his own dramatic contrivances . . . [Heywood] calls attention to them in order to share with his audience an inside perspective on the art of play-making and illusion-making'.[46] Heywood returned ten years later to this mixed mode, if his hand is present in *The Seven Champions of Christendom*, possibly a revision around 1614 of an earlier piece, a romance of knight-errantry with a melodramatic witch, Calib, and her son Suckabus, a typical Heywood clown.[47] Finally in 1643 he and Brome dealt with the late Lancashire witches in a combination of realism, sensationalism and low comedy that has not always found favour with critics.[48] It would appear that throughout his career Heywood viewed magic as simultaneously the province of charlatans and an area of psychic exploration, at the same time a fearsome and ill-understood phenomenon best treated with deflationary humour and a readily available source of comfort and assistance, consulted by people of all classes. The ambivalence of his plays probably reflects an almost identical uncertainty in the minds of the audience.

A kind of inclusiveness may be seen in the play's construction, as a single sprawling plot, animated by the surprises and reversals of its various deceptions, and drawing characters from city and country, high and low life, into one levelling action, symbolised finally by the gathering at the Wise-woman's universal meeting-place. This inclusiveness should not, however, be taken for lack of reflection on Heywood's part. So far from being, as Trollope considered it,[49] 'a very poor play indeed, in which the author has not taken the trouble so to digest the plot as to be able to command it in the writing', the play is carefully balanced between two pairs of contrasted themes. First, and most obviously, it expresses the tension between the dissolute prodigals of I.i and the wise and provident country Luce of I.ii, a tension not resolved until the final scene. Secondly, and more subtly, the play exploits the contrast between two forms of education, both introduced in the second act, the Wise-woman's earthy instruction in II.i, and Sir Boniface's sophisticated pedantry in II.ii. These themes are the core of the play, and can be seen to represent the moral reflection of the practical themes of prodigality and marriage. From this exploration of traditional and more self-conscious forms of instruction, Act III returns to the topics of Act I, in the Wise-woman's contrivance (on the country Luce's behalf) of the reversed marriages. In Act IV all new developments are in the hands of Senser. First this intriguer in disguise triumphs over the pedant (in IV.i), before preparing the ground for Chartley's and his own marriage (in another disguise, delivering invitations to the Wise-woman's house, IV.v). The fifth act, with the introduction of one further new character, Old Chartley, exposes the intrigues and prodigality and is resolved in marriage. Heywood's skill is evident in his technique of advancing the plot by association with a series of key characters (Chartley, the country Luce, the Wise-woman, Sir Boniface, Senser, Old Chartley), ensuring variety as each character becomes a spokesperson for the action. Less obvious is the patterned relationship of his four themes. In the first pair, Chartley's prodigality, which belongs to youth, is superseded by Luce's mature gift of marriage; in the second pair, the effective skills of the Wise-woman lead the action forward, while the pedantry of Sir Boniface is clearly retrograde. The play praises the future and finds ways to make the past obsolete. Its optimism, in equal parts disenchanted and hopeful, was designed to appeal to an audience increasingly conscious of moral dilemmas.

It is interesting, then, to consider how the last act's revelations might have been staged. Five different places of concealment appear to be demanded. In V.ii, Luce's father and Boister are hidden separately: 'Withdraw; I'll place you all in several rooms, / Where sit, see, but say nothing.' In V.iii, Gratiana is provided with a low stool and invited to 'withdraw'. In V.iv, Sir Harry is directed to enter 'this retiring chamber', which he calls a 'close chamber', and a chair and cushion are requested for him. In V.v, Old Chartley is asked to 'sit down', and is joined by the second Luce. At the start of V.vi, after the Wise-woman's summary ('Now they are placed in several rooms that look / Into this one'), a knock is heard, announcing Chartley, who in a perfectly naturalistic staging should enter by a sixth, unused, door. Of course such a literal staging is unnecessary. It is important only that the characters be 'concealed' from each other and from Chartley, and all but one of the hidden characters speak asides from their hiding-places before revealing themselves, which suggests that they remain visible to the audience. In addition, the repeated references to stools and sitting make little sense if the characters are out of sight. Two kinds of staging are possible. There is no evidence of as many as five doors or concealment spaces in the public theatres, two or at the most three being all that the extant texts require.[50] Rather than attempting to provide five concealment spaces and a sixth door, Heywood may have hit on the simple expedient here of placing five stools (or four stools and a cushioned chair) in different parts of the open stage, each seat establishing a hiding-place, from which the characters could play their reactions in full view, while 'invisible' to Chartley. The second possibility is that the play was not written for a public theatre (the Curtain, or later the Red Bull), but specifically for the Court performance suggested by Fleay. If the stage area were partly occupied by seated spectators, the characters to be concealed could easily disappear when placed among them. This would not have been an innovation by Heywood. There is byplay of a similar kind in a number of Inductions. As part of his gulling in *The Taming of the Shrew*, Christopher Sly is seated among lords and ladies to watch the main action, so transforming the Theatre into a private space. In *Cynthia's Revels* Jonson allows his competing child Prologues to consider taking their place among the gallants on stage, where this time the joke would be the difference in size. More tantalisingly, Marston's Induction to *The Malcontent* for its transfer to the Globe appears to confirm in its first exchange that seating on the stage was possible also in the public theatre. Finally, in *The Knight of the Burning Pestle* Induction, after considerable business with stools and climbing on to the Blackfriars stage, the citizens take their place among the gentlemen, an unambiguous instance (perhaps three or four years later than *The Wise-woman of Hogsdon*) of actors joining on-stage gallants. In the absence of specific stage-directions from Heywood, the use of on-stage stools is speculative, but no other staging will allow so easily for the asides to be made, nor explain the repeated calls for seats. In harmony with the remainder of the play, such a staging continues the interweaving of realism and imaginative fantasy by mingling performers with spectators, and offers the additional pleasure of a reversal of expectation, by making the stage a set of private rooms, an appropriate place for the scouring of Chartley's conscience, with the public world left offstage.

It was this possibility of an engaging closeness to its audience that may have caused the play to be taken in 1672 by John Coysh's provincial touring company to Norwich, apparently in tandem with *The Comedy of Errors*.[51] This production, in a heavily cut text (omitting for example I.i and all but the opening dialogue of III.iii, and removing the part of Haringfield entirely) is known to us from the prompt-book, a marked copy of the quarto, now in the Folger Library.[52] The association with Shakespeare's play (another comedy of mistaken identities, of characters sharing the same name, and of lightly handled enchantment) is attractive, especially if, according to Fleay's conjecture, the plays had been associated once before, in the Court winter festivities of 1604. Coysh's company of thirteen actors planned to present the play without doubling, though omitting Haringfield. Any Jacobean performances could have been played entire by nine men (assuming the Wise-woman to have been an adult role) and three boys, with stage-keepers as extras, Sir Boniface doubling with Luce's Father, and Old Chartley replacing Haringfield in the fifth act—an economical exchange of forces, Chartley's father being needed to expose his son's false alibi, while Haringfield, with no marriage partner, would disrupt the final symmetry, so carefully staged. There is no documentary record of contemporary or later performances of the play.

We can probably assign two of the play's roles to known actors of Queen Anne's Men.[53] Thomas Greene, the talented 'lean fool of the Bull',[54] must have originated the part of Taber, with a flamboyant performance that no text could reproduce. Some idea of Greene's virtuosity can be gained from his stage representation of a baboon: 'and you also, who with *Scylla*-barking, *Stentor*-throated bellowings, flash choaking squibbes of absurd vanities into the nosthrils of your spectators, barbarously diverting *Nature*, and defacing Gods owne image, by metamorphising humane shape into bestiall forme.'[55] The opening words of the quotation are Greene's catchphrase, 'tu quoque', famous enough to rename a play (*The City Gallant*) in which he played Bubble, as *Greene's Tu Quoque*. Richard Perkins, probably already a leader of the company (he was to be the first Flamineo in *The White Devil* of 1612) played the impetuous gallant Goodlack in Heywood's *1 The Fair Maid of the West* around 1604, and may well have taken the similar part of Young Chartley. Perkins is also known for a confident poem[56] in which (somewhat in the manner of a Donne satire) he rejects the tavern, lottery, dice-house and bowling-alley in favour of the playhouse, where he 'loves to sit . . . even in the stages front'. His ironic final couplet, contrasting hypocrites in the audience with the honest actor, indicates the level of intelligence and self-awarencess found in the best performers, even at the popular Red Bull: 'This is the difference: such would have men deeme / Them what they are not; I am what I seeme.'

THE ENGLISH TRAVELLER

In the early 1620s Heywood seems to have returned to playwriting after a ten-year hiatus, during which the fortunes of his company, Queen Anne's Men, had dwindled. As Bentley notes, 'none of his plays has been reasonably dated between 1614 and 1624'.[57] In the interim, he may have found employment with the Earl of Southampton and journeyed with him in 1614 to the Low Countries,[58] which would add an autobiographical touch to the opening scene of *The English Traveller*. Now he joined the Lady Elizabeth's Men, led by his colleague of over twenty years, Christopher Beeston, in the company's new theatre, the Cockpit, on fashionable Drury Lane. This theatre, also known as the Phoenix since its recovery from the Shrove Tuesday riot of 1617, had been purpose-built to a 1616 design by Inigo Jones, drawings for which are preserved.[59] It would have been an intimate space, with a stage fifteen feet deep and a little over twenty-one feet wide, about half the dimensions of the average public theatre, and with presumably a smaller audience. The difference in conditions from the Red Bull theatre must have been noticeable, for performers and spectators. In addition to residual associations of the cockpit (nervous tension, sudden eruptions of violent action, highly motivated spectators) the contemporary audience must have been reminded of an exactly comparable space, the anatomy theatre. Indeed, an eighteenth-century German visitor described the cockpit near Gray's Inn exactly in those terms: 'The building is round like a tower, and inside it resembles a "theatrum anatomicum", for all round it there are benches in tiers, on which the spectators sit.'[60] For his conversion of Best's original Cockpit to a theatre, Jones had apparently retained half of the original circular seating. In place of movement and spectacle across the Red Bull's broad stage, the new focus was upon individual conflicts, psychological analysis, personal sentiment. Now, perhaps for the first time, Heywood was encouraged to anatomise his characters' motives for a discriminating audience, comparable, according to Heminge and Condell in 1623, with that at the Blackfriars: 'And though you be a Magistrate of wit, and sit on the Stage at *Black-Friers*, or the *Cock-pit*, to arraigne Playes dailie.'[61] The second and third plays in this volume, *The English Traveller* and *The Captives*, were both probably written specifically for this new space, and both, as will be seen, show Heywood's response to the change in intimacy.

The English Traveller (registered and printed in 1633) has customarily been dated after 1624, on two assumptions, both open to challenge. The first, by Fleay (I, 297), was a proposed date of 1627, the third year after the accession of Charles, on the basis of 'We now / Write *anno tertio*' (I.ii.5–6). That line, however, a direct translation from the corresponding line of the Plautus source-play, *Mostellaria* 79 ('triennium qui iam hinc abest'), is of no use in dating. All other calculations of the play's date assume it to be a dramatisation of a story told as true in Heywood's 1624 *Gunaikeion*,[62] but it seems clear that here (and in the case of *The Captives*, one of whose plots is also told there) the prose version is in fact a recounting of the play for Heywood's hurriedly assembled compilation, 'a work planned, begun, finished and printed within seventeen weeks', as the author notes on the last of four hundred and sixty-six folio pages.[63] Of the dozen or so close verbal parallels between play and narrative, the following give a sense of the relationship: 'There's but one fire from which this smoke may grow' (III.i.218); 'how that fire was kindled from whence this smoke grew' (193). 'Bad tongues have been too busy with us all' (IV.iii.39); 'yet bad tongues had beene busie to their reproach' (194). 'The cause removed, to take away the effect' (IV.iii.63); 'his study was by taking away the cause to prevent the effect' (195). 'You dote upon the shadow, / But another he bears away the substance' (III.iii.71–2); 'she onely reserved him as a stale or shadow, whilest another carryed away the substance' (196).[64] These parallels show Heywood reconstructing his play in prose (from memory, since the echoes are not in play order) rather than the reverse. These cadences (in one case almost a complete iambic line) can hardly have been already present, available for use, in the prose text before the creation of the play. It is also noticeable that the prose retelling focuses most closely on a scene of dialogue, Geraldine's with the serving-girl Bess (III.iii), that is important in the play but could not have been a key element in the story as Heywood first heard it. We can be reasonably sure that the play was composed at leisure before 1624, when its story was retold in a book written under pressure, as the author admits: 'a suddaine Businesse, which began with the Presse, kept it still going, and ended some few dayes before it.'[65] The earliest date for the play's composition would be 1605, publication date of the Zachary Jones translation of Pierre le Loyer's *A Treatise of Specters*, the direct source of the drunken 'shipwreck by land' in II.i,[66] unless Reignald is an imitation also of Face, from the 1610 *Alchemist*, in addition to his obvious model, Tranio in *Mostellaria*. There are, however, similarities between *The English Traveller* and *The Captives* (certainly a 1624 play) that would encourage belief in a date in that region. Not only are plots from both plays retold in *Gunaikeion*, but both also contain companion plots derived from Plautus: *The English Traveller* from *Mostellaria*, and *The Captives* from *Rudens*.[67] The only other indication of date is the author's Prologue, presumably for first performance, which emphasises the play's simplicity, its dependence on 'bare lines'. The nostalgic tone, the apology for lack of spectacle ('song, dance, masque') may suggest a late Jacobean date, as would some features of the play's psychology, discussed below. But these are subjective criteria at best, and more specific evidence would be welcome.[68]

The main plot of *The English Traveller* has no known source. Perhaps it has no more distant model than *A Woman Killed with Kindness* and its unfaithful wife with her strict but forgiving husband; certainly Heywood revisited his earlier play to develop aspects left unexplored in 1603. When reconsidering the unhappy triangle of Frankford, Anne and Wendoll, Heywood left only the seducer unchanged. Dalavill is a close copy of Wendoll, though here we are given even less insight into motive. His escape at the play's end ('away he's galloped as if he were to ride a race for a wager') is indebted not only to Wendoll's abrupt introduction in *WKK* iv, 23–4 ('Sure he rid in fear / Or for a wager') but also to Wendoll's final decision 'to wander, like a Cain / In foreign countries and remoted climes'.[69] Paradoxically, this moment may also have suggested Geraldine's external character, returned from travel at the start of the play and almost exiled again at its close. The earlier Frankford, whose magnanimity in forgiving and sparing his wife was not entirely free of priggishness and even cruelty, now finds himself divided, into an older husband, Wincott, married for the second time, almost like a remarried Frankford, and Young Geraldine, the traveller, a childhood friend (and potential husband) of Mistress Wincott. This division allows the conflicting aspects of Frankford (his early carelessness and later outrage) to be separated. Old Wincott has an innocent trust in his wife; but the seduction, when it comes, is more a betrayal of Young Geraldine, pledged to Mistress Wincott on her husband's death. This scene (in II.i), an almost bigamous contract *de futuro*, is presented, over-optimistically, as forthright, pragmatic and delicately handled on both sides, a response to unequal marriage and the prospect of early widowhood that would not have troubled audiences accustomed to the moral tangles explored by Beaumont and Fletcher. The male-friendship bond between Young Geraldine and Old Wincott, itself perhaps influenced by the new drama, may have been suggested by the amity between Galgano and Sir Stricca in the forty-seventh novel of Painter's *Palace of Pleasure*, a frequent Heywood source;[70] the notion of Mistress Wincott taking Geraldine as second husband may possibly be an echo of the conclusion of *The Honest Man's Fortune* (1613), a story retold (see note 63) in *Gunaikeion*.

Heywood's most serious reconsideration, however, is in the character of the wife. Anne Frankford was an impulsive ingenue, surprised and confused by her fall into wantonness: 'What shall I say? / My soul is wand'ring and hath lost her way. / . . . This maze I am in / I fear will prove a labyrinth of sin' (*WKK* vi, 150f., 160f.). It was only in the last scenes of her play that she found moral direction, entering on the penitential fast that would end her life. By contrast, Mistress Wincott is fully conscious of her choices, completing Geraldine's tentative proposal ('Yet had the Fates so pleased—' 'I know your meaning. / It was once voiced that we two should have matched') and responding confidently, thirty lines later, to his explicit request ('Will you confer your widowhood on me?') with 'You ask the thing I was about to beg' (II.i.226f., 260). She is an independent woman, disposing of her own affections; but there is a penalty paid for this development. While *A Woman Killed with Kindness* left the characters bewildered at the moment of seduction, allowing them to find their direction with difficulty later, *The English Traveller* moves from confidence to uncertainty in the final scene. The wife's death offstage, delivering her repentance by letter, seems inadequate as a summary of her character. In the *Gunaikeion* retelling she is accused by letter, after the gentleman's self-exile. This may represent Heywood's second thoughts and rationalisations; the young gentleman, hearing of her death, returns freed from his vows, to be rewarded by the old man with land 'which he injoyes to this day, and in my opinion not altogether undeservedly' (196). The play lacks this leisurely movement. Having established the wife as an example of the new, self-confident woman, Heywood withdrew his support. But by this point, his interest had been captured by the dilemma of Geraldine, torn between his vows to his father and Old Wincott; in the end, Mistress Wincott and Dalavill had to fend for themselves.

This sense of *The English Traveller* as two plays, the first high-minded and the second sour, even disillusioned, is sharpened by the relationship of main story to subplot. Heywood has been taken to task for the incongruity of his double plots,[71] but more recent work[72] has taught us to consider apparent incongruities with a more attentive eye, and it is now clear that the Plautus plot of the invented ghost from *Mostellaria* (*The Ghost*) provides a witty and at times disturbingly reductive commentary on the main action. The Latin text is neatly modified (its first act becoming I.ii, the second II.ii, Act III divided between III.iii and IV.i, and the last two acts of Plautus compressed into the single long scene IV.vi) and Heywood is an economical and occasionally felicitous translator, as for example in 'The ghost and I am friends', (II.ii.211, 222, 225) for the repeated 'pax mihi est cum mortuis' (*Most.* 514, 524).[73] Yet the most striking use of Plautus is an interchange of thematic material between the Latin and English plots, in a series of images linking the concepts of travel, tempest, trade, usury and the play's two houses.[74] Travel, which prevented Geraldine's marriage to Mistress Wincott and is his first thought when betrayed by her, is also the burden of Old Lionel, another English Traveller, almost ruined in his absence by his prodigal son. The travel theme is counterpointed by images of violent storms, on land, in Young Lionel's description of himself as a house ruined by tempests and in the comic 'shipwreck on land', and at sea, culminating in two important metaphoric moments, when Geraldine is told by his father that he floats between two currents, Virtue and Vice: 'Take this, you steer to harbour, / Take that, to imminent shipwrack' (III.i.152–3), and in Dalavill's cowardly parting words: 'The storm's coming, I must provide for harbour' (V.i.207).

These linked images prepare for a persistent metaphor of trade in both plots. Many of the relationships in the play, most notably Lionel's with Blanda and Geraldine's with both Wincotts, are expressed in the language of money,[75] leading to Dalavill's sarcastic remark at III.i.24ff.: 'What strange felicity these rich men take / To talk of borrowing, lending and of use, / The usurer's language right.' The connected idea of property makes the two houses an important feature of both plots. The supposed haunting, leading to exclusion from one, and the corridors, chambers and passages which are the setting of the other, provide an interesting comment on Stone's remarks quoted earlier about the increase of privacy in the period. The contrast is surely deliberate between the outdoor action of the Plautine subplot, in front of the houses of Old Lionel and Ricott, and the indoor, increasingly claustrophobic, main plot. On a metaphorical level, the 'house' is that inheritance which Young Lionel threatens by his prodigality, and which Mistress Wincott destroys, in leaving her husband without an heir. Both houses are saved, by Lionel in his reformation and by Geraldine in being named Wincott's heir. Yet these well-managed conclusions half-conceal a basic irony, that while the restored prodigal Lionel guarantees repayment of his debts, Geraldine (whose rebuff of Mistress Wincott was the immediate cause of her death, a result already parodically foreshadowed in the bawd Scapha's faint when turned away by Lionel) will inherit her husband's estate unencumbered by guilt.[76] 'If she misfare,' says Wincott, 'I am a man more wretched in her loss / Than had I forfeited life and estate, / She was so good a creature' (V.i.213ff.). A moment later, on news of her death, Geraldine comments 'She hath made me then a free release / Of all the debts I owed her' (229–30). Both of these responses seem inadequate, Wincott's in the estimate of his wife, and Geraldine's in his apparent insouciance. It is as if the two men enter the satiric world of the subplot, to become the gulled *senex* and thoughtless *prodigus*. This is Reignald's biting opinion in the final scene: 'Burying of wives— / As stale as shifting shirts—or for some servants / To flout and gull their masters.'

Whether consciously or not, Heywood introduces a jarring note in the play's last words, given to the bereaved Wincott:

> First feast, and after mourn; we'll like some gallants
> That bury thrifty fathers, think't no sin
> To wear blacks without, but other thoughts within.

Such a close, coming at the end of a series of betrayals and deceptions in both plots,[77] is unnerving, not least because, uniquely in Heywood, this play deceives its audience at a number of points. Most importantly, Mistress Wincott's adultery surprises the audience no less than Geraldine, and Dalavill, even while denouncing Geraldine, is still not known to the audience as the wife's lover. It is also misleading, in this January–May marriage, that the young Mistress Wincott should prove the more experienced. Similarly the introductions of a bookish Dalavill and a travelled Geraldine are reversed by the play, without explanation. Finally, if the house of the subplot is possessed by an invented ghost (a fiction enjoyed by the audience) there is no prior warning that the Wincotts' home is truly haunted by a failed relationship, the ghost of a dead love, that is not fully understood even by the survivors.

It is possible, I think, to reconstruct the progress of the play's growth. Its first appeal to Heywood must have been as the tragedy, not unlike *Othello*, of a noble gentleman robbed of an honourable love by the devices of a villain (who echoes Iago in the deception scene, III.i.64, 75, 86) and prevented from revenge, or even complaint, by his vows to the wife and to his father. In his search for a balancing second plot Heywood ignored Shakespeare's lead (the linked Cassio subplot) and even his own pattern in *A Woman Killed with Kindness* of two near-tragic plots, preferring the rule outlined in the *Gunaikeion* preface:

> Why amongst sad and grave Histories, I have here and there inserted fabulous Jeasts and Tales, savouring of Lightnesse? I answer, I have therein imitated our Historicall and Comicall Poets, that write to the Stage; who least the Auditorie should be dulled with serious courses (which are meerely weightie and materiall) in everie Act present some Zanie with his Mimick action, to breed in the lesse capable, mirth and Laughter: For they that write to all, must strive to please all.

In this, the extreme statement of a 'comic relief' theory, the successful Heywood (who was trusted with alterations to *Sir Thomas More* in 1592 and enjoyed a literally royal success over forty years later with *Love's Mistress*) can be presumed to know his audiences. Yet such an approach in this case led to an unexpected result. Having chosen *Mostellaria* for its contrast of a prodigal with his virtuous Geraldine, in the writing he allowed the satire of the subplot to migrate into his main story, exposing even those characters as either deceitful, shallow or imperceptive. The clown Reignald is the only major character in either plot who escapes the general disenchantment, as being the one confessed dissembler in this parade of deceit and self-deception. The play's uncertain resolution shows Heywood, I believe, reluctant to confront the bleak truth of Old Wincott's and Geraldine's insufficiency. Yet he was honest enough to attempt an account of a house as filled with false hopes, half-truths and secret histories as Strindberg's *Ghost Sonata*, and he was led in that direction by the ghost-comedy of *Mostellaria*.

The play's attempted psychological dissection, which fails only in falling short of a conclusion, could not even have been begun without the conditions of the Cockpit and its audience, more discriminating, but also more cynical, than the spectators of *The Wise-woman of Hogsdon*. The difficult part of Geraldine, simultaneously admirable and morally pliable, might well have been taken by Richard Perkins, possibly, as suggested earlier, Heywood's first Chartley, probably Webster's first Flamineo, and at some time during the 1620s a successful Barabas in the Cockpit revival of *The Jew of Malta*. His refined, sardonic features, with one eyebrow quizzically raised, can be seen in the portrait at Dulwich,[78] his hand on his heart: 'I am what I seeme.' The clown of the Red Bull and Cockpit was the immensely popular Andrew Cane, linked with Timothy Reed of the Blackfriars in a 1641 dialogue *The Stage-Players' Complaint*. In the pamphlet Reed is made to comment: 'You incuse me of my nimble feet, but I think your tongue runnes a little faster, and you contend as much to out-strip facetious Mercury in your tongue, as [I] lame Vulcan in my feete.'[79] If Cane played Reignald, his quick tongue would have justified the line 'I'll be the Mercury for your release' (II.ii.97), an alchemical association (repeated at IV.i.12f.) made more amusing by Cane's other profession, as a goldsmith, who later coined money for the Royalist army while he also took part in surreptitious performances at the Red Bull.[80] In any case, it is a fair presumption that the two slippery characters, Geraldine and Reignald, were in good hands. *The English Traveller* could have been played by eleven men and two boys (with a perhaps suggestive doubling of Mistress Wincott with the whore Blanda or the bawd Scapha, and of Prudentilla with the honest servant Bess as well as Scapha or Blanda) and four non-speaking parts, two gallants and two wenches. I have found no record of a performance of the play since those 'Publikely acted at the Cock-pit in Drury-lane: By Her Majesties servants', as claimed on the 1633 title page.

THE CAPTIVES

On 3 September 1624 Sir Henry Herbert licensed 'For the Cockpit Company; A New Play, called *The Captive, or The Lost recovered*: Written by Hayward'.[81] In 1885 Bullen[82] identified this title with the third play in a collection of manuscript plays now in the British Library, reprinted here.[83] The manuscript lacks a title and indication of authorship, but Herbert's title and subtitle are so appropriate to this play that the identification has not been questioned, nor Heywood's authorship doubted. Since Bullen's ascription to Heywood, further scholarship on the question has simply added to the weight of supporting internal evidence, in particular the spelling 'ey' for 'aye', used only by Heywood in this period, other distinctive vocabulary choices, especially 'mechal', 'to entire', and 'to insidiate',[84] and a handwriting quirk that explains the printer's errors '*Actus 46*' and '*Actus 56*' in *The Wise-woman of Hogsdon*.[85] It is perhaps a little odd that Heywood should use the title of one Plautus play (*Captivi*) in naming a play based on another (*Rudens*), and it is possible that the Herbert entry refers to a now lost play based on *Captivi*, or one about a single captive, but these are hardly grounds for doubting the accepted identification. (It is equally possible that *The Captive* is the correct title of this play: 'It shall never / Be said you took a captive to your bed / But a free woman' (V.v.152ff.).)

That the manuscript is in Heywood's extremely difficult hand is clear from orthographic peculiarities paralleled in printed Heywood texts, and from numerous authorial alterations made *currente calamo*.[86] The special interest of this manuscript, however, lies not only in its authorial improvements, including cuts of over two hundred lines (printed in full in an Appendix to this edition) but also in the extensive annotations of a book-keeper preparing the play for performance. These annotations, recorded in the Collation (as *MS3*),[87] show a prompter clarifying exits and entrances, often with an asterisk in the margin, indicating sound effects and clearances of the stage, and noting the need for properties. That this work by the prompter was for a particular performance is shown by his distribution of some of the minor roles. For example, at III.ii.40 the 'country fellows' are allocated to 'Gibson', 'stagekeeper' and 'Taylor'; 'Gibson' takes the part of the Factor in V.i; and in V.iv the stage-keepers act as guards.[88] The prompter also suggested a number of cuts in the text (not followed in this edition, but recorded in the Collation), of which the most important are II.i.8–23 (religious caution), II.i.176 (removal of music), II.i.190–6 (religious caution), II.ii.15–20 (avoidance of class issues), II.ii.138–53 (unnecessary to main action), III.i.38 (to remove an age difference between Lord and Lady), and V.v.3–6, 13–15 (to remove Sarlabois from Act V). Many of these changes are practical; some reflect a kind of self-censorship in the theatre. The manuscript as annotated by the book-keeper was ready for transcription (needing only minor improvements, notably the addition of other exits and entrances) into a clean fair copy by a scribe for use in performance. That would probably have been the copy licensed by the censor Herbert and used in the theatre, since no licence appears on the surviving manuscript's blank last page.[89]

The date of performance (if the identification with *The Captives* is correct) will have been shortly after 3 September 1624. This accords well with the fact that the subplot of Friar John and the Lady d'Averne is retold in *Gunaikeion* (pp. 253–6) as 'The Faire Lady of Norwich'. As with *The English Traveller*, there can be little doubt that the play precedes the retelling in *Gunaikeion*. The story, though set in Norwich in the time of Henry V, is told with an unusual particularity of detail. The antagonistic friars' names are given, while the names of the Lord and Lady, more crucial to the story, are withheld, and details such as Friar John perfuming his cap before his assignation with the Lady, and Friar Richard sitting astride the monastery wall, are emphasised out of all proportion to their original importance. A number of phrases are quoted from the play, most strikingly 'as sudden extremities impresse in men as sudden shifts' (255) from 'These sudden mischiefs should have sudden shifts' (IV.ii.46), 'murther is one of the crying sinnes, and such a one as cannot be concealed' (155) from 'Murder is / A crying sin, and cannot be concealed' (IV.v.23–4) and 'hee thinkes it the safer course to trust to foure legges than to two' (255) from 'Far better than to two legs, trust to four' (IV.vi.24, the memorable closing line of an act). These are all quasi-proverbial phrases, but, in the question of priority, all can be presumed to have existed in the play before being quoted in *Gunaikeion*. While in his prose narrative Heywood sets the story in England, as one 'which I have often heard related' (253) and which 'remaines still recorded' (256),[90] the plot of the play in fact closely follows the first story in the 1476 collection *Il Novellino* of Masuccio di Salerno;[91] the few changes made by Heywood for dramatic effect (the monastery's dependence on the Lord's generosity, thus increasing the friar's guilt; the greater nobility of the Lady; the friar's involvement of the baker) are all reproduced in the prose retelling. The one element in which the prose version is closer to Masuccio is the final scene, where the Lord is pardoned without his wife's intercession. It may be that in this instance Heywood was hastening towards his rather abbreviated conclusion, and preferred to omit the wife's contribution, despite the general purpose of *Gunaikeion*. A final minor item of evidence is the date on Mirable/Palestra's handkerchief in the discovery scene (IV.i.257): 'born in Christ Church, London, *Anno* 1600'. In the manuscript (l. 2227) this date was first written '1600' by Heywood (suggesting a composition date of the early 1620s, the author imagining his heroine born at the start of the century) then altered by the prompter to '1530', so distancing the action of the play. The *Gunaikeion* retelling continues this distancing, into the heroic period of Henry V's 'warres in France' (253). We can feel confidence, then, in a terminal date of 1624 for the play's composition; if written earlier, that is unlikely to have been by more than a few years. The phrase 'anything for a quiet life' (III.iii.99–100) appears not to be on record before 1621, when it was the title of a Middleton play.

One other aspect of the subplot, the motif of the 'twice-killed friar', has occasioned comment, because of its appearance also in Marlowe's *The Jew of Malta*, played in the 1590s but seen through the press by Heywood in 1633. Heywood's biographer was of the opinion that the episode of the strangling of Friar Barnadine by Barabas and Ithamore, who then deceive Friar Jacomo into believing himself the murderer, is an insertion by Heywood, 'told in exactly the allusive way in which a person retells a story he has already told'.[92] *The Jew of Malta*'s most recent editors are divided on the question,[93] and it is not necessary to argue this thorny topic in full again here. One feature of the *Captives* text, however, is worth noting. At IV.ii.34.1, Heywood wrote 'Either strikes him with a staff or casts a stone', leaving the choice of weapon unresolved. Later, at V.v.299, Friar Richard confesses 'I hit him with a stone.' The weapon in Masuccio had been a stone, and in *Gunaikeion* (255) also it is a 'Brick-bat'. What is the source of the intrusive staff? It is the means used (somewhat puzzlingly) in *The Jew of Malta* both to prop up the strangled friar (at IV.i.155) and to 'kill' him again (IV.i.173), an event introducted by the inept line 'And see, a staff stands ready for the purpose'—with which one might compare Friar Richard's 'here's a ladder left!' at *Cap.* IV.ii.57. Marlowe's (or his reviser's) staff is derived from an English jest-book version of the same tale, 'Dan Hew, Monk of Leicester',[94] one of many versions of the widespread fabliau.[95] Heywood, using Masuccio for his version of the story in *The Captives* and *Gunaikeion*, nevertheless remembered the staff from early performances of *The Jew of Malta*, a play also recalled when the Lord d'Averne considers blowing up the monastery at III.i.79ff.[96]

The main plot of the play is closely imitated from Plautus, *Rudens* (*The Rope*), of which every scene finds an equivalent in *The Captives*, though transferred to a new setting near Marseilles. The temple of Venus becomes a monastery (which may have suggested the idea of the Masuccio subplot to Heywood) and Palestra's recovered casket contains 'not the Roman trinkets—the little golden sword and axe and the little silver knife—but embroidered handkerchiefs and baby clothes'.[97] While omitting little of interest in Plautus, apart from the striking lines 593–614, Daemones' dream of the monkey (see headnote to III.ii), Heywood did make additions. He inserted three musical numbers: an echo scene (II.i.76ff.), a grotesque duet between Palestra and Mildew (App. 122–40), and a song on poverty by Gripus (App. 193–224), though it is notable that two of the three additions were cut by Heywood on second thoughts.[98] He also developed a greater affection between Palestra and Scribonia, and introduced the quarrel between Ashburn and his wife in IV.i.103ff. His major alteration to the Latin is a considerable expansion of the abrupt, somewhat cynical, ending of *Rudens* into a harmonious conclusion involving the principal characters of both plots.[99] The most thoughtful recent essay on *The Captives*, by Carolyn Prager, regards Heywood's adaptation of *Rudens* as significant in its treatment of the morality of slavery. In Plautus, the father Daemones (after freeing the girls and his slave Gripus) invites the pimp Labrax home to dinner: 'Moral censure, if any, is directed against the conteporary evil of child-stealing. Chattel slavery and its moral ramifications are not controversial issues in the play.'[100] In *The Captives*, by contrast, Mildew is universally condemned. In the final scene he is 'denied the redemptive communal embrace of forgiveness that concludes the Latin play'.[101] His crime is not in the holding of slaves, since, as Sarlabois comments at I.i.190–7, slavery was commonplace in 1550, the play's dramatic date, and Marseilles was 'a thriving centre of a multi-ethnic slave trade well into the seventeenth century'.[102] Instead, Mildew's offence is the enslavement of free-born English women: 'I tell thee, peasant, / England's no brood for slaves' (III.ii.70f.). It is this moral indignation at the enslavement of Christians, found increasingly in seventeenth-century drama,[103] that can be seen in sharp focus in *The Captives*. If Heywood's first motive was patriotism and a belief in the freedom conferred by citizenship, he deserves credit for questioning a practice not generally regarded as reprehensible before the nineteenth century.[104]

Building on Prager's insight, it is possible to see a closer thematic relationship between the main and secondary plots of *The Captives* than its critics will allow. While the triangle of the Lord and Lady d'Averne and Friar John has little formal connexion with the loss, captivity and eventual rediscovery of the two English girls, the narratives echo each other, much in the manner of *The English Traveller*, and it may be that their very separation gives emphasis to the echoes. Heywood's crucial modifications of the Plautine original (his sensitivity to slavery, the praise of freedom, his development of Ashburn's wife Isabel as a speaking part, and the emphasis on the reunion of two families as brothers, daughters and cousins in the conclusion) allow him opportunities to explore in the main plot the linked themes of trade and inheritance, of sexuality as a form of commerce, and of marriage as a contract. The main plot begins with the attempt to sell two women as a commodity, and ends in their marriage. The procurer, a villainous outsider, a trader in flesh, is balanced by the respectable Thomas Ashburn, also an outsider (with no equivalent in Plautus), who appears in the fifth act to improve his older brother's fortunes and recover his own lost daughter. As in *The English Traveller*, the themes of storm and travel are linked with those of commerce and marriage; the storm of I.iii reverses the fortunes of Mildew and his captives, and it is the same storm that drives Thomas Ashburn out of his way to a fortunate reunion. The storm is not only a literal tempest, as described in I.iii and marked as continuing between the scene-break between II.i and II.ii; the off-stage thunder of the first two acts mutates into a series of directions for off-stage tumult. III.ii begins with the direction 'Enter after a great noise within, the Clown, meeting with John Ashburn and Godfrey', as the girls take sanctuary from Mildew. Soon Godfrey promises to 'go call the peasants / To raise another tempest', and is immediately rewarded with 'A tumult within and sudden noise' (III.ii.41.1), heralding the town's defence against Mildew. In the next act, however, a similar direction introduces a more domestic tumult, the jealous quarrel between Ashburn and his wife over Palestra and Scribonia: 'Enter after a noise or tumult John Ashburn, his wife, Palestra, Scribonia and Godfrey' (IV.i.104,1–2). The vigorous argument between Ashburn and his 'curst wife',[105] in which she claims to have been 'too long a grizel' and accuses him of earlier infidelities and now of making his 'private house a stews' (IV.i.108, 112), meets with the ironic aside from Godfrey, 'Why, this storm's worse than that untiled the house' (IV.i.122), and a similar comment from Palestra, 'The land's to us as dreadful as the seas, / For we are here, as by the billows, tossed / From one fear to another' (IV.i.142–4). By this device Heywood allows the sexual and domestic storms to develop out of the actual tempest, as preparation for the discoveries, later in the scene, that will produce 'a shower of joyful tears' (IV.i.336) and the final marriages: 'O, happy storm / That ends in such a calm!' (V.v.237–8).

Yet this device of the off-stage noise is not confined to the main plot. It appears again in literal form at the end of V.ii ('A noise within, trampling of horses'), an uproar that leads to the unmasking of Friar Richard, pursued by the 'ghost' of Friar John on horseback. The noise is a reminder that the domestic tempests (now calmed) of the main story have their counterpart in the subplot. This storm of jealousy, begun by Friar John's letter and leading to his murder, and now resolved in the tumult of horses, is handled most delicately in the 'unquiet sleeps' of the Lord's troubled conscience (IV.iii.1–18). In this encounter with his Lady, the Lord moves from bitterness ('You dog me, lady, / Like an ill genius'), countered with her mild reply ('You were wont to call me / Your better angel'), into a gentler resolution, marked by his refusal to make her a party to his guilt. The wife's quiet acceptance here, amid the storms surrounding her, contrasts with the less patient response of Ashburn's wife. The two domestic scenes (IV.i and IV.iii) parallel each other. Both move from quarrel to understanding, but by different routes, the Ashburns by discovery, the d'Avernes in a pact of secrecy. Even more strikingly, the slavery theme of the main plot, expressed literally in Mildew's ownership of the girls, and metaphorically in Ashburn's unhappy marriage, finds an answer in the trusting and co-operative equal marriage of the subplot. Here the Lady is open with her husband, supports him even after the friar's murder, and eventually, 'In the time / That you were seized with this deep melancholy / And inward sorrow' (V.v.321ff.) wins his pardon from the king, to save his life.

If the lines just quoted are reminiscent of Marina's role in *Pericles*, we should note other echoes of that romance in *The Captives*. Raphael's and Mildew's descriptions of Palestra / Mirabel in the play's opening scene are surely meant to recall Marina in Mytilene, and in the discovery (IV.i) Ashburn, like Pericles, by his own account 'so many years . . . Despoiled, / Neglected, scattered', is 'made up again, / Repaired and new created' by the reunion with his daughter, whom he asks, even after knowing her identity, to tell her mother's name. Like Marina, Perdita and Miranda, the rediscovered girl of *The Captives* also has a name that can be played upon meaningfully: 'O mirror of thy sex, my Mirabel' (IV.i.281). Heywood does not match *Pericles* V.i, either in psychological depth or in poetry—indeed, he sees fit to end his discovery scene with a passage of verbal foolery with the Clown (IV.i.300–23) that suggests an uncertainty about the scale of the emotions, similar to that at the end of *The English Traveller*—but it would seem that he wished to send his characters on a similar journey, from dislocation to wholeness, and in that he was not unsuccessful. If the tragicomedy of *The English Traveller* shows the influence of Fletcher, especially in the friendship between Geraldine and Old Wincott, *The Captives* explores themes found in all four of Shakespeare's late romances: an assault on innocence (by Mildew in one story and Friar John in the other), the regenerative power of children and (again in both plots) the restoration of harmony through marriage. In *The Captives*, less literally, and less magically, than their counterparts in *Pericles*, *Cymbeline* and *The Winter's Tale*, but no less meaningfully, both Ashburn and the Lord d'Averne rediscover their wives.

One influence remains to be considered. Only occasionally does the action of *The Captives* share the claustrophobic intimacy noted in the second half of *The English Traveller*, which may have been encouraged by the conditions of the indoor theatre. Other features, however, do suggest a response to those conditions. One, already discussed, is the frequent use of off-stage noise, probably most effective in the Cockpit's enclosed space. Another is the crucial series of night scenes in Acts III and IV, on which the subplot turns, just as the turning-point of Geraldine's fortunes in *The English Traveller* is played in darkness. This effect, which is both literal and emblematic in both plays, was no doubt easier to achieve indoors. Finally, both plays contain spectacular climbing scenes,[106] Reignald's climb to safety in *The English Traveller* IV.vi and the repeated use of the ladder by Friar Richard and Dennis in *Captives* IV.ii and IV.iv to transport Friar John's body back and forth across the monastery wall. Siege-scenes involving ladders and climbing were common in public theatre plays, but there is a virtuoso feel about the use of the *frons scenae* façade and the upper stage in both of these instances that suggests a particular delight in their use, and the effects (of comedy in one instance and of macabre farce in the other) must have been striking.

In presenting the play for performance, Heywood calls in the last scene for a total of fourteen adult speakers and four speaking boys, in addition to non-speaking officers and a maid. That the prompter cut one male part (Sarlabois) and one female (Isabel) from the scene is perhaps an indication that the forces proposed by the playwright were too large for the Lady Elizabeth's Men, though this need not mean that Heywood was less intimately connected with the company. With the exception of the allocations of minor roles discussed earlier, none of the parts can be assigned with certainty, but it is a fair presumption that the Clown was played by Andrew Cane, again with considerable additional business, no longer recoverable, and it is an intriguing possibility that Richard Perkins, who was a memorable Barabas in this company's revival of *The Jew of Malta*, may have brought similar skills to the part of Mildew. I am not aware of any professional performance of *The Captives* since its original presentation at the Cockpit in Drury Lane around 1624. The play might, if attempted, prove successful; like the other pieces in this volume, it has variety and energy, and was written to please.

HEYWOOD IN THE TWENTIETH CENTURY

Would these plays satisfy today's audiences? In the twentieth century, Heywood has been represented on the professional stage by very few of his works. *A Woman Killed with Kindness* has been revived with some frequency,[107] most recently by the Royal Shakespeare Company at The Other Place in October 1991. This production, by Katie Mitchell, was set in a wooden cottage with a peat floor, and had as its background a rustic carnival, thus diluting the author's critique of the minor gentry's slippery values. In a quite different vein, Heywood's sprawling romance *The Fair Maid of the West* has been successful in at least two modern renditions, both of them skilful conflations of the two parts into one. Jane Howell's 1971 version at Exeter's Northcott Theatre as a West Country musical, spiced with frequent songs and shanties, was an invigorating romp, and Trevor Nunn's 1986 Swan Theatre Stratford production, also ornamented with occasional songs fashioned from the more poetic passages of the text, provided a spectacular demonstration both of the versatility of the Swan's open stage and of Heywood's sure instincts for vivid theatre.

Heywood's episodic method and interest in dissonant effects (the much-derided songs in his *Rape of Lucrece*, or his ironic way with subplots) may, in the words of Simon Trussler, 'find a more open response in an age which has assimilated Brecht'.[108] He was not a philosopher or political theorist, but, as *An Apology for Actors* demonstrates throughout, he believed strongly in theatre as a means of instruction, and like Brecht, his ability to instruct was founded on close observation. He does not, in the manner of Jonson, invite the audience to inhabit a fully-realised locale and season of the year,[109] but the two London plays in this volume both make interesting use of contrasts between the more ordered business world of the City and the less disciplined life of the northern suburbs. Heywood's effects are for the most part quiet, the plots of his plays rapid and economical, and his themes generally taken from everyday life and treated with a lively sympathetic interest rather than high drama. The strengths and weaknesses of his method can be seen clearly in a comparison of *The Wise-woman of Hogsdon*'s final scene with that of *Volpone*. In both, a confidence trickster is brought to judgement and unmasked through a series of surprising reversals, and in both, the deceiver's closest associate holds the key to his unmasking. Jonson's version is a devastating exposé, which wounds almost all of its participants, a sardonic stripping-away of illusions, the true 'mortifying of a fox', and the punishments are savage. By comparison, Chartley's unmasking may seem slight, his gradual self-entrapment and confusion merely an embarrassment, and his eventual forgiveness too easily won. Yet Heywood's characteristically good-natured resolution required a whole play's intrigues to achieve, and harmony is as precious a commodity as disillusionment. Heywood may seem unambitious, too eager to please, when compared with the bright clangour of Jonson's language or the flamboyance of his revelations, but the arraignment of Chartley before a jury of his peers is as democratic and equitable as any trial scene of the period. If it was played at Court in December of 1604, it may, like *The Merry Wives of Windsor* a month earlier, have made a quietly revolutionary comment on society's ability to heal its own divisions through a kind of social theatre. At this level, in their insistence on considering perennial problems (fortune-hunting rogues, or the dangers of unequal marriage, or the threats to women in slavery and prostitution) all three plays in this volume still have some lessons to teach.

A NOTE ON THE TEXTS

The sole early printing of *The Wise-woman of Hogsdon* was the quarto from the press of Marmaduke Parsons in 1638.[110] Parsons, a printer active only between 1637 and 1639, also printed in 1638 texts by Heywood's associates Thomas Dekker, Henry Peacham and John Taylor, the Water Poet. [111] The compositors had considerable difficulty with their copy, which we can be certain was in Heywood's notoriously unreadable script, for which he himself apologises (as a 'difficult and unacquainted hand') on behalf of the compositor of *The Exemplary Lives . . . of Nine . . . Worthy Women* in 1640. The text preserves characteristic Heywood spellings (including twelve examples of the unique 'ey' for 'aye'), and the act headings '*Actus 46*' and '*Actus 56*' clearly derive from Heywood's style as seen in *The Captives* MS.[112] In addition the error (*Anne* for *Gratiana*) in the speech prefix at V.vi.14 must surely come from the author, who had married an Anne in June 1603,[113] and whose Woman Killed with Kindness in that same year also had that name. Other evidence of an authorial presence are the explanatory stage directions (e.g. '*Enter the second* Luce, *which was* Iack *in womans apparell . . .*', III.i.0.1) and the marginal information, such as '*Meaning* Boyster' at III.i.94.[114] Most striking is the additional note (in roman type) to the direction at IV.ii.59, '*shee faints*': '*Boyst.* held her up.' The past tense suggests reminiscence of a performance, and may represent commentary by an author making a fair copy for publication, as one of a number of texts which he edited in the 1630s. W. T. Jewkes notes [115] that act headings do not appear in Heywood texts before 1608, so that the careful divisions in this text may also indicate a later authorial copy rather than the original draft. There are no indications of a prompter/book-keeper's annotations. The evidence suggests that copy for the 1638 print is an annotated manuscript of Heywood's.

There is extensive proof-correction in almost every sheet of the text, about fifty out of the total of eighty corrections occurring in sigs F and G (from the start of Act IV). There was almost certainly a change of compositors at this point. Signatures A–E were probably set seriatim,

F–I certainly by forme;[116] there may well have been, as Greg suggests,[117] a change of type; and there are clear spelling variations, in act headings, running titles, the names Chartley and Haringfield, the u/v habit and the spellings sir/syr and I'le/Ile/ile.[118] There would seem to be evidence also of a pair of compositors at work within signatures F–I: on F4 the compositor set the spelling 'syr' seven times in the dialogue, at every appearance of the word, whereas on F2 the word is spelled 'sir' at every one of five appearances. There are variations also in the italicisation of stage directions and the abbreviation of speech prefixes that suggest two workers, but there is no clear pattern. Perhaps an experienced compositor was working with an apprentice. For this edition I have collated twenty-five copies of the 1638 quarto, and noted the readings of the modern editions (see Collation). There is no evidence of authorial involvement in the proof-reading of the quarto.

The English Traveller also appears in a single early quarto, that of Robert Raworth in 1633.[119] Raworth had a chequered career, printing from 1606 to 1608 and from 1633 to 1636. In 1635 and 1636 he published two other Heywood plays and one of his Lord Mayor's shows, in addition to works by Dekker, Peacham and the celebration of Dover's Cotswold games, Walbanke's *Annalia Dubrensia*, to which Heywood contributed. The printer's copy for *The English Traveller* seems to have been a theatre transcript: twenty of the entries are placed a line or two early (see Collation); the spelling 'Reighnald' in the stage direction at IV.vi.321 may well be that of a prompter/book-keeper; and there is a puzzling marginal note at IV.i.107, '*Bayes.*', in response to the text's mention of bay windows, that must be (however inexplicably) of playhouse origin. Some of the act divisions and exit markings also contain irregular Latin of a kind hardly likely in Heywood's copy. A marked change in spelling patterns between sigs F and G (at III.iii.71), from a combination of ile/Ile/il'e and bin/beene to a consistent I'le/bin habit, suggests a change of compositors, but the use throughout of a distinctive letter combination in place of a more normal ligature[120] raises the possibility of a single compositor setting from mixed copy. I have collated twenty-four copies of the 1633 quarto, and noted nine examples of press-correction; the relative ease of printing itself argues on behalf of scribal rather than authorial copy. None of the changes made in proof suggests authorial intervention; indeed, one of them, 'Gold' for 'Gould' at IV.i.12 (G2v), alters a characteristic Heywood spelling. I have also taken account (see Collation) of the emendations of modern editors.

This edition of *The Captives* is a modernised text of Heywood's autograph manuscript, in British Library MS Egerton 1994. This manuscript has been fully described by W. W. Greg, Arthur Brown and Ernst Honigmann, [121] the last of whom has established beyond doubt, through study of four types of copyist's error (eye-skip, omission, mishearing, mislineation), that the manuscript is an author's copy of a rougher draft, 'a transcript fouled by frequent bursts of free composition'. One might add a fifth category of copyist's error in support of these four: the copying of verse lines as prose. There are a number of speeches in the play (lines 462–5, 545–6, 597–600, 1509–12, 2328–31 and 2357–8 in the Malone Society reprint) that I feel should be relineated as verse. These key examples are spoken by Godfrey, a serving-man character, normally a verse-speaker, who shares the stage in the third scene with the prose-speaking Clown, and may have become assimilated in the author's mind with that type, so receiving some prose lines in error when the text was copied. (These speeches are at I.iii.4–7, 76–7, 112–14, III.ii.50–3, IV.i.338–41, 361–2.) Heywood's hand is present in two inks, called here *MS1* (corrected by him as *MS1b* and *MS1c*) and *MS2*, his later, final thoughts. The manuscript subsequently passed from Heywood to a prompter/book-keeper (*MS3* in the Collation), who annotated it carefully for performance, leaving it (though untidy) ready for transcript as a prompt-copy.[122] This would presumably have been the copy licensed by Herbert on 3 September 1624. My text follows, substantively, Heywood's final intentions, while modernising spelling and punctuation.[123] Very occasionally, Heywood's second thoughts are less effective (as at II.i.19, 'the heavens'', for his earlier, metrical, 'Heaven's') but even in such cases I follow his latest expressed intention. *MS1* and *MS2* variants within a line (excluding slips of the pen, mis-lineation, or other copying errors, which may be followed in the text and notes of the Malone Society edition)[124] are recorded in the Collation, variants and cuts of a whole line or more being collected in a separate Appendix. I collate *MS3*, the prompter's alterations, as editorial emendations, recording also, but not following, his proposed cuts. I have not collated his asterisks in the margin indicating entries, his comments (e.g. 'to them' or 'Manet') nor his instruction 'clere' to mark the ends of scenes, though I have allowed these to assist me in the vexed question of scene divisions in Acts IV and V, in the latter of which the book-keeper has five scenes for Heywood's three (see Collation to V.v, Scene heading). In addition to Brown's Malone Society reprint, there have been two previous editions, both in old spelling, by Bullen in 1885 and Judson in 1921. Judson and Brown in particular have been useful in their suggestions for missing entries and exits, and I am indebted to all three editions for necessary emendations, which are recorded in the Collation.

The present edition

This text follows the principles of modernised spelling and punctuation established for the Revels Plays and continued in the Revels Plays Companion Library. The collations record all substantive departures from my copytexts, the quartos and Heywood's manuscript respectively; editorial additions to stage directions (including those of the book-keeper for the presumed original production of *The Captives*) are enclosed in square brackets. The collations also list proof-corrections in the quartos, authorial and book-keeper alterations in the *Captives* MS, and emendations, including those of my predecessors in their editions of the three plays.

In my treatment of elisions in *The Captives* I have not followed Heywood's eccentric habit of eliding 'the' with a following consonant, as in lines 115, 'th' stooping' (I.i.69), 190, 'ith Cittye' (I.i.123) or 475, 'oth' topp' (I.iii.16). Like previous editors of Heywood, I have attempted to determine and restore verse lines printed as prose in the quartos. In the *Captives* MS, as discussed earlier, even the author seems occasionally to have mistaken verse lines for prose when making his fair copy. The compositors of *The Wise-woman of Hogsdon*, and in particular those of Acts IV and V, had special difficulty with their copy in the matter of verse, as may be seen from the tables at the close of its Textual Collation. *The English Traveller* quarto is more successful in identifying verse, but contains an unusual number of mislineations; these are also recorded at the end of that play's Collation. My text is somewhat more generous than previous editions in restoring verse lines, especially in *The Wise-woman*, but I have borne in mind the possibility (in all three plays) that heavily iambic prose may contain verse-fossils remaining from an earlier draft. One example, at *ET* IV.vi.39–41, is instructive. Old Lionel speaks verse:

> Yet I advise thee, fellow, for thy good...

to which the prose-speaking Clown replies:

> And I advise thee, friend, for thine own good...

In the latter case Heywood (in a speech undoubtedly intended as prose) has preserved an iambic line, adding the extra syllable 'own' when altering 'fellow' to 'friend'. Perhaps in this and other similar cases he unconsciously fell into verse. He was of course a writer of unusual speed and facility (as he himself notes in a famous comment in the *English Traveller* preface), and it would probably be a vain pursuit to attempt a precise distinction between his loosely accented, colloquial verse and its twin, his casual conversational prose.

NOTES

1 Titles of Heywood's likely or known domestic or marital dramas (dates as in Harbage) include *Joan as Good as my Lady*, 1599 (lost comedy); *1 and 2 Edward IV*, 1592–99 (history); *War without Blows and Love without Suit*, 1598–99 (lost comedy); *How a Man May Choose a Good Wife from a Bad*, 1601–02 (comedy); *The Blind Eats Many a Fly*, 1602 (lost comedy); *A Woman Killed with Kindness*, 1603 (tragedy); *How to Learn of a Woman to Woo*, 1604 (?lost comedy); *The Wise-woman of Hogsdon*, ?1604 (comedy); *The Rape of Lucrece*, 1606–08 (classical tragedy); *1 and 2 The Iron Age*, 1612–13 (classical legend); *The Captives*, 1624 (comedy); *The English Traveller*, ?1624 (tragi-comedy); *Love's Mistress*, 1634 (classical legend); *Love's Masterpiece*, 1640 (lost comedy).

2 Peter Ure, 'Marriage and the Domestic Drama in Heywood and Ford', *English Studies* 32 (1951), 200.

3 Set out at length in Louis B. Wright, *Middle-class Culture in Elizabethan England* (Chapel Hill, 1935), in C. L. Powell, *English Domestic Relations 1487–1653* (New York, 1917, 1972) and M. Grivelet, *Thomas Heywood et le drame domestique élisabéthain* (1959).

4 William Perkins, *Christian Oeconomie* (1590, trans. 1609) in *Works*, vol. III (1618), p. 669. Quoted by Catherine Belsey in *The Subject of Tragedy* (1985), p. 143.

5 William Gouge, *Of Domesticall Duties* (1622), sig. A4. This work was reprinted four times before 1629.

6 Quoted in Keith Wrightson, *English Society 1580–1680* (1982), p. 91.

7 Lawrence Stone, *Family, Sex and Marriage in England 1500–1800* (1977), pp. 7ff.

8 Stone, p. 8. Wrightson notes (p. 71) that Stone's evolutionary account may be valid for the 'aristocracy, upper gentry and leaders of urban society', but hardly universal.

9 Alan Macfarlane, *Marriage and Love in England: Modes of Reproduction 1300–1840* (Oxford, 1986), pp. 330–1.

10 A. (Aletheia?), *The Passionate Morris Dance* (1593), pp. 98–9. Quoted by Wright, p. 211.

11 *1 FMW* I.ii.80–4.

12 Aletheia, *Tell Trothes New Year's Gift* (1593), p. 5. Quoted by Wright, p. 210.

13 See Wallace Notestein, 'The English Woman 1580–1650', in *Studies in Social History*, ed. J. H. Plumb (1955), pp. 69–107. See also Kate McLuskie, '"Tis but a woman's jar": Family and Kinship in Elizabethan Domestic Drama', *Literature and History* 9:2 (Autumn 1983), 228–39.

14 See G. R. Hibbard, 'Love, Marriage and Money in Shakespeare's Theatre and Shakespeare's England', *Elizabethan Theatre VI*, ed. Hibbard (1978), p. 154.

15 See Andrew Clark, 'An Annotated List of Lost Domestic Plays, 1578–1624', *RORD* 18 (1975), 29–44, and A. Clark, 'An Annotated List of Sources and Related Material for Elizabethan Domestic Tragedy, 1591–1616', *RORD* 17 (1974), 25–33.

16 H. H. Adams, *English Domestic or Homiletic Tragedy 1575–1642* (New York, 1943).

17 Marilyn L. Johnson, *Images of Women in the Works of Thomas Heywood* (Salzburg, 1974), p. 102.

18 These domestic tragedies occupy a quite different world from that, for example, of Clytemnestra or Phaedra as mediated through Seneca.

19 See George Duckworth, *The Nature of Roman Comedy* (Princeton, 1952), pp. 396–433, and Alexander Leggatt, *Citizen Comedy in the Age of Shakespeare* (Toronto, 1973), pp. 33–53. See also E. Beck, 'The Paradigm of the Prodigal Son in English Renaissance Comedy', *Renaissance Drama* n.s. 6 (1973), 107–22, and Arthur Brown, 'Citizen Comedy and Domestic Drama', *Stratford upon Avon Studies* 1 (1960), pp. 63–83. For the longevity of the prodigal son tradition (a performance of 1724) see James E. May and Calhoun Winton, 'The "Prodigal Son" at Bartholomew Fair: A New Document', *Theatre Survey* 21:1 (May 1980), 63–72.

20 *WWH* contains a large number of close parallels with this play. The most significant are noted in the Commentary. For fuller discussion, see Leonard (1980), Introduction, pp. 6ff.

21 Cf. Francis Bacon, at the close of his cynical essay 'Of Marriage and Single Life' (*Essaies*, 1612): 'It is often seene, that bad *Husbands*, have very good *Wives*; whether it be, that it rayseth the Price of their *Husbands* Kindnesse, when it comes; Or that the *Wives* take a Pride, in their *Patience*.' Often enough, divorce being unavailable, as Wrightson has noted (pp. 96–101), patient endurance was the only reasonable course for an unhappy spouse.

22 See James G. MacManaway, 'Latin Title-page Mottoes as a Clue to Dramatic Authorship', *Library*, 4th ser., 26 (1946), 35–6.

23 Samuel King's commendatory poem makes Heywood's involvement in the 1638 printing almost certain.

24 Fleay, I, 291–2.

25 Henslowe, *Diary*, pp. 86, 134, 216, 225, 296. The play also contains references to the titles *A Pill to Purge Melancholy* (1599) and *Jack Drum's Entertainment* (1600); while many of these titles are proverbial, their clustering in this play is probably an indicator of date.

26 Possibly Munday's *John a Kent and John a Cumber* (1590), a magic and disguise play.

27 Henslowe, *Diary*, pp. 16, 24, 26, 59, 86, 104, 218. To these should be added *The White Witch of Westminster, or Love in a Lunacy*, a lost manuscript play of unknown date and authorship, seen by Abraham Hill around 1680: J. Q. Adams, *Library*, 4th ser., 20 (1940), 71–99. Similar surviving plays are Greene's *James the Fourth* (?1590) and the curious mixture of enchantment, love intrigue and low comedy, *The Wisdom of Doctor Doddipol*, played by the Children of Paul's around 1599.

28 Thomas, p. 292. In 1597 James had proposed the death penalty for resort to cunning-men (Thomas, p. 293). It is curious that of the other plays in this Court 'season' (*Othello*, *The Merry Wives of Windsor*, *Measure for Measure*, *The Comedy of Errors* and Chapman's *All Fools*), three contain a supernatural element, and all are 'marriage' plays. *Love's Labour's Lost* (later in January) and *The Merchant of Venice* (twice in three days in February) continue the pattern.

29 The quotations from Mannington's 1576 sonnet in this play (V.vi.10–12) and in the 1605 *Eastward Ho* are no indication of date, since the ballad was presumably popular throughout the period.

30 Charles Nicholl, *The Chemical Theatre* (1980), pp. 15–16.

31 Wayne Shumaker, *The Occult Sciences in the Renaissance* (Berkeley, 1972).

32 Frances A. Yates, *The Occult Philosophy in the Elizabethan Age* (1979), part 2.

33 Herford and Simpson, VII, 409.

34 Thomas Heywood, *An Apology for Actors* (1612), quoted in Chambers, IV, 251.

35 Thomas, p. 227.

36 Shakespeare, *The Winter's Tale* V.iii.110f.

37 J. Leeds Barroll, in Barroll et al., editors, *The Revels History of Drama in English*, vol. III, 1576–1613 (1975), p. 87.

38 Keith Sturgess, *Three Elizabethan Domestic Tragedies* (Harmondsworth, 1969), pp. 46–7.

39 A tablet of dubious authority in the entryway identifies the original owner as Jenny Bingham, 'Mother Damnable', the 'Shrew of Kentish Town', whose four husbands were either hanged or met with early deaths. Suspected of witchcraft, she would endure the abuse of her neighbours while seated with her cat outside her tavern, 'wearing her old red cap on her head, and her shawl (with black markings that resembled bats) around her shoulders.' See also Sugden, p. 335, who notes that the tavern is said to have been the favourite resort of Moll Cutpurse.

40 Cf. the brutal revenge on a bigamist by two of his sixteen wives, in *The Defence of Coney-catching* (1592), reprinted in Gāmini Salgādo, *Coney-catchers and Bawdy Baskets* (Harmondsworth, 1972), pp. 366–71.

41 T. S. Eliot, 'Thomas Heywood', in *Elizabethan Dramatists* (1963 ed.), p. 101.

42 See Madeline Doran, *Endeavors of Art* (Madison, 1954), p. 165.

43 Corbin and Sedge, *Three Jacobean Witchcraft Plays* (Manchester, 1986), p. 7.

44 Leonard (1967), pp. 77, 79ff.

45 Neil Carson, 'John Webster: The Apprentice Years', *Elizabethan Theatre VI*, ed. G. R. Hibbard (1978), pp. 76ff.

46 Barbara J. Baines, *Thomas Heywood* (Boston, 1984), p. 69.

47 Paul Merchant, 'Thomas Heywood's Hand in *The Seven Champions of Christendom*', *Library*, 5th ser., 33 (September 1978), 226–30.
48 Although its inversions of natural order are given serious consideration in a wide-ranging study by Stuart Clark, 'Inversion, Misrule and the Meaning of Witchcraft', *Past and Present* 87 (1980), 98–127.
49 Anthony Trollope, MS notes of 26 May 1880, in his copy of the Pearson *Heywood*, now in the Folger Library.
50 In Chambers, III, 85, the Globe illustration tentatively suggests five doors, but George F. Reynolds, *The Staging of Elizabethan Plays at the Red Bull Theatre 1605–1625* (New York, 1940), finds evidence of no more than three doors demanded by the texts for that theatre. He discusses this scene, p. 109, suggesting that three might be hidden (one at each end, one in the middle) behind the curtain of the central discovery space.
51 Sandra A. Burner, 'A Provincial Strolling Company of the 1670s', *ThN* 20 (1965/6), 74–8.
52 Copy 3. The prompt-book for Coysh's production of *The Comedy of Errors* is in the Edinburgh University Library. See G. Blakemore Evans, *Shakespearean Prompt Books of the Seventeenth Century* (Charlottesville, 1964).
53 The adult company is presumably represented by the first nine names in the list of 15 March 1604 (Chambers II, 229–30). Greene was apparently business manager.
54 Nungezer, p. 319.
55 Chambers, IV, 254, quoting from 'I.H.', *The World's Folly* (1615).
56 Contributed to Heywood's 1612 *An Apology for Actors*. Reprinted Nungezer, pp. 277–8.
57 Bentley, IV, 556.
58 Allan Holaday, 'Thomas Heywood and the Low Countries', *MLN* 66 (January 1951), 16–19.
59 Now at Worcester College, Oxford. See D. F. Rowan, 'A Neglected Jones/Webb Theatre Project: Barber-Surgeons Hall Writ Large', *New Theatre Magazine* 9 (1969), 6–15 and 'A Neglected Jones/Webb Theatre Project, Part II: A Theatrical Missing Link', *Elizabethan Theatre II*, ed. David Galloway (1970), pp. 60–73. The drawings are also reproduced in *ShS* 23 (1970), and also to accompany the most thorough analysis (where they were first identified as the designs for Beeston's new Cockpit) by John Orrell, *The Theatres of Inigo Jones and John Webb* (Cambridge, 1985), pp. 39–77. The Cockpit in Drury Lane should not be confused with the Cockpit at Court, also designed by Jones.
60 Orrell, pp. 46–7.
61 Epistle, 'To the Great variety of Readers' in the Shakespeare First Folio (1623).
62 'A Modern History of an Adulteresse' in Thomas Heywood, *Gunaikeion: or Nine Bookes of Various History, Concerning Women* (1624), pp. 193–196.
63 'Opus Excogitatum, Inchoatum, Explicitum, Et a Typographo excusum, inter septemdecim septimanas.' The plots of two other plays are also narrated in *Gunaikeion*. *The Honest Man's Fortune*, by Fletcher in collaboration, played by Heywood's company in 1613, is told as the final story (pp. 458–62); the play corresponds with the second half of Heywood's story, the first half being supplied out of hints in Erasmus or the *Golden Legend*. The story of Comiola Turinga, told (pp. 448–9) as out of Fulgosus, was used by Massinger for *The Maid of Honour*, a 1622 Cockpit play, based on Painter's *Palace of Pleasure*, a Heywood source. See R. G. Martin, 'A Critical Study of *Gunaikeion*', *SP* 20 (April 1923), 160–83. Martin regards all four plays as having been earlier than the *Gunaikeion* retellings. In the other direction, *Gunaikeion* has been suggested as a source for *'Tis Pity She's a Whore* (ed. Derek Roper (Manchester, 1975), p. xxix).
64 Other close echoes from *ET* (in order of their *Gun*. appearance) are at I.i.21, II.i.285–7, IV.iii.2–3, III.iii.79–80, III.iii.109–12, III.iii.104–6, III.iii.158–62, IV.iii.137, IV.iii.148–50.

65 *Gunaikeion*, Preface, 'To the Reader'.
66 See Franklin B. Williams Jr, 'Spenser, Shakespeare and Zachary Jones', *ShQ* 19 (1968), 205–12. The original source is Athenaeus, *Deipnosophists*, II, 37 (Loeb, ed. Gulick, I, pp. 162–5).
67 See Allan Gilbert, 'Thomas Heywood's Debt to Plautus', *JEGP* 12 (1913), 593–611.
68 We possess thirteen licences by Herbert for the company between May 1622 and February 1625, including *The Captives*, but *The English Traveller* is not among them (Bentley, I, 185–6).
69 R. W. Van Fossen, ed., *A Woman Killed with Kindness* (1961), pp. 16, 126ff.
70 William Painter, *The Palace of Pleasure* (1575), three-volume reprint, ed. Joseph Jacobs (1890). Painter's tale is a translation of the first story of *Il Pecorone* (1385) of Ser Giovanni Fiorentino, which Heywood may have known directly. Another version appears as the twenty-first novel of Masuccio's *Il Novellino* (1474), a certain source for *The Captives*. This version adds a cynical friend, who may have suggested hints for the character of Dalavill. Painter is the source of plots for *The Rape of Lucrece*, *Appius and Virginia*, *A Woman Killed with Kindness*, and *The Royal King and the Loyal Subject*. See Douglas Bush, 'William Painter and Thomas Heywood', *MLN* 54 (1939), 279ff.
71 Even Freda I. Townsend, in a generally appreciative essay, 'The Artistry of Thomas Heywood's Double Plots', *PQ* 25 (April 1946), 97–119, sees 'no thematic or causal relationship between the two plots' in either *The English Traveller* or *The Captives*.
72 Michel Grivelet, 'The Simplicity of Thomas Heywood', *ShS* 14 (1961), 56–65, and Norman Rabkin, 'Dramatic Deception in Heywood's *The English Traveller*', *SEL* 1:2 (1961), 1–16.
73 Martin, while criticising (p. 183) Heywood's pedestrian translations in *Gunaikeion*, notes that its verse translations 'have a higher degree of interest'.
74 Grivelet and Rabkin provide the first (and still the best) detailed accounts of the play. Their analyses are included in the following discussion.
75 Well summarised by Baines, pp. 127–30.
76 Baines, p. 127.
77 Well surveyed by Rabkin, *passim*, and by Baines, pp. 122–5.
78 Reproduced in Andrew Gurr, *The Shakespearean Stage 1574–1642* (Cambridge, 1970), plate III. See also Webster, *The White Devil*, ed. John Russell Brown (1960), Epilogue and p. xxiii.
79 Quoted by Nungezer, p. 83.
80 Nungezer, p. 84. For a list of the (seven) chief players in 1622, Perkins not yet having joined the company, see Bentley, I, 183.
81 Bentley, I, 185.
82 A. H. Bullen, *A Collection of Old English Plays* (1885), IV, 99–127.
83 BM MS Egerton 1994, folios 52a–73a.
84 See A. E. H. Swaen, *How a Man May Choose a Good Wife from a Bad*, Bang, *Materialen* (1912), viii; Judson, pp. 11ff; Brown, p. vii; Brown, 'Two Notes on Thomas Heywood', *MLR* 50 (1955), 497–8; Anthony Low, 'Thomas Heywood's Authorship of *The Captives*', *N & Q* 15 (1968), 252–3; Henry D. Janzen, 'A Note on the Authorship of *The Escapes of Jupiter*', *ELN* 10 (1973), 270–3. See Commentary in this edition on I.i.33, I.i.201, II.ii.144 and IV.ii.42. To these examples should be added the close echoes in *The Captives* of passages elsewhere in Heywood's work. See Commentary on *Appendix* 16–23 (first noted by Brown, 1955), and on I.iii.69–70, II.ii.108–9, III.ii.25–6, IV.i.296–7 and IV.i.361.
85 Brown, pp. vii–viii.
86 Brown, p. vi.
87 They are printed as a list in Greg, pp. 285–8, and may be followed in bold type in the Malone Society transcription.

88 Gibson is assigned to minor roles in two other plays in MS Egerton 1994: *Two Noble Ladies* and *Edmund Ironside*. Taylor had minor roles in *Two Noble Ladies*. See Greg, pp. 232, 257, 274.
89 Greg, pp. 203, 232.
90 These are typical story-tellers' tricks of attribution. Martin comments (p. 164) that 'the more exact and circumstantial Heywood becomes the more likely he is to be borrowing'.
91 Masuccio di Salerno, *Il Novellino* (1476), tr. W. G. Waters (1895, edition of 1903) vol. I, novel 1, pp. 12–99. See also Emil Koeppel, *Archiv für das Studium der Neueren Sprachen und Literaturen* 97 (1896), pp. 323–9 and Judson, pp. 17–25. Masuccio's story is set in Castile.
92 A. M. Clark, *Thomas Heywood, Playwright and Miscellanist* (Oxford, 1931), pp. 287–94.
93 Christopher Marlowe, *The Complete Works*, ed. Fredson Bowers, vol. I (Cambridge, 1973), pp. 255–7; *The Jew of Malta*, ed. N. W. Bawcutt (Manchester, 1978), pp. 39–46.
94 See Judson, pp. 18–19 and Otto Rauchbauer, 'The Subplot of Thomas Heywood's *The Captives*: Some Facts and Speculations', *Études Anglaises* 30.3 (1977), 343–5.
95 The motif is familiar as the Hunchback's Tale at the start of *The Arabian Nights*; it is number 1537 in the Aarne–Thompson catalogue, *The Types of the Folktale* (Helsinki, 1961). Cf. K. M. Briggs, *A Dictionary of British Folk-tales*, 4 vols (1970–1), part A vol. 2, p. 190. The motif appears also as a device in *The Revenger's Tragedy* V.i.
96 It is of course not impossible for Heywood to have revised *The Jew of Malta* in 1601 (with Dan Hew as his source) and to have used the story again (from Masuccio) in *The Captives*.
97 Judson, p. 15.
98 For the echo scene, see Commentary at II.i.76.
99 See Mowbray Velte, *The Bourgeois Elements in the Drama of Thomas Heywood* (1922, repr. New York, 1966), pp. 57–8, who feels that the ending 'introduces just the romantic and human element necessary to please a city crowd'.
100 Carolyn Prager, 'Heywood's Adaptation of Plautus' *Rudens*: The Problem of Slavery in *The Captives*', *Comparative Drama* 9 (1975), 117.
101 Prager, p. 119.
102 Prager, p. 119.
103 Prager, pp. 120ff., surveys the debate on the ethics of slavery in the sixteenth and seventeenth centuries, and cites a number of plays on the topic, by Beaumont, Fletcher, Massinger, Dekker, Fisher and Heywood, among others.
104 Prager, pp. 119ff.
105 She is so named twice, at III.ii.197 and IV.i.149.
106 Use of the upper stage at the Cockpit is discussed by T. J. King in 'Staging of Plays at the Phoenix in Drury-Lane, 1617–42' *ThN* 19 (1965), 160. King notes that the time of ascent or descent seems to require between six and twelve lines of dialogue, as would be the case with Reignald's (?interior) descent.
107 *WKK*, lxii–lxiv. Since Van Fossen's summary of the stage history was written, the play has also been produced at London's National Theatre, in 1971.
108 Thomas Heywood, *The Fair Maid of the West*, a text with commentary by Simon Trussler (1986), p. 11. See also Arthur Brown, 'Citizen Comedy and Domestic Drama', in *Jacobean Theatre*, ed. J. R. Brown and B. Harris, Stratford-upon-Avon Studies I (1960), pp. 63–83, for discussion of Heywood's moral purpose.
109 R. L. Smallwood, '"Here, in the Friars": Immediacy and Theatricality in *The Alchemist*', *RES* n.s. XXXII, 126 (1980), 142–60.
110 W. W. Greg, *Bibliography of the English Printed Drama to the Restoration* (1962), play 535.
111 Pantzer, *STC*, vol. 3, p. 132.

112 Brown, p. viii.
113 Clark, p. 58.
114 W. T. Jewkes, *Act Division in Elizabethan and Jacobean Plays 1583–1616* (1958), pp. 303–4.
115 Jewkes, pp. 42 (n. 23), 344–5.
116 Leonard (1967), pp. 131–47.
117 Greg, *Bibliography*, play 535.
118 Leonard (1980), pp. 49–50.
119 Greg, *Bibliography*, play 484; Pantzer, *STC*, vol. 3, p. 142.
120 Macdonald P. Jackson, 'A Curious Typesetting Characteristic in Some Elizabethan Quartos', *Library*, 6th ser., 2 (1980), 70–3.
121 W. W. Greg, *Dramatic Documents*, pp. 202ff, 231ff; 'The Escapes of Jupiter', in Greg, *Collected Papers*, ed. J. C. Maxwell (1966), pp. 156–62; Brown, pp. v–xii; Ernst Honigmann, *The Stability of Shakespeare's Text* (1965), pp. 200–6.
122 King, 'Staging of Plays', 152. King calls the text 'impossible to perform', but I find it (especially in its cuts) an intelligent revision. It does lack a number of exits and entrances, but Greg (*Documents*, p. 232) regards it as ready to be copied for playhouse use.
123 I have ventured to disagree substantively with Brown's transcript in four places: at 104 (I.i.58), where there is ample room for an extra letter; at 1194–207 (II.iii.60–6), where it seems clear from the manuscript that the whole speech was first cancelled in error by Heywood when revising, and then restored by him, leaving only 1198–204 (Appendix 113–19) deleted; at 2462 (Appendix 230), where the manuscript may read 'prevent'; and at 2790 (V.iii.39), where (with Greg, *Documents* transcript) I read an unjoined 'o' for 'a' in 'woken', since Heywood prefers to attach his 'a' to the following letter.
124 I have collated only those MS variants that illustrate changes of authorial intention. To have included the many dozens of copying errors would have burdened the collation with a mass of apparent revisions, obscuring the pattern of Heywood's second thoughts represented in this (possibly final) draft. There seemed no point in presenting readers with mistaken readings, even when their source was Heywood. For full consideration of Heywood's processes of composition and revision, interested readers will wish to consult the Malone Society reprints of *The Captives* and *The Escapes of Jupiter* (or their originals in British Library MS Egerton 1994) and the studies of Greg and Honigmann cited n. 121.

The VVise-woman Of Hogsdon.

A COMEDIE.

As it hath been sundry times Acted with great Applause.

Written by Tho: Heyvvood.

Aut prodesse solent, aut Delectare —

LONDON,

Printed by *M. P.* for *Henry Shephard*, and are to be sold at his Shop in *Chancerie-Lane*, at the Signe of the *Bible*, between *Serjeants-Inne* and *Fleet-street*. 1638.

THE WISE-WOMAN OF HOGSDON
A COMEDY

DRAMATIS PERSONAE

Young [Robin] CHARTLEY, *a wild-headed gentleman.*
BOISTER, *a blunt fellow.*
SENSER, *a conceited gentleman.*
HARINGFIELD, *a civil gentleman.*
LUCE, *a goldsmith's daughter.*
Luce's FATHER, *a goldsmith.*
JOSEPH, *the goldsmith's apprentice.*
[The SECOND LUCE.]
OLD Master CHARTLEY.
Young Chartley's Man.
[GILES,] Old Chartley's Man.
SIR HARRY, *a knight who is no piece of a scholar.*
GRATIANA, *Sir Harry's daughter.*
TABOR, *Sir Harry's Man.*
SIR BONIFACE [Abse], *an ignorant pedant or schoolmaster.*

Motto: Aut . . . Delectare—] A slight strengthening ('solent' for 'volunt', perhaps the result of quoting from memory) of Horace's comment in *Ars Poetica* that 'poets would either profit or delight', in Jonson's translation (Herford & Simpson VIII, 327). It was Heywood's motto in the second half of his career (see Introduction, note 22).

1. *Young [Robin] CHARTLEY*] Leonard notes that Robin was the first name of the impetuous Earl of Essex, a possible target for satire; in support, it may be added that Chartley (Staffordshire) was the Devereux country seat.
2. blunt] See especially I.i.122, and III.iii.197–201.
3. conceited] witty.
4. civil] refined.
5. *LUCE*] (The name also of the patient wife of the prodigal Flowerdale Junior in *The London Prodigal*, 1604.) Luce, identified as a goldsmith's daughter at II.i.129, is in a sempster's shop in I.ii.0.1. Leonard (1967) suggests that the family may have fallen on hard times. (cf. I.ii.120.1: *her* FATHER, *a plain citizen*, and I.i.131).
14. *TABOR*] The name perhaps pays tribute to the great comedian Richard Tarlton. (died 1588), portrayed as carrying a tabor. 'Tabrer' is also the name of a clown in Munday's *John a Kent and John a Cumber* (1590).
15. *SIR BONIFACE*] In the French commedia dell' arte, the name of the Doctor, the equivalent of Gratiano. The surname Abse (ABC) indicates his role as a pedant.

The WISE-WOMAN of Hogsdon, *who bears the name of the drama.*
A Countryman, *client to the Wise-woman.*
[Cicely,] *a kitchen-maid, and*
Two Citizens' Wives, *that come to the Wise-woman for counsel.*
[*Three or four* Serving-men.]

---

16. *Hogsdon*] Hoxton, a country resort north of London, noted for its diversions.

ACT I

SCENE i

Enter, as newly come from play, four young gentlemen: Master CHARTLEY, Master SENSER, Master BOISTER *and* Master HARINGFIELD.

Chartley. Price of my life! Now if the devil have bones
These dice are made of his. Was ever such
A cast seen in this age? Could any gull
In Europe, saving myself, fling such a cast?
Boister. Ay.
Chartley. No.
Boister. Yes.
Chartley. But I say no, I have lost
An hundred pound, and I will have my saying.
Boister. I have lost another hundred, I'll have mine.
Ay, yes, I flung a worse, a worse by odds.
Chartley. I cry you mercy, sir. Losers may speak.
I'll not, except 'gainst you. But let me see,
Which of these two that pocket up our cash
Dares contradict me?
Senser. Sir, not I,
I say you have had bad casting.
Haringfield. So say I.
Chartley. I say this hat's not made of wool.
Which of you all dares say the contrary?
Senser. It may be 'tis a beaver.
Haringfield. Very likely so, 'Tis not wool, but a plain beaver.
Chartley. 'Tis wool, but which of you dares say so? [*Aside*] I would

---

This vivid opening scene of dice-play, a game of In-and-In (see Charles Cotton, *The Compleat Gamester*, 1674, in C. H. Hartmann, *Games and Gamesters of the Restoration* (1930), pp. 80–1) provides a model for the play's larger action. Chartley and Boister have each lost a hundred pounds to Senser and Haringfield. They tempt the winners (first Haringfield, then Senser) back into play, until they recover their losses and make some gains. The game ends in their refusal to risk these winnings. This pattern of changing fortunes anticipates the play's denouement, in which Chartley and Boister, apparently thwarted, in the end prove lucky. More disturbingly, the prodigal Chartley benefits from others' generosity when in need, but when prosperous feels no urge to reciprocate, an ominous foretaste of his later duplicity.

0.1. play] gambling.

1–2. *devil . . . his*] proverbial (Tilley D250).

8. *by odds*] by a great deal.

9. *Losers . . . speak*] proverbial (L458).

16. *beaver*] hat made from beaver pelts.

fain pick a quarrel with them, to get some of my money again. But the slaves, now they have got it, are too wise to part with it.
[*To them*] I say it is not black.

Haringfield. So say we too.

Boister. 'Tis false. His cap's of wool, 'tis black and wool,
And wool and black.

Chartley. I have naught to say to losers.
[*Aside*] Have I nothing left to set at a cast? Ay, finger,
Must you be set in gold, and not a jot
Of silver in my purse?
[*To them*] A bale of fresh dice! Ho, come at this ring!

Senser. Fie, Master Chartley, 'tis time to give over.

Chartley. That's the winner's phrase. Hold me play, or he that hath uncrowned me, I'll take a speedy order with him.

Boister. Fresh dice! This jewel I will venture more.
Take this and all, I'll play in spite of luck.

Haringfield. Since you will needs, trip for the dice. I see
It is hard to go a winner from this company.

[*Chartley throws to begin.*]

Chartley. The dice are mine.
This diamond I value at twenty marks.
I'll venture it at a throw.

Haringfield. 'Tis set you.

Chartley. Then at all. [*Throws.*] All's mine. Nay, Master Boister,
I bar you. Let us work upon the winners. [*Throws.*]
Gramercy, cinques. Nay, though I owe you no
Quarrel, yet you must give me leave to draw.

Haringfield. I had rather you should draw your sword
Than draw my money thus.

Chartley. Again, sweet dice. [*Throws.*] Nay, I bar swearing.
Gentlemen, let's play patiently. Well, this
At the candlestick, so! *Chartley throws out.*

Boister. Now dice, at all!
'Totho', quoth the Spaniard. [*Throws.*]

Senser. Here's precious luck.

Boister. Why, via, I think 'tis quicksilver,
It goes and comes so fast. There's life in this.

29. Hold] Q; Help *L.* 47. 'Totho',] *this ed.*; To tho, Q; Todo, *V.*

---

27. *bale*] set (in the case of In-and-In, four dice).
29. *hold me play*] keep me in the game.
33. *trip for the dice*] throw to start (not in *OED*).
38. *at all*] winner take all.
40. *Gramercy*] Thank you. *cinques*] double fives.
41. *draw*] take winnings.
46. *at the candlestick*] This seems to be a prize; cf. line 38.
47. '*Totho*'] (Span.) everything (a phonetic spelling in Q).
48. *via*] (Ital.) Come on!
'tis quicksilver] proverbial (Dent Q14.1).
49. *There's . . . this*] proverbial (L265).

Haringfield. He passes all with treys.
Chartley. With treys? How say
By that: 'O, he's old dog at bowls and trays.'
Senser. Lend me some money, be my half, one cast.
I'll once out-brave this gamester with a throw.
So, now the dice are mine, wilt be my half?
Haringfield. I will.
Senser. Then once I'll play the frank gamester.
Let me but see how much you both can make
And I'll cast at all, all, every cross.
Chartley. Now bless us all, what, will you every cross?
Senser. I will not leave myself one cross to bless me.
Boister. I set.
Chartley. And so do I.
Senser. Why then, at all! *He flings out.*
How?
Chartley. Nay, swear not. Let's play patiently.
Senser. Damned dice, did ever gamester see the like?
Boister. Never, never.
Senser. Was ever known such casting?
Chartley. Drunk nor sober, I ne'er saw a man cast worse.
Senser. I'll prove this hat of mine an helmet.
Which of you here dares say the contrary?
Chartley. As fair an helmet as any man in Europe
Needs to wear.
Senser. Chartley, thy hat is black.
Chartley. Upon better recollection, 'tis so indeed.
Senser. I say 'tis made of wool.
Chartley. True, my losing had took away my senses
Both of seeing and feeling, but better luck
Hath brought them to their right temper. But come,
A pox of dice, 'tis time to give over.
Senser. All times are times for winners to give over,
But not for them that lose. I'll play till midnight
But I will change my luck.
Haringfield. Come, come, you shall not.
Give over. Tush, give over. Do, I pray,
And choose the fortune of some other hour.
Let's not, like deboshed fellows, play our clothes,
Belts, rapiers, nor our needful ornaments.
'Tis childish, not becoming gentlemen.

---

50. *treys*] double threes.

51. 'O . . . trays.'] *L* (1967) suspects a snatch of song here. The line may be a double pun, 'bowls and treys' representing the equally disreputable sports of bowling and dicing, while 'bowls and trays' might suggest drinking and eating to excess; 'old dog at', experienced in, is proverbial (D506).

55. *frank*] honest.

57. *cross*] a coin marked with a cross.

58. *cross*] sign of the cross.

59. *cross . . . me*] proverbial (C836).

Play was at first ordained to pass the time,
And, sir, you but abuse the use of play
To employ it otherwise.

Senser. You may persuade me—
For once I'll leave a loser.

Chartley. Then come, put on your helmet. Let's leave this abominable game and find out some better exercise. I canot endure this chafing when men lose.

Senser. And there's not a more testy waspish companion than thyself when thou art a loser, and yet thou must be vexing others with 'Play patiently, gentlemen, and let's have no swearing'.

Chartley. A sign that I can give good counsel better than take it. But say, where be the prettiest wenches, my hearts?

Senser. Well remembered. This puts me in mind of an appointment I had with a gentlewoman of some respect.

Chartley. I have you, sir, I have you. But I think you will never have her. 'Tis Gratiana, the knight's daughter in Gracious Street. Have I touched you?

Senser. You have come somewhat near me, but touched me not. Master Haringfield, will you bear me company thither? Have you seen the gentlewoman, Master Chartley?

Chartley. Never, sir.

Senser. How have you heard of her?

Chartley. That she hath, as other women have;
That she goes for a maid, as others do, etcetera.

Senser. I can assure you, she is a proper gentlewoman.

Chartley. Then if she have you, she is like to have a proper gentleman.

Senser. You should tell them so that know it not. Adieu, gentlemen.

Exeunt SENSER *and* HARINGFIELD.

Boister. I am glad yet they go so lightly away.

Chartley. What will you do, Master Boister?

Boister. Somewhat.

Chartley. You will not acquaint me with your business?

Boister. No. I am in love, my head is full of proclamations. There is a thing called a virgin. Nature hath showed her art in making her. Court her I cannot, but I'll do as I may.

Chartley. Do you go, or stay, sir?

Boister. Go.

Chartley. You before, I'll follow. *Exit* BOISTER.

---

117. *Boister.*] S; *Senc. Q.* 118.1. *Exit* BOISTER.] S; *Exit Sencer. Q.*

---

94. *give .. it*] proverbial (C688).

99. *Gracious*] Gracechurch.

106. *etcetera*] Q's extrametrical '&c.' may indicate either a suggestion of things unsaid or an invitation to the actor to invent material.

107. *proper*] honest.

108. *proper*] (*a*) handsome; (*b*) her own.

110. *lightly*] cheerfully, but also with less money.

113. *head . . . proclamations*] proverbial (H256); his thoughts are protestations of love.

He thinks with his blunt humour to enter as far as I with my sharp. No, my true Trojan, no. There is a fair, sweet, modest rogue, her name is Luce. With this dandiprat, this pretty little ape's face, is yon blunt fellow in love. And no marvel, for she hath a brow bewitching, eyes ravishing, and a tongue enchanting. And indeed she hath no fault in the world but one, and that is, she is honest. And were it not for that, she were the only sweet rogue in Christendom. As I live, I love her extremely, and to enjoy her would give anything. But the fool stands in her own light, and will do nothing without marriage. But what should I do marrying? I can better endure gyves than bands of matrimony. But in this meditation, I am glad I have won my money again. Nay, and she may be glad of it too. For the girl is but poor, and in my pocket I have laid up a stock for her; 'tis put to use already. And if I meet not with a dice-house or an ordinary by the way, no question but I may increase it to a sum. Well, I'll unto the Exchange to buy her some pretty novelty. That done, I'll visit my little rascal, and solicit instantly. *Exit.*

ACT I SCENE ii

Enter LUCE *in a sempster's shop, at work upon a laced handkercher, and* JOSEPH, *a prentice.*

Luce. Where is my father, Joseph?
Joseph. Mistress, above,
And prays you to attend below a little.
Luce. I do not love to sit thus publicly.
And yet upon the traffic of our wares
Our provident eyes and presence must still wait.
Do you attend the shop, I'll ply my work.
I see my father is not jealous of me,
That trusts me to the open view of all.

136. *Exit.*] V; *Exeunt.* Q. 0.1. *sempster's*] Q; Goldsmith's V.

---

120. *true Trojan*] fine fellow.
121. *dandiprat*] a small coin; a dwarf; a little boy. *OED* notes only this example in reference to a girl.
122. *ape's face*] like 'rogue' and 'dandiprat', an affectionately belittling term. Not in *OED*.
127. *stands . . . light*] proverbial (L276).
129. *gyves*] fetters.
132. *stock . . . use*] As spoken by Chartley, these financial terms have a bawdy undertone.
133. *ordinary*] public eating-house.
134. *Exchange*] the Royal Exchange, a place of business.
136. *solicit*] woo her.
0.1 s.d.] Cf. Dekker, *The Shoemaker's Holiday* (ed. Smallwood and Wells, Manchester, 1979), XII.0.1 and pp. 45–6. The setting is established, as Dessen (p. 94) suggests, by Luce's work on sewing the handkerchief.

The reason is, he knows my thoughts are chaste,
And my care such as that it needs the awe
Of no strict overseer.

Enter Master BOISTER.

Boister. [*Aside*] Yonder's Luce. [*To her*] Save thee.
Luce. And you too, sir, y'are welcome. Want you aught, I pray, in which our trade may furnish you?
Boister. Yes.
Luce. Joseph, show the gentleman.
Boister. 'Tis here that I would buy.
[*Exit* JOSEPH.]
Luce. What do you mean, sir? Speak, what is't you lack?
I pray you, wherefore do you fix your eyes
So firmly in my face? What would you have?
Boister. Thee.
Luce. Me?
Boister. Yes, thee.
Luce. Your pleasure is to jest, and so I take it.
Pray give me leave, sir, to intend my work.
Boister. You are fair.
Luce. You flout me.
Boister. You are, go to, you are.
I'd vex him that should say the contrary.
Luce. Well, you may say your pleasure.
Boister. I love thee.
Luce. O, sir!
Boister. As I live, I do.
Luce. Now as I am a true maid,
The most religious oath that I dare swear,
I hold myself indebted to your love,
And I am sorry there remains in me
No power how to requite it.
Boister. Love me, prithee now, do if thou canst.
Luce. I cannot.
Boister. Prithee, if thou canst.
Luce. Indeed, I cannot.
Boister. Yet ask thine heart, and see what may be done.
Luce. In troth, I am sorry you should spend a sigh
For my sake unrequited, or a tear,
Ay, or a word.
Boister. 'Tis no matter for my words, they are not many,
And those not very wise ones, neither.
Luce. Yet I beseech you, spend no more in vain.
I scorn you not. Disdain's as far from me
As are the two poles distant. Therefore, sir,

---

25. *intend*] look to.
26. *flout*] mock.

Because I would not hold you in suspense
But tell you what at first to trust unto,
Thus, in a word, I must not fancy you.

Boister. Must not?

Luce. I cannot, nor I may not.

Boister. I am gone.
Thou hast given me, Luce, a bone to gnaw upon. *Exit.*

Luce. Alas, that beauty should be sought of more
Than can enjoy it. Might I have my wish,
I would seem fair but only in his eye
That should possess me in a nuptial tie.

Enter young Master CHARTLEY, *with gloves, ring, purse, etc.*

Chartley. 'Morrow, Luce. In exchange of this kiss, see what I have brought thee from the Exchange.

Luce. What mean you, sir, by this?

Chartley. Guess that by the circumstance. Here's a ring, wear't for my sake; twenty angels—pocket them, you fool. Come, come, I know thou art a maid. Say nay, and take them.

Luce. Sweet Master Chartley, do not fasten on me
More than with ease I can shake off. Your gift
I reverence, yet refuse. And I pray, tell me
Why do you make so many errands hither,
Send me so many letters, fasten on me
So many favours? What's your meaning in't?

Chartley. Hark in thine ear, I'll tell thee. Nay, hear me out. Is't possible so soft a body should have so hard a soul? Nay, now I know my penance: you will be angry, and school me for tempting your modesty. A fig for this modesty! It hinders many a good man from many a good turn, and that's all the good it doth. If thou but knew'st, Luce, how I love thee, thou wouldst be far more tractable. Nay, I bar chiding when you speak. I'll stop thy lips if thou dost but offer an angry word. By this hand, I'll do't, and with this hand, too. Go to, now, what say you?

Luce. Sir, if you love me, as you say you do,
Show me the fruits thereof.

Chartley. The stock, I can. Thou mayest see the fruits hereafter.

Luce. Can I believe you love me, when you seek
The shipwrack of mine honour?

Chartley. Honour! There's another word to flap in a man's mouth. Honour! What shouldst thou and I stand upon our honour, that

---

53. *bone . . . upon*] proverbial (B522): a hope for the future, or something to consider.

62. *angels*] gold coins (with the figure of the Archangel Michael), worth at this time about half a pound.

63. *say . . . take*] proverbial (M34).

74. *a good turn*] (with a bawdy pun, 'lovemaking').

81. *stock . . . fruits*] For the bawdy, cf. I.i.132; but here 'stock' is a term from tree-grafting.

were neither of us yet Right Worshipful?

Luce. I am sorry, sir, I have lent so large an ear
To such a bad discourse, and I protest
After this hour never to do the like.
I must confess, of all the gentlemen
That ever courted me, you have possessed
The best part in my thoughts. But this coarse language
Exiles you quite from thence. Sir, had you come,
Instead of changing this mine honest name
Into a strumpet's, to have honoured me
With the chaste title of a modest wife,
I had reserved an ear for all your suits.
But since I see your rudeness finds no limit
I leave you to your lust.

Chartley. You shall not, Luce.

Luce. Then keep your tongue within more moderate bounds.

Chartley. I will. As I am virtuous, I will. [*Aside*] I told you the second word would be 'marriage'. It makes a man forfeit his freedom, and makes him walk ever after with a chain at his heels, or a jackanapes hanging at his elbow. Marriage is like Daedalus his labyrinth, and being once in, there's no finding the way out. Well, I love this little property most intolerably, and I must set her on the last, though it cost me all the shoes in my shop. [*To her*] Well, Luce, thou seest my stomach is come down.
Thou hast my heart already, there's my hand.

Luce. But in what way?

Chartley. Nay, I know not the way yet, but I hope to find it hereafter, by your good direction.

Luce. I mean, in what manner, in what way?

Chartley. In the way of marriage, in the way of honesty, in the way that was never gone yet. I hope thou art a maid, Luce.

Luce. Yes sir, and I accept it. In exchange
Of this your hand, you shall receive my heart.

Chartley. A bargain, and there's earnest on thy lips.

Luce. I'll call my father, sir, to witness it.
See, here he comes.

Enter her FATHER, *a plain citizen.*

Chartley. Father, save you. You have happened of an untoward son-in-law. Here I am; how do you like me?

---

104. *jackanapes*] ape chained to a clog; the marriage comparison was proverbial (J10, C426.1).

Daedalus] deviser of the Cretan maze that held the Minotaur.

106–7. *set . . . last*] work on her (with a bawdy meaning).

107. *cost . . . shop*] proverbial (S381.11).

108. *stomach*] pride.

109. *heart . . . hand*] proverbial (H339).

111–2.] (bawdy).

114. *In . . . honesty*] proverbial (W155, W582).

118. *earnest*] a pledge.

Father. Sir, I was nearer than you were aware,
And overheard both sum and circumstance.

Chartley. [*Aside*] Then I perceive you are an old eavesdropper. [*To him*] But what do you think of it, father?

Father. I entertain the motion with all love,
And I rejoice my daughter is preferred
And raised to such a match. I heard the contract,
And will confirm it gladly. But pray, sir,
When shall the merry day be?

Chartley. Marry, even tomorrow, by that we can see. Nay, we'll lose no more time, I'll take order for that.

Luce. Stay but a month.

Chartley. A month? Thou canst not hire me to't. Why, Luce, if thou beest hungry, canst thou stay a month from meat? Nay, if I see my diet before me, I love to fall to when I have a stomach. Here, buy thee a new smock. [*Gives her money.*] Let's have a new bed, too, and look it be strong. [*Gives her a box.*] There's a box of rings and jewels. Lay them up. [*Aside*] Ha, sirrah, methinks the very name of wedlock hath brought me to a night-cap already, and I am grown civil on the sudden. [*To Luce, giving her more money*] There's more money for dishes, platters, ladles, candlesticks, etcetera, as I shall find them set down in the inventory.

Father. But whom shall we invite unto the wedding?

Enter SECOND LUCE, *a young country gentlewoman, in the habit of a page, and overhears their discourse.*

Chartley. Ay, thereby hangs a tale. We will have no more at our marriage but myself, to say 'I take thee, Luce', thou to say 'I, Luce, take thee, Robin', the vicar to put us together, and you, father, to play the clerk, and cry 'Amen'.

Father. Your reason for that?

Chartley. I would not for a world it should be known to my friends, or come to my father's ear. It may be ten thousand pounds out of my way for the present. Therefore this is my conceit: let us be married privately, and Luce shall live like a maid still, and bear the name. 'Tis nothing, Luce. It is a common thing in this age to go for a maid, and be none. I'll frequent the house secretly. Fear not, girl. Though I revel abroad o' days, I'll be with thee to bring o' nights, my little whiting mop.

Luce. But so I may incur a public scandal,
By your so oft frequenting to my chamber.

Chartley. Scandal? What scandal? Why, to stop the mouth of all

---

141. *night-cap*] a sign of the taming effects of marriage.

146. *thereby . . . tale*] proverbial (T48).

153. *conceit*] plan.

157. *to bring*] 'A phrase usually implying getting the upper hand' (Skeat; not in *OED* in this sense, where there is a sexual implication).

158. *whiting mop*] young fish, here a term of endearment. Cf. *Cap*. II.ii.47 and App. 89.

scandal, after some few days do I appear in my likeness, married man and honest housekeeper, and then what becomes of your scandal? Come, send for Master Vicar, and what we do, let's do suddenly.

Second Luce. [*Aside*] Cold comfort for me.

Luce. If you purpose to be so privately married, I know one excellent at such an exploit. Are you not acquainted with the Wise-woman of Hogsdon?

Chartley. O, the witch, the beldam, the hag of Hogsdon.

Luce. The same, but I hold her to be of no such condition. I will anon make a step thither, and punctually acquaint her with all our proceedings. She is never without a Sir John at her elbow, ready for such a stratagem.

Chartley. Well, be't so, then.

Exeunt [CHARTLEY, LUCE *and her* FATHER].

Second Luce. Heigh ho! Have I disguised myself, and stolen out of the country thus far, and can light of no better news to entertain me? O, this wild-headed, wicked Chartley, whom nothing will tame. To this gallant was I, poor gentlewoman, betrothed, and the marriage-day appointed. But he, out of a fantastic and giddy humour, before the time prefixed, posts up to London. After him come I, thus habited, and you see my welcome, to be an ear-witness of his second contracting. Modesty would not suffer me to discover myself, otherwise I should have gone near to have marred the match. I heard them talk of Hogsdon, and a wise-woman, where these aims shall be brought to action. I'll see if I can insinuate myself into her service. That's my next project. And now, good luck of my side. *Exit.*

ACT II

SCENE i

Enter the WISE-WOMAN *and her clients, a* Countryman *with an urinal, two* Women *like citizens' wives,* TABOR, *a serving-man, and a* Kitchen-maid.

Wise-woman. Fie, fie, what a toil and a moil it is

188.1] *Explicit Actus Primus.* Q.

---

162. *appear . . . likeness*] proverbial (L293.1).
166. *cold comfort*] proverbial (C542).
173. *Sir John*] jocular name for a priest.

For a woman to be wiser than all her neighbours!
I pray, good people, press not too fast upon me.
Though I have two ears, I can hear but one at once.
You with the urine.

Countryman. Here, forsooth, mistress.

Enter SECOND LUCE [*in boy's disguise*], *and stands aside.*

Wise-woman. And who distilled this water?
Countryman. My wife's limbeck, if it please you.
Wise-woman. And where doth the pain hold her most?
Countryman. Marry, at her heart, forsooth.
Wise-woman. Ay, at her heart, she hath a griping at her heart.
Countryman. You have hit it right.
Wise-woman. Nay, I can see so much in the urine.
Second Luce. [*Aside*] Just so much as is told her.
Wise-woman. She hath no pain in her head, hath she?
Countryman. No, indeed, I never heard her complain of her head.
Wise-woman. I told you so, her pain lies all at her heart.
Alas, good heart! But how feels she her stomach?
Countryman. O, queasy and sick at stomach.

Wise-woman. Ay, I warrant you. I think I can see as far into a millstone as another. You have heard of Mother Nottingham, who for her time was pretty well skilled in casting of waters, and after her, Mother Bombie. And then there is one Hatfield, in Pepper Alley; he doth pretty well for a thing that's lost. There's another in Coleharbour that's skilled in the planets. Mother Sturton in Golden Lane is for forespeaking, Mother Phillips of the Bankside for the weakness of the back, and then there's a very reverend matron on Clerkenwell Green, good at many things. Mistress Mary on the Bankside is for recting a figure, and one

0.2. *two*] *V*; foure *Q*. 0.3. Kitchen-maid.] *V*; *Chamber-mayd. Q.*

0.2. two] *V*'s emendation of *Q*'s 'foure' (a misreading of MS 'some'?) to match the number given in the Dramatis Personae seems sensible; only one of the women speaks in this scene.

1. *moil*] labour.

7. *limbeck*] alembic for distilling liquid; here, the bladder.

19–20. *see ... millstone*] proverbial (M965).

20. *Mother Nottingham*] unidentified.

21. *casting of waters*] diagnosis by urine (satirised in lines 6–13).

22. *Mother Bombie*] The central character of Lyly's play (see Introduction). Hatfield, in Pepper Alley, is unidentified, as also is Mother Sturton, l. 25.

25. *forespeaking*] fortune-telling (with a hint of 'forspeaking', bewitching).
Phillips] Perhaps the Judith Philips, a 'professed cunning woman', whose exploits, and punishment by whipping, were described in a 1595 pamphlet, Pantzer, *STC* 19855. See Barbara Rosen, *Witchcraft* (1969) pp. 214–18.

27. *matron ... Green*] a neighbour of Heywood's; her story of being persecuted by a witch is told in *Gunaikeion*, pp. 414–15.

28. *Mistress Mary*] possibly Mary Frith, the Roaring Girl, cutpurse and fortune-teller, who was named as 'Merry Mall of the Bankside' in the title of a lost work of 1610. She would have been about nineteen or twenty in 1604.
recting a figure] casting a horoscope, possibly also with a sexual implication.

(what do you call her?) in Westminster that practiseth the Book and the Key, and the Sieve and the Shears. And all do well, according to their talent. For myself, let the world speak. Hark, you, my friend, you shall take— *She whispers.*

[*Exit* Countryman.]

Second Luce. [*Aside*] 'Tis strange the ignorant should be thus fooled.
What can this witch, this wizard, or old trot
Do by enchantment or by magic spell?
Such as profess that art should be deep scholars.
What reading can this simple woman have?
'Tis palpable gross foolery.

Wise-woman. Now, friend, your business.

Tabor. I have stolen out of my master's house, forsooth, with the kitchen-maid, and I am come to know of you whether it be my fortune to have her or no.

Wise-woman. And what's your suit, lady?

Kitchen-maid. Forsooth, I come to know whether I be a maid or no.

Wise-woman. Why, art thou in doubt of that?

Kitchen-maid. It may be I have more reason than all the world knows.

Tabor. Nay, if thou comest to know whether thou beest a maid or no, I had best ask to know whether I be with child or no.

Wise-woman. Withdraw into the parlour there. I'll but talk with this other gentlewoman, and I'll resolve you presently.

Tabor. Come, Cicely, if she cannot resolve thee, I can, and in the case of a maidenhead do more than she, I warrant thee.

Exeunt [TABOR *and* Kitchen-maid].

Woman. Forsooth, I am bold, as they say—

Wise-woman. You are welcome, gentlewoman.

Woman. I would not have it known to my neighbours that I come to a wise-woman for anything, by my truly.

Wise-woman. For should your husband come and find you here—

Woman. My husband, woman? I am a widow.

Wise-woman. Where are my brains? 'Tis true, you are a widow. And you dwell, let me see, I can never remember that place—

Woman. In Kent Street.

Wise-woman. Kent Street, Kent Street! And I can tell you wherefore you come.

Woman. Why? And say true.

Wise-woman. You are a wag, you are a wag! Why, what do you think now I would say?

Woman. Perhaps to know how many husbands I should have.

Wise-woman. And if I should say so, should I say amiss?

---

29. *what . . . Westminster*] possibly a reference to Long Meg of Westminster, another notorious roaring girl, described in a pamphlet of 1582 and a (lost) Admiral's men play performed sixteen times between 1595 and 1597.

29–30. *Book . . . Shears*] two methods of divination; at the calling of the thief's name, a key jumped out of the Bible, or the sieve revolved on the point of the shears. See Thomas, pp. 252–5.

34. *trot*] hag.

Woman. I think you are a witch.

Wise-woman. In, in. I'll but read a little of Ptolemy and *Erra Pater.* And when I have cast a figure, I'll come to you presently.

Exeunt Women.

Now, wag, what wouldst thou have?

Second Luce. [*Aside*] If she were a wise-woman, she could tell that without asking. Now, methinks, I should come to know whether I were a boy or a girl. [*To her*] Forsooth, I lack a service.

Wise-woman. By my fidelity, and I want a good trusty lad.

Second Luce. [*Aside*] Now could I sigh, and say, alas, this is some bawd trade-fallen, and out of her wicked experience is come to be reputed wise. I'll serve her, be't but to pry into the mystery of her science.

Wise-woman. [*Aside*] A proper stripling, and a wise, I warrant him. [*To her*] Here's a penny for thee. I'll hire thee for a year by the Statute of Winchester. Prove true and honest, and thou shalt want nothing that a good boy—

Second Luce. [*Aside*] Here, wise-woman, you are out again. I shall want what a good boy should have, whilst I live. Well, here I shall live both unknown and my sex unsuspected. But whom have we here?

Enter Master HARINGFIELD, *and* CHARTLEY *half drunk.*

Chartley. Come, Haringfield, now we have been drinking of Mother Redcap's ale, let us now go make some sport with the wise-woman.

Haringfield. We shall be thought very wise men of all such as shall see us go in to the wise-woman's.

72.1. *Exeunt* Women.] *V subst*; *Exit Wom. Q.*

---

70. *I . . . witch*] cf. 2 *FMW* I.i.55: 'A foolish proverb we use in our country, . . . as much as to say you have hit the nail on the head.'

71. *Ptolemy and* Erra Pater] Ptolemy of Alexandria's *Tetrabiblos* was a source text for astrologers. It was not translated into English until 1701, but a crude astrological almanac, *The Compost of Ptolemaeus*, was popular in the sixteenth century. *Erra Pater* (named after Esdras) was a naive book of prognostication first published in 1536. The Wise-woman would have read neither; she is illiterate (III.i.40ff.).

72. *cast a figure*] calculated a horoscope.

79. *trade-fallen*] out of business.

84. *Statute of Winchester*] An ordinance governing service. Heywood was hired by Henslowe under this statute on 25 March 1598 (*Diary*, p. 241). The Wise-woman is offering the correct contract fee. There may also be a sly joke alluding to the Bishop of Winchester's jurisdiction over the Southwark brothels.

86. *out*] mistaken.

87. *want*] lack.

90–1. *Mother Redcap's ale*] Here, as at IV.iii.5, the Wise-woman's house is described as being near Mother Redcap's Tavern, though that was in Kentish Town (see Introduction). Mother Redcap was the subject of an Admiral's men play in 1598 (Henslowe, pp. 86, 320) by Munday and Drayton. In 1609 the poem *Pimlyco. Or, Runne Red-Cap. 'Tis a mad world at Hogsdon* (*STC* 19936) compares Ben Pimlico's ale with Redcap's.

Chartley. See, here she is. How now, witch? How now, hag? How now, beldam? You are the wise-woman, are you? And have wit to keep yourself warm enough, I warrant you.

Wise-woman. Out, thou knave.

Second Luce. [*Aside*] And will these wild oats never be sown?

Chartley. You enchantress, sorceress, she-devil. You Madam Hecate, Lady Proserpine, you are too old, you hag, now, for conjuring up spirits yourself, but you keep pretty young witches under your roof that can do that.

Wise-woman. I or my family conjure up any spirits? I defy thee, thou young hare-brained—

Haringfield. Forbear him till he have his senses about him, and I shall then hold thee for a wise-woman indeed. Otherwise, I shall doubt thou hast thy name for nothing. Come, friend, away, if thou lovest me.

Chartley. Away, you old dromedary. I'll come one of these nights and make a racket amongst your she-caterwaulers.

Haringfield. I prithee, let's be civil.

Chartley. Out of my sight, thou she-mastiff.

Exeunt [HARINGFIELD *and* CHARTLEY].

Second Luce. Patience, sweet mistress.

Wise-woman. Now bless me, he hath put me into such a fear as makes all my bones to dance and rattle in my skin. I'll be revenged on that swaggering companion.

Second Luce. Mistress, I wish you would. He's a mere madcap, and all his delight is in misusing such reverend matrons as yourself.

Wise-woman. Well, what's thy name, boy?

Second Luce. I am even little better than a turn-broach, for my name is Jack.

Wise-woman. Honest Jack, if thou couldst but devise how I might cry quittance with this Cutting Dick, I will go near to adopt thee my son and heir.

Second Luce. Mistress, there is a way, and this it is:
Tomorrow morning doth this gentleman

96–7. *wit . . . warm*] proverbial (K10).

99. *wild oats*] proverbial (O6).

100–1. *Hecate . . . Proserpine*] In Roman religion, the goddess of magic and the queen of the Underworld.

101–2. *conjuring up spirits*] (with a sexual innuendo)

104. *family*] household, including her prostitutes. cf. l. 130. and *Cap.* I.i.111.

110. *dromedary*] 'a rogue, especially a thief' (Partridge, *Dict. of Underworld*, New York, 1950); also a name for a cargo vessel, and so of a prostitute. cf. *Cap.* I.i.48–51.

116. *bones . . . skin*] proverbial (B528.1).

121. *turn-broach*] turn-spit.

122. *Jack*] (with a pun on 'jack', the mechanism of a roasting-spit)

124. *Cutting Dick*] a swaggering cutpurse and roaring boy, hero of a (lost) Worcester's Men play, for which Heywood wrote additions in September 1602 (Henslowe, p. 216). He is mentioned again in *1FMW* III.i.7. Clark (pp. 28–9) identifies him as Cutting Dick Evans, a highwayman.

Intend to marry with one Mistress Luce,
A goldsmith's daughter. Do you know the maid?

Wise-woman. My daughter, and a pretty, smug-faced girl.
I had a note but late from her, and she means
To be with me in th'evening, for I have bespoke
Sir Boniface to marry her in the morning.

Second Luce. Do but prevent this gallant of his wife,
And then your wrongs shall be revenged at full.

Wise-woman. I'll do't, as I am matron. Ay, and show him a new trick for his learning.

Enter Master BOISTER.

Boister. 'Morrow.

Wise-woman. Y'are welcome, sir.

Boister. Art wise?

Second Luce. [*Aside*] He should be wise, because he speaks few words.

Wise-woman. I am as I am, and there's an end.

Boister. Canst conjure?

Wise-woman. O, that's a foul word! But I can tell you your fortune, as they say. I have some little skill in palmistry, but never had to do with the devil.

Boister. And had the devil never anything to do with thee? Thou lookest somewhat like his dam. Look on me, canst tell what I ail?

Wise-woman. Can you tell yourself? I should guess you be mad, or not well in your wits.

Boister. Th'art wise. I am so. Men being in love are mad, and I being in love, am so.

Wise-woman. Nay, if I see your complexion once, I think I can guess as near as another.

Boister. One Mistress Luce I love. Know'st thou her, grannam?

Wise-woman. As well as the beggar knows his dish. Why, she is one of my daughters.

Boister. Make her my wife, I'll give thee forty pieces.

Second Luce. Take them, mistress, to be revenged on Chartley.

Wise-woman. A bargain! Strike me luck, cease all your sorrow.
Fair Luce shall be your bride betimes tomorrow.

Boister. Th'art a good grannam, and but that thy teeth stand like hedge-stakes in thy head, I'd kiss thee. *Exit.*

---

130. *My daughter*] Prostitutes could be known as the bawd's 'daughters'. cf. l. 157, *Cap.* I.i.121 and V.v. 84–5, and *How a Man*, 953. Not in *OED* in this sense.

134. *prevent*] cheat (by an earlier marriage).

141. *wise . . . words*] proverbial (W799).

147–8. *devil . . . dam*] proverbial (D225).

155. *grannam*] affectionate term for an old woman.

156. *beggar . . . dish*] proverbial (B234).

157. *daughters*] Here the Wise-woman presumably claims a friendly, not financial, relationship with the London Luce.

160. *Strike me luck*] Clap hands on a bargain.

Wise-woman. Pray, will you in? Come hither, Jack, I have
A new trick come into my head. Wilt thou
Assist me in't?
Second Luce. If it concern the crossing of the marriage
With Mistress Luce, I'll do't, whate'er it be.
Wise-woman. Thou shalt be tired like a woman. Can you make a curtsy, take small strides, simper and seem modest? Methinks thou hast a woman's voice already.
Second Luce. Doubt not of me. I'll act them naturally.
Wise-woman. I have conceited to have Luce married to this blunt gentleman, she mistaking him for Chartley. And Chartley shall marry thee, being a boy, and take thee for Luce. Will't not be excellent?
Second Luce. O, super, super-excellent!
Wise-woman. Play but thy part as I'll act mine, I'll fit him with a wife, I warrant him.
Second Luce. [*Aside*] And a wife I'll warrant him. *Exeunt.*

[ACT II SCENE ii]

Enter old SIR HARRY *and his man* TABOR.

Sir Harry. Ha, then; thou sawest them whispering with my daughter.
Tabor. I saw them, if it shall please you, not whisper, but—
Sir Harry. How, then, thou knave?
Tabor. Marry, sir knight, I saw them in sad talk. But to say they were directly whispering, I am not able.
Sir Harry. Why, Tabor, that sad talk was whispering.
Tabor. Nay, they did not greatly whisper, for I heard what was said, and what was said I have the wit to keep to myself.
Sir Harry. What said the unthrift, Tabor? Tell me, knave.
Tell me, good knave, what did the unthrift say?
Tabor. I am loath to be called in question about men and women's matters, but as soon as ever he saw your daughter, I heard what was spoke.
Sir Harry. Here, sirrah, take thy quarter's wages aforehand, and tell me all their words, and what their greeting was at their first encounter. Hold thine hand. [*Gives him money.*]
Tabor. Thanks, noble sir, and now I'll tell you. Your daughter being walking to take the air of the fields, and I before her, whom should we meet, just in the nick?
Sir Harry. Just in the nick, man?
Tabor. In the highway, I meant, sir.
Sir Harry. Ha, and what conference passed betwixt them, Tabor?

1. them] *Q*; him *L*.

---

169. *tired*] clothed.
17. *noble*] (perhaps with a pun on 'noble', a gold coin)
19. *in the nick*] proverbial (N160), but Sir Harry suspects bawdy.

Tabor. As well as my pipe can utter, you shall know, sir. This gentleman meeting with my young mistress full butt—imagine you were she, and I young Master Senser—now, there you come, and here I meet you. He comes in this manner, and put off his hat in this fashion.

Sir Harry. Ay, but what said he?

Tabor. 'Be with you, fair gentlewoman.' And so goes quite away, and scarce so much as once looked back. And if this were language to offer to a young lady, judge you.

Sir Harry. But spake he nothing else?

Tabor. Nothing, as I am true.

Sir Harry. Why, man, all this was nothing.

Tabor. Yes, sir, it was as much as my quarter's wages aforehand.

Enter Master SENSER, Master HARINGFIELD *and* GRATIANA.

Gratiana. Here are two gentlemen with great desire
Crave conference with my father. Here he is.
Now, gallants, you may freely speak your minds.

Senser. Save you, sir. My name is Senser, I am a Northamptonshire gentleman, born to a thousand pound land by the year. I love your daughter, and I am come to crave your goodwill.

Sir Harry. Have you my daughter's, that you covet mine?

Senser. No, sir, but I hope in time I shall have.

Sir Harry. So hope not I, sir. Sir, my daughter's young,
And you a gentleman unknown. Senser?
Ha, Senser!
O, sir, your name I now remember well.
'Tis ranked 'mongst unthrifts, dicers, swaggerers
And drunkards. Were not you brought before me
Some moneth since, for beating of the watch?
By the same token, I sent you to the Counter.

Senser. I confess myself to have been in that action, but note the cause, sir. You could not have pleasured me so much, in giving me a piece of gold, as at the same time to help me to that Counter.

Sir Harry. Why, sir, what cause had you to beat the watch,
And raise a midnight tumult in the streets?

Senser. Nay, but hear me, sweet Sir Harry. Being somewhat late at supper at the Mitre, the doors were shut at my lodging. I knocked at three or four places more. All were abed, and fast. Inns, taverns, none would give me entertainment. Now, would you have had me despaired, and lain in the streets? No, I bethought me of a trick worth two of that, and presently devised, having at

---

23. *pipe*] throat; tabor and pipe made a frequent combination.

24. *full butt*] point-blank (*OED* v[1], 6).

50. *moneth*] month (the old spelling retained as necessary for scansion).

51. *Counter*] a London prison.

58. *Mitre*] One of two London taverns, one in Bread Street, Cheapside, the other in Fleet Street.

62. *trick . . . that*] proverbial (T518).

that time a charge of money about me, to be lodged, and safely, too.

Sir Harry. As how, I pray you?

Senser. Marry, thus: I had knocked my heels against the ground a good while, knew not where to have a bed for love nor money. Now what did I, but spying the watch, went and hit the constable a good souse on the ear, who provided me of a lodging presently. And the next day, being brought before your worship, I was then sent thither back again, where I lay three or four days without control.

Sir Harry. Oh, you're a gallant! Is that gentleman
A suitor, too?

Haringfield. I am a suitor in my friend's behalf,
No other wise. I can assure you, sir,
He is a gentleman descended well,
Derived from a good house, well qualified,
And well possessed. But that which most should move you,
He loves your daughter.

Gratiana. [*Aside*] But were I to choose
Which of these two should please my fancy best,
I sooner should affect this gentleman
For his mild carriage and his fair discourse
Than my hot suitor. Ruffians I detest.
A smooth and square behaviour likes me best.

Senser. What say you to me, lady?

Gratiana. You had best ask my father what I should say.

Senser. Are you angry, sweet lady, that I asked your father's consent?

Gratiana. No. If you can get his consent to marry him, shall it displease me?

Haringfield. Indeed, you therein much forget yourself,
To sound her father ere you tasted her.
You should have first sought means for her goodwill,
And after, compassed his.

Sir Harry. He can prevail with neither. Gentlemen,
If you will come to revel, you are welcome;
If to my table, welcome; if to use me
In any grateful office, welcome, too.
But if you come as suitors, there's the door.

Senser. The door?

Sir Harry. I say the door.

Senser. Why, sir, tell not me of your door, nor going out of it. Your company is fair and good, and so is your daughter's. I'll stay here this twelve-month ere I'll offer to trouble your door.

Sir Harry. Sir, but you shall not. [*Calls*] Tabor! Where's that knave?

---

63. *charge*] heavy weight.
67. *for . . . money*] proverbial (L484).
69. *souse*] blow.
85. *likes*] suits.
89. *to marry him*] a joke perhaps repeated from *MND* I.i.93–4.

Senser. Why, sir, I hope you do not mean to make us dance, that you call for a tabor.

Haringfield. Nay, Master Senser, do not urge the knight.
He is incensed now, choose a fitter hour,
And tempt his love in that. Old men are testy.
Their rage, if stood against, grows violent,
But suffered and forborne, confounds itself.

Sir Harry. Where's Tabor?

Tabor. At hand, noble master.

Sir Harry. Show them the door.

Tabor. That I will, and take money, too, if it please them.

Senser. Is thy name Tabor?

Tabor. I am so yclept, sir.

Senser. And Tabor, are you appointed to give us Jack Drum's entertainment?

Tabor. Why, sir, you do not play upon me.

Senser. Though I cannot, yet I have known an hare that could. But knight, thou dost not forbid us thine house?

Sir Harry. Yes, and forewarn it, too.

Senser. But, by thy favour, we may choose whether we will take any warning or no. Well, farewell, old knight. Though thou forbiddest me thine house, I'll honour thee and extol thee. And though thou keep'st me from thy daughter, thou shalt not hinder me to love her and admire her, and, by thy favour, sometimes to see her. A cat may look at a king, and so may I at her. Give me thine hand, knight. The next time I come into thy company, thou shalt not only bid me welcome, but hire me to stay with thee and thy daughter.

Sir Harry. When I do that, enjoy my full consent
To marry Gratiana.

Senser. 'Tis a match.
[*To Haringfield*] Strike me luck. [*To Gratiana*] Wife that may be, farewell. [*To Sir Harry*] Father-in-law that must be, adieu. Tabor, play before. My friend and I will dance after.

Exeunt [TABOR, SENSER and HARINGFIELD].

Sir Harry. [*Aside*] When I receive thee gladly to mine house
And wage thy stay, thou shalt have Gratiana,
Doubt not, thou shalt. Here's a strange humourist
To come a-wooing.

[*Enter* TABOR.]

Tabor, are they gone?

Tabor. I have played them away, if it please your worship. And

---

116. *yclept*] named (a comical archaism).

117–18. *Jack Drum's entertainment*] a beating; Marston used this proverbial phrase (J12) for the title of his 1600 play.

120. *hare*] *L* notes that hares drum with their feet, and quotes a proverb (H160) on the impossibility of catching a hare with a tabor.

128. *cat . . . king*] proverbial (C141).

yonder at the door attends a schoolmaster. You sent for him, if you remember, to teach my little young master and mistress.

Sir Harry. A proper scholar. Pray him to come near.

Enter a pedantical schoolmaster, SIR BONIFACE.

Sir Boniface. Eques honoratus,
Ave salutatus.
Non video quod est in tergo,
Sed salve, bona virgo.

Sir Harry. Sir, you may call me nicknames. If you love me,
Speak in your mother tongue. Or at the least,
If learning be so much allied unto you
That Latin unawares flows from your lips,
To make your mind familiar with my knowledge
Pray utter it in English. What's your name?

Sir Boniface. Sit faustum tibi omen,
I'll tell you my *nomen.*

Sir Harry. Will you tell it to no men?
I'll entertain none ere I know their names.
Nay, if you be so dainty of your name
You are not for my service.

Sir Boniface. Intende, vir nobilis.

Sir Harry. Not for twenty nobles?
Trust me, I will not buy your name so dear.

Sir Boniface. O, ignorantia! What it is to deal with stupidity. Sir Henry, Sir Henry, hear me one word. I see, *Preceptor legit, vos vero negligitis.*

147. *quod*] *this ed.*; *quid Q.*

144.1. *SIR BONIFACE*] A character resembling Shakespeare's Holofernes (*LLL*) in his pedantry, and Sir Hugh Evans (*Wiv.*) in the comic Latin lesson. Sir Boniface repeats (often verbatim) much of the language of Aminadab in *How a Man*, presumably also by Heywood. The Latin in this scene, in III.i and in IV.i derives mainly from the two editions of William Lily's Grammar, *Brevissima Institutio* (1540) and *A Shorte Introduction of Grammar* (1567). The earlier edition, made compulsory for schools in 1540, was authorised again in 1604. The references are from such widely separated parts of the texts that they are clearly quoted from memory, an easy task for any normally educated Elizabethan schoolboy.

145–8. Eques . . . virgo] Honoured knight, welcome with greetings. I do not see behind me, but greetings, good maid. The nonsense line 147, presumably invented to rhyme with 148, is based on the final line of Catullus, poem 22, 'We cannot see the knapsack on our back', quoted in Lily (1540), Eiiiv.

155. sit . . . omen] may the omen favour you.

156. nomen] name.

159. *dainty of*] reluctant to give.

161. Intende . . . nobilis] Take note, noble sir.

162. *nobles*] gold coins, each worth a third of a pound.

164. O, ignorantia] O, ignorance.

165–6. Praeceptor . . . negligitis] From Lily (1567), Ciiiiv, where it is translated as 'The Maister readeth, and ye regard not.'

Tabor. I think he saith we are a company of fools and nidgets. But I hope you shall not find us such, master schoolmaster.

Sir Harry. Friend, friend, to cut off all vain circumstance,
Tell me your name, and answer me directly,
Plainly, and to my understanding, too,
Or I shall leave you. Here's a deal of gibberish.

Sir Boniface. Vir bone—

Sir Harry. Nay, nay, make me no bones, but do't.

Sir Boniface. Then in plain vulgar English, I am called
Sir Boniface Abse.

Sir Harry. Why, this is somewhat like, Sir Boniface.
Give me thine hand. Thou art a proper man,
And, in my judgement, a great scholar, too.
What shall I give thee by the year?

Sir Boniface. I'll trust, sir, to your generosity.
I will not bargain, but account myself
Mille et mille modis bound to you.

Sir Harry. I cannot lease my mills, they're farmed already.
The stipend that I give shall be in money.

Tabor. Sure, sir, this is some miller that comes to undermine you, in the shape of a schoolmaster.

Gratiana. You both mistake the scholar.

Sir Harry. I understand my English, that I know.
What's more than modern doth surpass my reach.
Sir Boniface, come to me two days hence,
You shall receive an answer. I have now
Matters of some import that trouble me.
Thou shouldst be else dispatched.

Tabor. Sir Boniface, if you come to live in our house and be a familist amongst us, I shall desire you better acquaintance. Your name and my phiznomy should have some consanguinity, good Sir Boniface.

Sir Boniface. Quomodo vales? Quomodo vales?

Tabor. Go with you to the ale-house? I like the motion well. I'll make an excuse out of doors and follow you. I am glad yet we shall have a good-fellow come into the house amongst us.

184. lease] *conj. Da*; leave *Q*.

---

167. *nidgets*] idiots.

173. Vir bone] Good man.

174. *make ... bones*] proverbial (B527).

183. Mille ... modis] In thousands of ways.

184. *farmed*] rented out.

194. *dispatched*] dealt with immediately.

195. *familist*] one of the household; perhaps with reference to the notorious sect the Family of Love.

197. *phiznomy*] face.

199. Quomodo vales?] How do you do? With this line and a joke based on it, *L* compares *The Fair Maid of the Exchange* (Pearson, II, 56). There is a similar joke in *How a Man* (quoted Fleay, I, 290), in a form ('Come out of alehouse') that clarifies the jest's origin.

202. *good-fellow*] jovial companion.

Sir Boniface. *Vale, vir magne.*

Sir Harry. You shall not have me at Saint Magnus. My house is here in Gracious Street.

Sir Boniface. I know it, sweet knight, I know it. Then *virgo formosa et domine gratiose, valete.*

Sir Harry. Ay, in Gracious Street you shall hear of me, Sir Boniface.

[*Exit* SIR BONIFACE.]

He shall instruct my children, and to thee
Fair Gratiana, read the Latin tongue.

Tabor. Who shall, Sir Bawdy-face?

Sir Harry. Sir Boniface, you fool.

Tabor. His name is so hard to hit on.

Sir Harry. Come, daughter. If things fall out as I intend,
My thoughts shall peace have, and these troubles end. *Exeunt.*

ACT III

SCENE i

Enter the SECOND LUCE, *which was* Jack, *in woman's apparel, and the* WISE-WOMAN.

Wise-woman. Jack, thou art my boy.

Second Luce. Mistress!

Wise-woman. I'll be a mother to thee, no mistress. Come, lad, I must have thee sworn to the orders of my house, and the secrets thereof.

Second Luce. As I am an honest lad, I am yours to command. But mistress, what mean all these women's pictures hanged here in your withdrawing-room?

Wise-woman. I'll tell thee, boy. Marry, thou must be secret. When any citizens or young gentlemen come hither, under a colour to know their fortunes, they look upon these pictures, and which of

208. me, Sir Boniface.] *V*; me. *Sir Bonif.* (*as speech prefix*) *Q*. 215.1] *Explicit Actus secundus. Q.*

203. Vale, vir magne] Farewell, great sir.

204. *Saint Magnus*] One of the City churches, close to London Bridge.

206–7. virgo . . . valete] Farewell pretty maid and gracious sir.

213. *hit on*] remember, but with pun on 'strike'.

For this pivotal scene in the disguise plot, the opening stage direction establishes the levels of deception: a boy playing a girl, disguised as a boy, disguised as a woman.

10. *colour*] pretence.

them they best like, she is ready with a wet finger. Here they have all the furniture belonging to a private chamber, bed, bedfellow and all. But mum, thou knowest my meaning, Jack?

Second Luce. But I see coming and going, maids, or such as go for maids, some of them as if they were ready to lie down, sometimes two or three delivered in one night, then suddenly leave their brats behind them, and convey themselves into the city again. What becomes of their children?

Wise-woman. Those be kitchen-maids, and chamber-maids, and sometimes good men's daughters. Who, having catched a clap, and growing near their time, get leave to see their friends in the country for a week or so. Then hither they come, and for a matter of money here they are delivered. I have a midwife or two belonging to the house, and one Sir Boniface, a deacon, that makes a shift to christen the infants. We have poor, honest and secret neighbours that stand for common gossips. But dost not thou know this?

Second Luce. Yes, now I do. But what after becomes of the poor infants?

Wise-woman. Why, in the night we send them abroad, and lay one at this man's door, and another at that, such as are able to keep them. And what after becomes of them, we inquire not. And this is another string to my bow.

Second Luce. [*Aside*] Most strange, that woman's brain should apprehend
Such lawless, indirect and horrid means
For covetous gain! How many unknown trades
Women and men are free of, which they never
Had charter for. [*To her*] But mistress, are you so
Cunning as you make yourself? You can
Neither write nor read. What do you with those
Books you so often turn over?

Wise-woman. Why, tell the leaves. For to be ignorant and seem ignorant, what greater folly?

Second Luce. [*Aside*] Believe me, this is a cunning woman, neither hath she her name for nothing, who out of her ignorance can fool so many that think themselves wise. [*To her*] But wherefore have you built this little closet close to the door, where sitting, you may hear every word spoken by all such as ask for you?

---

12. *with a wet finger*] at once, easily; proverbial (F234).
16. *lie down*] go into labour.
21. *clap*] misfortune; here, pregnancy.
25. *deacon*] an assistant priest, qualified only for secular ministry.
27. *gossips*] godparents.
33. *another . . . bow*] proverbial (S937).
42. *tell the leaves*] count the pages.
47. *little closet*] Rosen, *Witchcraft*, pp. 223–4, quotes the identical device of John and Alice West, 'falsely called the King and Queene of Fayries'. Alice had 'by the porch and door to her house a little closet where she might hear every word spoken'. Her activities are described in a text of 1613.

Wise-woman. True. And therefore I built it. If any knock, you must to the door and question them to find what they come about, if to this purpose or to that. Now they, ignorantly telling thee their errand, which I sitting in my closet overhear, presently come forth, and tell them the cause of their coming, with every word that hath passed betwixt you in private. Which they admiring and thinking it to be miraculous, by their report I become thus famous.

Second Luce. This is no trade, but a mystery. And were I a wise-woman, as indeed I am but a foolish boy, I need not live by your service. But mistress, we lose ourselves in this discourse. Is not this the morning in which I should be married?

Wise-woman. Now how had I forgot myself? Mistress Luce promised to be with me half an hour ago, but masked and disguised, and so shalt thou be, too. Here's a black veil to hide thy face against the rest come. [*Gives her a veil.*]

Enter SIR BONIFACE.

Sir Boniface. Sit tibi bona dies,
Salus et quies.

Wise-woman. Into the withdrawing-room, Sir Boniface.

Sir Boniface. Without any compunction
I will make the conjunction. *Exit.*

Wise-woman. Now, keep thy countenance, boy.

Second Luce. Fear not me, I have as good a face in a mask as any lady in the land could wish to have. [*Aside*] But to my heart, he comes or he comes not, now am I in a pitiful perplexity until I see the event of all.

Wise-woman. No more 'Jack' now, but 'Mistress Luce'.

Second Luce. I warrant you, mistress. [*Aside*] That it happens so luckily that my name should be Luce, too, to make the marriage more firm!

Enter CHARTLEY *disguised, and in a vizard.*

Chartley. My honey-sweet hag, where's Luce?

Wise-woman. Here, sweet heart, but disguised and veiled, as you are vizarded.

Chartley. But what's the reason we are thus hoodwinked?

---

56. *mystery*] art.
62. *against*] when.
64–5. Sit . . . quies] May you have a good day, health and peace.
68. *conjunction*] (in marriage)
71–2. *he . . . not*] whether or not he comes.
75–6. *happens so luckily*] Heywood playfully acknowledges the coincidence necessary to his plot.
76–7. *Luce . . . firm*] a play on words (loose/firm).
77.1. vizard] mask.
81. *hoodwinked*] Chartley refers to his disguise; the meaning 'deceived' is also appropriate.

Wise-woman. No discovery of yourselves for a million. There's Sir Boniface within, shall he blab who you are? Besides, there's a young heir that hath stolen a lord's daughter from the Court, and would not have their faces seen for a world. Cannot you be content to fare well, and keep your own counsel? And see, yonder they come.

Enter at several places BOISTER *vizarded and* LUCE *masked.*

Chartley. Gramercy, my sugar-candy-sweet trot.

Wise-woman. Mum, no more words.

Chartley. If the great heir and the young lady be so dainty of their complexions, they shall see, my sweet Luce, we can vizard it with the best of them.

Luce. [*Aside*] That gentleman, by the wise-woman's description, should be Master Chartley. (*Meaning Boister.*)

Boister. That gallant wench, if my grannam fable not,
Should be Luce. But what be those other?

Wise-woman. You wrong me but to ask. Who but a young heir and a lady of the Court? That's Luce. Take her, and keep your promise.

Boister. Pocas palabras.

Wise-woman. That's Chartley. Take him, Luce.

Luce. But who be they?

Wise-woman. A lord and lady. Shall Sir Boniface stay?
Rather than so, strive who should lead the way.

Exeunt CHARTLEY *with* [SECOND LUCE *as*] Jack, BOISTER *with* LUCE.

Wise-woman [*Alone*]. Now Jack, my boy, keep thine own counsel and countenance, and I shall cry quittance with my young gallant. Well, by this time Sir Boniface is at his book. But because there is a mistake, known only to my boy and myself, the marriage shall be no sooner ended but I'll disturb them by some sudden outcry, and that, too, before they have leisure to unmask and make known themselves one to another. For if the deceit were known, I should fall into the danger of that young mad rascal. And now this double apprehension of the lord and the lady shall fetch me off from all. I know it is Sir Boniface his custom to make short work, and hath dispatched by this. And now, wise-woman, try if thou canst bestir thyself like to a mad-woman—[*Cries out.*] Shift for yourselves! Warrants and pursuivants! Away! Warrants and pursuivants! Shift for yourselves!

---

82. *No . . . million*] proverbial (M963.11).
86. *keep . . . counsel*] proverbial (C694).
87.1. several places] separate entrances.
89. *Mum . . . words*] proverbial (W767).
99. Pocas palabras] (Span.) Few words.
105. *cry quittance*] proverbial (Q18).
106. *at his book*] reading the marriage service.
112–3. *fetch me off*] keep me in the clear.
116. *Warrants and pursuivants*] Officers, and their authority to make searches.

Enter, as affrighted and amazed, CHARTLEY, BOISTER, SIR BONIFACE *and others* [*including* LUCE *and* SECOND LUCE].

Chartley. I'll take this way.
Boister. I this. *Exeunt* [CHARTLEY and BOISTER].
Sir Boniface. Curro, curris, cucurri,
My cheeks are all murrey,
And I am gone in an hurry. *Exit.*

Luce. O heaven, what shall become of me?

Second Luce. [*Aside*] I know what shall become of me, already.

Wise-woman. [*To Luce*] O sweet daughter, shift clothes with this lady. Nay, as thou lov'st thy credit and mine, change habits. So, if thou be'st taken in her garments, finding the mistake will let thee pass. And should they meet her in thine, not knowing her, would no way question her. And this prove to both your securities and my safety. [*They change clothes.*]

Luce. As fast as I can, good mother. [*To Second Luce.*] So, madam, farewell. [*Exit.*]

Second Luce. All happy joys betide you. *Exit.*

Wise-woman [*Alone*]. Ha, ha, let me hold my sides and laugh. Here were even a plot to make a play on. But that Chartley is so fooled by my boy, Jack! Well, he'll make a notable wag, I'll warrant him. All the jest will be, if Boister should meet with him in Luce's habit which he hath now on, he would think himself merely gulled and cheated. And should Chartley meet with Luce as she is now robed, he would be confident he had married her. Let me see, how many trades have I to live by? First, I am a wise-woman and a fortune-teller, and under that I deal in physic and forespeaking, in palmistry and recovering of things lost. Next, I undertake to cure mad folks. Then I keep gentlewomen lodgers, to furnish such chambers as I let out by the night. Then I am provided for bringing young wenches to bed. And, for a need, you see I can play the match-maker.
She that is but one, and professeth so many,
May well be termed a wise woman, if there be any. *Exit.*

[ACT III SCENE ii]

Enter BOISTER.

Boister. Why, run away, and leave my wench behind? I'll back. What have warrants and pursuivants to do with me? With me? Why should I budge? Why should I wear mask or vizard? If lords or ladies offend, let lords and ladies answer. Let me better bethink

---

120. Curro . . . cucurri] I run, you run, I ran. This declension is illustrated by the same verb in Lily (1540), Cviii.

121. *murrey*] dark red.

148–9.] The Wise-woman's aphorism, reminiscent in form to those of Lear's Fool (e.g. *Lear* I.v.48f.) is not recorded in Tilley or Dent. It is a nice irony that she should speak an apparent proverb in a play so well stocked with real ones.

me. Why should I play at hob-man blind? Hum. Why marry *in tenebris*? Ha! Is there no trick in it? If my grannam should make me a younger brother now, and instead of Luce pop me off with some broken commodity, I were finely served. Most sure I am to be in for better and worse, but with whom, Heaven and my grannam knows.

Enter half ready and masked SECOND LUCE [*after changing clothes with* LUCE].

Second Luce. [*Aside*] I am stolen out of doors, to see if I can meet my husband, with whom I purpose to make some sport, ere I suddenly disclose myself. [*Sees Boister.*] What's he?

Boister. [*Aside*] Heyday, what have we here, an hobbledehoy? [*To her*] Come hither, you.

Second Luce. [*Aside*] 'Tis Mistress Luce's husband.
I'll not leave him thus.

Boister. What art thou?

Second Luce. Do you not know me?

Boister. That mask and robe I know.

Second Luce. I hope so, or else I were in a woe case.

Boister. That mask, that gown, I married.

Second Luce. Then you have no reason but to enjoy
Both them and me, too. And so you are like—
I should be loath to divorce man and wife.

Boister. I am fooled. But what cracked ware are you, forsooth?

Second Luce. I belong to the old gentlewoman of the house.

Boister. I'll set her house on fire. I am finely bobbed.

Second Luce. But I hope you will not bob me.

Boister. No, Ise warrant thee. What art thou, girl or boy?

Second Luce. Both, and neither. I was a lad last night,
But in the morning I was conjured into
A lass. And being a girl now, I shall be
Translated to a boy anon. Here's all
I can at this time say for myself: farewell. [*Exit.*]

Boister [*Alone*]. Yes, and be hanged withal. O, for some gunpowder to blow up this witch, this she-cat, this damned sorceress! O, I

---

5. *hob-man blind*] blind-man's buff.
in tenebris] in the shadows.
7. *younger brother*] i.e., dispossessed; proverbial (B686).
9. *in*] married.
10.1. half ready] partly dressed.
14. *hobbledehoy*] youth between boyhood and manhood.
21. *in a woe case*] in a sorry state.
26. *set . . . fire*] (in revenge); a common treatment of suspected witches.
bobbed] fooled.
27. *bob*] strike.
28. *Ise*] I shall. *OED* gives the form 'I swarand' from *c.* 1440 (warrant 4a), the next use of the dialect phrase being from 1786.
33–4. *farewell . . . hanged*] proverbial (H130.1).

could tear her to fitters with my teeth! Yet I must be patient, and put up all, lest I be made a jeer to such as know me. Fooled by a boy! Go to; of all the rest, the girl Luce must not know it. *Exit.*

[ACT III SCENE iii]

Enter CHARTLEY *and his* [*serving-*] Man, *meeting* LUCE [*entering separately*].

Chartley. So, now am I the same man I was yesterday. Who can say I was disguised, or who can distinguish my condition now, or read in my face whether I be a married man or a bachelor?

Luce. [*Aside*] Who's that?

Chartley. Luce!

Luce. Sweet husband, is it you?

Chartley. The news?

Luce. Never so frighted in my days.

Chartley. What's become of the lord and the lady?

Luce. The lord fled after you, the lady stayed.
Who, masked and half unready, ran fast after
Her poor affrighted husband. Now all's quiet.

Chartley. This storm is then well past. And now, convey yourself home as privately as you can, and see you make this known to none but your father.

Luce. I am your wife and servant. *Exit.*

Chartley. This name of 'Luce' hath been ominous to me. One Luce I should have married in the country, and just the night before, a toy took me in the head, and mounting my horse I left capons, ducks, geese, poultry, wildfowl, father and bride and all, and posted up to London, where I have ever since continued bachelor till now. And now—

Enter GRATIANA *in haste, a* Serving-man *before her, and* TABOR *after her.*

Gratiana. Nay, on, I prithee fellow, on. My father will wonder where I have been visiting. Now, what had I forgot? Tabor, there's money, go to the goldsmith's, bid him send me my fan, and make a quick return. On, fellow, on.

Exeunt [Serving-man *and* GRATIANA].

---

36. *fitters*] fragments.

An important scene, beginning with Chartley's thoughts on the restrictions of marriage, his first sight of Gratiana, and his complicated deception of Luce and her father. These are contrasted with Boister's blunt wooing of Luce, in which both keep their true feelings from each other, but for different reasons. The clumsy tenderness of this closing encounter of Act III is made more resonant by the irony that the couple are (unknown to themselves) already man and wife.

8. *half unready*] cf. III.ii.10.1.

16. *toy*] foolish whim; proverbial (T456.1).

Tabor. [*Aside*] Her fan at the goldsmith's! Now had I forgot to ask her his name or his sign. But I will after, to know.

Chartley. Sirrah, go call me back that serving-man,
And ask him what's the gentlewoman's name.

[*Chartley's*] *serving-man.* I shall. [*Calls.*] Ho, you! Friend, you!

Tabor. Who's that calls?

Serving-man. 'Twas I.

Tabor. Your business? You should be one, though not of my cognisance, yet of my condition: a serving-creature, as I take it. Pray, what's your will with me?

Serving-man. Pray sir, what might I call that gentlewoman on whom you were attendant?

Tabor. You may call her what you please, but if you call her otherwise than in the way of honesty, you may perchance hear on't.

Serving-man. Nay, be not offended. I say, what do you call her?

Tabor. Why, sir, I call her as it shall best please me: sometimes 'young lady', sometimes 'young mistress'. And what hath any man to do with that?

Chartley. Are you so captious, sirrah? What's her name? Speak, and be brief.

Tabor. Ay, marry, sir, you speak to purpose, and I can resolve you. Her name is Gratiana. [*Aside*] But all this while I have forgot my mistress' fan.

Exeunt [TABOR *and* Chartley's serving-man].

Chartley. Gratiana! Oft have I heard of her, but saw her not till now. 'Tis a pretty wench, a very pretty wench. Nay, a very, very, very pretty wench. But what a rogue am I of a married man, nay, that have not been married this six hours, and to have my shittle-wits run a-woolgathering already? What would poor Luce say if she should hear of this? I may very well call her 'poor Luce', for I cannot presume of five pounds to her portion. What a coxcomb was I, being a gentleman, and well derived, to match into so beggarly a kindred! What needed I to have grafted in the stock of such a choke-pear, and such a goodly poppering as this to escape me? Escape me, said I? If she do, she shall do it narrowly. But I am married already, and therefore it is not possible, unless I should make away my wife, to compass her. Married? Why, who knows it? I'll outface the priest, and then there is none but she and her father, and their evidence is not good in law. And if they put me in suit, the best is, they are poor, and cannot follow it. Ay, marry, sir, a man may have some credit by such a wife as this. I

46.1. *Exeunt.*] *this ed.; Exit.* Q.

---

37. *in . . . honesty*] proverbial (W155).
50. *shittle-wits*] fickleness.
51. *run a-woolgathering*] proverbial (W582).
56. *choke-pear*] unpalatable pear, used to make perry.
poppering] This kind of pear has bawdy connotations (pop-her-in); see Partridge.
59. *compass*] win.
62. *put . . . suit*] take me to law.

could like this marriage well, if a man might change away his wife still as he is aweary of her, and cope her away like a bad commodity. If every new moon a man might have a new wife, that's every year a dozen. But this 'Till death us depart' is tedious. I will go a-wooing to her; I will. But how shall I do for jewels and tokens? Luce hath mine in her custody, money and all. Tush, I'll juggle them from her well enough. See, here she comes.

Enter LUCE *and her* FATHER.

Luce. Here is my husband. I pray, move him in it.

Father. It toucheth both our reputations nearly,
For by his oft repair now, whilst the marriage
Is kept from public knowledge, your good name
May be by neighbours hardly censured of.

Chartley. Th'art sad, th'art sad, Luce. What, melancholy already, ere thou hast had good cause to be merry, and knew'st what sport was?

Luce. I have great reason, when my name is tossed
In every gossip's mouth, and made a byword
Unto such people as it least concerns.
Nay, in my hearing, as they pass along,
Some have not spared to brand my modesty,
Saying 'There sits she whom young Chartley keeps,
There hath he entered late, betimes gone forth'.
Where I with pride was wont to sit before
I'm now with shame sent blushing from the door.

Chartley. Alas, poor fool, I am sorry for thee, but yet cannot help thee, as I am a gentleman. Why, say, Luce, thou losest now forty shillings' worth of credit; stay but a time, and it shall bring thee in a thousand pounds' worth of commodity.

Father. Son, son, had I esteemed my profit more
Than I have done my credit, I had now
Been many thousands richer. But you see,
Truth and good dealing bear an humble sail.
That little I enjoy, it is with quiet,
Got with good conscience, kept with good report,
And that I still shall labour to preserve.

Chartley. But do you hear me?

Father. Nothing I'll hear that tends unto the ruin
Of mine or of my daughter's honesty.
Shall I be held a broker to lewd lust

65. *cope*] barter.

67. *depart*] separate; Cranmer's original term in the Order of Matrimony, 1549; regularised in 1662 to 'do part'.

70. *juggle . . . her*] cheat her out of them.

73. *oft repair*] frequent visits.

91. *commodity*] profit.

95. *Truth . . . sail*] proverbial (S24.1).

Now, in my wane of years?
Chartley. Will you but hear me?
Father. Not in this case. I, that have lived thus long,
Reported well, esteemed a welcome guest
At every burdened table, there respected,
Now to be held a pandar to my daughter?
That I should live to this!
Chartley. But hark you, father!
Father. A bawd to mine own child!
Chartley. Father!
Father. To my sweet Luce!
Chartley. Father!
Father. Deal with me like a son; then call me 'father'.
I, that have had the tongues of every man
Ready to crown my reputation,
The hands of all my neighbours to subscribe
To my good life, and such as could not write
Ready with palsy and unlettered fingers
To set their scribbling marks.
Chartley. Why, father-in-law!
Father. Thou hadst a mother, Luce. 'Tis woe with me
To say thou hadst, but hast not. A kind wife
And a good nurse she was. She, had she lived
To hear my name thus canvassed and thus tossed
Seven years before she died, I had been a widower
Seven years before I was. Heaven rest her soul.
She is in heaven, I hope. (*He wipes his eyes.*)
Chartley. Why, so now, these be good words. I knew these storms would have a shower, and then they would cease. Now, if your anger be over, hear me.
Father. Well, say on, son.
Chartley. Stay but a month. 'Tis but four weeks. Nay, 'tis February, the shortest month of the year, and in that time I shall be at full age, and the land being entailed, my father can disinherit me of nothing. Is your spleen down now? Have I satisfied you? Well, I see you choleric-hasty men are the kindest, when all is done. [*Aside*] Here's such wetting of handkerchers. He weeps to think of his wife, she weeps to see her father cry. Peace, fool. We shall else have thee claim kindred of the woman killed with kindness!
Father. Well, son, my anger's past. Yet I must tell you
It grieves me that you should thus slight it off
Concerning us, to such a dear degree.
In private be it spoke, my daughter tells me

117. life,] *V*; like; *Q*. 141. to] *L*; no *Q*; in *V*.

123. *canvassed*] tossed in a blanket for sport; criticised.
138. *woman . . . kindness*] proverbial (K51), but Heywood is here surely referring to the title of his own 1603 play.

She's both a wife and maid.

Chartley. [*Aside*] That may be helped.

[*To Luce*] Now, Luce, your father's pacified. Will you be pleased? I would endure a quarter's punishment for thee, and wilt not thou suffer a poor month's penance for me? 'Tis but eight and twenty days, wench. Thou shalt fare well all the time, drink well, eat well, lie well. Come, one word of comfort at the later end of the day.

Luce. Yours is my fame, mine honour; and my heart
Linked to your pleasure, and shall never part.

Chartley. Gramercy, wench. [*Removes her chain.*] Thou shalt wear this chain no longer, for that word. I'll multiply the links in such order that it shall have light to shine about thy neck oftener than it doth. [*Takes her jewel.*] This jewel, a plain Bristow stone, a counterfeit. How base was I, that coming to thee in the way of marriage, courted thee with counterfeit stones! Thou shalt wear right, or none. Thou hast no money about thee, Luce?

Luce. Yes, sir, I have the hundred pounds that you gave me to lay up last.

Chartley. Fetch it.

[*Exit* LUCE.]

Let me see, how much branched satin goes to a petticoat? And how much wrought velvet to a gown? Then for a beaver for the city, and a black bag for the country—[*Aside*] I'll promise her nothing, but if any such trifles be brought home, let her not thank me for them.

Enter LUCE *with the bag.*

Gramercy, Luce. Nay, go in, Gravity and Modesty. [*Aside*] Ten to one but you shall hear of me ere you see me again.

Father. I know you kind. Impute my hasty language
Unto my rage, not me.

Chartley. Why, do not I know you, and do not I know her? [*Aside*] I doubt you'll wish shortly that I had never known either of you. [*To Luce*] Now what sayest thou, my sweet Luce?

Luce. My words are yours, so is my life. I am now
Part of yourself, so made by nuptial vow.

Chartley. [*Aside*] What a pagan am I to practise such villainy against this honest Christian. If Gratiana did not come into my thoughts I should fall into a vein to pity her. But now that I talk of her, I have a tongue to woo her, tokens to win her. And that done, if I do not find a trick both to wear her and weary her, it may

175. vow.] *V*; vowes. *Q*. 177. did not] *V*; did *Q*.

143. *helped*] remedied (with bawdy sense).
155. *Bristow stone*] rock-crystal mined near Bristol.
162–3. *branched . . . wrought*] two terms for embroidery.
167. *Gravity and Modesty*] (i.e. Father and Luce).
180. *wear . . . weary her*] possess in marriage (cf. 'win and wear') and then exploit.

prove a piece of a wonder. [*To her*] Thou seest, Luce, I have some store of crowns about me. There are brave things to be bought in the city. Cheapside and the Exchange afford variety and rarity. This is all I will say now, but thou mayest hear more of me hereafter. *Exit.*

Luce. Heaven speed you where you go, sir. Shall we in?
Though not from scandal, we live free from sin.
Father. I'll in before. *Exit.*

Enter Master BOISTER.

Boister. I am still in love with Luce, and I would know
An answer more directly. Fie, fie, this love
Hangs on me like an ague, makes me turn fool,
Coxcomb and ass. Why should I love her? Why?
A rattle-baby, puppet, a slight toy!
And now I could go to buffets with myself
And cuff this love away. But see, that's Luce.
Luce. [*Aside*] I cannot shun him, but I'll shake him off.
Boister. 'Morrow.
Luce. As much to you.
Boister. I'll use few words. Canst love me?
Luce. 'Deed sir, no.
Boister. Why then, farewell. The way I came, I'll go. *Exit.*
Luce. This is no tedious courtship. He's soon answered.
So should all suitors else be, were they wise.
For, being repulsed, they do but waste their days
In thankless suits and superficial praise.

Enter BOISTER *again.*

Boister. Swear that thou wilt not love me.
Luce. Not, sir, for any hate I ever bare you,
Or any foolish pride or vain conceit,
Or that your feature doth not please mine eye,
Or that you are not a brave gentleman,
But for concealèd reasons I am forced
To give you this cold answer. And to swear
I must not. Then with patience, pray, forbear.
Boister. Even farewell, then. *Exit.*
Luce. The like to you, and save your hopes in me.
Heaven grant you your best wishes. All this strife
Will end itself, when I am known a wife. *Exit.*

216. *Exit.*] V; *Exeunt. Q.* 216.1] *Explicit Actus tertius. Q.*

183. *Cheapside*] London's old Market Square, north-east of St Paul's.
193. *rattle-baby, puppet, . . . toy*] contemptuous terms comparing Luce to a doll.
209. *brave*] fine.

ACT IV

SCENE i

Enter SIR HARRY, Master HARINGFIELD [*and*] GRATIANA, *with others.*

Sir Harry. I am satisfied, good Master Haringfield,
Touching your friend, and since I see you have left
His dangerous company, I limit you
To be a welcome guest unto my table.
Haringfield. You have been always noble.

Enter TABOR.

Sir Harry. Tabor, the news with thee?
Tabor. May it please the right worshipful to understand that there are some at the gate who dance a turn or two without, and desire to be admitted to speak with you within.
Sir Harry. The scholar, is it not?
Tabor. Nay, sir, there are two scholars, and they are spouting Latin one against the other. And in my simple judgement the stranger is the better scholar, and is somewhat too hard for Sir Boniface, for he speaks louder, and that, you know, is ever the sign of the most learning. And he also hath a great desire to serve your worship.
Sir Harry. Two scholars! My house hath not place for two.
Thus it shall be: Tabor, admit them both. [*Exit* TABOR.]
We, though unlearned, will hear them two dispute,
And he that of the two seems the best read
Shall be received, the other quite cashiered.
Haringfield. In that you show but justice. In all persons
Merit should be regarded.

Enter TABOR, *ushering* SIR BONIFACE, *and* SENSER *disguised like a pedant.*

Sir Boniface. Venerabiles magistri,
Absint vobis capistri.

Scene heading] *V*; *Actus 46. Scena prima. Q.* 17.1. *Exit* TABOR.] *L*; *not in Q.* 23. *Venerabiles*] *V*; Venerabilis *Q.*

This long scene presents two unfair competitions: the debate between Sir Boniface and Senser to be Gratiana's tutor (a deception by false Latin) and the contest of Chartley with Senser (deception by a forged letter).

3. *limit*] appoint, allow.

8. *dance . . . two*] dance attendance, wait.

23–4. Venerabiles . . . capistri] Venerable masters, may you be spared halters (i.e., nooses; cf. l. 40). See Lily (1540), Bvi verso.

Senser. Et tu, domine calve,
Iterum atque iterum salve.
Amo, amas, amavi,
Sweet lady, Heaven save ye.
Sir Harry. This approves him to be excellent,
But I thank my breeding I understand not a word.
You tongue-men, you whose wealth lies in your brains
Not in your budgets, hear me. Be it known,
My house affords room for one schoolmaster,
But not for more. And I am thus resolved—
Take you that side, gentle Sir Boniface,
And, sir, possess you that—
He of you two in arguing proves the best,
To him will I subscribe. Are you agreed?
Sir Boniface. Nec animo, nec corde, nec utroque!
Senser. No more of that 'neck cordy'. Noble knight,
He wishes you 'neck cordy'. Think of that!
Sir Harry. A cord about my neck, Sir Boniface?
Speak, do you use me well?
Sir Boniface. *Domine, cur rogas?*
Senser. Is this to be endured, to call a knight
'Cur', 'rogue' and 'ass'?
Sir Harry. I find myself abused.
Haringfield. Yet patience, Good Sir Harry, and hear more.
Pray, Sir Boniface, of what university
Were you of?
Sir Boniface. I was student in Brasenose.
Haringfield. A man might guess so much by your pimples.
And of what place were you?
Senser. Petrus dormit securus,
I was, sir, of Peterhouse.
Sir Boniface. Natus eram in Woxford,
And I proceeded in Oxford.

25. *domine*] *V*; domini *Q*. 40. 'neck cordy'] *this ed.*; nec corde, *Q*. 41. 'neck cordy'] *this ed.*; nec corde, *Q*. 48. Brazenose.] *V*; Brazen nose. *Q*.

25–7. Et . . . amavi] And you, bald sir, greetings again and again. I love, you love, I loved (fragment of the most familiar conjugation).
29. *approves*] demonstrates.
32. *budgets*] wallets.
39. nec . . . utroque!] not in mind or spirit, in neither.
43. Domine . . . rogas?] Sir, why do you ask?
48. *Brasenose*] an Oxford college.
49. *pimples*] (giving his 'nose' a 'braised' appearance?)
51. Petrus . . . securus] See Lily (1567), Cviii verso: 'Petrus dormit securus, Peter slepeth void of care.'
52. *Peterhouse*] a Cambridge college.
53. Natus eram] I was born.
Woxford] a name invented for the rhyme.

Senser. Est mihi bene nostrum,
Thou wouldest say, 'in Gotham'.
For my part, Sir Harry,
I can read service and marry,
Quae genus aut flexum,
Though I go in jeans fustian,
Scalpellum et charta,
I was not brought up at plough and cart,
I can teach *Qui mihi*
And neither laugh nor tee-hee,
Sed -as in praesenti,
If your worship at this present,
Iste, ista, istud,
Will do me any good
To give me *legem pone*
In gold or in money,
Piper atque papaver,
I'll deserve it with my labour.
Haringfield. But when go you to dispute?
Sir Boniface. Nominativo: hic pediculus.
His words are most ridiculous.
But *tu*, thou, *qui*, the which, *derides*, deridest those that be rich,

59. *Quae genus aut*] *this ed.*; *Que genus et Q.* 65. *praesenti,*] *V subst.*; *presente, Q.* 74. *Nominativo*:] *S*; Nomnativo *Q. pediculus.*] *conj. L*; prediculus, *Q.* 76. *derides*, deridest] *this ed.*; deridest *Q.*

---

55. Est mihi bene nostrum] Our (recipe, medicine) is good. (An apothecary's motto?)

56. *Gotham*] famous for its wise fools; proverbial (M636).

59. Quae genus aut flexum] see Lily (1540), Bvi: 'Quae genus aut flexum, variant nouns of uncertain gender, nouns of alternate gender or declension.'

60. *jeans fustian*] heavy cotton cloth from Genoa.

61. scalpellum et charta] penknife and paper. See Lily (1567), Dv, in the poem *Carmen de Moribus* beginning 'Qui mihi discipulus puer es' ('You, boy, my pupil'): 'Scalpellum, calami, atramentum, charta, libelli, / Sint semper studiis arma parata tuis' ('Let penknife, pen, ink, paper, books, always be ready as weapons for learning').

62. *brought . . . cart*] proverbial (C102.11).

63. Qui mihi] See note to l. 61. Quoted also in *How a Man* 645–9.

65. Sed -as in praesenti] But (the ending) -as in the present tense. See Lily (1540), Cvi. Quoted also in Heywood, *Late Lancashire Witches* IV.175 and *How a Man* 1257.

67. Iste, ista, istud] declension of pronoun 'iste' (that). Lily (1567), Bi. cf. *How a Man* 1121.

69. legem pone] teach me thy laws; Psalm 119.33, associated with Quarter Day, and so used colloquially for the payment of debts.

71. Piper atque papaver] pepper and poppy; Lily (1567), Bii verso.

74. Nominativo: hic pediculus] In the nominative; this louse. cf. Lily (1540), Avi verso: 'Nominativo, hic magister (this teacher)' and *How a Man* 644: 'O pediculus, a louse.' 'Pediculus' is used of a pedant in Marston, *Fidele and Fortunio* (ed. R. Hosley, 1981), IV.vi.113.

76. tu . . . qui . . . derides] You who mock (a phrase from Plautus, e.g. *Amph.* 3.3.8 and *Bacch.* 4.9.87).

construe hanc sententiam, construe me this sentence: *Est modus in rebus; sunt certi denique fines.*

Senser. *Est modus in rebus*, there is mud in the rivers; *sunt certi denique fines*, and certain little fishes.

Sir Harry. I warrant you, he hath his answer ready.

Sir Boniface. *Di boni, boni*!

Haringfield. He'll give you more bones than those to gnaw on, Sir Boniface.

Senser. *Kartere Mousotrophos, poluphiltate phile poetatis,*
tes logikes rhetōn ouk elachiste sophōn.
That is as much as to say, in our *materna lingua*, I will make you, Sir Boniface, confess yourself an ass in English, speak open and broad words for want of Latin, and *denique* instruct me to resolve such questions as I shall ask you in our modern tongue.

Sir Harry. Confess himself an ass? Speak obscene words?
After, intreat thee to resolve thy questions?
Do that, possess the place.

Senser. *Di*, *do* and *dum*,
No more words, but mum.

Sir Boniface. Noble Sir Harry, *numquam sic possit*?

Sir Harry. Sir Boniface is sick already, and calls
For a posset. No marvel, being so threatened.

Senser. You Boniface, decline me 'I am an o' after the first conjugation: *amo*, *amavi*; *vocito*, *vocitavi*; *titubo*, *titubavi*.

77. *construe*] *V*; *consterue Q*. 85. *Mousotrophos*,] *this ed.*; Moosotropos *Q*. 86.] *this ed* (elachiste *V*); Tes Logikes retoon, onch elashiste sophoon. *Q*. 87. *materna lingua*,] *S*; *muterna lingna Q*. 91. himself] *V*; him *Q*. 99. 'I am an o'] *this ed.*; I am a no *Q*.

79–80. Est . . . fines] There is measure in things; in the end, limits are set. Horace, *Sat.* I.i.106; quoted Lily (1540), Dviii verso.

82. Di . . . boni] Ye good, good gods.

85–6. Kartere . . . sophōn] 'Staunch friend of the Muses, much loved patron of poetry, Not the least of the famed savants of logic.' A clumsy elegiac couplet in Greek, with false quantities in 'phile' and 'poetatis' and an unclassical formation, 'Mousotrophos'. *Q*'s misspelled 'elashiste' is a guide to Elizabethan pronunciation. Heywood's Greek was probably (see Martin, 180–2) inferior to his Latin.

87. materna lingua] mother tongue.

88–9. *open and broad*] brazen and indecent.

89. denique] finally; common in Lily to conclude a series.

94. Di, do and dum] case-endings of the gerund (Lily, 1540, Diiii verso) with a schoolboy pun on 'dumb'. Perhaps also with an echo of the folk incantation 'Fee Fi Fo Fum'? (cf. Lyly, *Mother Bombie*, ed. Tydeman (in *Four English Comedies*, Harmondsworth, 1984), 1305ff.: 'I woulde have likte well if all the gerundes had been there: *di*, *do* and *dum*; but all in "die", that's too deadly.' Tydeman notes that the correct order would be -dum, -di, -do.).

95. *no . . . mum*] proverbial (W767).

96. numquam sic possit?] can this ever be allowed?

98. *posset*] hot mixture of milk and wine.

100. amo . . . titubavi] present and perfect tenses of the verbs 'love', 'shout' and 'stagger'; Lily (1567), Biii verso, (1540), Cvi, Dii.

Sir Boniface. I am not the preceptor to a pupil,
But can decline it. Mark, Sir Timothy:
I am an o.
Senser. *Bene, bene.*
Sir Boniface. I am an as?
Senser. Most true, most true!
Vos estis!
Ut ego sum testis
That what he confessed is
As true as the *pestis*.
Sir Harry. This scholar works by magic.
He hath made him confess himself an ass.
Sir Boniface. *Per has meas manus*
Vir, tu es insanus.
Senser. I'll make him fret worse yet. Sir Boniface,
Quid est grammatica?
Sir Boniface. *Grammatica est ars—*
Sir Harry. Fie, fie!
No more of these words, good Sir Boniface.
Senser. Attend again. Proceed me with this verse
Of reverend Cato: *Si deus est animus—*
Sir Boniface. *Nobis ut carmina dicunt.*
Tabor. Die—, quotha? Out on him for a beastly man!
Sir Harry. I would not have him teach my children so
For more than I am worth.
Sir Boniface. O, but reverend Sir Harry,
You must *subaudi.*
Sir Harry. I'll never be so bawdy whilst I live,
Nor any of mine, I hope.
Sir Boniface. O, *propria quae maribus—*
Sir Harry. Ay, Boniface, it is those marrowbones
That makes you talk so broadly!

106. *ego sum*] *V*; *egosum Q*. 120. Die——, quotha?] *this ed.*; di quoth ha, *Q*; Di——quotha! *V*.

---

101. *preceptor ... pupil*] *L* (1967) notes a comic confusion here; but cf. l. 136, where Sir Boniface is correct.

103. Bene, bene] good, good.

105–6. Vos ... testis] You are. As I am witness.

108. pestis] plague.

111–12. Per ... insanus] By these hands of mine, sir, your are insane.

114–15. Quid ... ars] What is grammar? Grammar is an art. Lily (1540), Aii. cf. *How a Man* 669.

118–19. Si ... dicunt] If God is a spirit, as poems tell us. The opening of the popular school-text *Disticha Catonis*.

120. *Die*—] Both words (the second bowdlerised in *Q*) are bawdy.

123. subaudi] understand. See Lily (1540), Eiiii: 'subaudi servum' ('slave', understood). cf. also *How a Man* 2255.

126. propria quae maribus] masculine attributes; Lily (1540), Avi verso. *L* (1967) notes the phrase in *How a Man* 680 and in two other Heywood plays.

127. *marrowbones*] (with phallic connotations); marrow was also considered an aphrodisiac; Partridge glosses 'marrow' as semen.

Sir Boniface. Venerabilis vir, homo ille est ebrius.
Sir Harry. What doth he mean by that?
Senser. He saith I can speak Hebrew.
Sir Harry. I believe 't.
But if Sir Boniface still con these lessons
He'll speak the French tongue perfect.
Senser. Now to the last. I'll task Sir Boniface
But with an easy question. Tell me, sir,
What's Latin for 'this earth'?
Sir Boniface. Facile and easy,
More fit for the pupil than the preceptor.
What's Latin for 'this earth'? *Tellus.*
Senser. Tell you?
No, sir, it belongs to you to tell me.
Sir Boniface. I say *tellus*, that is Latin for 'the earth'.
Senser. And I say, I will not tell you what is Latin
For 'the earth', unless you yield me victor.
Sir Harry. You have no reason. Good Sir Timothy,
The place is yours.
Haringfield. He hath deserved it well.
Senser. But I'll deserve it better. Why, this fellow
Is frantic. You shall hear me make him speak
Idly and without sense. *He whispers to Sir Harry.*
I'll make him say
His nose was husband to a queen.
Sir Harry. Sir Timothy, not possible.
Tabor. He will not speak it, for shame.
Senser. That you shall hear. *Magister* Boniface—
Sir Boniface. Quid ais, domine Timothy?
Senser. Who was Pasiphae's husband, Queen of Crete?
Sir Boniface. Who knows not that? Why, Minos was her husband.
Senser. That his nose was! Did I not tell you so?
Sir Boniface. I say that Minos was.
Senser. That his nose was! *[He]ha-has.*
Sir Harry. I'll not believe it.
Sir Boniface, there are a brace of angels,
You are not for my turn. Sir Timothy,
You are the man shall read unto my daughter
The Latin tongue in which I am ignorant.

140. *tellus*, that is] *this ed.; Tellus* is *Q*; *Tellus*, which is *conj. Da.* 153. Pasiphae's] *this ed.*; *Pasiphas Q*; Pasiphe's *V*. 156. was! *[He] ha-has.*] *this ed.*; was ha has. *Q*; was ha ha *S*; was—ha ha! *V*.

129. Venerabilis . . . ebrius] Revered sir, this man is drunk.
133. *French tongue*] perhaps bawdy.
138. Tellus] Earth.
148. *nose*] bawdy.
151. Magister] Master.
152. Quid . . . domine] What are you saying, sir?
156. ha-has] *Q* appears to have a direction for laughter here. *S* emends to make the laughter part of the line.

[*To Sir Boniface*] Confess yourself an ass, speak bawdy words,
And after, to talk idly? Hence, away!
You shall have my good word, but not my pay.

Sir Boniface. Opus et usus,
Sir Timothy, you abuse us.
I swear by a noun,
Had I thy hose down,
Qui, quae, quod
I would so smoke thee with the rod
Ille, illa, illud
Until I fetch blood.
But, *nobiles, valete,*
Remain *in quiete.* *Exit* [*with* TABOR].

Sir Harry. Sir Timothy, there is some gold in earnest.
[*Gives him money.*]
I like you well. Take into your tuition
My daughter Gratiana.

Enter TABOR.

The news, Tabor?

Tabor. Of another gallant, noble sir, that pretends to have business both with you and my mistress.

Sir Harry. Admit him.

Enter CHARTLEY *very gallant, in his hand a Letter.*

Tabor. Lusty Juventus, will it please you to draw near?

Chartley. Noble knight, whilst you peruse that, sweet lady tell me, how you like this. (*Kisseth her.*)

Gratiana. You press so suddenly upon me, sir,
I know not what to answer.

Senser. [*Aside*] Mad Chartley! What makes desperation here?

Chartley. To the word 'wooer' let me add the name 'speeder'. My father hath written to your father, and the cause of his writing at this present is to let you understand that he fears you have lived a maid too long. And therefore, to prevent all diseases incident to

165. *et*] *conj. L*; est *Q*. 180.1. *Letter.*] conj. *Da*; *Lady. Q*.

165. opus et usus] work and practice; Lily (1540), Eiiii, (1567), Cvii.
169. Qui, quae, quod] relative pronoun 'who' in three forms; Lily (1540), Ci verso, (1567), Bi verso.
170. *smoke*] punish, originally by burning.
171. Ille, illa, illud] demonstrative pronoun 'that' in three forms. Fleay (I, 290) compares 'Iste, ista, istud ... until he fetcht blood', *How a Man* III.i.
173. nobiles, valete] nobles, farewell.
174. in quiete] in peace.
175. *in earnest*] as a first instalment.
181. *Lusty Juventus*] Vigorous Youth; the type of the prodigal, as in R. Weaver's play of this title, *c.* 1550.
187. *speeder*] successful suitor.

the same, as the green-sickness and others, he sent me, like a skilful physician, to take order with you against all such maladies. If you will not credit me, list but how fervently my father writes in my behalf.

Sir Harry. [*Reads*] 'He is my only son, and she I take as
Your only daughter. What should hinder, then,
To make a match between them?' Well! 'Tis well!
'Tis good, I like it. 'I will make her jointure
Three hundred pounds a year.'

Chartley. How say you by that, sweet lady? Three hundred pounds a year, and a proper man, to boot?

Sir Harry. All's good, I like it. Welcome, Master Chartley.
Thou, Gratiana, art no child of mine
Unless thou bidst him welcome. [*To Chartley*] This I presume
To be your father's hand?

Chartley. [*Aside*] But I'll be sworn
He never writ it.

Sir Harry. And this, his seal at arms?

Chartley. [*Aside*] Or else I understand it very poorly.
[*To Gratiana*] But lady, in earnest of further acquaintance
Receive this chain, these jewels, hand and heart.
[*Gives her the jewel-bag.*]

Sir Harry. Refuse no chain nor jewels, heart nor hand,
But in exchange of these bestow thyself,
Thine own dear self, upon him.

Gratiana. Myself on him, whom I till now ne'er saw?
Well, since I must, your will's to me a law.

Senser. Nay, then, 'tis time to speak. Shall I stand here waiting like a coxcomb and see her given away before my face? Stay your hand, Sir Harry, and let me claim my promise.

Sir Harry. My promise I'll perform, Sir Timothy.
You shall have all your wages duly paid.

Senser. I claim fair Gratiana by your promise.
No more 'Sir Timothy', but Senser now. [*Takes off his disguise.*]
You promised me, when you received my service
And with your liberal hand did wage my stay,
To endow me freely with your daughter's love.
That promise now I claim.

Sir Harry. Mere cosenage, knavery!
I tied myself to no conditions
In which such guile is practised. Come, son Chartley,
To cut off all disasters incident

213. I till now ne'er] *V*; I tell now I neere *Q*; I tell now neere *S*. 228. off] *V*; of *Q*.

---

191. *green-sickness*] anaemia in young women, seen as symbolic of love-sickness.

209. jewel-bag] Chartley gave jewels in a box at I.ii.141; Luce returned them in a bag at III.iii.166.1.

210. *heart . . . hand*] proverbial (H339).

214. *your . . . law*] proverbial (W391.10).

To these proceedings, we will solemnise
These nuptial rites with all speed possible.
Chartley. Farewell, good 'Sir Timothy'. Farewell,
Learned 'Sir Timothy'. *Exeunt* [*all but* SENSER].
Senser. Why, and farewell, learned Sir Timothy.
For now Sir Timothy and I am two.
Boast on, brag on, exult, exalt thyself,
Swim in a sea of pleasure and content
Whilst my barque suffers wrack. I'll be revenged,
Chartley; I'll cry *Vindicta*! for this scorn.
Next time thou gorest, it must be with thy horn. *Exit*.

[ACT IV SCENE ii]

Enter Master BOISTER.

Boister. I am mad, and know not at what.
I could swagger, but know not with whom.
I am at odds with myself, and know not why.
I shall be pacified, and cannot tell when.
I would fain have a wife, but cannot tell where.
I would fasten on Luce, but cannot tell how.
How, where, when, why, whom, what.
Feeding sure makes me lean, and fasting fat.

Enter LUCE *and* JOSEPH.

Luce. Not all this while once see me?
Joseph. His occasions
Perhaps enforce his absence.
Luce. His occasions?
Unless he find occasion of new love
What could enforce such absence from his spouse?
Am I grown foul and black since my espousals?
It should not seem so, for the shop is daily
Customed with store of chapmen such as come
To cheapen love. O no, I am myself!
But Chartley, he is changed.
Joseph. [*Seeing Boister*] You know that gentleman.
Luce. Escape him, if thou canst.

235. exult, exalt] *this ed.*; exalt, exalt Q. 238. scorn.] S; Horne, Q.

236. *swim . . . content*] proverbial (S184.11).

238. Vindicta!] Hieronymo's celebrated cry for revenge in Kyd, *The Spanish Tragedy* (ed. Philip Edwards, 1959) III.xiii. cf. *Cap*. IV.v.17.

9, 10. *occasions*] necessary business. In her reply, Luce plays on the meaning 'opportunity'.

15–16. *chapmen . . . cheapen*] from the Old English verb for buying and selling; but Luce intends also the other, pejorative, sense of 'cheapen', to 'make less valuable'.

Boister. He cannot, I arrest you.
Luce. At whose suit?
Boister. Not at mine own, that's dashed. I love thee not.
Thou art a Spaniard, gipsy, a mere blackamoor.
Again I say I love thee not.
Luce. A blackamoor? A gipsy?
Sure, I am changed indeed, and that's the cause
My husband left me so. This gentleman
Once termed me beautiful. How look I, Joseph?
Joseph. As well as e'er you did—fat, fresh and fair.
Boister. You lie, boy. Pocket that, and now be gone. [*Gives money.*]
Joseph. And what shall then become of my mistress?
Boister. I'll wait upon your mistress.
Luce. I know you will not wait on such a gipsy.
Boister. Yes, Luce, on such a gipsy. Boy, *abi*, *abi*.
Joseph. Abide, sir? You need not fear that. I have no purpose to leave her.
Boister. Now you are going to the wedding-house.
You are bid to be a bridemaid, are you not?
Luce. What wedding, sir, or whose?
Boister. Why, Chartley's. Luce, hath he been thy friend so long
And would not bid thee to wait on his bride?
Why lookst thou red and pale, and both, and neither?
Luce. To Master Chartley's bridals? Why, to whom
Should he be married?
Boister. To Grace, of Gracious Street.
Luce. To Gratiana?
Beshrew you, sir, you do not use me well
To buzz into mine ears these strange untruths.
I tell you, sir, 'tis as impossible
They two should match, as earth and heaven to meet.
Boister. You'll not believe it? Pray then, hark within
The nuptial music echoing to their joys.
But you give credit to no certainties—
I told you but a tale, a lie, a fable,
A monstrous, a notorious, idle untruth,
That you were black and that I loved you not,
And you could credit that.

Enter SIR HARRY *and* HARINGFIELD, CHARTLEY *leading* GRATIANA *by the arm,* TABOR, *and attendants.*

Who's tell-truth now?
Know you that man, or know you that fine virgin
Whom by the arm he leads?

28. e'er] *V*; ere *Q*.

---

28. *e'er*] Q's 'ere', 'before', is only slightly less attractive than Verity's emendation 'e'er', 'ever'.
fat] in good condition.
33. abi] go away.

Luce. I'll not endure it. Heaven give you joy, sir!
Chartley. I thank you. Luce? *She faints.* BOISTER *held her up.*
Sir Harry. Look to the maid; she faints.
Chartley. Grace, come not near her, Grace.
Father, keep off. On, gentlemen, apace.
She's troubled with the falling-sickness, for
Oft hath she fallen before me.
Sir Harry. Nay, if it be no otherwise, on, gentlemen.
Let those with her strive to recover her.
Keep off; the disease is infectious.
Chartley. If it were in a man, it were nothing.
But the falling-sickness in a woman is dangerous.

Enter Luce's FATHER.

[*Aside*] My t'other father-in-law! Now shall I be
Utterly shamed. If he assure to know me,
I'll outface him.
Father. Son, you're well met.
Chartley. How, fellow?
Father. I cry you mercy, sir.
Chartley. No harm done, friend, no harm done.

Exeunt SIR HARRY, HARINGFIELD, CHARTLEY, GRATIANA, TABOR, *and attendants.*

Father. [*Aside*] If he, he could not but have known me there.
Yet he was wondrous like him.
Boister. How cheer you, Luce? Whence grew this passion?
Luce. Pardon me, sir, I do not know myself.
I am apt to swound, and now the fit is past me.
I thank you for your help. Is Master Chartley
Vanished so soon?
Boister. Yes. And to supply his place
See where thy father comes.
Father. [*Aside*] He hath not such a suit. Besides, this gallant
Led by the arm a bride, a lusty bride!
How much might I have wronged the gentleman
By craving his acquaintance. This it is
To have dim eyes. Why looks my daughter sad?
[*To Boister*] I cry you mercy, sir. I saw not you.
Boister. [*Aside*] I would I had not seen you at this time,
Neither. [*To them*] Farewell. *Exit.*

59.1. held] For the textual implications of the past tense, see Introduction.

60. *Grace, come*] Metrically, this should read 'Gratiana, come'; possibly the compositor amended to normalise the names. cf. IV.v.101.

62. *falling-sickness*] epilepsy; in l. 68, Chartley plays on a bawdy sense.

71. *outface*] contradict.

Luce. [*Aside*] If he be gone, then call me vent my grief.
[*To Father*] Father, I am undone!
Father. Forbid it, Heaven!
Luce. Disgraced, despised, discarded and cast off.
Father. How, mine own child?
Luce. My husband, O my husband!
Father What of him?
Luce. Shall I the shower of all my grief at once
Pour out before you? Chartley, once my husband,
Hath left me to my shame. Him and his bride
I met, within few minutes.
Father. Sure, 'twas they.
I met them two. 'Twas he! Base villain, Jew!
I'll to the wedding board, and tell him so.
I'll do't , as I am a man!
Luce. Be not so rash.
Father. I'll live and die upon him. He's a base fellow,
So I'll prove him, too. Joseph, my sword!
Luce. This rashness will undo us.
Father. I'll have my sword.
It hath been twice in France, and once in Spain
With John o' Gaunt. When I was young like him
I had my wards, and foins, and quarter-blows,
And knew the way into St George's Fields
Twice in a morning. Tothill, Finsbury!
I knew them all. I'll to him. Where's my sword?
Luce. Or leave this spleen, or you will overthrow
Our fortunes quite. Let us consult together
What we were best to do.
Father. I'll make him play at leap-frog! Well, I hear thee.
Luce. I cannot prove our marriage; it was secret,
And he may find some cavil in the law.

90. call] *Q*; let *V*. 99. two] *Q*; too *V*. 104. prefix *Luce*.] *S*; *given to Father*, *Q*. 104. prefix *Father*.] *S*; *Luce*. Q (where Father's speech begins l. 105). 111. prefix *Luce*.] *S*; *not in Q*.

---

90. *call ... grief*] invite me to weep. For omission of 'to', cf. *Sir Thomas More* (ed. Gabrieli and Melchiori, Manchester, 1990), p. 226, l. 4: 'Point me meet the block.'

99. *Jew*] Heywood's casual anti-Semitism, here and elsewhere, is of a piece with his equally unqualified national chauvinism. cf. *ET* I.i.146–72.

100. *board*] feast.

106. *John o' Gaunt*] The fourteenth-century pedigree makes the sword either a valued possession or an absurdly antiquated prop. John of Gaunt's victory in Spain was a popular legend. See Kyd, *Spanish Tragedy* (ed. Edwards) I.iv.140–57 and note.

107. *wards, foins and quarter-blows*] fencing terms for defensive, stabbing and slashing strokes.

108–9. *St George's ... Tothill ... Finsbury*] open fields near London used for exercise, including duelling and military drills.

111. *Or*] Either.

Father. I'll to him with no law but Stafford law.
I'll ferret the false boy. Nay, on, good Luce.
Luce. Part of your spleen if you would change to counsel,
We might revenge us better.
Father. Well I hear thee.
Luce. To claim a public marriage at his hands
We want sufficient proof, and then the world
Will but deride our folly, and so add
Double disgrace unto my former wrong.
To law with him? He hath a greater purse
And nobler friends. How, then, to make it known?
Father. Is this his 'damasked kirtle fringed with gold',
His 'black bag', and his 'beaver'? 'Tis well yet
I have a sword.
Luce. And I have a project in my brain begot
To make his own mouth witness to the world
My innocence and his incontinence.
Leave it to me. I'll clear myself from blame.
Though I the wrong, yet he shall reap the shame. *Exeunt.*

[ACT IV SCENE iii]

Enter SENSER *like a serving-man.*

Senser. Now or never! Look about thee, Senser. Tomorrow is the marriage-day, which to prevent lies not within the compass of my apprehension. Therefore I have thus disguised myself, to go to the cunning woman's, the fortune-teller's, the anything, the nothing. This, over against Mother Redcap's, is her house. I'll knock.

Enter SECOND LUCE *in her boy's shape.*

Second Luce. Who's there? What would you have?
Senser. I would speak with the wise gentlewoman of the house.
Second Luce. O, belike you have lost somewhat?
Senser. You are in the wrong, sweet youth.
Second Luce. I am somewhat thick of hearing; pray speak out.
Senser. I say, I have not lost anything but wit and time, and neither of those she can help me to.
Second Luce. Then you, belike, are crossed in love, and come to know what success you shall have?

127. fringed] *V*; frendge *Q*. 3. cunning] *conj. Da*; Looming *Q*.

117. *Stafford law*] a beating; proverbial (S808).
118. *ferret*] expose.
1. *Now or never*] proverbial (N351).
Look about thee] proverbial (L427.1).
3. *cunning*] wise.
5. *Mother Redcap's*] see note to II.i.90–1.

Senser. Thou hast hit it, sweet lad, thou hast hit it.
Second Luce. What is it you say, sir?
Senser. Thou hast hit it!
Second Luce. I pray, come in. I'll bring you to my mistress.
Exeunt.

[ACT IV SCENE iv]

Enter LUCE and JOSEPH.

Luce. This is the house. Knock, Joseph. My business craves dispatch.
Joseph. Now am I as angry as thou art timorous. And now, to vent the next thing I meet. O, 'tis the door. (*Knocks.*)

Enter SECOND LUCE [*in her boy's disguise*].

Second Luce. Who's there? What are you?
Luce. A maid, and a wife.
Second Luce. And that would grieve any wench to be so.
[*Aside*] I know that by myself, not Luce.
Luce. Boy, where's your mistress?
Second Luce. In some private talk with a gentleman.
I'll fetch her to you presently. *Exit.*
Luce. [*Aside*] If she and you see me not, I am but dead.
I shall be made a byword to the world,
The scorn of women, and my father's shame.

Enter WISE-WOMAN *and* SENSER [*followed by* SECOND LUCE].

Wise-woman. You tell me your name is Senser; I knew it before. And that Chartley is to be married tomorrow; I could have told it you.
Second Luce. [*Aside*] Married tomorrow? O, me!
Senser. Ay, but you tell me that Chartley before tomorrow shall be disappointed of this. Make that good, thou shalt have twenty angels.
Wise-woman. I'll do't. Stand aside, I'll have but a word or two with this gentlewoman, and I am for you presently.
Luce. O, mother, mother! (*They whisper.*)
Second Luce. [*Aside*] My husband marry another wife tomorrow? O, changeable destiny. No sooner married to him, but instantly to lose him. Nor doth it grieve me so much that I am a wife, but that I am a maid, too. To carry one of them well is as much as any is bound to do, but to be tied to both is more than flesh and blood can endure.

2. vent] Q; vent on *V*. 14. married tomorrow;] *this ed.* (sugg. Smallwood); married, Q. 17. this.] *this ed.*; his, Q; his wife; *V*. 24. doth it grieve] *V*; death it grieves Q.

---

2. *vent*] break open.
26–7. *more . . . endure*] proverbial (F361.12).

Wise-woman. [*To Luce*] Well, trust to me, and I will set all things straight.

Enter BOISTER.

Boister. Where's this witch, this hag, this beldam, this wizard? And have I found thee? Thus will I tear, mumble and maul thee!
Wise-woman. Help, help, and if you be a gentleman!
Senser. Forbear this rudeness. He that touches her
Draws against me. [*Draws his sword.*]
Boister. Against you, sir? Apply thou, that shall be tried. [*Draws.*]
All. Help, help! Part them! Help!
Senser. With patience hear her speak.
Boister. Now, trot! Now, grannam! What canst thou say for thyself? [*Aside.*] What, Luce here? Be patient, and put up, then. We must now see the end. [*Puts up his sword.*]
Senser. Then truce of all sides. If we come for counsel,
Let us with patience hear it. [*Puts up.*]
Luce. Then first to me.
Wise-woman. You would prevent young Chartley's marriage? You shall.
Hark in your ear. [*She whispers.*]
Luce. It pleaseth me.
Wise-woman. [*To Senser*] You, forestall Gratiane's wedding? 'Tis but thus.
[*She whispers.*]
Senser. I'll do it.
Wise-woman. [*To Boister*] You would enjoy Luce as your wife, and lie
With her tomorrow night? Hark in your ear. [*She whispers.*]
Boister. Fiat.
Wise-woman. Away! You shall enjoy him, you are married, Luce. Away! You shall see Chartley discarded from Gratiana, Senser. Be gone. And if I fail in any of these or the rest, I lay myself open to all your displeasures.
Boister. Farewell till soon.
Wise-woman. You know your meeting-place?
All. We do.
Wise-woman. You shall report me wise, and cunning, too.
Exeunt [*all except* SECOND LUCE].

28. set] *S*; sell *Q*. 30. beldam,] *V*; beldan, *Q*. 39. then.] them, *Q*; thou: *V*. 39. We must now] *this ed.*; shee must not *Q*. 41. Then truce] *S subst.*; Than trince *Q*. 46. Gratiane's] *Q*; Gratiana's *V*. 56. wise,] *S*; wiser *Q*.

31. *mumble*] beat.

39–40. *We . . end*] *Q*'s 'shee must not see the end.' is surely corrupt. An alternative to the emendation proposed here would be 'She must not see thee mad.'

46. *Gratiane's*] A trisyllable, for the metre. The Wise-woman speaks a mixture of prose and verse.

49. Fiat] So be it.

Second Luce. I'll add one night more to the time I have stayed.
I have not many, I hope, to live a maid. *Exit.*

[ACT IV SCENE V]

Enter TABOR *and* SIR BONIFACE *with a trencher, with broken meat and a napkin.*

Tabor. Fie, fie, what a time of trouble is this 'tomorrow'. Tomorrow is my mistress to be married, and we serving-men are so puzzled.

Sir Boniface. The dinner's half done, and before I say grace,
And bid the old knight and his guest proface,
A medicine from your trencher, good Master Tabor,
As good a man as e'er was Sir Sabre,
We'll think it no shame; men of learning and wit
Say, study gets a stomach. Friend Tabor, a bit.

Tabor. Lick clean, good Sir Boniface, and save the scraper a labour.

Enter SENSER *like a serving-man.*

Sir Boniface. But soft, let me ponder,
Know you him that comes yonder?

Tabor. [*To Senser*] Most heartily welcome; would you speak with any here?

Senser. Pray, is the young gentleman of the house at leisure?

Tabor. Mean you the bridegroom, Master Chartley?

Senser. I have a letter for him. You seem to be a gentleman yourself. Acquaint him with my attendance, and I shall rest yours in all good offices.

Tabor. Sir Boniface, pray keep the gentleman company. I will first acquaint your lips with the virtue of the cellar.

Sir Boniface. *Adesdum*, come near
And taste of our beer.
Welcome, *sine dolo*,

57. stayed.] *conj. L*; said. *Q*. 1. this 'tomorrow'. Tomorrow is] *Q*; this! Tomorrow is *V*. 22. our] *S*; your *Q*. 23. *dolo*,] *conj. L*; *dole*, *Q*.

This scene, like the last scene in Act III, contrasts Chartley's predatory sexuality with a gentler form of wooing, in this case Senser's. See note to ll. 126–9.

0.1. trencher] a wooden platter.

0.2. broken meat] food remnants.

4. *proface*] a greeting, 'good health', from Latin.

6. *Sir Sabre*] obscure; *OED* lists no use of 'sabre' before 1680, though the 1617 spelling 'sable' may suggest an earlier use. If *Q*'s 'Saber' is a misprint, possible corrections might be 'Scraper' (cf. l. 9) or 'Salver', but neither fits the rhyme.

8. *study . . . stomach*] *L* (1967) notes proverbs expressing the contrary (e.g. 'A belly full of gluttony will never study willingly', B285); cf. B293.

21. Adesdum] Come here.

23. sine dolo] without guile.

For *paucis te volo*.

Exit [TABOR].

Senser. When I taste of your liquor,
Gramercy, Master Vicar.

Enter TABOR *with a bowl of beer and a napkin*.

Tabor. Most heartily welcome. Your courtesy, I beseech you. Ply it off, I entreat you. Pray, Sir Boniface, keep the gentleman company, till I acquaint my young master with his business. *Exit*.

Sir Boniface. Tabor, I shall *besolas manus*.

Senser. Ah, *vostre servitor*. (*They dissemble one to another*.)

Enter HARINGFIELD.

Haringfield. Hey, what art thou?

Senser. A hanger-on, if it please you.

Haringfield. And I a shaker-off. I'll not bear you, gallows. You shall not hang on me.

Enter CHARTLEY *with his napkin as from dinner*.

O, Master Bridegroom.

Chartley. Gentlemen, the ladies call upon you to dance. They will be out of measure displeased if, dinner being done, you be not ready to lead them a measure.

Haringfield. Indeed, women love not to be scanted of their measure.

Chartley. Fie, Sir Boniface, have you forgot yourself? Whilst you are in the hall, there's never a whetstone for their wits in the parlour.

Sir Boniface. I will enter and set an edge upon their ingenies.

[*Exeunt* SIR BONIFACE *and* HARINGFIELD.]

Chartley. [*To Senser, who hands him a letter*] To me, sir? From whom? A letter? [*Reads*] 'To her most dear, most loving, most kind friend Master Chartley these be delivered.' Sure, from some wench or other. I long to know the contents.

Senser. [*Aside*] Now to cry quittance with you for my 'farewell, learned Sir Timothy'.

24. *paucis te volo.*] *conj.* L; *puntis te vole*, Q. 32. Hey,] V; Hee Q. 34. bear you,] *this ed.*; beare your Q; be your *conj. Da.*

---

24. paucis te volo] I'd like a few words with you. Heywood is quoting from the opening lines of Terence, *Andria*.

27–8. *Your courtesy . . . Ply it off*] Tabor is either teaching manners to the guests, inviting them to bow to each other (where 'ply' has the meaning 'bend'), or he offers them the chance to apply themselves to the beer. The former is more characteristic of his wit.

30. besolas manus] corruption of Spanish 'beso las manos', 'kiss the hands'.

31. vostre servitor] corruption of early French 'vostre serviteur', 'your servant'.

34. *gallows*] villain (gallows-meat).

38–40. *measure . . . measure . . . measure*] (*a*) proportion; (*b*) dance; (*c*) portion (bawdy).

42. *whetstone . . . wits*] proverbial (W299).

43. *ingenies*] intellects.

Chartley. Good news, as I live. There's for thy pains, my good sir Pandarus. [*Gives Senser money.*] Hadst thou brought me word my father had turned up his heels, thou couldst scarcely have pleased me better. (*He reads*) 'Though I disclaim the name of "wife", of which I account myself altogether unworthy, yet let me claim some small interest in your love. This night I lie at the house where we were married, the wise-woman's I mean, where my maidenhead is to be rifled. Bid fair for it, and enjoy it. See me this night, or never. So may you, marrying Gratiana and loving me, have a sweet wife and a true friend. This night or never, your quondam wife; heareafter, your poor sweetheart, no other, Luce.' [*Aside*] So, when I am tired with Gratiana, that is, when I am past grace, with her I can make my rendezvous. I'll not slip this occasion, nor sleep till I see her. [*To Senser*] Thou art an honest lad, and mayest prove a good pimp, in time. Canst thou advise me what colour I may have to compass this commodity?

Senser. Sir, she this night expects you, and prepares a costly banquet for you.

Chartley. I'll go, although the devil and mischance look big.

Senser. Feign some news that such a piece of land is fallen to you, and you must instantly ride to take possession of it. Or, which is more probable, cannot you persuade them you have received a letter that your father lies a-dying?

Chartley. You rogue, I would he did. But the name of that news is called 'too good to be true'.

Senser. And that if ever you will see him alive, you must ride post into the country.

Chartley. Enough; if ever I prove knight errant, thou shalt be mine own proper squire for this. Thou hast fitted me with a plot; do but wait here. Note how I will manage it. [*Calls*] Tabor, my horse; for I must ride tonight.

[*Enter* TABOR].

Tabor. Tonight, sir?
Chartley. So tell my bride and father.
I have news that quite confounds my senses.

[*Exit* TABOR.]

Enter SIR HARRY, GRATIANA *and* HARINGFIELD.

Gratiana. How, ride tonight, the marriage-day tomorrow
And all things well provided for the feast?
O, tell me, sweet, why do you look so pale?

78. squire for this. Thou] *this ed.*; squire, for this thou *Q.*

---

51. *Pandarus*] Troilus and Cressida's go-between.
52. *turned . . . heels*] proverbial (H392). cf. V.vi.52.
68. devil . . . big] proverbial (D226.11).
73–4. *news . . . true*] proverbial (N156); used as Worcester's Men play title in 1602 by Chettle, Hathway and Smith.

Chartley. My father, O, my father!
Gratiana. What of him?
Sir Harry. What of your father, son?
Chartley. If ever I will hear his aged tongue
Preach to me counsel, or his palsy hand
Stroke my wild head and bless me, or his eyes
Drop tear by tear, which they have often done
At my misgoverned, rioting youth—
[*Aside*] What should I more? [*To them*] If ever I would see
The good old man alive—O! O!
Senser. [*Aside*] Go thy ways, for thou shalt ha't.
Gratiana. But do you mean to ride?
Chartley. Ay, Grace, all this night.
Senser. [*Aside*] Not all the night without alighting, sure.
You'll find more in't than to get up and ride.
Haringfield. The gentleman's riding boots and spurs. Why, Tabor!
Chartley. Nay, Grace, now's no time to stand
On scrupulous parting. Knewest thou my business—
Senser. [*Aside*] As she shall know it.
Chartley. And how I mean this night to toil myself—
Senser. [*Aside*] Marry, hang you, brock.
Chartley. Thou would bemoan my travel.
Senser. [*Aside*] I know 'twould grieve her.
Chartley. You father, Grace, good Master Haringfield,
You sir, and all, pray for me, gentlemen,
That in this dark night's journey I may find
Smooth way, sweet speed, and all things to my mind.
Sir Harry. We'll see my son take horse.
Gratiana. But I will stay.
I want the heart to see him post away.
Exeunt [CHARTLEY, SIR HARRY *and* HARINGFIELD].
Senser. Save you, gentlewoman. I have a message to deliver to one Mistress Gratiana. This should be the knight's house, her father.
Gratiana. It is. The message that you have to her
You may acquaint me with, for I am one
That knows the inside of her thoughts.
Senser. Are you the lady?
Gratiana. Sir, I am the poor gentlewoman.
Senser. There is a cunning woman dwells not far,
At Hogsdon, lady, famous for her skill.
Besides some private talk that much concerns
Your fortunes in your love, she hath to show you
This night, if it shall please you walk so far

96–7.] Senser picks up the (proverbial) bawdy (N284) in 'ride', as he does with 'business', 'toil' and 'travel' in the following lines.

101. *Grace*] Metrically, as at IV.ii.60, this should read 'Gratiana', but emendation is not justified in this passage of irregular prose and verse.

105. *brock*] trickster (lit., 'badger').

As to her house, an admirable suit
Of costly needlework, which if you please
You may buy under rate for half the value
It cost the making. About six o' clock
You may have view thereof, but otherwise
A lady that hath craved the sight thereof
Must have the first refusal.
Gratiana. I'll not fail her.
My husband being this day rid from home
My leisure fitly serves me. Thank your mistress.
Senser. At six o' clock?
Gratiana. I will not fail the hour. *Exit.*
Senser. Now to Sir Harry; his is the next place,
To meet at Hogsdon his fair daughter Grace. *Exit.*

ACT V

SCENE i

Enter OLD Master CHARTLEY *as new come out of the country to enquire after his son, and three or four serving-men with blue coats to attend him* [*, one of them named* GILES].

Old Chartley. Good heaven, this London is a stranger grown,
And out of my acquaintance. This seven years
I have not seen Paul's steeple, or Cheap Cross.
Giles. Sir?
Old Chartley. Hast thou not made enquiry for my son?
Giles. Yes, sir, I have asked about everywhere for him,
But cannot hear of him.
Old Chartley. Disperse yourselves,

128. buy] *V*; by *Q*. 134. your mistress.] *conj. L*; you Mistresse? *Q*; you, mistress. *V, following S in giving speech to Senser.* Scene heading] *V*; *Actus 56. Scena prima. Q*.

126–9. *suit . . . making*] A gentle pun; Senser's 'admirable suit' to Gratiana has cost him more than she will recognise.

128. *under rate*] wholesale.

2. *This . . . years*] proverbial (Y25): a long time.

3. *Paul's steeple*] *L* (1967) notes that St Paul's lost its steeple in 1561, while in I.i. and III.iii Chartley refers to the Exchange, built in 1566. The dramatic date is presumably close to 1600, when 'Paul's steeple' was still in common speech.

Cheap Cross] a cross in Cheapside.

Enquire about the taverns, ordinaries,
Bowl-alleys, tennis-courts, gaming-houses,
For there, I fear, he will be found.
Giles. But where shall we hear of your worship again?
Old Chartley. At Grace Church, by the Conduit, near Sir Harry.
But stay, leave off a while your bootless search.
[*Aside*] Had e'er man such a wild-brain to his sorrow
Of such small hope? Who when he should have married
A fair, a modest and a virtuous maid,
Rich, and revenued well, and even the night
Before the marriage day, took horse, rode thence,
Whither, heaven knows. Since, the distracted virgin
Hath left her father's house, but neither found,
Yet in their search we have measured out much ground.

Enter SIR HARRY *and* SENSER.

Senser. Your worship will be there?
Sir Harry. Yes, not to fail,
At half an hour past six, or before seven.
Senser. You shall not find us at six and at seven,
I'll warrant you. Good health to your worship. *Exit.*
Sir Harry. Farewell, good fellow.
[*Aside*] At the wise-woman's house? I know it well.
Perhaps she knows some danger touching me.
I'll keep mine hour.
Old Chartley. Sir Harry!
A hand, a hand! To balk you, it were sin.
I shall be bold to make your house mine inn.
Sir Harry. Brother Chartley, I am glad to see you.
Old Chartley. Methinks, Sir Harry, you look strangely on me,
And do not bid me welcome with an heart.
Sir Harry. And blame me not, to look amazedly
To see you here.
Old Chartley. Why me?
Sir Harry. Come, come, y'are welcome.
And now I'll turn my strangeness to true joy.
I am glad to see you well, and safe recovered
Of your late grievous sickness.
Old Chartley. The strange amazèd looks that you cast off
You put on me; and blame me not to wonder
That you should talk of sickness to sound men.
I thank my stars I did not taste the grief
Of inward pain or outward malady
This seven years' day.
Sir Harry. But, by your favour, brother,

19. found,] *S*; feumd, *Q*. 30. sin.] *S*; siun. *Q*.

---

23. *at . . . seven*] proverbial (A208).
30. *balk*] avoid.
45. *This . . . day*] cf. V.i.2 and note.

Then let me have my wonder back again.
Old Chartley. Before I quite part with it, let me know
Why you the name of 'brother' put upon me
In every clause, a name as strange to me
As my recovered sickness.
Sir Harry. You are pleasant,
And it becomes you well. Welcome again,
The rather, you are come just to the wedding.
Old Chartley. What wedding, sir?
Sir Harry. That you should ask that question!
Why, of my daughter Grace.
Old Chartley. Is Grace bestowed?
Of whom, I pray?
Sir Harry. Of whom, but of your son?
I wonder, brother Chartley, and my friend,
You should thus play on me.
Old Chartley. But, by your favour,
Were you ten knights, Sir Harry—take me with you!—
My son match with your daughter? My consent
Not worthy to be craved?
Sir Harry. Nay then, I see
You'll stir my patience. Know, this forward match
Took its first birth from you.
Old Chartley. From me?
Sir Harry. From you.
Peruse this letter. Know you your own hand?
'Twas well that I reserved your hand a witness
Against your tongue. You had best deny the jointure
Of the three hundred pounds made to my daughter—
'Tis that I know you aim at. But your seal— [*Shows the letter.*]
Old Chartley. Shall not make me approve it. I deny
This seal for mine, nor do I vouch that hand.
Your daughter and the dower, letter and all,
I quite disclaim. Sir Harry, you much wrong me.
Sir Harry. I can bear more than this. Heap wrong on wrong,
And I'll support it all. I for this time
Will cast my spleen behind me. And yet hear me:
This letter your son Chartley as from you
Delivered me. I like the motion well.
Old Chartley. My spleen is further thrown aside than yours,
And I am full as patient. And yet hear me:
My son's contracted to another maid—
Nay, I am patient, still—yet that I writ
This letter, sealed this impress, I deny.
Sir Harry. Why then, the jack your hand did counterfeit.

81. sealed this impress,] *V*; seald, this impresse *Q*.

58. *take . . . you*] proverbial (T28.1).
81. *impress*] wax impression.
82. *jack*] knave.

Old Chartley. Why then, he did so. Where's that unthrift, speak?
Sir Harry. Some hour ago, he mounted and rid post
To give you visit, whom he said lay sick
Upon your death-bed.
Old Chartley. You amaze me, sir.
It is an ill presage. Hereon, I see,
Your former salutation took its ground,
To see me safe recovered of my sickness.
Sir Harry. Indeed it did. Your welcome is a subject
I cannot use too oft. Welcome again.
I am sorry you this night must sup alone,
For I am elsewhere called about some business,
Concerning what, I know not. Hours run on,
I must to Hogsdon, high time I were gone. *Exit.*
Old Chartley. [*Aside*] Perhaps to the wise-woman's. She may tell me
The fortunes of my son. This accident
Hath bred in me suspicion and strange fears.
I will not sup alone, but I protest
'Mongst some this night I'll play the intruding guest.
Exit with his serving-men.

[ACT V SCENE ii]

Enter the WISE-WOMAN, SENSER [*as serving-man*], LUCE *and her* FATHER [*and*] SECOND LUCE [*in boy's clothes*].

Wise-woman. But will Sir Harry come?
Senser. Presume he will,
And Chartley, too.
Father. I'll have the knave by the ears!
Luce. Nay, patience, sir, leave your revenge to me.

Enter Master BOISTER.

Boister. Grannam, I am come, according to promise.
Wise-woman. And welcome to the best hole that I have
In Hogsdon.
Boister. [*To Luce*] Good even.
Luce. Thanks, sir. A good even may it prove,
That each may reap the fruits of their own love.
Second Luce. That shall be my prayer, too.
Boister. Come, what shall 's do?
Wise-woman. Withdraw; I'll place you all in several rooms,
Where sit, see, but say nothing.
[*She hides Luce's Father and Boister separately.*]

5. *hole*] room (commonly, a prison cell); also with presumed bawdy.

[ACT V SCENE iii]

Enter TABOR, *ushering* GRATIANA.

Tabor. Here, sweet mistress. I know the place well, ever since I was here to know my fortune.

Gratiana. Call me some half an hour hence.

Exit [TABOR].

Enter the WISE-WOMAN *and* SECOND LUCE.

Wise-woman. Your ladyship is most lovingly welcome.
[*To Second Luce*] A low stool for the gentlewoman, boy.
[*She fetches a stool*.]
[*To Gratiana*] I made bold to send to you to take view
Of such a piece of work as I presume
You have seldom seen the like.

Gratiana. Of whose doing, I pray?

Wise-woman. A friend of yours and mine. Please you withdraw,
I'll bring you to't. [*Hides Gratiana*.]

Second Luce. Mistress!

Wise-woman. One calls. Sweet lady, I shall do you wrong,
But pray you, think my little stay not long.
[*Exeunt* WISE-WOMAN *and* SECOND LUCE.]

[ACT V SCENE iv]

Enter SENSER, SIR HARRY *and* LUCE.

Senser. Here, sir, in this retiring chamber. [*Hides him*.]

Sir Harry. Gramercy, friend. How now? What's here to do?
A pretty wench, and a close chamber, too?

Luce. That you have so much graced my mother's house
With your desirèd presence, worthy knight,
Receive a poor maid's thanks. [*Calls*] Who's there? A chair
And cushion for Sir Harry! [*A chair is brought*.]

Sir Harry. Thanks, most fair.

Luce. Please you but a few minutes here to stay
Till my return. I'll not be long away. [*Exit*.]

Senser. The gentlewoman will wait on you by and by, sir.

Sir Harry. And I'll attend her, friend.
[*Exit* SENSER.]
Of all those doubts I long to know the end. [*Conceals himself*.]

[ACT V SCENE v]

[*Enter* SECOND LUCE *and* OLD CHARTLEY.]

Second Luce. The knight you seek was here, or will be straight,
And if you be the man you name yourself

You are most welcome, and you shall not back
Till you have seen Sir Harry.
Old Chartley. Gentle youth,
I saw him enter here, and under privilege
Of his acquaintance made I bold to stay.
Second Luce. And you are welcome, sir. Sit down, I pray.
[*Hides herself with him.*]

[ACT V SCENE vi]

[*Enter* WISE-WOMAN, SENSER *and* LUCE.]

Wise-woman. Now they are placed in several rooms that look
Into this one. Were Chartley come, we had all
Our company. [*A knock at the door.*]
Senser. Hark, there's one knocks. 'Tis Chartley, on my life.
Luce. One of you, let him in whilst I prepare me
To entertain his coming. [*Exit* SENSER.]

Enter Young CHARTLEY, *ushered in by* SENSER.

[*Exeunt* SENSER *and* WISE-WOMAN.]
Chartley. What, old acquaintance Luce? Not a word?
Yet some lip-labour, if thou lovest me. [*Attempts to kiss her.*]
Gratiana. [*Within*] My husband?
Sir Harry. [*Within*] What, young Chartley?
Old Chartley. [*Within*] How, my son?
Chartley. Come, come, away with this wailing in woe.
If thou putst finger in the eye a little longer,
I shall plunge in pain too, presently.
Luce. O, husband, husband!
Gratiana. [*Within*] Husband?
Chartley. What sayest thou, my sweet wife?
Gratiana. [*Within*] Wife? O, my heart!
Second Luce. [*Within*] In that name 'wife' I claim a poor child's part.
Luce. O husband, how have you used me!
Chartley. Nay, how do I mean to use thee? But as a man
Should use his wife.

14. prefix *Gratiana.*] *V*; *Anne. Q.*

For a discussion of the staging of this scene, see Introduction. In the disguise plot, the last and most pleasing reversal is for the usually well-informed Wise-woman to find that her boy Jack has been a girl.

1. *several*] separate.

10–12. *wailing . . . pain*] 'I wail in woe, I plunge in pain' was the first line of a sonnet made by George Manningham before his execution in 1576 and published in *A Handful of Pleasant Delights* (1584). See Hyder E. Rollins, *An Analytical Index to the Ballad-Entries 1557–1709* (Chapel Hill, 1924, repr. 1967), item 1617. A parodic repentance song was performed to the ballad's tune in 1605 in Jonson, Chapman and Marston's *Eastward Ho* (V.v) by the prodigal Quicksilver.

Gratiana. [*Within*] I hope he doth not mean to use her so.
Second Luce. [*Within*] I hope so, too.
Boister. [*Within*] My grannam is a witch.
Chartley. Nay Luce, sweet wife, leave weeping if thou lov'st me.
Luce. O, can you blame me, knowing that the fountain
Of all these springs took their first head from you?
You know, you too well know, not three days since
Are past since we were married.
Gratiana. [*Within*] Married? I can endure no longer.
Sir Harry. [*Within*] It cannot be.
Old Chartley. [*Within*] It is not possible.
Boister. [*Within*] I'll be even with thee for this, old grannam.
Luce. And though we wanted witness upon earth,
Yet heaven bears record of our nuptial tie.
Chartley. Tush, when we meet in heaven let's talk of that.
Nay, come, you ass, you fool; what's past is past.
Though man and wife, yet I must marry now
Another gallant. Here's thy letter, Luce,
And this night I intend to lodge with thee.
Second Luce. [*Within*] I'll scratch her eyes out first, although I love her.
Chartley. Prithee, be merry.
I have made a gull of Grace, and old Sir Harry
Thinks me a great way off. I told the knight
My father lay a-dying, took post-horse,
Rid out of Holborn, turned by Islington,
So hither, wench, to lodge all night with thee.
Second Luce. [*Within*] Here's one saith nay to that.
Old Chartley. [*Within*] Was that your journey?
Chartley. Why, I have too much of Grace already.
Boister. [*Within*] Thou hast no grace at all.
Chartley. Nay, let's to bed. If thou couldst but imagine how I love thee, Luce.
Luce. How is it possible you can love me, and go about to marry another?
Chartley. Dost thou not know she's rich? Why, you fool, as soon as I have got her dower, it is but giving her a dram, or a pill to purge melancholy, to make her turn up her heels, and then with all that wealth come I to live with thee, my sweet rascal.
Gratiana. [*Revealing herself*] She thanks you, and is much beholding to you.
Chartley. I am betrayed!
Gratiana. Art thou my suitor? Wouldst thou marry me

24. well] *V*; will *Q*.

32. *what's ... past*] proverbial (P90.11).
52. *dram*] (of poison).
pill ... melancholy] proverbial (P324.11), this being the first appearance noted by Dent, and also the title of a 1599 pamphlet (Pantzer, *STC*, 19933.5).

And thy first wife alive? Then poison me
To purchase my poor dower?

Chartley. [*Aside*] What shall I say, or think, or do? I am
At a nonplus.

Gratiana. Hast thou the face, thou brazen impudence,
To look on me past grace?

Chartley. Thou canst not properly call me 'past Grace',
For I never enjoyed thee yet. I cannot tell
Whether I blush or no, but I have now at this time
More Grace than I can tell what to do with.

Gratiana. Who drew thee to this folly?

Chartley. Who but the old dotard thy father, who, when I was honestly married to a civil maid, he persuaded me to leave her. I was loath at first, but after entreating, urging, and offering me large proffers, I must confess I was seduced to come a-wooing to thee.

Gratiana. My father, villain?

Chartley. Ay, thy father, Grace. And were he here,
I would justify it to the old dotard's face.

Sir Harry. [*Revealing himself*] Vile boy, thou dar'st not be so impudent!
When did I meet thee, seek or sue to thee?
When? Name the day, the month, the hour, the year.

Chartley. Plots, plots. I can but cry you mercy, both, say that I have done you wrong; I can be but sorry for it. But indeed, to clear you, and lay the fault where it ought to be, all this comes from mine own father in the country, who, hearing I had married with Luce, sends me word of his blessing to be divorced from her, and to come a suitor to your daughter. I think you have his hand and seal to show.

Old Chartley. [*Revealing himself*] My hand and seal? When was that letter writ?

Chartley. Heyday!
If you get one word more of me tonight
But scurvy looks, I'll give you leave to hang me.

Sir Harry. Vile boy!

Old Chartley. Ungracious villain!

Gratiana. Treacherous youth!

Sir Harry. No grace at all?

Chartley. No grace.

Old Chartley. This is bad company! Who hath seduced thee?
Speak, on my blessing, who hath thus misled thee?
But no more lies, I charge thee.

Chartley. Bad company hath been the shame of me. I was
As virtuously given as any youth in Europe
Till I fell into one Boister's company.
'Tis he that hath done all the harm upon me.

93. prefix *Old Chartley.*] *1672*, *S*; *Chart.* *Q* (*catchword Old Chartly.*).

---

61. *At a nonplus*] proverbial (N206).
77. *vile*] with associations also of 'wild' (Q: vild).

Boister. [*Within*] I?

Chartley. And if he should deny it—

Boister. [*Revealing himself*] What then? You'd cry him mercy?

Chartley. [*Aside*] I had best bite out my tongue, and speak no more. What shall I do, or what shall I say? There is no outfacing them all. [*To them*] Gentlemen, fathers, wives, or what else, I have wronged you all. I confess it that I have. What would you more? Will any of you rail of me? I'll bear it. Will any of you beat me? So they strike not too hard, I'll suffer it. Will any of you challenge me? I'll answer it. What would you have me say, or do? One of these I have married, the other I have betrothed, yet both maids for me. Will you have me take one, and leave the t'other? I will. Will you have me keep them both? I will.

Father. [*Revealing himself*] Perjured, not mine!

Chartley. What, you here, too? Nay then I see all my good friends are met together. Wilt thou have me, Luce? I am thy husband, and had I not loved thee better than Grace, I had not disappointed the marriage day tomorrow.

Luce. Lascivious, no.

Chartley. Wilt thou have me, Grace? For had I not loved thee better than Luce, I would never, after I had married her, been contracted to thee.

Grace. Inconstant, no.

Chartley. Then neither married man, widow nor bachelor, what's to be done? Here's even the proverb verified: between two stools, the tail goes to ground.

Sir Harry. Now I bethink me,
This our meeting here is wondrous strange.
Call in the gentlewoman that owns this house.

Enter SENSER *and the* WISE-WOMAN, *he like a gentleman.*

Boister. Old trot, I'll trounce thee.
Here is the marriage proved 'twixt Luce and Chartley.
Witch, this was not your promise.

Wise-woman. Have patience, and in the end we'll pay you all. Your worships are most heartily welcome. I made bold to send for you, and you may see to what end, which was to discover unto you the wild vagaries of this—of this wanton wagpasty, a wild oats, I warrant him. And Sir Harry, that your daughter hath scaped this scouring, thank this gentleman, and then make of him as he deserves.

135. of this—of this] *this ed.*; of this, of this *Q*; of this *S*.

124–5. *between . . . ground*] as Chartley notes, proverbial (S900).

135. *wagpasty*] Not in *OED*. It appears in Udall's *Ralph Roister Doister* (ed. Tydeman in *Four English Comedes*, Harmondsworth, 1984), 814, where it is glossed 'mischievous rogue'.

136–7. *scaped . . . scouring*] avoided being harmed (*OED* scouring 6).

Sir Harry. O, I remember him.
Gratiana. He never pleased mine eye so well as now.
I know his love, and he in Chartley's place
My favour shall possess.
Senser. Thanks, my sweet Grace.
Sir Harry. Ay, and the more the inconstant youth to spite,
Senser, I give her thee in Chartley's sight.
Chartley. There's one gone already,
But this is my wife, and her I'll keep
In spite both of the devil and his dam.
Wise-woman. Not from her lawful husband.
Chartley. That am I.
Wise-woman. [*Indicating Boister*] That is the gentleman. Accept him, Luce,
And you the like of her. Nay, I'll make it good:
This gentleman married you vizarded,
You him disguised, mistaking him for Chartley,
Which none but my boy Jack was privy to.
After, she changed her habit with him,
And you met Jack in mistress Luce's habit.
Luce. May I believe you, mother?
Wise-woman. This be your token.
[*She joins their hands.*]
Boister. Her that I married, I wrung twice by the finger.
Luce. Of that token my hand was sensible.
Boister. And ere the clamorous and loud noise begun,
I whispered to her, thus— [*He whispers.*]
Luce. You are the man.
Boister. Thanks, grannam. What thou promised, thou hast done.

144. give] *S*; gaue *Q*. 150. the like] *S*; then like *Q*. 155. And you met Jack in] *this ed.*; as / you with Iack. / And you in *Q*. 159. begun,] *V*; bee gone, *Q*.

---

155. I assume that Heywood's manuscript originally read:
After shee chang'd her habit with him,
And you in mistresse *Luces* habit
He then interlined the omission:
After shee chang'd her habit with him,
you mett Iack
And you in mistresse *Luces* habit
This was set, wrongly emended, as:
after shee chang'd her habit with him, as
you with Iack.
And you in mistresse *Luces* habit.
Heywood's intention was:
After, she changed her habit with him,
And you met Jack in mistress Luce's habit.
156. s.d.] follows *L*'s suggestion (1967).
157. *I . . . finger*] *L* (1967) compares *How a Man* 405, where the words are part of a song.

Father. And leaving him, I take you for my son.
Chartley. Two gone. Then where's the third? This makes me mad.
Where is my wife, then? For a wife I had.
Wise-woman. Not see thy wife? Come hither, Jack my boy.

[SECOND LUCE *steps out, still disguised*.]

Nay, take him to thee, and with him all joy.
Old Chartley. Well art thou served, to be a general scorn
To all thy blood. And, if not for our sakes,
For thy soul's health and credit of the world,
Have some regard to me, to me thy father.
Chartley. Enough, sir. If I should say I would
Become a new man, you would not take my word.
If I should swear I would amend my life,
You would not take mine oath. If I should bind
Myself to become an honest man,
You would scarce take my bond.
Old Chartley. I should do none of these.

Chartley. Then see, sir, when to all your judgements I see me past grace, do I lay hold of grace and here begin to retire myself. This woman hath lent me a glass in which I see all my imperfections, at which my conscience doth more blush inwardly than my face outwardly, and now I dare confidently undertake for myself, I am honest.

Second Luce. Then I dare confidently undertake
To help you to a wife who desires to have
An honest man or none. Look on me well.
Simple though I stand here, I am your wife.
Blush not at your folly, man. Perhaps
I have more in me than you expect from me.
Chartley. Knavery and riot, both which are now to me
Mean forage.
Second Luce. You and I have been better acquainted, and yet
Search me not too far, lest you shame me.
Look on me well. Nay better, better yet.
I'll assure you, I left off a petticoat
When I put on these breeches. *She scatters her hair.*
What say you now?
Chartley. First love, and best beloved!

170. regard] *S*; regarded *Q*. 179. of grace] *V*; of *Grace*, *Q*. 195. off] *V*; of *Q*.

179. *retire*] Chartley proposes a change of occupation, perhaps to a more contemplative life.

191. *Mean forage*] distasteful food (with a hint that his former life was beastly).

196. s.d.] Unbound hair was a sign of virginity, specified in stage marriages in Jonson's *Hymenaei* and Shakespeare and Fletcher's *Two Noble Kinsmen*. In removing her boy's disguise, Luce at the same time proclaims her innocence.

197. *first . . . beloved*] proverbial (L478).

Second Luce. Let me be both, or neither.
Wise-woman. [*Aside*] My boy turned girl! I hope she'll keep my
counsel.
From henceforth, I'll never entertain
Any servant but I'll have her searched.
Old Chartley. Her love hath drawn her hither after him.
My loving daughter, welcome. Thou hast run
A happy course. To see my son thus changed!
Chartley. Father, call me once again your son,
And Sir Harry, me your friend,
Senser, an hand, and Mistress Grace, an heart,
In honourable love. Where I have wronged
You, Luce, forgive. Impute my errors to
My youth, not me. With Grace I interchange
An embrace, with you, Luce, a parting buss.
I wish you all joy; divide my heart amongst you.
Thou, my soul.
Nay, Mother Midnight, there's some love for you.
Out of thy folly, being reputed wise,
We, self-conceited, have our follies found.
Bear thou the name of all these comic acts.
Luce, Luce and Grace—O, covetous man—I see
I sought to engross what now sufficeth three.
Yet each one, wife enough. One nuptial feast
Shall serve three bridals. Where be thou chief guest.
Exeunt omnes.

221.2. *Explicat Actus 56. Q.*

---

209. *Luce*] the London Luce? Lines 208–12 seem like farewells to his failed loves.
211. *Luce*] (the London Luce)
buss] kiss.
213. *Thou*] (the Second Luce); the unfinished line is suggestive of a pause, during which Chartley and the Second Luce are brought together, but the verse is not so regular in this final speech (see l. 206) that such an intention can be assumed.
214. *Mother Midnight*] 'a Midwife (often a Bawd)': B.E., *A New Dictionary . . . of the Canting Crew* (before 1700), *OED*.
216. *self-conceited*] blinded by vanity.
219. *engross*] monopolise.
220. *thou*] (the Wise-woman).

TO HIS CHOSEN FRIEND
the learned author Master Thomas Heywood

Thou wants no herald to divulge thy fame;
'T needs no apology, only thy name
Into judicious readers doth infuse
A will to add a laurel to thy Muse.
Was now Maecenas living, how would he
Support thy learned wit? Whose industry
Hath purchased such a knowing skill, that those
Who read admire thee, 'less some critic shows
His ignorance in seeking with new songs
To gain the honour which to thee belongs.
But let pale envy belch forth all her spite;
Thy candid fame shall still continue white,
Unspotted, pure and fair, till memory
Be turned oblivion, or a deity
Prove mortal. And when Atropos shall do
The fatal office her belongs unto,
Apollo will rebreathe a life in thee
In length to equal all eternity,
Where in Elysian joys he will so raise
Thy worth where never wither shall the bays
Wherewith he crowns thee. So thy works will show
The debt I pay's no more but what I owe.

Samuel King

FINIS

---

5. *Maecenas*] patron of the poets Virgil and Horace.

12. *candid*] pure.

15. *Atropos*] One of the Fates; she cuts life's thread.

20. *bays*] laurel (worn both by the god Apollo and by the poets he favours).

23. *Samuel King*] A Clerkenwell neighbour of Heywood, he wrote a poem also for *The Nipping or Snipping of Abuses* (1614), by their mutual friend John Taylor, the Water Poet, who himself contributed verses to Heywood's *An Apology for Actors* (1612). Little more is known of King beyond the date (1601) of his marriage (Clark, p. 59).

THE ENGLISH TRAVELLER.

AS IT HATH BEENE Publikely acted at the COCK-PIT in *Drury-lane*: By Her Maiesties seruants.

Written by THOMAS HEYVVOOD.

Aut prodesse solent, aut delectare ——

LONDON,
Printed by *Robert Raworth*: dwelling in Old Fish-street, neere Saint *Mary Maudlins* Church. 1633.

THE ENGLISH TRAVELLER

DRAMATIS PERSONAE

[YOUNG] GERALDINE, [*and*]
DALAVILL, *two young gentlemen.*
Old WINCOTT, *the husband.*
His WIFE, *a young gentlewoman.*
PRUDENTILLA, *sister to the Wife.*
REIGNALD, *a parasitical serving-man.*
ROBIN, *a country serving-man.*
[YOUNG] LIONEL, *a riotous citizen.*
BLANDA, *a whore.*
SCAPHA, *a bawd.*
RIOTER, *a spendthrift.*
Two Gallants, *his companions.*
Roger *the* CLOWN, *servant to Old Wincott.*
Two Prostitutes, *companions with Blanda.*
OLD LIONEL, *a merchant, father to Young Lionel.*
A [*pair of*] Servant[s] *to Old Lionel.*
[*Watermen.*]
OLD Master GERALDINE, *father to Young Geraldine.*
An Usurer *and his man.*
A Gentleman, *companion with Dalavill.*
BESS, *chambermaid to Mistress Wincott.*
A Tavern Drawer.

Motto: See note on *WWH* title page.
Device: The classically-costumed knight with spear and shield under a blazing sun can hardly have been engraved for this play. It was presumably part of Raworth's old stock.

Many of the characters are given appropriate names, some obvious (Prudentilla, Rioter) others more subtle. Reignald is the foxy servant (Reynard) of two 'lions', Old and Young Lionel; his last speech begins 'I was the fox' (IV. vi. 328). Dalavill, the 'man about town' is the more worldly of the two young men, though the opening dialogue misleadingly suggests otherwise (see Introduction); by the play's end, he has become a 'devil', at which time his name's ending may suggest 'villain'. Grivelet comments that the name of Wincott, January married to May, represents the 'wintry house'. Finally, from Plautus, Blanda ('flattering, enticing') and Scapha ('skiff') are suitable for a whore and a bawd, light craft easily manned.

Master RICOTT, *a merchant.*
The Owner *of the house supposed to be possessed.*

THE EPISTLE DEDICATORY

To the Right Worshipful Sir Henry Appleton, Knight, Baronet, &c.
Noble Sir,
For many reasons I am induced to present this poem to your favourable acceptance; and not the least of them, that alternate love and those frequent courtesies, which interchangeably passed betwixt yourself and that good old gentleman mine uncle (Master Edmund Heywood) whom you pleased to grace by the title of Father. I must confess, I had altogether slept (my weakliness and bashfulness discouraging me) had they not been wakened and animated by that worthy gentleman, your friend and my countryman, Sir William Elvish, whom (for his unmerited love many ways extended towards me) I much honour. Neither, sir, need you to think it any undervaluing of your worth to undertake the patronage of a poem in this nature, since the like hath been done by Roman Laelius, Scipio, Maecenas, and many other mighty princes and captains, nay, even by Augustus Caesar himself, concerning whom Ovid is thus read (*Trist.* 2):

Inspice ludorum sumptus, Auguste, tuorum:
empta tibi magno talia multa leges.
Haec tu spectasti, spectandaque saepe dedisti—
maiestas adeo comis ubique tua est.

13. (*Trist.* 2):] *this ed.*; *De trist*: *lib.* 2. *Q.* 16. dedisti—] *Di*; de desti *Q.*

Dedicatee: *Sir Henry Appleton*] an Essex landowner, married to a young woman of Lincolnshire, Heywood's county. The dramatist's uncle, Edmund Heywood (l. 4), a gentleman in the Exchequer office, mentions Appleton twice in his will of 7 October 1624, where he also leaves a bequest to 'Thomas Heywoode and his wief' (see Katherine L. Bates, 'A conjecture as to Thomas Heywood's family', *JEGP* 12 (1913), 93–109).

4. *Master Edmund Heywood*] Bates suggests that Edmund's brother, the prodigal Christopher, whom their father tried to disinherit on his death in 1570, may have been the dramatist's father.

8. *Sir William Elvish*] son of Sir Gervase Helwysse (Ellwis, Elvish), Lieutenant of the Tower at the time of Overbury's murder (Clark, p. 1).

12. *Laelius, Scipio*] Republican patrons of the playwright Terence, the Greek historian Polybius and the Roman satirist Lucilius.

12–13. *Maecenas . . . Augustus*] patrons of Virgil and Horace.

14. *Ovid*] author of the *Amores* and *Metamorphoses*, and of the *Tristia*, written in exile.

15–18. Inspice . . . est] *Tristia* II.509–12: 'Consider the expenses of your shows, Augustus, and you will see many such things bought at great cost. You were their spectator, and often laid them on for others, so kind and wide-ranging was your power.' The contest in the original (of risqué entertainments) is glossed over here, as it is in Heywood's *Apology for Actors*, where the same passage is quoted, with a translation of the opening couplet: 'Behold, Augustus, the great pompe and state, / Of these thy playes payd deere for, at hye rate.'

So highly were they respected in the most flourishing estate of the Roman Empire; and if they have been vilified of late by any separistical humorist (as in the now questioned *Histrio-mastix*) I hope by the next term (*Minerva assistente*) to give such satisfaction to the world, by vindicating many particulars in that work maliciously exploded and condemned, as that no gentleman of quality and judgement but shall therein receive a reasonable satisfaction. I am loath by tediousness to grow troublesome, therefore conclude with a grateful remembrance of my service, intermixed with myriads of zealous wishes for your health of body and peace of mind, with superabundance of earth's blessings, and Heaven's graces, ever remaining,

Yours most observant,
Thomas Heywood.

TO THE READER

If, reader, thou hast of this play been an auditor, there is less apology to be used by entreating thy patience. This tragicomedy (being one reserved amongst two hundred and twenty in which I have had either an entire hand or at the least a main finger) coming accidentally to the press, and I having intelligence thereof, thought it not fit that it should pass as *filius populi*, a bastard without a father to acknowledge it. True it is that my plays are not exposed unto the world in volumes, to bear the title of *Works* (as others); one reason is that many of them by shifting and change of companies have been negligently lost; others of them are still retained in the hands of some actors, who think it against their peculiar profit to have them come in print; and a third, that it never was any great ambition in me to be in this kind

---

20. *separistical*] separatist, sectarian.

21. Histrio-mastix] Not John Marston's burlesque of *c.* 1598, but the 1633 attack on the theatre by the Puritan William Prynne, target of Heywood's 1634 masque *Love's Mistress*.

29. Minerva assistente] with the help of the goddess of wisdom.

3. *two hundred and twenty*] Approximately forty titles, including lost and joint-authored plays, are known, some thirty of them surviving. Analyses of Heywood's contribution to the stage are based on less than a seventh of his claimed output.

6. filius populi] an orphan.

8. Works] The target of Heywood's scorn here is presumably Jonson, whose carefully edited *Workes* appeared in folio in 1616. The jibe was common, appearing in verses attached to plays by Massinger and Ford (see Colin Gibson, 'Elizabethan and Stuart Dramatists in *Wits Recreations*, 1640', *RORD* 29 (1986–7), 22).

9. *shifting ... companies*] Heywood was a member of at least three companies: the Admiral's Men (1596–99), Worcester's/Queen Anne's Men (1600–19), and the Lady Elizabeth's/Queen Henrietta's companies at the Cockpit, from perhaps 1624.

11. *against ... profit*] This statement implies that a dramatist's most successful plays might escape print.

12. *ambition*] There is a clear contrast between Heywood's concern for his non-dramatic works (*An Apology for Actors*, the translation of Sallust, *Troia Britannica*, *England's Elizabeth*, *Gunaikeion*, *The Exemplary Lives of ... the Most Worthy Women, The Hierarchy of the Blessed Angels*) and his more casual attitude, especially before 1630, towards his plays. Cf. the 'modesty' of his preface to *1FMW*.

volumniously read. All that I have further to say at this time is only this: censure, I entreat, as favourably as it is exposed to thy view freely. Ever

studious of thy pleasure and profit,
Thomas Heywood.

THE PROLOGUE

A strange play you are like to have, for know,
We use no drum, nor trumpet, nor dumb show
No combat, marriage, not so much today
As song, dance, masque, to bombast out a play.
Yet these all good, and still in frequent use
With our best poets; nor is this excuse
Made by our author as if want of skill
Caused this defect; it's rather his self-will.
Will you the reason know? There have so many
Been in that kind, that he desires not any
At this time in this scene; no help, no strain,
Or flash that's borrowed from another's brain;
Nor speaks he this, that he would have you fear it,
He only tries if once bare lines will bear it.
Yet may't afford, so please you silent sit,
Some mirth, some matter, and perhaps some wit.

---

12. *volumniously*] i.e., in volumes, rather than 'read' in performance. For the form, apparently only in Heywood, cf. his 'Volumne', Preface to 2 *IAge* (A4).

2. *no . . . trumpet*] Cf. Anon., *The Two Merry Milkmaids* (1619), Prologue: 'expect no noise of Guns, Trumpets, nor Drum'.

4. *bombast*] pad, inflate; Heywood claims *The English Traveller* as a play of dialogue ('bare lines', l. 14) rather than action or spectacle. Cf. the epilogues of *Arden of Faversham* ('this naked tragedy') and *A Warning for Fair Women*, and the prologue of *A Woman Killed with Kindness* ('a bare subject, a bare scene'). Doran (p. 145) explains this attitude by the domestic drama's debt to the morality play 'tradition of realism in scenes of common life'. Heywood's defensive tone here suggests that this style of theatre needed apology in 1624.

16. *Some . . . wit*] This line (with a more contrived companion rhyme) is quoted in the prologue to *1FMW*. Unlike the Epistle, datable to 1633, the Prologue more likely dates from the (?1624) first performance.

ACT I

SCENE i

Enter YOUNG GERALDINE *and* Master DALAVILL.

Dalavill. O friend, that I to mine own notion
Had joined but your experience. I have
The theoric, but you the practic.
Young Geraldine. I
Perhaps have seen what you have only read of.
Dalavill. There's your happiness.
A scholar in his study knows the stars,
Their motion and their influence, which are fixed
And which are wandering, can decipher seas
And give each several land his proper bounds,
But set him to the compass, he's to seek,
When a plain pilot can direct his course
From hence unto both th' Indies, can bring back
His ship and charge with profits quintuple.
I have read Jerusalem, and studied Rome,
Can tell in what degree each city stands,
Describe the distance of this place from that—
All this the scale in every map can teach—
Nay, for a need could punctually recite
The monuments in either, but what I have
By relation only, knowledge by travel,
Which still makes up a complete gentleman,
Proves eminent in you.
Young Geraldine. I must confess
I have seen Jerusalem and Rome, have brought
Mark from the one, from th' other testimony,
Know Spain and France, and from their airs have sucked
A breath of every language; but no more

1. *notion*] abstract knowledge.
8. *wandering*] (planets).
10. *to seek*] at a loss.
13. *charge*] cargo.
15. *degree*] (of latitude).
18. *punctually*] accurately.
24. *Mark*] Jerusalem pilgrims were tattooed with a cross; but 'mark' here probably means 'remark', as in the comparable passage of *Hierarchy of the Blessed Angels* (1636), Book IV, p. 254: 'To whom he related his journey, and what he had seene in the Holy City; describing punctually every Monument and place of remarke: which agreed with the relations of such Travellers and Pilgrims as had beene there and brought Certificate and assured testimonie from thence.'

Of this discourse, since we draw near the place
Of them we go to visit.

Enter [Roger, Old WINCOTT's] CLOWN.

Clown. Noble Master Geraldine, worshipful Master Dalavill.

Dalavill. I see thou still remember'st us.

Clown. Remember you? I have had so many memorandums from the multiplicities of your bounties that not to remember you were to forget myeself. You are both most ingeniously and nobly welcome.

Young Geraldine. And why ingeniously and nobly?

Clown. Because had I given your welcomes other attributes that I have done, the one being a soldier and the other seeming a scholar, I should have lied in the first and showed myself a kind of blockhead in the last.

Young Geraldine. I see your wit is nimble as your tongue.
But how doth all at home?

Clown. Small doings at home, sir, in regard that the age of my master corresponds not with the youth of my mistress, and you know cold January and lusty May seldom meet in conjunction.

Dalavill. I do not think but this fellow in time may for his wit and understanding make almanacs.

Clown. Not so, sir; you being more judicious than I, I'll give you the pre-eminence in that, because I see by proof you have such judgement in times and seasons.

Dalavill. And why in times and seasons?

Clown. Because you have so seasonably made choice to come so just at dinner-time. You are welcome, gentlemen. I'll go tell my master of your coming. *Exit.*

Dalavill. A pleasant knave.

Young Geraldine. This fellow, I perceive,
Is well acquainted with his master's mind.
O, 'tis a good old man.

Dalavill. And she a lady
For beauty and for virtue unparalleled,
Nor can you name that thing to grace a woman
She has not in a full perfection.
Though in their years might seem disparity,
And therefore at the first a match unfit,
Imagine but his age and government,

28.1. *Clown*] Of the play's two clowns, Roger (from the 'English' main plot) is a household Fool of the Feste type, while Reignald (the equivalent of Tranio in *Mostellaria*) is a crafty slave typical of Plautus and of later *commedia dell' arte*.

35–8.] Roger ironically reverses the usual categories, making the soldier intelligent and the scholar noble.

41. *doings*] (bawdy).

43. *January . . . May*] Cf. Chaucer, *The Merchant's Tale*; proverbial (M768).

50. *just*] precisely.

61. *government*] both discretion and authority.

Withal her modesty and chaste respect,
Betwixt them there's so sweet a sympathy
As crowns a noble marriage.
Young Geraldine. 'Tis acknowledged.
But to the worthy gentleman himself
I am so bound in many courtesies
That not the least, by all th' expression
My labour or my industry can show,
I will know how to cancel.
Dalavill. O, you are modest.
Young Geraldine. He studies to engross me to himself
And is so wedded to my company
He makes me stranger to my father's house
Although so near a neighbour.
Dalavill. This approves you
To be most nobly propertied, that from one
So exquisite in judgement can attract
So affectionate an eye.
Young Geraldine. Your character
I must bestow on his unmerited love
As one that know I have it, and yet ignorant
Which way I should deserve it. Here both come.

Enter Old Master WINCOTT, [*his*] WIFE [*and*] PRUDENTILLA *her sister.*

Wincott. Gentlemen, welcome. But what need I use
A word so common, unto such to whom
My house was never private? I expect
You should not look for such a needless phrase,
Especially you, Master Geraldine.
Your father is my neighbour, and I know you
Even from the cradle. Then I loved your infancy
And since, your riper growth bettered by travel.
My wife and you in youth were playfellows
And nor now be strangers; as I take it
Not above two years different in your age.
Wife. So much he hath outstripped me.
Wincott. I would have you
Think this your home, free as your father's house,
And to command it as the master on't,
Call boldly here, and entertain your friends

68. will] *Q*; well *conj. Di, Da.* 79.2. *her sister.*] *this ed.*; *the sister, and the* Clowne. *Q.* 89. nor] *Q*; must not *V.*

69. *cancel*] repay.
70. *engross*] monopolise.
74. *nobly propertied*] noble in quality.
76. *character*] description.
79.2 s.d.] *Q*'s '*and the* Clowne' may be a prompter's note. But the entry is not till l. 189.

As in your own possessions. When I see't
I'll say you love me truly, not till then.
O what a happiness your father hath,
Far above me, one to inherit after him
Where I (heaven knows) am childless.
Young Geraldine. That defect
Heaven hath supplied in this your virtuous wife,
Both fair and full of all accomplishments.
My father is a widower, and herein
Your happiness transcends him.
Wife. O, Master Geraldine,
Flattery in men's an adjunct of their sex.
This country breeds it, and for that, so far
You needed not to have travelled.
Young Geraldine. Truth's a word
That should in every language relish well,
Nor have I that exceeded.
Wife. Sir, my husband
Hath took much pleasure in your strange discourse
About Jerusalem and the Holy Land,
How the new city differs from the old,
What ruins of the Temple yet remain
And whether Sion and those hills about
With their adjacent towns and villages
Keep that proportioned distance as we read.
And then in Rome, of that great pyramis
Reared in the front, on four lions mounted,
How many of those idol temples stand,
First dedicated to their heathen gods,
Which ruined, which to better use repaired,
Of their Pantheon and their Capitol
What structures are demolished, what remain.
Wincott. And what more pleasure to an old man's ear,
That never drew save his own country's air,
Than hear such things related? I do exceed him
In years, I must confess, yet he much older

114. their] *Di*; these *Q*; the *V*.

115. *as we read*] (in the Old Testament); Heywood distinguishes here (and in his *Four Prentices of London*) between Solomon's extended New City and David's old Jerusalem on the hill of Zion or Sion.

116. *pyramis*] the Vatican obelisk, moved in 1586 to St Peter's Square. See S. M. Beach, *MLN* 35 (1920), 27–31. A similar obelisk stands at the perspective point in Serlio's *scena tragica* (1545), in contrast with the middle-class houses of his *scena comica*. One of this play's tensions is the meeting of an old-fashioned with a modern morality.

117. *Reared . . . front*] Set up prominently.

120. *better*] (i.e., Christian).

Than I in his experience.
Prudentilla. Master Geraldine,
May I be bold to ask you but one question
The which I'd be resolved in?
Young Geraldine. Anything
That lies within my knowledge.
Wincott. Put him to't,
Do, sister, you shall find him (make no doubt)
Most pregnant in his answer.
Prudentilla. In your travels
Through France, through Savoy and through Italy,
Spain and the Empire, Greece and Palestine,
Which breeds the choicest beauties?
Young Geraldine. In troth, lady,
I never cast on any in those parts
A curious eye of censure, since my travel
Was only aimed at language, and to know.
These passed me but as common objects did,
Seen, but not much regarded.
Prudentilla. O, you strive
To express a most unheard-of modesty
And seldom found in any traveller,
Especially of our country, thereby seeking
To make yourself peculiar.
Young Geraldine. I should be loath—
Profess in outward show to be one man
And prove myself another.
Prudentilla. One thing more:
Were you to marry, you that know these climes,
Their states and their conditions, out of which
Of all these countries would you choose your wife?
Young Geraldine. I'll answer you in brief. As I observe,
Each several clime, for object, fare or use
Affords within itself for all of these
What is most pleasing to the man there born.
Spain, that yields scant of food, affords the nation
A parsimonious stomach, where our appetites
Are not content but with the large excess
Of a full table. Where the pleasingest fruits
Are found most frequent, there they best content.
Where plenty flows, it asks abundant feasts.
For so hath provident Nature dealt with all.

---

127. *experience*] For the ironies in the claims of innocence and experience in this first scene, see Introduction.
132. *pregnant*] full, clear.
134. *Empire*] the German territories of the Holy Roman Empire.
137. *censure*] judgement.
144. *peculiar*] distinguished.
151. *fare or use*] diet or custom.

So in the choice of women. The Greek wantons,
Compelled beneath the Turkish slavery,
Vassal themselves to all men, and such best
Please the voluptuous that delight in change.
The French is of one humour, Spain another,
The hot Italian, he's a strain from both,
All pleased with their own nations. Even the Moor,
He thinks the blackest the most beautiful.
And, lady, since you so far tax my choice,
I'll thus resolve you: being an Englishman
'Mongst all these nations I have seen or tried
To please me best, here would I choose my bride.

Prudentilla. And happy were that lady, in my thoughts,
Whom you would deign that grace to.

Wife. How now, sister?
This is a fashion that's but late come up
For maids to court their husbands.

Wincott. I would, wife,
It were no worse, upon condition
They had my helping hand and purse to boot,
With both in ample measure. O this gentleman
I love, nay almost dote on.

Wife. You've my leave
To give it full expression.

Wincott. In these arms, then. [*Embraces him.*]
O, had my youth been blest with such a son
To have made my estate to my name hereditary,
I should have gone contented to my grave
As to my bed, to death as to my sleep.
But heaven hath will in all things. Once more welcome,
And you, sir, for your friend's sake.

Dalavill. Would I had in me
That which he hath, to have claimed it for mine own.
However, I much thank you.

Enter CLOWN.

Wincott. Now sir, the news with you?

Clown. Dancing news, sir, for the meat stands piping hot upon the dresser, the kitchen's in a heat, and the cook hath so bestirred himself that he's in a sweat, the jack plays music, and the spits turn round to't.

171. he's] *Q*; has *V*.

---

161. *Greek wantons*] Heywood shares the traditional Elizabethan bias, exemplified in Shakespeare's 'merry Greek', Cressida.

163. *vassal*] enslave.

169. *tax*] challenge.

184–5. *grave . . . bed*] proverbial (B192.1).

186. *heaven hath will*] proverbial (cf. H348).

193. *jack*] a triple pun, comparing the mechanism to turn a spit with the figure striking a clock bell and the plectrum of a harpsichord.

Wincott. This fellow's my best clock. He still strikes true
To dinner.

Clown. And to supper, too, sir. I know not how the day goes with you, but my stomach hath struck twelve, I can assure you that.

Wincott. You take us unprovided, gentlemen,
Yet something you shall find, and we would rather
Give you the entertain of household guests
Than compliment of strangers. I pray, enter.

Exeunt. Manet CLOWN.

Clown. I'll stand to't, that in good hospitality there can be nothing found that's ill. He that's a good housekeeper keeps a good table; a good table is never without good stools; good stools seldom without good guests; good guests never without good cheer; good cheer cannot be, without good stomachs; good stomachs, without good digestion. Good digestion keeps men in good health, and therefore, all good people that bear good minds, as you love goodness, be sure to keep good meat and drink in your houses, and so you shall be called good men, and nothing can come on't but good, I warrant you. *Exit.*

ACT I SCENE ii

Enter two serving-men, REIGNALD *and* ROBIN.

Reignald. Away, you Corydon.

Robin. Shall I be beat out of my master's house thus?

Reignald. Thy master? We are lords amongst ourselves
And here we live and reign. Two years already
Are past of our great empire, and we now
Write *anno tertio.*

Robin. But the old man lives
That shortly will depose you.

Reignald. I'the meantime

207. be,] *this ed.*; be Q.

196–7. *dinner . . . supper*] meals eaten before midday and soon after five respectively.

198. *stomach . . . twelve*] proverbial (S872).

202. *compliment*] formal courtesy.

203. *stand to*] affirm.

This scene is a free rendering of the first act of Plautus, *Mostellaria* (see Introduction); the exchange between Reignald and Young Lionel (54–91) and the scene with Rioter and the gallants (205–end) are largely Heywood's invention. He is closest to Plautus in Young Lionel's comparison of young man and house (92–129), a key source of imagery for both plots.

1. *Corydon*] generic name (in Theocritus, Vergil and Spenser) for a rustic; the name of the Clown in Heywood's *Love's Mistress.*

6. anno tertio] (Lat.) in the third year (of our reign).

I, as the mighty lord and seneschal
Of this great house and castle, banish thee
The very smell o'the kitchen. Be it death
To appear before the dresser.

Robin. And why so?

Reignald. Because thou stink'st of garlic. Is that breath
Agreeing with our palace, where each room
Smells with musk, civet and rich ambergris,
Aloes, cassia, aromatic gums,
Perfumes and powders? One whose very garments
Scent of the folds and stables? O, fie, fie,
What a base nasty rogue 'tis!

Robin. Yet your fellow.

Reignald. Then let us put a cart-horse in rich trappings
And bring him to the tilt-yard.

Robin. Prank it, do,
Waste, riot and consume, misspend your hours
In drunken surfeits, lose your days in sleep
And burn the nights in revels, drink and drab,
Keep Christmas all year long, and blot lean Lent
Out of the calendar; all that mass of wealth
Got by my master's sweat and thrifty care
Havoc in prodigal uses, make all fly,
Pour't down your oily throats, or send it smoking
Out at the tops of chimneys. At his departure,
Was it the old man's charge to have his windows
Glister all night with stars, his modest house
Turned to a common stews, his beds to pallets
Of lusts and prostitutions, his buttery hatch
Now made more common than a tavern's bar,
His stools, that welcomed none but civil guests,
Now only free for pandars, whores and bawds,
Strumpets and such?

Reignald. I suffer thee too long.
What is to me thy country, or to thee
The pleasure of our city? Thou hast cows,

17. folds] *Q* (fowlds); fowls *V*.

---

8. *seneschal*] steward; Reignald's language is comically inflated throughout this dialogue.

14. *musk, civet, ambergris*] perfumes derived from animals.

15. *Aloes, cassia . . . gums*] perfumes from trees and plants.

20. *Prank*] dance, caper.

23. *drab*] visit whores; the phrase 'drink and drab' is repeated at IV.vi.88, and may be a catchphrase.

24. *Keep . . . year*] proverbial (C372).

27. *Havoc*] waste (verb). *uses*] consumption of food and drink.

28. *oily*] unctuous, flattering.

32. *stews*] brothel. *pallets*] straw mattresses.

33. *buttery hatch*] serving hatch.

Cattle and beeves to feed, *oves* and *boves*.
These that I keep and in this pasture graze
Are dainty damosellas, bonny girls.
If thou be'st born to hedge, ditch, thresh and plough
And I to revel, banquet and carouse,
Thou, peasant, to the spade and pickaxe, I
The baton and stiletto, think it only
Thy ill, my good. Our several lots are cast
And both must be contented.

Robin. But when both
Our services are questioned—

Reignald. Look thou to one.
My answer is provided.

Enter YOUNG LIONEL.

Robin. Farewell, musk-cat. *Exit.*

Reignald. Adieu, good cheese and onions. Stuff thy guts
With speck and barley-pudding for disgestion,
Drink whig and sour milk, whilst I rinse my throat
With Bordeaux and canary.

Young Lionel. What was he?

Reignald. A spy, sir.
One of their hinds o'the country, that came prying
To see what dainty fare our kitchen yields,
What guests we harbour and what rule we keep,
And threats to tell the old man when he comes.
I think I sent him packing.

Young Lionel. It was well done.

Reignald. A whoreson jackanapes, a base baboon,
To insinuate in our secrets.

Young Lionel. Let such keep
The country, where their charge is.

Reignald. So I said, sir.

Young Lionel. And visit us when we command them thence,
Not search into our counsels.

Reignald. 'Twere not fit.

Young Lionel. Who in my father's absence should command
Save I, his only son?

Reignald. It is but justice.

---

40. oves . . . boves] sheep, oxen.
42. *damosellas*] maidens.
46. *baton and stiletto*] cudgel and dagger.
49. *Look . . . one*] proverbial, 'every man for himself' (o50, M112).
50. *musk-cat*] scented fop.
52. *speck and barley-pudding*] fat meat and gruel.
53. *whig*] whey or buttermilk.
54. *canary*] a wine from the Canary Islands.
60. *jackanapes*] ape, fool.

Young Lionel. For am not I now Lord?
Reignald. *Dominus factotum.*
And am not I your steward?
Young Lionel. Well remembered.
This night I have a purpose to be merry,
Jovial and frolic. How doth our cash hold out?
Reignald. The bag's still heavy.
Young Lionel. Then my heart's still light.
Reignald. I can assure you, yet 'tis pretty deep,
Though scarce a mile to the bottom.
Young Lionel. Let me have
To supper, let me see, a duck—
Reignald. Sweet rogue!
Young Lionel. A capon—
Reignald. Geld the rascal!
Young Lionel. Then a turkey—
Reignald. Now spit him for an infidel!
Young Lionel. Green plover, snipe,
Partridge, lark, cock and pheasant.
Reignald. Ne'er a widgeon?
Young Lionel. Yes, wait thyself at table.
Reignald. Where I hope
Yourself will not be absent.
Young Lionel. Nor my friends.
Reignald. We'll have them then in plenty.
Young Lionel. Caviar,
Sturgeon, anchovies, pickle-oysters. Yes,
And a potato pie. Besides all these
What thou think'st rare and costly.
Reignald. Sir, I know
What's to be done, the stock that must be spent
Is in my hands, and what I have to do
I will do suddenly.
Young Lionel. No butcher's meat;
Of that beware, in any case.
Reignald. I still remember
Your father was no grazier. If he were,
This were a way to eat up all his fields,

76. snipe,] *Di*; Snite, *Q*.

---

67. Dominus factotum] (Lat.) Lord Do-all.
71. *bag's . . . light*] proverbial (P655).
74. *duck*] term of endearment.
75. *capon*] castrated cockerel; so, a fool. *turkey*] (with pun on 'Turk')
76. *plover*] In *Bartholomew Fair* (ed. Horsman, 1960) IV.v.16, a 'bird of the game', and so a prostitute.
77. *widgeon*] a species of wild duck, a simpleton.
87. *of that beware*] The joke is obscure; in *The Knight of the Burning Pestle* V.v, the 'butchers' hooks at Whitechapel' seem to carry the same associations as 'fleshmonger'; Partridge records sexual connotations for women under 'beef', 'flesh', 'meat' and 'mutton'.

Hedges and all.
Young Lionel. You will be gone, sir?
Reignald. Yes,
And you are i'the way going. *Exit.*
Young Lionel. To what may young men best compare themselves?
Better to what, than to a house new built,
The fabric strong, the chambers well contrived,
Polished within, without well beautified,
When all that gaze upon the edifice
Do not alone commend the workman's craft
But either make it their fair precedent
By which to build another, or at least
Wish there to inhabit? Being set to sale,
In comes a slothful tenant, with a family
As lazy and deboshed. Rough tempests rise,
Untile the roof, which by their idleness
Left unrepaired the stormy showers beat in,
Rot the main posts and rafters, spoil the rooms,
Deface the ceilings, and in little space
Bring it to utter ruin; yet the fault
Not in the architector that first rearèd it
But him that should repair it. So it fares
With us young men: we are those houses made,
Our parents raise these structures, the foundation
Laid in our infancy; and as we grow
In years, they strive to build us by degrees
Storey on storey higher. Up at height
They cover us with counsel, to defend us
From storms without; they polish us within
With learnings, knowledge, arts and disciplines;
All that is naught and vicious they sweep from us
Like dust and cobwebs, and our rooms concealed
Hang with the costliest hangings, 'bout the walls
Emblems and beauteous symbols pictured round.
But when that lazy tenant, love, steps in
And in his train brings sloth and negligence,
Lust, disobedience and profuse excess,
The thrift with which our fathers tiled our roofs
Submits to every storm and winter's blast,
And, yielding place to every riotous sin,
Gives way without, to ruin what's within.
Such is the state I stand in.

90. *hedges and all*] A comment on the enclosure of arable land for grazing, which had driven labourers like Robin to the towns in search of work.

91. *i' the way going*] (i.e., downhill): a direct translation of Plautus. Cf. Reignald's 'now I am gone', III.ii.64. 'Going the wrong way' (to the gallows) was proverbial (W168).

114. *up at height*] i.e., at full growth.

118. *naught*] wicked.

Enter BLANDA, *a whore and* SCAPHA, *a bawd.*

[YOUNG LIONEL *steps aside.*]

Blanda. And how doth this tire become me?

Scapha. Rather ask, how your sweet carriage and court behaviour doth best grace you. For lovers regard not so much the outward habit as that which the garment covers.

Young Lionel. [*Aside*] O here's that hail, shower, tempest, storm and gust
That shattered hath this building, let in lust,
Intemperance, appetite to vice; withal,
Neglect of every goodness. Thus I see
How I am sinking in mine own disease
Yet can I not abide it.

Blanda. And how this gown? I prithee, view me well
And speak with thy best judgement.

Scapha. What do you talk of gowns and ornaments
That have a beauty precious in itself
And becomes anything?

Young Lionel. [*Aside*] Let me not live, but she speaks naught but truth,
And I'll for that reward her.

Blanda. All's one to me, become they me or not,
Or be I fair or foul in others' eyes,
So I appear so to my Lionel.
He is the glass in whom I judge my face,
By whom in order I will dress these curls
And place these jewels, only to please him.
Why dost smile?

Scapha. To hear a woman that thinks herself so wise speak so foolishly; that knows well, and does ill.

Blanda. Teach me wherein I err.

Scapha. I'll tell thee, daughter: in that thou knowest thyself to be beloved of so many, and settlest thy affection only upon one. Doth the mill grind only when the wind sits in one corner, or ships only sail when it's in this or that quarter? Is he a cunning fencer that lies but at one guard, or he a skilful musician that plays but on one string? Is there but one way to the wood, and but one bucket that belongs to the well? To affect one and despise all other becomes the precise matron, not the prostitute; the loyal wife, not the loose wanton. Such have I been, as you are now and should learn to sail with all winds, defend all blows, make music

---

130. *tire*] dress, or head-gear.

139. *abide*] redeem, expiate; by confusion with 'abye' (*OED*).

158–63] Scapha's string of proverbs (Tilley nos M942, F187, S936 and W179) all advise against specialisation.

162. *bucket*] ?proverbial (cf. W264, 'Many wells, many buckets').

with all strings, know all the ways to the wood, and, like a good travelling hackney, learn to drink of all waters.

Young Lionel. [*Aside*] May I miscarry in my Blanda's love
If I that old damnation do not send
To hell before her time.

Blanda. I would not have you, mother, teach me aught
That tends to injure him.

Scapha. Well, look to't when 'tis too late, and then repent at leisure, as I have done. Thou seest here's nothing but prodigality and pride, wantoning and wasting, rioting and revelling, spoiling and spending, gluttony and gormandising. All goes to havoc. And can this hold out? When he hath nothing left to help himself, how can he harbour thee? Look at length to drink from a dry bottle and feed from an empty knapsack. Look to't, 'twill come to that.

Young Lionel. [*Aside*] My parsimony shall begin in thee
And instantly; for from this hour, I vow
That thou no more shalt drink upon my cost
Nor taste the smallest fragment from my board.
I'll see thee starve i'the street first.

Scapha. Live to one man? A jest! Thou may'st as well tie thyself to one gown; and what fool but will change with the fashion? Yes, do, confine thyself to one garment and use no variety, and see how soon it will rot and turn to rags.

Young Lionel. [*To Scapha*] Those rags be thy reward! [*To Blanda*] O,
my sweet Blanda,
Only for thee I wish my father dead
And ne'er to rouse us from our sweet delight.
But for this hag, this beldam, she whose back
Hath made her items in my mercers' books,
Whose ravenous guts I have stuffed with delicates,
Nay, even to surfeit, and whose frozen blood
I have warmed with aqua-vitae: be this day
My last of bounty to a wretch ingrate,
But unto thee a new indenture sealed
Of an affection fixed and permanent.
I'll love thee still, be't but to give the lie
To this old cankered worm.

Blanda. Nay, be not angry.

Young Lionel. With thee my soul shall ever be at peace,
But with this love-seducer, still at war.

Enter RIOTER *and two gallants.*

194. mercers'] *this ed.* (Mercers Q); mercer's *Di*, *V.*

---

167. *hackney*] hired horse, hack; a prostitute.
drink . . . waters] proverbial (W131.11).
193. *beldam*] witch.
194. *items . . . books*] debts with silk merchants.
197. *aqua-vitae*] distilled liquor.
198. *ingrate*] ungrateful.

Scapha. Hear me but speak.
Young Lionel. Ope but thy lips again, it makes a way
To have thy tongue plucked out.
Rioter. What, all in tempest?
Young Lionel. Yes, and the storm raised by that witch's spells.
O, 'tis a damned enchantress!
Rioter. What's the business?
Blanda. Only some few words, slipped her unawares.
For my sake, make her peace.
Rioter. You charge me deeply.
Come, friend, will you be moved at women's words,
A man of your known judgement?
Young Lionel. Had you but heard
The damned erroneous doctrine that she taught,
You would have judged her to the stake.
Blanda. But sweet heart,
She now recants those errors. Once more number her
Amongst your household servants.
Rioter. Shall she beg,
And be denied aught from you?
Blanda. Come, this kiss
Shall end all former quarrels.
Rioter. 'Tis not possible
Those lips should move in vain, that two ways plead,
Both in their speech and silence.
Young Lionel. You have prevailed,
But upon this condition, no way else:
I'll censure her as she hath sentenced thee,
But with some small inversion.
Rioter. Speak, how's that?
Blanda. Not too severe, I prithee. See, poor wretch,
She at the bar stands quaking.
Young Lionel. Now, hold up—
Rioter. How, man, how?
Young Lionel. Her hand, I mean. And now I'll sentence thee
According to thy counsel given to her:
Sail by one wind, thou shalt; to one tune sing;
Lie at one guard; and play but on one string.
Henceforth I shall confine thee to one garment
And that shall be a cast one, like thyself
Just: past all wearing, as thou, past all use,
And not to be renewed till 't be as ragged

234. Just: past] *this ed.* (Iust, past *Q*); Just past *Di*, *V*.

---

215. *to the stake*] (as a witch).
224. *inversion*] turning of Scapha's arguments against herself.
228. *hand*] Rioter had vulgarly assumed 'skirts'.
233. *cast*] discarded.

As thou art rotten.
Blanda. Nay, sweet!
Young Lionel. That for her habit.
Scapha. A cold suit I have on't.
Young Lionel. To prevent surfeit,
Thy diet shall be to one dish confined
And that, too, rifled with as unclean hands
As e'er were laid on thee.
Scapha. What he scants me
In victuals, would he but allow me in drink.
Young Lionel. That shall be the refuse of the flagons: jacks
And snuffs, such as the nastiest breaths shall leave.
Of wine and of strong-water, never hope
Henceforth to smell.
Scapha. O me, I faint already!
Young Lionel. If I sink in my state, of all the rest
Be thou excused. What thou proposed to her,
Beldam, is now against thyself decreed:
Drink from dry springs, from empty knapsacks feed.
Scapha. No burnt wine, nor hot-waters! *She swoons.*
Young Lionel. Take her hence.
Blanda. Indeed, you are too cruel.
Young Lionel. Yes, to her,
Only of purpose to be kind to thee.
Are any of my guests come?
Rioter. Fear not, sir,
You will have a full table.
Young Lionel. What, and music?
Rioter. Best consort in the city for six parts.
Young Lionel. We shall have songs, then?
Rioter. By th'ear.
Young Lionel. (*Whispers*) And wenches?
Rioter. Yes, by th'eye.
Blanda. Ha, what was that you said?
Rioter. We shall have such to bear you company
As will no doubt content you.
Young Lionel. Enter then.
In youth there is a fate that sways us still
To know what's good, and yet pursue what's ill.
Exeunt omnes.

244. and of strong-water,] *Di*; and Strong-water *Q*. 256. s.d.] *Di*; *one line earlier*, *Q*. 259. Enter then.] *Q*; Euer then: *S*; Ever thine: *V*.

236. *rotten*] diseased.
239. *rifled*] plundered, picked over.
242. *jacks*] tiny amounts (*OED*, 17).
243. *snuffs*] dregs.
250. *burnt . . . hot-waters*] mulled wine and distilled spirits.
255. *consort*] group of musicians.
257. *by th' eye*] without limit; proverbial (E249).
260–1. *a fate . . . ill*] proverbial (B325).

ACT II

SCENE i

Enter Old Master WINCOTT *and his* WIFE.

Wincott. And what's this Dalavill?
Wife. My apprehension
Can give him no more true expression
Than that he first appears a gentleman
And well conditioned.
Wincott. That for outward show.
But what in him have you observèd else
To make him better known?
Wife. I have not eyes
To search into the inward thoughts of men
Nor ever was I studied in that art
To judge of men's affection by the face.
But that which makes me best opinioned of him
Is that he's companion and the friend
Beloved of him whom you so much commend,
The noble Master Geraldine.
Wincott. Thou hast spoke
That which not only crowns his true desert
But now instates him in my better thoughts,
Making his worth unquestioned.
Wife. He pretends
Love to my sister Pru. I have observed him
Single her out to private conference.
Wincott. But I could rather for her own sake wish
Young Geraldine would fix his thoughts that way
And she towards him. In such affinity,
Trust me, I would not use a sparing hand.
Wife. But love in these kinds should not be compelled,
Forced nor persuaded. When it freely springs
And of itself takes voluntary root
It grows, it spreads, it ripens and brings forth

8. was I studied] *Di*; was studied *Q*.

This scene, with its typically abrupt opening, begins with Wincott's mistaken assessment of Dalavill and the Clown's misleading 'massacre of meat' narrative, and Geraldine's account of the self-deceiving 'shipwreck by land'. It ends in the troth-plighting *de futuro* between Geraldine and Mistress Wincott, a relationship whose promise is coloured for the audience by the scene's earlier misconceptions.

8–9. *art . . . face*] Cf. *Mac.* I.iv.11–12: 'There's no art / To find the mind's construction in the face', also spoken in advance of a deception.

Such an usurious crop of timely fruit
As crowns a plenteous autumn.

Wincott. Such a harvest
I should not be th' ungladdest man to see,
Of all thy sister's friends.

Enter CLOWN.

Now, whence come you?

Clown. Who, I, sir? From a lodging of largesse, a house of hospitality, and a palace of plenty; where there's feeding like horses, and drinking like fishes; where for pints we're served in pottles, and instead of pottle-pots, in pails; instead of silver tankards we drink out of water tankards; claret runs as freely as the cocks, and canary, like the conduits of a coronation day. Where there's nothing but feeding and frolicking, carving and kissing, drinking and dancing, music and madding, fiddling and feasting.

Wincott. And where, I pray thee, are all these revels kept?

Clown. They may be rather called reaks than revels. As I came along by the door, I was called up amongst them, he-gallants and she-gallants. I no sooner looked out, but saw them out with their knives, slashing of shoulders, mangling of legs and launching of loins, till there was scarce a whole limb left amongst them.

Wincott. A fearful massacre!

Clown. One was hacking to cut off a neck. This was mangling a breast, his knife slipped from the shoulder, and only cut off a wing. One was picking the brains out of a head, another was knuckle-deep in a belly. One was groping for a liver, another searching for the kidneys. I saw one pluck the soul from the body—goose that she was to suffer't—another pricked into the breast with his own bill—woodcock to endure it.

Wife. How fell they out at first?

Clown. I know not that, but it seems one had a stomach and another

37. and kissing,] *Di*; in kissing *Q*. 47. slipped] *Di*; slip *Q*. cut off] *Di*; cut of *Q*. 52. own] *Di*; one *Q*.

---

27. *usurious*] abundant (*OED* 3, earliest ref. 1780).
33. *pottles*] half-gallon jugs.
34–5. *silver . . . tankards*] In place of (large) mugs, the guests drink from great vats of wood or leather.
35. *cocks*] water-pipes.
36. *conduits . . . day*] On special occasions, public drinking fountains ran with wine.
38. *madding*] unruly behaviour.
40. *reaks*] wanton or riotous pranks.
43. *launching*] wounding, lancing.
50. *soul*] soft flesh of a goose about the lungs.
50–1. *goose . . . woodcock*] simpletons; cf. I.ii.75–8. 'Goose' is also slang for a prostitute.
51–2. *pricked . . . bill*] Woodcocks were skewered with their own bills for roasting.
54–5. *stomach . . . stomach*] The Clown plays misleadingly on two senses, 'appetite' and 'anger'.

had a stomach. But there was such biting and tearing with their teeths that I am sure I saw some of their poor carcasses pay for't.

Wincott. Did they not send for surgeons?

Clown. Alas, no; surgeons' help was too late. There was no stitching up of those wounds where limb was plucked from limb, nor any salve for those scars which all the plaster of Paris cannot cure.

Wincott. Where grew the quarrel first?

Clown. It seems it was first broached in the kitchen, certain creatures being brought in thither by some of the house. The cook, being a choleric fellow, did so touse them and toss them, so pluck them and pull them, till he left them as naked as my nail, pinioned some of them like felons, cut the spurs from others off their heels. Then down went his spits; some of them he ran in at the throat and out at the backside. About went his basting-ladle, where he did so besauce them that many a shrewd turn they had amongst them.

Wife. But in all this, how did the women scape?

Clown. They fared best, and did the least hurt that I saw, but for quietness' sake were forced to swallow what is not yet digested. Yet everyone had their share, and she that had least, I am sure by this time hath her belly full.

Wincott. And where was all this havoc kept?

Clown. Marry, sir, at your next neighbour's, young Master Lionel. Where there is nothing but drinking out of dry-fats and healthing in half-tubs. His guests are fed by the belly, and beggars served at his gate in baskets. He's the adamant of this age, the daffodil of these days, the prince of prodigality and the very Caesar of all young citizens.

Wincott. Belike then 'twas a massacre of meat,
Not as I apprehended?

Clown. Your gravity hath guessed aright. The chiefest that fell in this battle were wild fowl and tame fowl; pheasants were wounded instead of alferes, and capons for captains; anchovies stood for ancients, and caviar for corporals; dishes were assaulted instead of ditches, and rabbits were cut to pieces upon the ravelins; some lost their legs, whilst other of their wings were forced to fly; the pioneer undermined nothing but pie-crust, and—

Wincott. Enough, enough; your wit hath played too long

67. off their] *Di*; of their *Q*. 88. ravelins;] *Di* (*footnote*); rebellings, *Q*.

---

62. *broached*] another pun, on 'begun' and 'pierced with a spit'.
64. *touse*] tear, handle roughly.
65. *naked . . . nail*] proverbial (N4).
69. *shrewd turn*] misfortune; proverbial (T617).
74. *belly full*] (with a sexual double entendre)
77. *dry-fats*] large barrels.
79. *adamant*] centre of attention, magnet.

daffodil] For his alliteration on 'd', the Clown picks out an image of brightness and youth, perhaps with a reference to the self-absorbed Narcissus.

86–7. *alferes . . . ancients*] standard-bearers or ensigns.
88. *ravelins*] fortifications.

Upon our patience. Wife, it grieves me much
Both for the young and old man; the one greys
His head with care, endures the parching heat
And biting cold, the terrors of the lands
And fears at sea in travel, only to gain
Some competent estate to leave his son.
Whiles all that merchandise through gulfs, cross-tides,
Pirates and storms he brings so far, the other
Here shipwracks in the harbour.

Wife. 'Tis the care
Of fathers, and the weakness incident
To youth that wants experience.

Enter YOUNG GERALDINE, DALAVILL [*and*] PRUDENTILLA, *laughing*.

Clown. I was at the beginning of the battle, but here comes some that it seems were at the rifling of the dead carcasses, for by their mirth they have had part of the spoil.

Wincott. You are pleasant, gentlemen. What, I entreat,
Might be the subject of your pleasant sport?
It promiseth some pleasure.

Prudentilla. If their recreation
Be, as I make no question, on truth grounded,
'Twill beget sudden laughter.

Wife. What's the project?

Dalavill. Who shall relate it?

Wincott. Master Geraldine,
If there be anything can please my ear
With pleasant sounds, your tongue must be the instrument
On which the string must strike.

Dalavill. Be't his, then.

Prudentilla. Nay, hear it, 'tis a good one.

Wife. We entreat you,
Possess us o'the novel.

Wincott. Speak, good sir.

Young Geraldine. I shall with a kind of babarism
Shadow a jest that asks a smoother tongue,
For in my poor discourse, I do protest,
It will but lose his lustre.

Wife. You are modest.

Wincott. However, speak, I pray; for my sake do't.

Clown. [*Aside*] This is like a hasty pudding, longer in eating than it was in making.

93. greys] *this ed.*; graces Q. 120. It will] *V*; 'twill Q.

---

93. *greys*] The emendation is supported by IV.iii.153. (Q's 'Graces', which I take to be a misreading of MS 'Graies', would, if correct, suggest a halo of white hair.)

108. *recreation*] recounting.

116. *novel*] news, story. For the source of the comic shipwreck, see Introduction; Baskerville (*The Elizabethan Jig* (Chicago, 1929), pp. 300 ff.) proposes that a similar stage shipwreck was a popular jig, based on the familiar emblem of the Ship of Fools.

122. *hasty pudding*] a kind of porridge.

Young Geraldine. Then thus it was: this gentleman and I
Passed but just now by your next neighbour's house,
Where, as they say, dwells one young Lionel.
Clown. Where I was tonight at supper.
Wincott. An unthrift youth, his father now at sea.
Young Geraldine. Why, that's the very subject upon which
It seems this jest is grounded. There this night
Was a great feast.
Clown. Why, so I told you, sir.
Wincott. Be thou still dumb. 'Tis he that I would hear.
Young Geraldine. In the height of their carousing, all their brains
Warmed with the heat of wine, discourse was offered
Of ships, and storms at sea; when suddenly
Out of his giddy wildness one conceives
The room wherein they quaffed to be a pinnace
Moving and floating, and the confused noise
To be the murmuring winds, gusts, mariners;
That their unsteadfast footing did proceed
From rocking of the vessel. This conceived,
Each one begins to apprehend the danger
And to look out for safety. 'Fly', saith one,
'Up to the main-top, and discover.' He
Climbs by the bed-post to the tester, there
Reports a turbulent sea and tempest towards,
And wills them, if they'll save their ship and lives,
To cast their lading overboard. At this
All fall to work, and hoist into the street,
As to the sea, what next come to their hand:
Stools, tables, trestles, trenchers, bedsteads, cups,
Pots, plate and glasses. Here a fellow whistles;
They take him for the boatswain. One lies struggling
Upon the floor, as if he swum for life.
A third takes the bass viol for the cock-boat,
Sits in the belly on't, labours and rows,
His oar the stick with which the fiddler played.
A fourth bestrides his fellows, thinking to scape
As did Arion on the dolphin's back,
Still fumbling on a gittern.
Clown. Excellent sport.
Wincott. But what was the conclusion?
Young Geraldine. The rude multitude,
Watching without, and gaping for the spoil
Cast from the windows, went by th'ears about it.

158. fellows,] Q; fellow, *conj. La.*

145. *tester*] canopy.
155. *cock-boat*] small dinghy, towed behind a larger vessel.
159. *Arion*] Greek musician saved from drowning by dolphins drawn to his lyre-playing.
160. *gittern*] instrument resembling a guitar.
162–3. *spoil . . . windows*] proverbial for a scene of merrymaking (H785).

The constable is called to atone the broil,
Which done, and hearing such a noise within.
Of imminent shipwrack, enters the house and finds them
In this confusion: they adore his staff
And think it Neptune's trident, and that he
Comes with his Tritons (so they called his watch)
To calm the tempest and appease the waves;
And at this point we left them.

Clown. Come what will, I'll steal out of doors and see the end of it, that's certain. *Exit.*

Wincott. Thanks, Master Geraldine, for this discourse.
In troth, it hath much pleased me, but the night
Begins to grow fast on us. For your parts
You are all young, and you may sit up late.
My eyes begin to summon me to sleep,
And nothing's more offensive unto age
Than to watch long and late.

Young Geraldine. Now good rest with you.

[*Exit* WINCOTT.]

Dalavill. What says fair Prudentilla? Maids and widows
And we young bachelors, such as indeed
Are forced to lie in solitary beds
And sleep without disturbance, we methinks
Should desire later hours, when married wives,
That in their amorous arms hug their delights,
To often wakings subject, their more haste
May better be excused.

Prudentilla. How can you,
That are, as you confess, a single man,
Enter so far into these mystical secrets
Of marriage, which as yet you never proved?

Dalavill. There's lady, an instinct innate in man
Which prompts us to the apprehensions
Of th'uses we were born to, such we are
Aptest to learn, ambitious most to know,
Of which our chief is marriage.

Prudentilla. What you men
Most meditate, we women seldom dream of.

Dalavill. When dream maids most?

Prudentilla. When think you?

Dalavill. When you lie upon your backs.
Come, come, your ear.

Exeunt DALAVILL *and* PRUDENTILLA.

Young Geraldine. We now are left alone.

Wife. Why, say we be; who should be jealous of us?

185. when] *Q*; than *V*.

169. *Tritons*] half-human, half-fish children of Neptune.
191. *proved*] experienced.

This is not first of many hundred nights
That we two have been private; from the first
Of our acquaintance, when our tongues but clipped
Our mother's-tongue and could not speak it plain,
We knew each other. As in stature, so
Increased our sweet society. Since your travel
And my late marriage, through my husband's love
Midnight hath been as mid-day, and my bedchamber
As free to you as your own father's house,
And you as welcome to't.

Young Geraldine. I must confess
It is in you your noble courtesy,
In him a more than common confidence,
And in this age can scarce find precedent.

Wife. Most true; it is withal an argument
That both our virtues are so deep impressed
In his good thoughts, he knows we cannot err.

Young Geraldine. A villain were he to deceive such trust,
Or (were there one) a much worse character.

Wife. And she no less, whom either beauty, youth,
Time, place or opportunity could tempt
To injure such a husband.

Young Geraldine. You deserve,
Even for his sake, to be for ever young,
And he for yours, to have his youth renewed,
So mutual is your true conjugal love.
Yet had the Fates so pleased—

Wife. I know your meaning.
It was once voiced that we two should have matched.
The world so thought, and many tongues so spake.
But heaven hath now disposed us otherways,
And being as it is (a thing in me
Which, I protest, was never wished nor sought)
Now done, I not repent it.

Young Geraldine. In those times,
Of all the treasures of my hopes and love
You were th'exchequer, they were stored in you,
And had not my unfortunate travel crossed them,
They had been here reserved still.

Wife. Troth, they had;
I should have been your trusty treasurer.

Young Geraldine. However, let us love still, I entreat.
That, neighbourhood and breeding will allow.
So much the laws divine and human both
'Twixt brother and a sister will approve;
Heaven then forbid that they should limit us

---

204. *clipped*] abbreviated, cut short.

235. *unfortunate*] (in separating the two speakers); the adjective may have been suggested by the title of Nashe's famous narrative.

Wish well to one another.
Wife. If they should not,
We might proclaim they were not charitable,
Which were a deadly sin but to conceive.
Young Geraldine. Will you resolve me one thing?
Wife. As to one
That in my bosom hath a second place
Next my dear husband.
Young Geraldine. That's the thing I crave,
And only that: to have a place next him.
Wife. Presume on that already. But perhaps
You mean to stretch it further?
Young Geraldine. Only thus far:
Your husband's old, to whom my soul doth wish
A Nestor's age, so much he merits from me.
Yet if (as proof and Nature daily teach
Men cannot always live, especially
Such as are old and crazed) he be called hence,
Fairly, in full maturity of time,
And we two be reserved to after life,
Will you confer your widowhood on me?
Wife. You ask the thing I was about to beg.
Your tongue hath spake mine own thoughts.
Young Geraldine. Vow to that.
Wife. As I hope mercy.
Young Geraldine. 'Tis enough; that word
Alone instates me happy. Now, so please you,
We will divide, you to your private chamber,
I to find out my friend.
Wife. Nay, Master Geraldine.
One ceremony rests yet unperformed.
My vow is past, your oath must next proceed,
And as you covet to be sure of me
Of you I would be certain.
Young Geraldine. Make ye doubt?
Wife. No doubt. But Love's still jealous, and in that
To be excused. You, then, shall swear by Heaven,
And as in all your future acts you hope
To thrive and prosper, as the day may yield
Comfort, or the night rest, as you would keep
Entire the honour of your father's house
And free your name from scandal and reproach,
By all the goodness that you hope to enjoy
Or ill to shun—
Young Geraldine. You charge me deeply, lady.
Wife. Till that day come, you shall reserve yourself

253. *Nestor*] Greek hero noted for longevity.
256. *crazed*] infirm.
263. *instates*] establishes.

A single man, converse nor company
With any woman, contract nor combine
With maid or widow. Which expected hour,
As I do wish not haste, so when it happens
It shall not come unwelcome. You hear all;
Vow this.
Young Geraldine. By all that you have said, I swear,
And by this kiss confirm.
Wife. You're now my brother,
But then, my second husband. *Exeunt.*

[ACT II SCENE ii]

Enter YOUNG LIONEL, RIOTER, BLANDA, SCAPHA, *two* Gallants *and two* Wenches, *as newly waked from sleep.*

Young Lionel. We had a stormy night on't.
Blanda. The wine still works,
And with the little rest they have took tonight
They are scarce come to themselves.
Young Lionel. Now 'tis a calm,
Thanks to those gentle sea-gods that have brought us
To this safe harbour. Can you tell their names?
Scapha. He with the painted staff I heard you call
Neptune.
Young Lionel. The dreadful god of seas,
Upon whose back ne'er stuck March fleas.
First Gallant. One with the bill keeps Neptune's porpoises,
So Ovid says in's *Metamorphoses*.
Second Gallant. A third the learned poets write on,
And as they say, his name is Triton.
Young Lionel. These are the marine gods to whom my father
In his long voyage prays, too. Cannot they,
That brought us to our haven, bury him
In their abyss? For if he safe arrive,
I, with these sailors, sirens and what not,
Am sure here to be shipwracked.
First Wench. [*To Rioter*] Stand up stiff.
Rioter. But that the ship so totters; I shall fall.
First Wench. If thou fall, I'll fall with thee.
Rioter. Now I sink,

---

280. *company*] keep company.

283. *not haste*] not to hurry.

With the entrance of Reignald (l. 22), Heywood returns to the dramatisation of *Mostellaria*, Act II of which (ll. 348–531) forms this scene.

8. *March fleas*] Because more active in Spring, or from the proverbial (R18) association with rain?

10. Metamorphoses] Ovid's mythological epic, a source for Heywood's *Ages* plays.

12. *Triton*] sea god, half man half fish.

And, as I dive and drown, thus by degrees
I'll pluck thee to the bottom. *They fall.*

Enter REIGNALD

Young Lionel. Amain for England! See, see,
The Spaniard now strikes sail.
Reignald. So must you all.
First Gallant. Whence is your ship? From the Bermoothes?
Reignald. Worse, I think: from Hell.
We are all lost, split, shipwracked and undone;
This place is a mere quicksands.
Second Gallant. So we feared.
Reignald. Where's my young master?
Young Lionel. Here man. Speak. The news?
Reignald. The news is, I, and you—
Young Lionel. What?
Reignald. She, and all these—
Blanda. I?
Reignald. We, and all ours, are in one turbulent sea
Of fear, despair, disaster and mischance
Swallowed. Your father, sir—
Young Lionel. Why, what of him?
Reignald. He is —
O, I want breath—
Young Lionel. Where?
Reignald. Landed, and at hand.
Young Lionel. Upon what coast? Who saw him?
Reignald. I, these eyes.
Young Lionel. O Heaven, what shall I do, then?
Reignald. Ask ye me
What shall become of you that have not yet
Had time of study to dispose myself?
I say again, I was upon the quay,
I saw him land and this way bend his course.
What drunkard's this, that can outsleep a storm
Which threatens all our ruins? Wake him.
Blanda. Ho, Rioter, awake!
Rioter. Yes, I am wake.
How dry hath this salt water made me. Boy,
Give me th'other glass.
Young Lionel. Arise, I say.
My father's come from sea.
Rioter. If he be come,
Bid him be gone again.
Reignald. Can you trifle

18–22. *Stand . . . bottom*] (with bawdy innuendo).
25. *Bermoothes*] Bermuda; 'The Bermudas', at the west end of the Strand, were a haunt of prostitutes.

At such a time, when your inventions, brains,
Wits, plots, devices, stratagems and all
Should be at one in action? Each of you
That love your safeties, lend your helping hands,
Women and all, to take this drunkard hence
And to bestow him elsewhere.
Blanda. Lift, for heaven's sake! *They carry him in.*
Reignald. But what am I the nearer? Were all these
Conveyed to sundry places, and unseen,
The stain of our disorders still remain,
Of which the house will witness, and the old man
Must find when he enters; and for these
I am left here to answer.

Enter again [YOUNG LIONEL *and the others*].

What, is he gone?
Young Lionel. But whither? But into the self-same house
That harbours him, my father's, where we all
Attend from him surprisal.
Reignald. I will make
That prison of your fears your sanctuary.
Go, get you in together.
Young Lionel. To this house?
Reignald. Your father's, with your sweetheart, these and all.
Nay, no more words, but do't.
Blanda. That were
To betray us to his fury.
Reignald. I have't here
To bail you hence at pleasure. And in th'interim
I'll make this supposed gaol to you as safe
From th'injured old man's just incensèd spleen
As were you now together i'the Low Countries,
Virginia, or i'th'Indies.
Blanda. Present fear
Bids us to yield unto the faint belief
Of the least hopèd safety.
Reignald. Will you in?
All. By thee we will be counselled.
[*All except* YOUNG LIONEL *and* REIGNALD *go in.*]
Reignald. Shut them fast.
Young Lionel. And thou and I to leave them?
Reignald. No such thing,
For you shall bear your sweetheart company,
And help to cheer the rest.
Young Lionel. And so thou

62. find] *Q*; find them *Di*; find it *V*.

60. *Stain . . . remain*] The verb is made plural by association with 'disorders'.

Meanest to escape alone?
Reignald. Rather, without
I'll stand a champion for you all within.
Will you be swayed? One thing in any case
I must advise: the gates bolted and locked,
See that 'mongst you no living voice be heard,
No, not so much as a dog to howl
Or cat to mew. All silence, that I charge,
As if this were a mere forsaken house
And none did there inhabit.
Young Lionel. Nothing else?
Reignald. And though the old man thunder at the gates
As if he meant to ruin what he had reared,
None, on their lives, to answer.
Young Lionel. 'Tis my charge.
Remains there nothing else?
Reignald. Only the key,
For I must play the gaoler for your durance,
To be the Mercury in your release.
Young Lionel. Me and my hope I in this key deliver
To thy safe trust. [*Gives him the key.*]
Reignald. When you are fast, you are safe.
[YOUNG LIONEL *goes in.*]
And with this turn 'tis done. [*Locks door.*] What fools are these,
To trust their ruined fortunes to his hands
That hath betrayed his own, and make themselves
Prisoner to one deserves to lie for all,
As being cause of all! And yet something prompts me,
I'll stand it at all dangers, and to recompense
The many wrongs unto the young man done,
Now if I can doubly delude the old—
My brain, about it, then. All's hushed within;
The noise that shall be, I must make without,
And he, that part for gain and part for wit
So far hath travelled, strive to fool at home.
Which to effect, art must with knavery join
And smooth dissembling meet with impudence.

88. as a dog] *Q*; as but a dog *V*.

---

93. *reared*] built (though Old Lionel is not the house's first owner).
97. *Mercury*] god of thieves and eloquence, and deliverer of dead souls. In alchemy, mercury was a releasing agent. Cf. IV.i.12 f. and *Cap.* I.iii.69.
99. *fast*] locked in.
101. *his*] (i.e., Reignald's).
103. *lie*] be imprisoned.
106. *many wrongs*] This is the one suggestion in the play that Young Lionel has a grievance; it may well be an instinctive invention by his 'parasitical serving-man', as he is described in Dramatis Personae.
110. *he*] (i.e., Old Lionel); the apparent subject of the sentence becomes the object of the final verb.

I'll do my best, and howsoe'er it prove
My praise or shame, 'tis but a servant's love.
[REIGNALD *withdraws.*]

Enter OLD LIONEL *like a civil merchant, with watermen and two servants with burdens and caskets.*

Old Lionel. Discharge these honest sailors that have brought
Our chests ashore, and pray them have a care
Those merchandise be safe we left aboard.
As heaven hath blessed us with a fortunate voyage,
In which we bring home riches with our healths,
So let not us prove niggards in our store.
See them paid well and to their full content.
First Servant. I shall, sir. [*Exit.*]
Old Lionel. Then return; these special things
And of most value we'll not trust aboard.
Methinks they are not safe till they see home
And there repose where we will rest ourselves
And bid farewell to travel. For I vow
After this hour no more to trust the seas
Nor throw me to such danger.
Reignald. [*Aside*] I could wish
You had took your leave o'the land, too.
Old Lionel. And now it much rejoiceth me to think
What a most sudden welcome I shall bring
Both to my friends and private family.

[*Enter* First Servant.]

Reignald. [*Aside*] O, but how much more welcome had he been
That had brought certain tidings of thy death.
Old Lionel. But soft, what's this? My own gates shut upon me
And bar their master entrance? Who's within there?
How, no man speak? Are all asleep, or dead,
That no soul stirs to open? *Knocks aloud.*
[REIGNALD *comes forward.*]
Reignald. What madman's that who, weary of his life,
Dares once lay hand on these accursèd gates?
Old Lionel. Who's that? My servant Reignald.
Reignald. My old master,
Most glad I am to see you. Are you well, sir?
Old Lionel. Thou seest I am.
Reignald. But are you sure you are?
Feel you no change about you? Pray you, stand off.
Old Lionel. What strange and unexpected greeting's this
That thus a man may knock at his own gates,
Beat with his hands and feet and call thus loud,

121. *let . . . niggards*] The generosity of Old Lionel's first speech contrasts with his son's and Reignald's portrait of him.

And no man give him entrance?
Reignald. Said you, sir,
Did your hand touch that hammer?
Old Lionel. Why, whose else?
Reignald. But are you sure you touched it?
Old Lionel. How else, I prithee,
Could I have made this noise?
Reignald. You touched it, then?
Old Lionel. I tell thee yet, I did.
Reignald. O, for the love I bear you—
O, me most miserable! You, for your own sake,
Of all alive most wretched! Did you touch it?
Old Lionel. Why, say I did?
Reignald. You have then a sin committed
No sacrifice can expiate to the dead.
But yet I hope you did not.
Old Lionel. 'Tis past hope,
The deed is done, and I repent it not.
Reignald. You and all yours will do't. In this one rashness
You have undone us all. Pray be not desperate,
But first thank heaven that you have escaped thus well.
Come from the gate. Yet further; further yet,
And tempt your fate no more. Command your servants
Give off and come no nearer. They are ignorant
And do not know the danger, therefore pity
That they should perish in't. 'Tis full seven months
Since any of your house durst once set foot
Over that threshold.
Old Lionel. Prithee, speak the cause.
Reignald. First look about; beware that no man hear;
Command these to remove.
Old Lionel. Begone.
[*Exeunt servants and watermen.*]
Now speak.
Reignald. O, sir, this house is grown prodigious,
Fatal, disastrous unto you and yours.
Old Lionel. What fatal? What disastrous?
Reignald. Some host that hath been owner of this house
In it his guest hath slain, and we suspect
'Twas he of whom you bought it.
Old Lionel. How came this
Discovered to you first?
Reignald. I'll tell you, sir.
But further from the gate. Your son one night
Supped late abroad, I within—O, that night
I never shall forget. Being safe got home,
I saw him in his chamber laid to rest,
And after went to mine, and being drowsy

172. *prodigious*] ominous.

Forgot by chance to put the candle out.
Being dead asleep, your son affrighted calls
So loud that I soon wakened, brought in light
And found him almost drowned in fearful sweat.
Amazed to see't, I did demand the cause,
Who told me that this murdered ghost appeared,
His body gashed and all o'erstuck with wounds,
And spake to him as follows.

Old Lionel. O, proceed,
'Tis that I long to hear.

Reignald. 'I am', quoth he,
'A transmarine by birth, who came well stored
With gold and jewels to this fatal house,
Where seeking safety I encountered death.
The covetous merchant, landlord of this rent,
To whom I gave my life and wealth in charge,
Freely to enjoy the one robbed me of both.
Here was my body buried, here my ghost
Must ever walk, till that have Christian rite;
Till when, my habitation must be here.
Then fly, young man, remove thy family
And seek some safer dwelling. For my death
This mansion is accursed; 'tis my possession,
Bought at the dear rate of my life and blood.
None enter here, that aims at his own good.'
And with this charge he vanished.

Old Lionel. O my fear,
Whither wilt thou transport me?

Reignald. I entreat,
Keep further from the gate, and fly.

Old Lionel. Fly whither?
Why dost not thou fly too?

Reignald. What need I fear?
The ghost and I am friends.

Old Lionel. But Reignald—

Reignald. [*Speaking towards the house*] Tush,
I nothing have deserved, nor aught transgressed;
I came not near the gate.

Old Lionel. To whom was that
Thou spakest?

Reignald. Was't you, sir, namèd me?
Now as I live, I thought the dead man called
To enquire for him that thundered at the gate
Which he so dearly paid for. Are you mad,

200. rite;] *this ed.*; right; Q. 214. namèd] *this ed.*; nam'd Q.

193. *transmarine*] foreigner; this rare term (a direct translation from *Most.* 497) gives memorable weight to the ghost's invented words; it also focuses the travel/commerce theme in both plots.

To stand a foreseen danger?
Old Lionel. What shall I do?
Reignald. Cover your head and fly, lest looking back
You spy your own confusion.
Old Lionel. Why dost not thou fly, too?
Reignald. I tell you, sir,
The ghost and I am friends.
Old Lionel. Why didst thou quake, then?
Reignald. In fear lest some mischance may fall on you
That have the dead offended. For my part,
The ghost and I am friends. Why fly you not,
Since here you are not safe?
Old Lionel. Some blest powers guard me!
Reignald. Nay sir, I'll not forsake you. [*Aside*] I have got the start,
But ere the goal 'twill ask both brain and art. *Exeunt.*

ACT III

SCENE i

Enter OLD *Master* GERALDINE, YOUNG GERALDINE, Master WINCOTT *and* [*his*] WIFE, DALAVILL [*and*] PRUDENTILIA.

Wincott. We are bound to you, kind Master Geraldine,
For this great entertainment. Troth, your cost
Hath much exceeded common neighbourhood.
You have feasted us like princes.
Old Geraldine. This, and more
Many degrees, can never countervail
The oft and frequent welcomes given my son.
You have took him from me quite, and have I think
Adopted him into your family,
He stays with me so seldom.
Wincott. And in this
By trusting him to me, of whom yourself
May have both use and pleasure, you're as kind
As moneyed men, that might make benefit
Of what they are possessed, yet to their friends
In need will lend it gratis.
Wife. And like such
As are indebted more than they can pay

219. your] *Di*; you *Q*.

We more and more confess ourselves engaged
To you for your forbearance.
Prudentilla. Yet you see,
Like debtors such as would not break their day
The treasure late received we tender back,
The which the longer you can spare, you still
The more shall bind us to you.
Old Geraldine. Most kind ladies,
Worthy you are to borrow, that return
The principal with such large use of thanks.
Dalavill. [*Aside*] What strange felicity these rich men take
To talk of borrowing, lending and of use,
The usurer's language right.
Wincott. You've, Master Geraldine,
Fair walks and gardens; I have praisèd them
Both to my wife and sister.
Old Geraldine. You would see them?
There's no pleasure that the house can yield
That can be debarred from you. Prithee, son,
Be thou the usher to those mounts and prospects
May one day call thee master.
Young Geraldine. Sir, I shall.
Please you to walk?
Prudentilla. What, Master Dalavill,
Will you not bear us company?
Dalavill. 'Tis not fit
That we should leave our noble host alone.
Be you my friend's charge, and this old man mine.
Prudentilla. Well, be't then at your pleasure.
Exeunt. Manent DALAVILL *and* OLD GERALDINE.
Dalavill. [*Aside*] You to your prospects, but there's project here
That's of another nature. [*To Old Geraldine*] Worthy sir,
I cannot but approve your happiness
To be the father of so brave a son,
So every way accomplished and made up,
In which my voice is least. For I, alas,
Bear but a mean part in the common choir,
When with much louder accents of his praise
So all the world reports him.
Old Geraldine. Thank my stars
They have lent me one who, as he always was
And is my present joy, if their aspect
Be no ways to our goods malevolent,

37.1. *Manent*] Di; *Manet Q*.

18. *break . . . day*] fail to meet payment date.
23. *use*] interest.
38. *project*] a scheme.
41. *brave*] worthy.
48. *aspect*] astrological alignment.

May be my future comfort.
Dalavill. Yet must I hold him happy above others,
As one that solely to himself enjoys
What many others aim at but in vain.
Old Geraldine. How mean you that?
Dalavill. So beautiful a mistress.
Old Geraldine. A mistress, said you?
Dalavill. Yes, sir, or a friend,
Whether you please to style her.
Old Geraldine. Mistress? Friend?
Pray, be more open-languaged.
Dalavill. And indeed
Who can blame him to absent himself from home
And make his father's house but as a grange,
For a beauty so attractive? Or blame her,
Hugging so weak an old man in her arms,
To make a new choice of an equal youth
Being in him so perfect? Yet in troth
I think they both are honest.
Old Geraldine. You have, sir,
Possessed me with such strange fancies.
Dalavill. For my part
How can I love the person of your son
And not his reputation? His repair
So often to the house is voiced by all
And frequent in the mouths of the whole country.
Some, equally addicted, praise his happiness,
But others, more censorious and austere,
Blame and reprove a course so dissolute.
Each one in general pity the good man
As one unfriendly dealt with; yet in my conscience
I think them truly honest.
Old Geraldine. 'Tis suspicious.
Dalavill. True, sir, at best; but what when scandalous tongues
Will make the worst, and what good in itself
Sully and stain by fabulous misreport?
For let men live as chary as they can
Their lives are often questioned; then no wonder
If such as give occasion of suspicion
Be subject to this scandal. What I speak
Is as a noble friend unto your son,

77. what *Q*; what's *Di.*

---

59. *grange*] country house infrequently visited.

64. *I think . . . honest*] The phrase here, and in ll. 75 and 86, recalls Iago's repeated use of the same construction (*Oth.* III.iii.129, 133) to plant doubts in Othello's mind. The play on 'reputation' in Dalavill's next speech may well be remembered from Cassio (*Oth.* II.iii.153ff.).

77. *what*] Dilke's suggestion ('what's') clarifies the elliptical syntax.

79. *chary*] carefully.

And therefore, as I glory in his fame
I suffer in his wrong. For, as I live,
I think they both are honest.
Old Geraldine. Howsoever,
I wish them so.
Dalavill. Some course might be devised
To stop this clamour ere it grow too rank,
Lest that which yet but inconvenience seems
May turn to greater mischief. This I speak
In zeal to both: in sovereign care of him
As of a friend, and tender of her honour
As one to whom I hope to be allied
By marriage with her sister.
Old Geraldine. I much thank you,
For you have clearly given me light of that
Till now I never dreamt on.
Dalavill. 'Tis my love,
And therefore, I entreat you, make not me
To be the first reporter.
Old Geraldine. You have done
The office of a noble gentleman,
And shall not be so injured.

Enter again as from walking WINCOTT, [*his*] WIFE, YOUNG GERALDINE [*and*] PRUDENTILLA [*with flowers*].

Wincott. See, Master Geraldine,
How bold we are; especially these ladies
Play little better than the thieves with you,
For they have robbed your garden.
Wife. You might, sir,
Better have termed it sauciness than theft.
You see we blush not, what we took in private
To wear in public view.
Prudentilla. Besides, these cannot
Be missed out of so many; in full fields
The gleanings are allowed.
Old Geraldine. These and the rest
Are, ladies, at your service.
Wincott. Now to horse.
But one thing ere we part I must entreat,
In which my wife will be joint suitor with me,
My sister, too.
Old Geraldine. In what, I pray?
Wincott. That he
Which brought us hither may but bring us home:
Your much respected son.
Old Geraldine. [*Aside*] How men are born

88. *rank*] excessive.

To woo their own disasters.
Wife. But to see us
From whence he brought us, sir, that's all.
Old Geraldine. [*Aside*] This second motion makes it palpable.
To note a woman's cunning: make her husband
Bawd to her own lascivious appetite
And to solicit his own shame.
Prudentilla. Nay, sir,
When all of us join in so small a suit
It were some iniury to be denied.
Old Geraldine. [*Aside*] And work her sister, too! What will not woman
To accomplish her own ends? But this disease
I'll seek to physic ere it grow too far.
[*To them*] I am most sorry to be urged, sweet friends
In what at this time I can no ways grant.
Most, that these ladies should be aught denied
To whom I owe all service; but occasions
Of weighty and important consequence
Such as concern the best of my estate
Call him aside. Excuse us both this once;
Presume, this business is no sooner over
But he's at his own freedom.
Wincott. 'Twere no manners
In us to urge it further. We will leave you,
With promise, sir, that he shall in my will
Not be the last remembered.
Old Geraldine. We are bound to you.
See them to horse, and instantly return;
We have employments for you.
Young Geraldine. Sir, I shall.
Dalavill. Remember your last promise.
Old Geraldine. Not to do't
I should forget myself.
[*Exeunt* WINCOTT *and his wife*, DALAVILL, PRUDENTILLA *and* YOUNG GERALDINE.]
If I find him false
To such a friend, be sure he forfeits me.
In which to be more punctually resolved
I have a project how to sift his soul
How 'tis inclined, whether to yonder place,
The clear bright palace, or black dungeon.

116. woo] *V*; woe *Q*.

---

116. *woo*] *Q*'s 'woe' suggests a pun, but *OED* records no verbal use of 'woe'.
144. *punctually*] accurately.
146. *yonder place*] (i.e., heaven, contrasted below with hell's 'black dungeon').

Enter YOUNG GERALDINE.

See,
They are onward on the way, and he returned.
Young Geraldine. I now attend your pleasure.
Old Geraldine. You are grown perfect man, and now you float
Like to a well-built vessel 'tween two currents,
Virtue and vice. Take this, you steer to harbour,
Take that, to imminent shipwrack.
Young Geraldine. Pray, your meaning?
Old Geraldine. What fathers' cares are, you shall never know
Till you yourself have children. Now my study
Is how to make you such that you in them
May have a feeling of my love to you.
Young Geraldine. Pray, sir, expound yourself, for I protest
Of all the languages I yet have learned
This is to me most foreign.
Old Geraldine. Then I shall:
I have lived to see you in your prime of youth
And height of fortune, so you will but take
Occasion by the forehead. To be brief
And cut off all superfluous circumstance,
All the ambition that I aim at now
Is but to see you married.
Young Geraldine. Married, sir?
Old Geraldine. And to that purpose, I have found out one
Whose youth and beauty may not only please
A curious eye, but her immediate means
Able to strengthen a state competent
Or raise a ruined fortune.
Young Geraldine. Of all which
I have, believe me, neither need nor use,
My competence best pleasing as it is
And this my singularity of life
Most to my mind contenting.
Old Geraldine. [*Aside*] I suspect,
But yet must prove him further.
[*To him*] Say to my care I add a father's charge
And couple with my counsel my command?
To that how can you answer?
Young Geraldine. That I hope
My duty and obedience still unblamed
Did never merit such austerity,
And from a father never yet displeased.
Old Geraldine. Nay then, to come more near unto the point,

162–3. *take . . . forehead*] proverbial: 'take Time by the forelock, for she is bald behind' (T311).
169. *curious*] discriminating.
170. *state competent*] comfortable financial position.

Either you must resolve for present marriage
Or forfeit all your interest in my love.

Young Geraldine. Unsay that language, I entreat you, sir,
And do not so oppress me. Or if needs
Your heavy imposition stand in force.
Resolve me by your counsel: with more safety
May I infringe a sacred vow to heaven
Or to oppose me to your strict command,
Since one of these I must?

Old Geraldine. [*Aside*] Now, Dalavill,
I find thy words too true.

Young Geraldine. For marry, sir,
I neither may nor can.

Old Geraldine. Yet whore you may,
And that's no breach of any vow to heaven;
Pollute the nuptial bed with mechal sin,
Asperse the honour of a noble friend,
Forfeit thy reputation here below
And th'interest that thy soul might claim above
In yon blest city; these you may, and can,
With untouched conscience. O, that I should live
To see the hopes that I have stored so long
Thus in a moment ruined, and the staff
On which my old decrepit age should lean
Before my face thus broken, on which trusting
I thus abortively, before my time,
Fall headlong to my grave. *Falls on the earth.*

Young Geraldine. It yet stands strong,
Both to support you unto future life
And fairer comfort.

Old Geraldine. Never, never, son;
For till thou canst acquit thyself of scandal
And me of my suspicion, here, even here,
Where I have measured out my length of earth
I shall expire my last.

Young Geraldine. Both these I can;
Then rise, sir, I entreat you; and that innocency
Which poisoned by the breath of calumny
Cast you thus low, shall, these few stains wiped off,
With better thoughts erect you. [*He helps him to his feet*].

Old Geraldine. Well, say on.

Young Geraldine. There's but one fire from which this smoke may grow,
Namely the unmatched yoke of youth and age;
In which, if ever I occasion was

219. youth and age;] *V*; youth; And *Q*.

---

196. *mechal*] adulterous (a coinage from Latin, used only by Heywood).
219. *unmatched yoke*] unequal marriage (of the Wincotts).

Of the smallest breach, the greatest implacable mischief
Adultery can threaten fall on me;
Of you may I be disavowed a son,
And unto heaven a servant. For that lady,
As she is beauty's mirror, so I hold her
For chastity's examples: from her tongue
Never came language that arrived my ear
That even censorious Cato, lived he now,
Could misinterpret; never from her lips
Came unchaste kiss; or from her constant eye
Look savouring of the least immodesty.
Further—

Old Geraldine. Enough. One only thing remains,
Which on thy part performed assures firm credit
To these thy protestations.

Young Geraldine. Name it then.

Old Geraldine. Take hence th'occasion of this common fame
Which hath already spread itself so far
To her dishonour and thy prejudice.
From this day forward to forbear the house,
This do, upon my blessing.

Young Geraldine. As I hope it,
I will not fail your charge.

Old Geraldine. I am satisfied. *Exeunt.*

[ACT III SCENE ii]

Enter at one door an Usurer *and his man, at the other* OLD LIONEL *with his servant, in the midst* REIGNALD.

Reignald. [*Aside*] To which hand shall I turn me? Here's my master
Hath been to inquire of him that sold the house
Touching the murder. Here's an usuring rascal
Of whom we have borrowed money to supply
Our prodigal expenses, broke our day,
And owe him still the principal and use.
Were I to meet them single, I have brain
To oppose both and to come off unscarred.
But if they do assault me, and at once,
Not Hercules himself could stand that odds,

226. examples:] *Q*; example: *Di.*

---

228. *censorious Cato*] Cato the Censor, renowned for his temperance.

235. *take... occasion*] proverbial, 'the cause taken away, the effect vanisheth' (C202); *fame*] rumour.

This scene translates the first scene of Act III (536–689) of *Mostellaria*.

6. *use*] interest.

Therefore I must encounter them by turns;
And to my master first. [*To him*] O, sir, well met.
Old Lionel. What, Reignald? I but now met with the man
Of whom I bought yon house.
Reignald. What, did you, sir?
But did you speak of aught concerning that
Which I last told you?
Old Lionel. Yes, I told him all.
Reignald. [*Aside*] Then am I cast. [*To him*] But I pray tell me, sir,
Did he confess the murder?
Old Lionel. No such thing;
Most stiffly he denies it.
Reignald. Impudent wretch;
Then serve him with a warrant. Let the officer
Bring him before a justice; you shall hear
What I can say against him. 'Sfoot, deny't!
But I pray, sir, excuse me; yonder's one
With whom I have some business. Stay you here,
And but determine what's best course to take,
And note how I will follow't.
Old Lionel. Be brief, then.
Reignald. [*Aside*] Now if I can as well put off my use-man,
This day I shall be master of the field.
Usurer. That should be Lionel's man.
Man. The same, I know him.
Usurer. After so many frivolous delays
There's now some hope. He that was wont to shun us
And to absent himself, accosts us freely
And with a pleasant countenance. Well met, Reignald;
What, is this money ready?
Reignald. Never could you
Have come in better time.
Usurer. Where's your master,
Young Lionel? It something troubles me
That he should break his day.
Reignald. A word in private.
Usurer. Tush, private me no privates. In a word,
Speak, are my moneys ready?
Reignald. Not so loud.
Usurer. I will be louder yet. Give me my moneys;
Come, tender me my moneys.
Reignald. We know you have a throat wide as your conscience,
You need not use it now. Come, get you home.
Usurer. Home?
Reignald. Yes, home, I say. Return by three o' clock,
And I will see all cancelled.

34. What, is] *V*; What's *Q*.

27. *use-man*] money-lender, usurer (only example in *OED*).

Usurer. 'Tis now past two, and I can stay till three;
I'll make that now my business. Otherways,
With these loud clamours I will haunt thee still:
Give me my use, give me my principal.
Reignald. [*Aside*] This bur will still cleave to me. What, no means
To shake him off? I ne'er was caught till now.
[*To him*] Come, come, you're troublesome.
Usurer. Prevent that trouble,
And without trifling pay me down my cash.
I will be fooled no longer.
Reignald. So, so, so.
Usurer. I have been still put off from time to time
And day to day. These are but cheating tricks,
And this is the last minute I'll forbear
Thee or thy master. Once again I say
Give me my use, give me my principal.
Reignald. [*Aside*] Pox o' this use, that hath undone so many,
And now will confound me.
Old Lionel. Hast thou heard this?
Servant. Yes, sir, and to my grief.
Old Lionel. Come hither, Reignald.
Reignald. Here, sir. [*Aside*] Nay, now I am gone.
Old Lionel. What use is this,
What principal he talks of, in which language
He names my son, and thus upbraideth thee?
What is't you owe this man?
Reignald. A trifle, sir.
Pray stop his mouth and pay't him.
Old Lionel. I, pay? What?
Reignald. If I say pay't him, pay't him.
Old Lionel. What's the sum?
Reignald. A toy: the main about five hundred pounds,
And the use fifty.
Old Lionel. Call you that a toy?
To what use was it borrowed? At my departure
I left my son sufficient in his charge,
With surplus, to defray a large expense
Without this need of borrowing.
Reignald. 'Tis confessed,
Yet stop his clamorous mouth, and only say
That you will pay't tomorrow.
Old Lionel. I, pass my word?
Reignald. Sir, if I bid you, do't. Nay, no more words,
But say you'll pay't tomorrow.
Old Lionel. Jest indeed.
But tell me how these moneys were bestowed.

51. *bur . . . cleave*] To 'stick like a bur' is proverbial (B723, 724).
70. *toy*] trifle, triviality.

Reignald. Safe, sir, I warrant you.
Old Lionel. The sum still safe?
Why do you not then tender it yourselves?
Reignald. Your ear, sir. This sum joined to the rest, your son
Hath purchased land and houses.
Old Lionel. Land, dost thou say?
Reignald. A goodly house and gardens.
Old Lionel. Now joy on him,
That whilst his father merchandised abroad
Had care to add to his estate at home.
But Reignald, wherefore houses?
Reignald. Now Lord, sir,
How dull you are. This house possessed with spirits,
And there no longer stay, would you have had
Him, us, and all your other family
To live and lie i'the streets? It had not, sir,
Been for your reputation.
Old Lionel. Blessing on him
That he is grown so thrifty.
Usurer. 'Tis struck three;
My money's not yet tendered.
Reignald. Pox upon him.
See him discharged, I pray, sir.
Old Lionel. Call upon me
Tomorrow, friend, as early as thou wilt;
I'll see thy debt defrayed.
Usurer. It is enough,
I have a true man's word.
Exeunt Usurer *and* [*his*] *man.*
Old Lionel. Now tell me, Reignald,
For thou hast made me proud of my son's thrift,
Where, in what country, doth this fair house stand?
Reignald. [*Aside*] Never in all my time so much to seek;
I know not what to answer.
Old Lionel. Wherefore studiest thou?
Use men to purchase lands at a dear rate
And know not where they lie?
Reignald. 'Tis not for that,
I only had forgot his name that sold them.
'Twas—let me see, see—
Old Lionel. Call thyself to mind.
Reignald. [*Aside*] Nonplussed or never, now. Where art thou, brain?
[*To him*] O, sir, where was my memory? 'Tis this house
That next adjoins to yours.
Old Lionel. My neighbour Ricott's?

83. This sum] *Q*; With this sum *Di.* 95. thrifty] *Di*; thiftie *Q.* 100.1. *Exeunt*] *V*; *Exit. Q.*

102. *country*] region.
103. *to seek*] at a loss.

Reignald. The same, the same, sir. We had pennyworths in't,
And I can tell you have been offered well
Since, to forsake our bargain.
Old Lionel. As I live,
I much commend your choice.
Reignald. Nay, 'tis well seated,
Roughcast without, but bravely lined within.
You have met with few such bargains.
Old Lionel. Prithee knock
And call the master or the servant on't
To let me take free view on't.
Reignald. [*Aside*] Puzzle again on puzzle. [*To him*] One word, sir:
The house is full of women; no man knows
How on the instant they may be employed.
The rooms may lie unhandsome, and maids stand
Much on their cleanliness and housewifery.
To take them unprovided were disgrace,
'Twere fit they had some warning. Now do you
Fetch but a warrant from the justice, sir—
You understand me?
Old Lionel. Yes I do.
Reignald. To attach
Him of suspected murder; I'll see't served.
Did he deny't? And in the interim I
Will give them notice you are now arrived
And long to see your purchase.
Old Lionel. Counselled well.
And meet some half-hour hence.
Reignald. [*Aside*] This plunge well past
All things fall even, to crown my brain at last. *Exeunt.*

[ACT III SCENE iii]

Enter DALAVILL *and a* Gentleman.

Gentleman. Where shall we dine today?
Dalavill. At th'ordinary.
I see, sir, you are but a stranger here.
This Barnet is a place of great resort,

129–30. served. / Did] *Q*; served, / Did *V*.

---

112. *We . . . in't*] We bought it cheaply.
116. *bravely lined*] handsomely panelled.
118–19. *on't . . . on't*] The first of these may perhaps be a misreading of 'out', but the repetition could as easily be the result of hasty writing.
1. *ordinary*] public eating-house.
3. *Barnet*] market town north of London. In Jonson's *New Inn* (1629), set in Barnet, the house of the title was called The Light Heart, as being, like other coaching inns, a place for lovers to meet. By his choice of place, Heywood may suggest both associations, the mercantile and the amatory.

And commonly upon the market days
Here all the country gentlemen appoint
A friendly meeting; some about affairs
Of consequence and profit, bargain, sale,
And to confer with chapmen; some for pleasure,
To match their horses, wager in their dogs
Or try their hawks; some to no other end
But only meet good company, discourse,
Dine, drink and spend their money.

Gentleman. That's the market
We have to make this day.

Dalavill. 'Tis a commodity
That will be easily vented.

Enter OLD GERALDINE *and* YOUNG GERALDINE.

What, my worthy friend,
You are happily encountered. O, you're grown strange
To one that much respects you. Troth, the house
Hath all this time seemed naked without you.
The good old man doth never sit to meat
But next his giving thanks he speaks of you;
There's scarce a bit that he at table tastes
That can digest without a Geraldine,
You are in his mouth so frequent, he and she
Both wondering what distaste from one or either
So suddenly should alienate a guest
To them so dearly welcome.

Old Geraldine. Master Dalavill,
Thus much let me for him apology:
Divers designs have thronged upon us late
My weakness was not able to support
Without his help; he hath been much abroad
At London, or elsewhere; besides, 'tis term
And lawyers must be followed; seldom at home,
And scarcely then at leisure.

Dalavill. I am satisfied,
And I would they were so, too. [*Whispers.*] But I hope, sir,
In this restraint you have not used my name?

Old Geraldine. Not as I live.

Dalavill. You're noble. [*To both*] Who had thought
To have met with such good company. You're, it seems,
But new alighted. Father and son, ere part,

9. wager in *Q*; wager on *Di.* 26. apology:] *Q*; apologise: *V.* 36. seems,] *V*; seeme *Q*.

---

8. *chapmen*] traders.
14. *vented*] sold (the object for sale is not specified).
26. *apology*] apologise; this rare verbal use seems to originate with Heywood.
30. *term*] court sessions.

I vow we'll drink a cup of sack together;
Physicians say it doth prepare the appetite
And stomach against dinner.
Old Geraldine. We old men
Are apt to take these courtesies.
Dalavill. What say you, friend?
Young Geraldine. I'll but inquire for one at the next inn
And instantly return.
Dalavill. 'Tis enough.
Exeunt [DALAVILL, Gentleman, OLD GERALDINE].

Enter BESS *meeting* YOUNG GERALDINE.

Young Geraldine. Bess, how dost thou, girl?
Bess. Faith, we may do how we list for you, you are grown
So great a stranger. We are more beholding
To master Dalavill; he's a constant guest,
And howsoe'er to some that shall be nameless
His presence may be graceful, yet to others—
I could say somewhat.
Young Geraldine. He's a noble fellow,
And my choice friend.
Bess. Come, come, he is what he is,
And that the end will prove.
Young Geraldine. And how's all at home?
Nay, we'll not part without a glass of wine,
And meet so seldom. Boy!

Enter Drawer.

Drawer. Anon, anon, sir.
Young Geraldine. A pint of claret, quickly.
Exit Drawer.
Nay, sit down.
The news, the news, I pray thee. I am sure
I have been much inquired of thy old master,
And thy young mistress, too.
Bess. Ever your name
Is in my master's mouth, and sometimes, too,
In hers, when she hath nothing else to think of.
Well, well, I could say somewhat.

Enter Drawer.

Drawer. Here's your wine, sir.
Young Geraldine. Fill, boy. [*Drawer fills glasses.*]
Exit [Drawer].
Here, Bess; this glass to both their healths.

43. 'Tis] Q; It is *V*. 43.1. *Exeunt*] *V*; *Exit Q*.

38. *sack*] white wine.
51–2. *he is . . . prove*] With Bess's dismissive comment, compare the Wise-woman's ironic 'I am as I am, and there's an end' (*WWH* II.i.142).

Why dost weep, my wench?
Bess. Nay, nothing, sir.
Young Geraldine. Come, I must know.
Bess. In troth, I love you, sir,
And ever wished you well. You are a gentleman
Whom always I respected; know the passages
And private whisperings of the secret love
Betwixt you and my mistress, I dare swear
On your part well intended, but—
Young Geraldine. But what?
Bess. You bear the name of landlord, but another
Enjoys the rent; you dote upon the shadow,
But another he bears away the substance.
Young Geraldine. Be more plain.
Bess. You hope to enjoy a virtuous widowhood,
But Dalavill, whom you esteem your friend,
He keeps the wife in common.
Young Geraldine. You're to blame,
And Bess, you make me angry. He's my friend,
And she my second self. In all their meetings
I never saw so much as cast of eye
Once entertained betwixt them.
Bess. That's their cunning.
Young Geraldine. For her, I have been with her at all hours,
Both late and early; in her bedchamber,
And often singly ushered her abroad.
Now, would she have been any man's alive,
She had been mine. You wrong a worthy friend
And a chaste mistress; you're not a good girl. [*Gives money.*]
Drink that; speak better of her. I could chide you,
But I'll forbear. What you have rashly spoke
Shall ever here be buried.
Bess. I am sorry
My freeness should offend you, but yet know
I am her chambermaid.
Young Geraldine. Play now the market maid,
And prithee, 'bout thy business.
Bess. Well, I shall—
That man should be so fooled! *Exit.*
Young Geraldine. She a prostitute?
Nay, and to him? My troth-plight and my friend?
As possible it is that heaven and earth

63. dost weep] *Q*; dost thou weep *V*. 76. to blame] *Di*; too blame *Q*.

71–2. *shadow . . . substance*] Hudson compares Aesop's fable of the dog and the bone, but Heywood was generally interested in the contrast of illusion with reality; see the similar use of 'shadow' in the *Apology* passage quoted in the Introduction, and (contrasted with 'substance') in *Cap*. IV.i.296–7.

76. *in common*] jointly with her husband.

94. *troth-plight*) betrothed.

Should be in love together, meet and kiss,
And so cut off all distance. What strange frenzy
Came in this wench's brain, so to surmise?
Were she so base, his nobleness is such
He would not entertain it, for my sake;
Or he so bent, his hot and lust-burnt appetite
Would be soon quenched at the mere contemplation
Of her most pious and religious life.
The girl was much to blame; perhaps her mistress
Hath stirred her anger by some word or blow
Which she would thus revenge, not apprehending
At what a high price honour's to be rated;
Or else someone that envies her rare virtue
Might hire her thus to brand it; or who knows
But the young wench may fix a thought on me
And to divert me from her mistress' love
May raise this false aspersion? Howsoever,
My thoughts on these two columns fixèd are:
She's good as fresh, and purely chaste as fair.

Enter CLOWN *with a letter* [*and a pint pot*].

Clown. O sir, you are the needle, and if the whole county of Middlesex had been turned to a mere bottle of hay, I had been enjoined to have found you out, or never more returned back to my old master. There's a letter, sir.

[*Gives him the letter.*]

Young Geraldine. I know the hand that superscribed it well.
Stay but till I peruse it, and from me
Thou shalt return an answer.

Clown. I shall, sir.
[*Aside, while* Young Geraldine *reads*] This is market-day, and here acquaintance commonly meet. And whom have I encountered? My gossip Pint-pot, and brimful; nay, I mean to drink with you before I part. And how doth all your worshipful kindred: your sister Quart, your pater Pottle (who was ever a gentleman's fellow) and your old grandsire Gallon? They cannot choose but be all in health, since so many healths have been drunk out of them. I could wish them all here, and in no worse state than I see you are in at this present. Howsoever, gossip, since I have met you hand to hand, I'll make bold to drink to you—nay, either you must pledge me, or get one to do't for you. Do you open your mouth towards me? Well, I know what you would say: 'Here, Roger, to your master and mistress and all our good friends at home.' Gramercy, gossip; if I should not pledge thee, I were worthy to be turned out to grass and stand no more at livery. And now in requital of this courtesy I'll begin one health to you and all your

115–16. *needle . . . hay*] proverbial (N97), with 'bottle (bundle) of hay' for the more familiar 'haystack'.

124. *gossip*] familiar friend.

society in the cellar: to Peter Pipe, Harry Hogshead, Bartholomew Butt and little master Randal Runlet, to Timothy Taster and all your other great and small friends.

Young Geraldine. He writes me here
That at my discontinuance he's much grieved,
Desiring me, as I have ever tendered
Or him or his, to give him satisfaction
Touching my discontent, and that in person
By any private meeting.

Clown. Ay, sir, 'tis very true; the letter speaks no more than he wished me to tell you by word of mouth.

Young Geraldine. Thou art, then, of his council?

Clown. His privy, an't please you.

Young Geraldine. [*Aside*] Though ne'er so strict hath been my father's charge,
A little I'll dispense with't, for his love.
[*To Clown*] Commend me to thy master; tell him from me
On Monday night (then will my leisure serve)
I will by heaven's assistance visit him.

Clown. On Monday, sir? That's, as I remember, just the day before Tuesday.

Young Geraldine. But 'twill be midnight first, at which late hour
Please him to let the garden door stand ope;
At that I'll enter, but conditionally
That neither wife, friend, servant, no third soul
Save him and thee to whom he trusts this message,
Know of my coming in or passing out.
When, tell him, I will fully satisfy him
Concerning my forced absence.

Clown. I am something oblivious; your message would be the trulier delivered if it were set down in black and white.

Young Geraldine. I'll call for pen and ink,
And instantly dispatch it. *Exeunt.*

150. an't] *V* (an' *Di*); and *Q*.

138–9. *Pipe . . . Hogshead . . . Butt . . . Runlet . . . Taster*] wine-containers of varying size, in approximate descending order, from a giant barrel to a tasting-cup.
150. *privy*] (i.e., council, but the Clown seizes any opportunity for a jest).
166. *oblivious*] forgetful.

ACT IV

SCENE i

Enter REIGNALD.

Reignald. Now impudence but steel my face this once,
Although I ne'er blush after. Here's the house.
[*Calls*] Ho, who's within? What, no man to defend
These innocent gates from knocking?

Enter Master RICOTT.

Ricott. Who's without there?
Reignald. One, sir, that ever wished your worship's health,
And those few hours I can find time to pray in
I still remember it.
Ricott. Gramercy, Reignald,
I love all those that wish it. You are the men
Lead merry lives, feast, revel and carouse;
You feel no tedious hours, time plays with you;
This is your golden age.
Reignald. It was; but now, sir,
That gold is turned to worse than alchemy,
It will not stand the test. Those days are past,
And now our nights come on.
Ricott. Tell me, Reignald, is he returned from sea?
Reignald. Yes, to our grief, already; but we fear
Hereafter it may prove to all our costs.
Ricott. Suspects thy master anything?
Reignald. Not yet, sir.
Now my request is, that your worship being
So near a neighbour, therefore most disturbed,
Would not be first to peach us.
Ricott. Take my word;
With other neighbours make what peace you can,
I'll not be your accuser.
Reignald. Worshipful sir,

2. ne'er] Q; e'er *Di.*

This scene adapts the remainder of *Mostellaria* Act III (700–857).

2. *ne'er blush*] Dilke's emendation 'e'er' is one solution to this apparent non-sequitur. But Reignald may mean that this ultimate piece of impudence eliminates whatever remained of his sense of shame.

12. *alchemy*] counterfeit gold.

21. *peach*] betray.

I shall be still your beadsman. Now, the business
That I was sent about: the old man, my master,
Claiming some interest in acquaintance past,
Desires (might it be no way troublesome)
To take free view of all your house within.
Ricott. View of my house? Why, 'tis not set to sale,
Nor bill upon the door. Look well upon't.
View of my house?
Reignald. Nay, be not angry, sir;
He no way doth disable your estate;
As far to buy, as you are loath to sell.
Some alterations in his own he'd make,
And hearing yours by workmen much commended
He would make that his precedent.
Ricott. What fancies
Should at this age possess him, knowing the cost,
That he should dream of building?
Reignald. 'Tis supposed
He hath late found a wife out for his son.
Now, sir, to have him near him, and that nearness
Too without trouble, though beneath one roof
Yet parted in two families, he would build
And make what's picked a perfect quadrangle
Proportioned just with yours, were you so pleased
To make it his example.
Ricott. Willingly.
I will but order some few things within
And then attend his coming. *Exit.*
Reignald. Most kind coxcomb.
Great Alexander and Agathocles,
Caesar, and others, have been famed, they say,
And magnified for high facinorous deeds;
Why claim not I an equal place with them,
Or rather, a precedent? These commanded
Their subjects and their servants; I, my master
And every way his equals, where I please
Lead by the nose along. They placed their burdens
On horses, mules and camels; I, old men
Of strength and wit load with my knavery

---

24. *beadsman*] obedient servant (a formula); for the (equally ironic) prayer associations, cf. ll. 5–7.
32. *disable*] disparage.
43. *what's picked*] what he chose.
48–9. *Alexander . . . Agathocles . . . Caesar*] Greek, Sicilian and Roman military commanders. For Agathocles, cf. *Cap.* I.iii.21. Caesar, naturally, is Heywood's addition to Plautus.
50. *facinorous*] infamous.
52. *precedent*] (accent on second syllable) predecessor, superior.
55. *Lead . . . nose*] proverbial (N233) for making an 'ass' of someone.

Till both their backs and brains ache. Yet, poor animals,
They ne'er complain of weight.

Enter OLD LIONEL.

O, are you come, sir?
Old Lionel. I made what haste I could.
Reignald. And brought the warrant?
Old Lionel. See, here I have't.
Reignald. 'Tis well done, but speak, runs it
Both without bail and mainprize?
Old Lionel. Nay, it carries
Both form and power.
Reignald. Then I shall warrant him.
I have been yonder, sir.
Old Lionel. And what says he?
Reignald. Like one that offers you
Free ingress, view and regress, at your pleasure,
As to his worthy landlord.
Old Lionel. Was that all?
Reignald. He spake to me, that I would speak to you,
To speak unto your son; and then again,
To speak to him, that he would speak to you,
You would release his bargain.
Old Lionel. By no means.
Men must advise before they part with land,
Not after to repent it. 'Tis most just
That such as hazard and disburse their stocks
Should take all gains and profit that accrue
As well in sale of houses as in barter
And traffic of all other merchandise.

Enter Master RICOTT *again walking before the gate.*

Reignald. See, in acknowledgement of a tenant's duty
He attends you at the gate. Salute him, sir.
Old Lionel. My worthy friend.
Ricott. Now as I live, all my best thoughts and wishes
Impart with yours, in your so safe return.
Your servant tells me you have great desire
To take surview of this my house within.
Old Lionel. Be't, sir, no trouble to you.
Ricott. None; enter boldly
With as much freedom as it were your own.
Old Lionel. As it were mine? Why, Reignald, is it not?
Reignald. Lord, sir, that in extremity of grief
You'll add unto vexation. See you not
How sad he's on the sudden?
Old Lionel. I observe it.

62. *mainprize*] release under surety.
84. *surview*] survey.

Reignald. To part with that which he hath kept so long,
Especially his inheritance. Now, as you love
Goodness and honesty, torment him not
With the least word of purchase.
Old Lionel. Counselled well;
Thou teachest me humanity.
Ricott. Will you enter?
Or shall I call a servant to conduct you
Through every room and chamber?
Old Lionel. By no means;
I fear we are too much troublesome of ourselves.
Reignald. See, what a goodly gate!
Old Lionel. It likes me well.
Reignald. What brave carved posts! Who knows but here
In time, sir, you may keep your shrievalty,
And I be one o' the serjeants.
Old Lionel. They are well carved.
Ricott. And cost me a good price, sir. Take your pleasure;
I have business in the town. *Exit.*
Reignald. Poor man, I pity him.
H'ath not the heart to stay and see you come,
As 'twere, to take possession. Look that way, sir,
What goodly fair bay windows!
Old Lionel. Wondrous stately.
Reignald. And what a gallery, how costly ceiled,
What painting round about!
Old Lionel. Every fresh object
To good adds betterness.
Reignald. Tarrassed above,
And how below supported! Do they please you?
Old Lionel. All things beyond opinion. Trust me, Reignald,
I'll not forgo the bargain for more gain
Than half the price it cost me.
Reignald. If you would,
I should not suffer you; was not the money
Due to the usurer took upon good ground
That proved well built upon? We were no fools
That knew not what we did.
Old Lionel. It shall be satisfied.
Reignald. Please you to trust me with't, I'll see't discharged.

107.] *Bayes. marginal note, Q.*

---

100. *brave carved posts*] The description appeals to the audience's imagination, but Heywood may have in mind the ornate pillars of the new Cockpit. In Plautus (l. 819) they are 'firm' and 'thick'.

101. *shrievalty . . . serjeants*] When his master is sheriff, Reignald will be an officer.

107. *bay windows*] Q's marginal note '*Bayes.*' is puzzling; it is presumably a book-keeper's annotation, but its purpose is obscure.

108. *ceiled*] panelled or roofed.

110. *tarrassed*] plastered or galleried (another theatre term).

Old Lionel. He hath my promise, and I'll do't myself.
Never could son have better pleased a father
Than in this purchase. Hie thee instantly
Unto my house i'the country, give him notice
Of my arrive, and bid him with all speed
Post hither.
Reignald. Ere I see the warrant served?
Old Lionel. It shall be thy first business; for my soul
Is not at peace till face to face I approve
His husbandry, and much commend his thrift.
Nay, without pause, begone.
Reignald. [*Aside*] But a short journey,
For he's not far that I am sent to seek.
I have got the start, the best part of the race
Is run already; what remains is small,
And tire now, I should but forfeit all.
Old Lionel. Make haste, I do entreat thee. *Exeunt.*

[ACT IV SCENE ii]

Enter the CLOWN.

Clown. This is the garden gate, and here am I set to stand sentinel and to attend the coming of young Master Geraldine. Master Dalavill's gone to his chamber, my mistress to hers. 'Tis now about midnight, a banquet prepared, bottles of wine in readiness, all the whole household at their rest; and no creature by this honestly stirring, save I and my old master; he in a by-chamber prepared of purpose for their private meeting; and I here to play the watchman against my will.

Enter YOUNG GERALDINE.

Chavelah? Stand! Who goes there?
Young Geraldine. A friend.
Clown. The word?
Young Geraldine. Honest Roger!
Clown. That's the word, indeed; you have leave to pass freely without calling my corporal.
Young Geraldine. How go the affairs within?
Clown. According to promise: the business is composed, and the servants disposed; my young mistress reposed; my old master,

1. *This . . . gate*] Just as previously in *A Woman Killed with Kindness* ('This is the key that opes my outward gate', sc. xiii) the opening of gates and doors becomes a metaphor for moral discoveries, here and in IV.iii.120.1.
4. *banquet*] a dessert of sweetmeats and fruit.
5. *no creature . . . stirring*] cf. *WKK* xii.29; 'To bed, good honest serving creatures.'
9. *Chavelah?*] Who goes there? (Corruption of French 'Qui va là?')
11. *word*] (i.e., password).

according as you proposed, attends you, if you be exposed to give him meeting; nothing in the way being interposed, to transpose you to the least danger; and this I dare be deposed, if you will not take my word, as I am honest Roger.

Young Geraldine. Thy word shall be my warrant, but secured
Most in thy master's promise; on which building,
By this known way I enter.

Clown. Nay, by your leave, I that was late but a plain sentinel will now be your captain conductor. Follow me. *Exeunt.*

[ACT IV SCENE iii]

Table and stools set out. Lights, a banquet, wine.
Enter Master WINCOTT.

Wincott. I wonder whence this strangeness should proceed,
Or wherein I, or any of my house,
Should be th'occasion of the least distaste.
Now, as I wish him well, it troubles me.
But now the time grows on from his own mouth
To be resolved, and I hope satisfied.

Enter CLOWN *and* YOUNG GERALDINE.

Sir, as I live, of all my friends, to me
Most wishedly you are welcome. Take that chair,
I this; nay, I entreat, no compliment.
Attend; fill wine.

Clown. Till the mouths of the bottles yawn directly upon the floor, and the bottoms turn their tails up to the ceiling, Whilst there's any blood in their bellies, I'll not leave them.

Wincott. I first salute you thus.

Young Geraldine. It could not come
From one whom I more honour. Sir, I thank you.

Clown. Nay, since my master begun it, I'll see't go round to all three.

Wincott. Now give us leave.

Clown. Talk you by yourselves, whilst I find something to say to this; I have a tale to tell him shall make his stony heart relent. *Exit.*

Young Geraldine. Now first, sir, your attention I entreat;
Next, your belief that what I speak is just,

---

18. *exposed*] perhaps in the sense of 'open'.

20. *deposed*] sworn on oath.

0.1] The setting marks the last moment of harmony and conviviality in Geraldine's relationship with the house. The disruption of both marriage and friendship is given more force (as it was in *A Woman Killed with Kindness*) by this generous sharing of hospitality, an effect analogous to the large number of interrupted banquets in Shakespeare.

19. *stony*] (because stoneware).

Maugre all contradiction.
Wincott. Both are granted.
Young Geraldine. Then I proceed, with due acknowledgement
Of all your more than many courtesies:
You've been my second father, and your wife
My noble and chaste mistress; all your servants
At my command, and this your bounteous table
As free and common as my father's house.
Neither 'gainst any or the least of these
Can I commence just quarrel.
Wincott. What might then be
The cause of this constraint, in thus absenting
Yourself from such as love you?
Young Geraldine. Out of many,
I will propose some few: the care I have
Of your (as yet unblemishèd) renown;
The untouched honour of your virtuous wife;
And (which I value least, yet dearly, too)
My own fair reputation.
Wincott. How can these
In any way be questioned?
Young Geraldine. O, dear sir,
Bad tongues have been too busy with us all;
Of which I never yet had time to think
But with sad thoughts and griefs unspeakable.
It hath been whispered by some wicked ones,
But loudly thundered in my father's ears
By some that have maligned our happiness
(Heaven, if it can brook slander, pardon them)
That this my customary coming hither
Hath been to base and sordid purposes:
To wrong your bed, injure her chastity,
And be mine own undoer. Which, how false—
Wincott. As heaven is true, I know't.
Young Geraldine. Now, this calumny
Arriving first unto my father's ears,
His easy nature was induced to think
That these things might perhaps be possible.
I answered him as I would do to heaven,
And cleared myself in his suspicious thoughts
As truly as the high all-knowing Judge
Shall of these stains acquit me, which are merely
Aspersions and untruths. The good old man,
Possessed with my sincerity, and yet careful
Of your renown, her honour, and my fame,

34. unblemishèd] *La*; vnblemisht *Q*.

---

22. *Maugre*] despite.

To stop the worst that scandal could inflict
And to prevent false rumours, charges me,
The cause removed, to take away the effect,
Which only could be, to forbear your house;
And this upon his blessing. You hear all.

Wincott. And I of all acquit you. This your absence,
With which my love most cavilled, orators
In your behalf. Had such things passed betwixt you,
Not threats nor chidings could have driven you hence.
It pleads in your behalf, and speaks in hers,
And arms me with a double confidence
Both of your friendship and her loyalty.
I am happy in you both, and only doubtful
Which of you two doth most impart my love.
You shall not hence tonight.

Young Geraldine. Pray pardon, sir.

Wincott. You are in your lodging.

Young Geraldine. But my father's charge.

Wincott. My conjuration shall dispense with that.
You may be up as early as you please,
But hence tonight you shall not.

Young Geraldine. You are powerful.

Wincott. This night, of purpose, I have parted beds,
Feigning myself not well, to give you meeting,
Nor can be aught suspected by my wife,
I have kept all so private. Now 'tis late;
I'll steal up to my rest. But howsoever,
Let's not be strange in our writing; that way daily
We may confer without the least suspect
In spite of all such base calumnious tongues.
So now, goodnight, sweet friend.

Young Geraldine. May he that made you
So just and good still guard you.

Exit WINCOTT.

Not to bed;
So I perhaps might oversleep myself
And then my tardy waking might betray me
To the more early household. Thus as I am
I'll rest me on this pallet. [*Lies down.*] But in vain;
I find no sleep can fasten on mine eyes,
There are in this disturbèd brain of mine
So many mutinous fancies. This to me

---

67. *orators*] pleads (not in *OED* as a verb).

74. *impart*] have a share in.

77. *conjuration*] entreaty.

80. *parted beds*] slept apart (*OED* gives no use before 1710, when the phrase has associations of 'divorce').

94. *no sleep . . . eyes*] cf. *WKK* viii.214: 'No sleep will fasten on my eyes, you know, until you come.'

Will be a tedious night. How shall I spend it?
No book that I can spy? No company?
A little let me recollect myself.
O, what more wished company can I find,
Suiting the apt occasion, time and place,
Than the sweet contemplation of her beauty
And the fruition, too, time may produce
Of what is yet lent out? 'Tis a sweet lady,
And every way accomplished. Hath mere accident
Brought me thus near, and I not visit her?
Should it arrive her ear, perhaps might breed
Our lasting separation; for 'twixt lovers
No quarrel's to unkindness. Sweet opportunity
Offers prevention, and invites me to't;
The house is known to me, the stairs and rooms,
The way unto her bedchamber frequently
Trodden by me at midnight and all hours.
How joyful to her would a meeting be,
So strange and unexpected; shadowed, too,
Beneath the veil of night. I am resolved
To give her visitation in that place
Where we have passed deep vows: her bedchamber.
My fiery love this darkness makes seem bright,
And this the path that leads to my delight.

He goes in at one door and comes out at another.

And this the gate unto't. I'll listen first
Before too rudely I disturb her rest
And gentle breathing. Ha! She's sure awake,
For in the bed two whisper, and their voices
Appear to me unequal: one a woman's,
And hers. Th'other should be no maid's tongue,
It bears too big a tone. And hark, they laugh.
Damnation! But list further: t'other sounds—
Like—'tis the same false perjured traitor, Dalavill,
To friend and goodness. Unchaste, impious woman,
False to all faith and true conjugal love.
There's met a serpent and a crocodile,
A Sinon and a Circe. O, to what
May I compare you? But my sword—
I'll act a noble execution

129. traitor, Dalavill,] *Q*; Delavil, traitor *V*. 134. But] *Q*; Out, *V*.

---

109. *No quarrel's to unkindness*] Cruelty has no justification.

120–1. *This the path ... this the gate*] cf. *WKK* xiii.9–10: 'This is the hall door, this the withdrawing chamber. But this, that door that's bawd unto my shame.'

129–30.] *V*'s suggestion ('Delavil, traitor / to') clarifies the speaker's tumbling syntax.

133. *Sinon ... Circe*] the Greek who deceived Troy, and the enchantress who delayed Odysseus.

On two unmatched for sordid villainy.
I left it in my chamber, and thanks, heaven,
That I did so: it hath prevented me
From playing a base hangman. Sin securely,
Whilst I, although for many, yet less, faults
Strive hourly to repent me. I once loved her,
And was to him entired. Although I pardon,
Heaven will find time to punish; I'll not stretch
My just revenge so far as once by blabbing
To make your brazen impudence to blush.
Damn on; revenge too great; and, to suppress
Your souls yet lower, without hope to rise,
Heap Ossa upon Pelion. You have made me
To hate my very country, because here bred
Near two such monsters. First I'll leave this house
And then my father's; next I'll take my leave
Both of this clime and nation, travel till
Age snow upon this head. My passions now
Are unexpressable. I'll end them thus:
Ill man, bad woman; your unheard-of treachery
This unjust censure on a just man give,
To seek out place where no two such can live. *Exit.*

[ACT IV SCENE iv]

Enter DALAVILL *in a night-gown*, [WINCOTT'S] WIFE *in a night-tire, as coming from bed.*

Dalavill. A happy morning now betide you, lady,
To equal the content of a sweet night.
Wife. It hath been to my wish and your desire,
And this your coming, by pretended love
Unto my sister Pru, cuts off suspicion
Of any such converse 'twixt you and me.
Dalavill. It hath been wisely carried.
Wife. One thing troubles me.
Dalavill. What's that, my dearest?
Wife. Why your friend Geraldine
Should on the sudden thus absent himself.
Has he had, think you, no intelligence
Of these our private meetings?
Dalavill. No, on my soul,
For therein hath my brain exceeded yours;
I, studying to engross you to myself,

142. entired.] *Q*; entire. *V*.

142. *entired*] attached exclusively (usage peculiar to Heywood; cf. *Cap*. I.i.33).
148. *Ossa . . . Pelion*] mountains piled by the giants fighting the gods; proverbial (O81).

Of his continued absence have been cause;
Yet he of your affection no way jealous,
Or of my friendship. How the plot was cast
You at our better leisure shall partake.
The air grows cold, have care unto your health;
Suspicious eyes are o'er us, that yet sleep,
But with the dawn will open. Sweet, retire you
To your warm sheets, I now to fill my own
That have this night been empty.

Wife. You advise well.
O, might this kiss dwell ever on thy lips
In my remembrance.

Dalavill. Doubt it not, I pray,
Whilst day frights night, and night pursues the day.
Good morrow. *Exeunt.*

[ACT IV SCENE V]

Enter REIGNALD, YOUNG LIONEL, BLANDA, SCAPHA, RIOTER *and two gallants,* REIGNALD *with a key in his hand.*

Reignald. Now is the jail-delivery; through this back gate
Shift for yourselves; I here unprison all.

Young Lionel. But tell me, how shall we dispose ourselves?
We are as far to seek now as at the first.
What is it to reprieve us for few hours
And now to suffer? Better had it been
At first to have stood the trial, so by this
We might have passed our penance.

Blanda. Sweet Reignald.

Young Lionel. Honest rogue.

Rioter. If now thou failest us, then we are lost for ever.

Reignald. This same 'sweet Reignald', and this 'honest rogue',
Hath been the burgess under whose protection
You all this while have lived free from arrests;
But now the sessions of my power's broke up
And you exposed to actions, warrants, writs,
For all the hellish rabble are broke loose
Of serjeants, sheriffs and bailiffs.

All. Guard us, heaven!

Reignald. I tell you as it is. Nay, I myself
That have been your protector, now as subject
To every varlet's pestle, for you know
How I am engaged with you—[*He starts.*] At whose suit, sir?

All. Why didst thou start? *All start.*

Reignald. I was afraid some catchpole stood behind me

---

6. *now*] (i.e., still).
21. *varlet*] serjeant.
24. *catchpole*] sheriff's officer.

To clap me on the shoulder.
Rioter. No such thing,
Yet I protest thy fear did fright us all.
Reignald. I knew your guilty consciences.
Young Lionel. No brain left?
Blanda. No crochet, for my sake?
Reignald. One kiss then, sweet,
Thus shall my crochets and your kisses meet.
Young Lionel. Nay, tell us what to trust to.
Reignald. Lodge yourselves
In the next tavern. There's the cash that's left. [*Gives money.*]
Go, health it freely for my good success,
Nay, drown it all; let not a tester 'scape
To be consumed in rot-gut. I have begun,
And I will stand the period.
Young Lionel. Bravely spoke.
Reignald. Or perish in the conflict.
Rioter. Worthy Reignald.
Reignald. Well, if he now come off well, fox you all;
Go, call for wine; for singly of myself
I will oppose all danger. But I charge you,
When I shall faint or find myself distressed
If I like brave Orlando wind my horn,
Make haste unto my rescue.
Young Lionel. And die in't.
Reignald. Well hast thou spoke, my noble Charlemagne
With these thy peers about thee.
Young Lionel. May good speed
Attend thee still.
Reignald. The end still crowns the deed. *Exeunt.*

[ACT IV SCENE vi]

Enter OLD LIONEL *and the first* Owner *of the house.*

Owner. Sir, sir, your threats nor warrants can fright me.
My honesty and innocency's known

36–7. Reignald. / Well,] Q; Reignald— / Will, *conj. Da.*

---

28. *crochet*] clever idea (with a bawdy play in the next line).

33. *tester*] sixpence.

37. *fox*] proverbial (F651 'to catch a fox') for getting drunk (cf. ll. 30–5, 38); at the same time, the speaker is the 'foxy' Reignald.

41. *Orlando*] hero of the *Chanson de Roland*, who dies sounding his horn at Roncesvalles. In *The Distracted Emperor* (printed by Bullen, III.161, from Egerton MS 1994, which includes *Cap.*) 'Reinaldo' is a friend of Orlando and Charlemagne. 'Renaldo' is an eloquent character, Orlando's cousin, in Ariosto's *Orlando Furioso*.

45. *end . . . deed*] proverbial (E116), 'all's well that ends well'.

From the entry of Robin (l. 69), Heywood completes the dramatisation of *Mostellaria*, compressing the last two acts of Plautus into the remainder of the scene. The one major change is Reignald's escape by climbing; in *Most.*, Tranio takes refuge at the altar.

Always to have been unblemished. Would you could
As well approve your own integrity
As I shall doubtless acquit myself
Of this surmisèd murder.

Old Lionel. Rather surrender
The price I paid, and take into thy hands
This haunted mansion, or I'll prosecute
My wrongs, even to the utmost of the law,
Which is no less than death.

Owner. I'll answer all,
Old Lionel, both to thy shame and scorn.
This for thy menaces! [*He makes a gesture.*]

Enter the CLOWN.

Clown. [*Aside*] This is the house, but where's the noise that was wont to be in't? I am sent hither to deliver a note to two young gentlemen that here keep revel-rout; I remember it since the last massacre of meat that was made in't; but it seems that the great storm that was raised then is chased now. I have other notes to deliver, one to Master Ricott, and—I shall think on them all in order. My old master makes a great feast for the parting of young Master Geraldine, who is presently upon his departure for travel, and the better to grace it, hath invited many of his neighbours and friends, where will be old Master Geraldine, his son, and I cannot tell how many. But this is strange, the gates shut up at this time o' day; belike they are all drunk and laid to sleep. If they be, I'll wake them, with a murrain! *Knocks.*

Old Lionel. What desperate fellow's this, that ignorant
Of his own danger thunders at these gates?

Clown. Ho, Reignald! Riotous Reignald! Revelling Reignald!

Old Lionel. What madness doth possess thee, honest friend,
To touch that hammer's handle?

Clown. What madness doth possess thee, honest friend,
To ask me such a question?

Old Lionel. Nay, stir not yòu.

Owner. Not I; the game begins.

Old Lionel. How dost thou? Art thou well?

Clown. Yes, very well, I thank you. How do you, sir?

Old Lionel. No alteration? What change about thee?

Clown. Not so much change about me at this time as to change you a shilling into two testers.

Old Lionel. Yet I advise thee, fellow, for thy good,
Stand further from the gate.

Clown. And I advise thee, friend, for thine own good, stand not betwixt me and the gate, but give me leave to deliver my errand. Ho, Reignald, you mad rascal!

Old Lionel. In vain thou thunder'st at these silent doors
Where no man dwells to answer, saving ghosts,
Furies and sprites.

25. *with a murrain*] a plague on them.

Clown. Ghosts! Indeed, there has been much walking in and about the house after midnight.

Old Lionel. Strange noise oft heard?

Clown. Yes, terrible noise, that none of the neighbours could take any rest for it; I have heard it myself.

Old Lionel. You hear this? Here's more witness.

Owner. Very well, sir.

Old Lionel. Which you shall dearly answer. Whooping?

Clown. And hallooing.

Old Lionel. And shouting?

Clown. And crying out, till the whole house rung again.

Old Lionel. Which thou hast heard?

Clown. Oftener than I have toes and fingers.

Old Lionel. Thou wilt be deposed of this?

Clown. I'll be sworn to't, and that's as good.

Old Lionel. Very good still. [*To Owner*] Yet you are innocent?
[*To Clown*] Shall I entreat thee, friend, to avouch as much
Hereby, to the next justice?

Clown. I'll take my soldier's oath on't.

Old Lionel. A soldier's oath, what's that?

Clown. My corporal oath. And you know, sir, a corporal is an office belonging to a soldier.

Old Lionel. [*To Owner*] Yet you are clear? Murder will come to light.

Owner. So will your gullery, too.

Enter ROBIN, *the old serving-man.*

Robin. [*Aside*] They say my old master's come home. I'll see if he will turn me out of doors as the young man has done. I have laid rods in piss for somebody, 'scape Reignald as he can; and with more freedom than I durst late, I boldly now dare knock.

Robin knocks.

Old Lionel. More madmen yet. I think, since my last voyage,
Half of the world's turned frantic. [*To Robin*] What dost mean?
Or long'st thou to be blasted?

Robin. O sir, you are welcome home; 'twas time to come
Ere all was gone to havoc.

Old Lionel. My old servant?
Before I shall demand of further business,
Resolve me why thou thunder'st at these doors
Where thou know'st none inhabits?

Robin. Are they gone, sir?
'Twas well yet they have left the house behind,
For all the furniture, to a bare bench,

73. durst] *Di*; dust *Q*.

---

68. *gullery*] deception.
71–2. *laid . . . piss*] proverbial (R157), for keeping a punishment in store.

I am sure is spent and wasted.
Old Lionel. Where's my son,
That Reignald, posting for him with such speed,
Brings him not from the country?
Robin. Country, sir?
'Tis a thing they know not. Here they feast,
Dice, drink and drab. The company they keep,
Cheaters and roaring lads, and these attended
By bawds and queans. Your son hath got a strumpet
On whom he spends all that your sparing left,
And here they keep court, to whose damned abuses
Reignald gives all encouragement.
Old Lionel. But stay, stay;
No living soul hath for these six months' space
Here entered, but the house stood desolate.
Robin. Last week I am sure, so late, and th'other day,
Such revels were here kept.
Old Lionel. And by my son?
Robin. Yes, and his servant Reignald.
Old Lionel. And this house
At all not haunted?
Robin. Save, sir, with such sprites.
Owner. This murder will come out.

Enter Master RICOTT.

Old Lionel. But see, in happy time here comes my neighbour
Of whom he bought this mansion. He, I am sure,
More amply can resolve me. I pray, sir,
What sums of moneys have you late received
Of my young son?
Ricott. Of him? None, I assure you.
Old Lionel. What of my servant Reignald?
Ricott. But devise
What to call less than nothing, and that sum
I will confess received.
Old Lionel. Pray sir, be serious.
I do confess myself indebted to you
A hundred pound.
Ricott. You may do well to pay't then, for here's witness
Sufficient of your words.
Old Lionel. I speak no more
Than what I purpose; just so much I owe you,
And ere I sleep will tender.
Ricott. I shall be
As ready to receive it, and as willing
As you can be to pay't.
Old Lionel. But provided
You will confess seven hundred pounds received
Beforehand of my son.
Ricott. But by your favour,

Why should I yield seven hundred pounds received
Of them I never dealt with? Why? For what?
What reason? What condition? Where or when
Should such a sum be paid me?

Old Lionel. Why? For this bargain. And for what? This house.
Reason? Because you sold it. The conditions? Such
As were agreed between you. Where and when?
That only hath escaped me.

Ricott. Madness, all.

Old Lionel. Was I not brought to take free view thereof
As of mine own possession?

Ricott. I confess
Your servant told me you had found out a wife
Fit for your son, and that you meant to build,
Desired to take a friendly view of mine
To make it your example. But for selling,
I tell you, sir, my wants be not so great
To change my house to coin.

Old Lionel. Spare, sir, your anger
And turn it into pity. Neighbours and friends,
I am quite lost. Was never man so fooled,
And by a wicked servant. Shame and blushing
Will not permit to tell the manner how,
Lest I be made ridiculous to all.
My fears are, to inherit what's yet left
He hath made my son away.

Robin. That's my fear, too.

Old Lionel. Friends, as you would commiserate a man
Deprived at once both of his wealth and son,
And in his age, by one I ever tendered
More like a son than servant, by imagining
My case were yours, have feeling of my griefs
And help to apprehend him. Furnish me
With cords and fetters; I will lay him safe
In prison within prison.

Ricott. We'll assist you.

Robin. And I.

Clown. And all. [*Aside*] But not to do the least hurt to my old friend
Reignald.

Old Lionel. His legs will be as nimble as his brain,
And 'twill be difficult to seize the slave,
Yet your endeavours, pray. Peace, here he comes.

Enter REIGNALD *with a horn in his pocket;*
they withdraw behind the arras.

119. hundred pounds] *Di*; hundred *Q*.

---

141. *made . . . away*] put to death.
155.2. arras] curtain.

Reignald. My heart misgives, for 'tis not possible
But that in all these windings and indents
I shall be found at last. I'll take that course
That men both troubled and affrighted do:
Heap doubt on doubt, and as combustions rise
Try if from many I can make my peace
And work mine own atonement.
Old Lionel. Stand you close,
Be not yet seen, but at your best advantage
Hand him and bind him fast, whilst I dissemble
As if I yet knew nothing. [*He comes forward.*]
Reignald. [*Aside*] I suspect,
And find there's trouble in my master's looks;
Therefore I must not trust myself too far
Within his fingers.
Old Lionel. Reignald?
Reignald. Worshipful sir.
Old Lionel. What says my son i'the country?
Reignald. That tomorrow
Early i'the morning he'll attend your pleasure
And do as all such duteous children ought:
Demand your blessing, sir.
Old Lionel. Well; 'tis well.
Reignald. [*Aside*] I do not like his countenance.
Old Lionel. But Reignald, I suspect the honesty
And the good meaning of my neighbour here,
Old Master Ricott. Meeting him but now,
And having some discourse about the house,
He makes all strange, and tells me in plain terms
He knows of no such matter—
Reignald. Tell me that, sir?
Old Lionel. I tell thee as it is—nor that such moneys,
Took up at use, were ever tendered him
On any such conditions.
Reignald. I cannot blame
Your worship to be pleasant, knowing at what
An under-rate we bought it; but you ever
Were a most merry gentleman.
Old Lionel. [*Aside*] Impudent slave!
[*To him*] But Reignald, he not only doth deny it
But offers to depose himself and servants
No such thing ever was.
Reignald. Now, heaven to see
To what this world's grown to. I will make him—
Old Lionel. Nay more, this man will not confess the murder.

185. s.d. *Old Lionel.*] *Di*; *Y. Lio. Q* (*catchword Old Lio.*).

157. *indents*] irregularities (as in a coastline).
181. *Took . . . use*] borrowed on interest.

Reignald. Which both shall dearly answer; you have warrant
For him already. But for the other sir,
If he deny it, he had better—
Old Lionel. (*Softly.*) Appear, gentlemen,
'Tis a fit time to take him.
Reignald. [*Aside*] I discover
The ambush that's laid for me.
Old Lionel. Come nearer, Reignald.
Reignald. First, sir, resolve me
One thing: amongst other merchandise
Bought in your absence by your son and me
We engrossed a great commodity of combs;
And how many sorts, think you?
Old Lionel. You might buy
Some of the bones of fishes, some of beasts,
Box combs, and ivory combs.
Reignald. But besides these, we have for horses, sir,
Mane-combs and curry-combs. Now sir, for men
We have head-combs, beard-combs; ay, and coxcombs, too;
Take view of them at your pleasure, whilst for my part
I thus bestow myself.

They all appear with cords and shackles, whilst he gets up.

Clown. Well said, Reignald; nobly put off, Reignald; look to thyself, Reignald.
Old Lionel. Why dost thou climb thus?
Reignald. Only to practise
The nimbleness of my arms and legs
Ere they prove your cords and fetters.
Old Lionel. Why to that place?
Reignald. Why? Because, sir, 'tis your own house;
It hath been my harbour long, and now it must be
My sanctuary; dispute now, and I'll answer.
Owner. Villain, what devilish meaning hadst thou in't
To challenge me of murder?
Reignald. O sir, the man you killed is alive
At this present to justify it: 'I am', quoth he,
'A transmarine by birth'—
Ricott. Why challenge me
Receipt of moneys, and to give abroad
That I had sold my house?
Reignald. Why? Because, sir,
Could I have purchased houses at that rate
I had meant to have bought all London.

192. other sir,] *Q*; other, sir, *Di.*

---

198. *engrossed*] bought up.
202. *box combs*] presumably combs made from boxwood.
204. *curry-combs*] metal combs used in grooming horses.
207.1. gets up] climbs to the upper acting level.
212. *prove*] test.

Clown. Yes, and Middlesex, too, and I would have been thy half, Reignald.
Old Lionel. Yours are great,
My wrongs insufferable: as, first, to fright me
From mine own dwelling till they had consumed
The whole remainder of the little left;
Besides, out of my late stock got at sea
Discharge the clamorous usurer; make me accuse
This man of murder; be at charge of warrants;
And challenging this my worthy neighbour of
Forswearing sums he never yet received;
Fool me to think my son that had spent all
Had by his thrift bought land; ay, and him too
To open all the secrets of his house
To me, a stranger. O, thou insolent villain,
What to all these canst answer?
Reignald. Guilty, guilty.
Old Lionel. But to my son's death, what, thou slave?
Reignald. Not guilty.
Old Lionel. Produce him, then. I'the meantime—and—
Honest friends, get ladders.
Reignald. Yes, and come down
In your own ropes.
Owner. I'll fetch a piece and shoot him.
Reignald. So the warrant in my master's pocket
Will serve for my murder, and ever after
Shall my ghost haunt this house.
Clown. And I will say like Reignald, 'This ghost and I am friends.'
Old Lionel. Bring faggots; I'll set fire upon the house
Rather than this endure.
Reignald. To burn houses is felony, and I'll not out
Till I be fired out. But since I am besieged thus,
I'll summon supplies unto my rescue.

He winds a horn. Enter YOUNG LIONEL, RIOTER, *two gallants,* BLANDA *and others.*

Young Lionel. Before you chide, first hear me. Next, your blessing
That on my knees I beg. I have but done
Like mis-spent youth, which, after wit dear bought,
Turns his eyes inward, sorry and ashamed.
These things in which I have offended most
Had I not proved, I should have thought them still
Essential things, delights perdurable,
Which now I find mere shadows, toys and dreams,
Now hated more than erst I doted on.

245–6. *come . . . ropes*] ?be hanged in your own nooses.
254. *fired out*] (like the fox that Reignald's name suggests).
261. *proved*] tried.
262. *perdurable*] lasting.

Best natures are soonest wrought on; such was mine.
As I the offences, so the offenders throw
Here at your feet, to punish as you please. [*He kneels.*]
You have but paid so much as I have wasted
To purchase to yourself a thrifty son
Which I from henceforth vow.

Old Lionel. See what fathers are,
That can three years' offences, foul ones too,
Thus in a minute pardon, and thy faults
Upon myself chastise in these my tears.
Ere this submission I had cast thee off;
Rise in my new adoption. But for these—

Clown. The one you have nothing to do withal; here's his ticket for his discharge. [*Gives out letters.*] Another for you, sir, to summon you to my master's feast; for you, and you, where I charge you all to appear, upon his displeasure and your own apperils.

Young Lionel. This is my friend; the other one I loved.
Only because they have been dear to him
That now will strive to be more dear to you
Vouchsafe their pardon.

Old Lionel. All dear to me, indeed,
For I have paid for't soundly; yet for thy sake
I am atoned with all. Only that wanton,
Her and her company abandon quite;
So doing, we are friends.

Young Lionel. A just condition, and willingly subscribed to.

Old Lionel. But for that villain, I am now devising
What shame, what punishment remarkable
To inflict on him.

Reignald. Why, master, have I laboured,
Plotted, contrived, and all this while for you,
And will you leave me to the whip and stocks,
Not mediate my peace?

Old Lionel. Sirrah, come down.

Reignald. Not till my pardon's sealed; I'll rather stand here
Like a statue in the forefront of your house
For ever, like the picture of Dame Fortune
Before the Fortune playhouse.

Young Lionel. If I have here
But any friend amongst you, join with me
In this petition.

265. soonest] *Q*; soon'st *V*.

---

265. *best . . . wrought on*] ?proverbial (cf. H304: 'A gentle heart is tied with an easy thread'). Young Lionel's self-characterisation here may seem optimistic; it might be classed with his other moment of sensitivity, at I.ii.260–1, after his description (92–129) of the dangers of youth.

279. *apperils*] risks.

297. *picture*] effigy, either on the old Fortune, burned in December 1621, or on the new, rebuilt in 1623 (Chambers, II, 442–3).

Clown. Good sir, for my sake! I resolved you truly concerning whooping, the noise, the walking, and the sprites, and for a need can show you a ticket for him, too.

Owner. I impute my wrongs rather to knavish cunning
Than least pretended malice.

Ricott. What he did
Was but for his young master; I allow it
Rather as sports of wit than injuries;
No other, pray, esteem them.

Old Lionel. Even as freely
As you forget my quarrels made with you,
Raised from the errors first begot by him,
I here remit all free. I now am calm,
But had I seized upon him in my spleen—

Reignald. I knew that; therefore this was my invention,
For policy's the art still of prevention.

Clown. Come down, then, Reignald, first on your hands and feet, and then on your knees to your master. Now gentlemen, what do you say to your inviting to my master's feast?

Ricott. We will attend him.

Old Lionel. Nor do I love to break good company,
For Master Wincott is my worthy friend
And old acquaintance.

Enter REIGNALD [*after descending*].

O thou crafty wag-string,
And couldst thou thus delude me? But we are friends.
Nor, gentlemen, let not what's hereto passed
In your least thoughts disable my estate:
This my last voyage hath made all things good,
With surplus, too; be that your comfort, son.
Well, Reignald—but no more.

Reignald. I was the fox,
But I from henceforth will no more the cox-
Comb put upon your pate.

Old Lionel. Let's walk, gentlemen. *Exeunt omnes.*

324. passed] *this ed.*; past Q.

314. *policy*] diplomacy; the sentence is proverbial (P548).
321. *wag-string*] person destined to be hanged.

ACT V

SCENE i

Enter OLD GERALDINE *and* YOUNG GERALDINE.

Old Geraldine. Son, let me tell you, you are ill advised
And doubly to be blamed, by undertaking
Unnecessary travel, grounding no reason
For such a rash and giddy enterprise.
What profit aim you at you have not reaped?
What novelty affords the Christian world
Of which your view hath not participated
In a full measure? Can you either better
Your language or experience? Your self-will
Hath only purpose to deprive a father
Of a loved son, and many noble friends
Of your much wished acquaintance.
Young Geraldine. O, dear sir,
Do not, I do entreat you, now repent you
Of your free grant, which with such care and study
I have so long, so often, laboured for.
Old Geraldine. Say that may be dispensed with, show me reason
Why you desire to steal out of your country
Like some malefactor that had forfeited
His life and freedom. Here's a worthy gentleman
Hath for your sake invited many guests
To his great charge, only to take of you
A parting leave. You send him word you cannot,
After, you may not come. Had not my urgence,
Almost compulsion, driven you to his house,
Th'unkindness might have forfeited your love
And rased you from his will, in which he hath given you
A fair and large estate; yet you of all this strangeness
Show no sufficient ground.
Young Geraldine. Then understand,
The ground thereof took his first birth from you;
'Twas you first charged me to forbear the house,
And that upon your blessing. Let it not then
Offend you, sir, if I so great a charge
Have strived to keep so strictly.
Old Geraldine. Me perhaps

23. *urgence*] insistence (most early citations in *OED* of this form are from Heywood).
26. *rased*] removed, erased.
26, 27] Both lines are extrametrical, and suggest extremely hasty writing.

You may appease, and with small difficulty
Because a father; but how satisfy
Their dear, and on your part unmerited, love?
But this your last obedience may salve all.
We now grow near the house.

Young Geraldine. [*Aside*] Whose doors to me
Appear as horrid as the gates of hell.
Where shall I borrow patience, or from whence,
To give a meeting to this viperous brood
Of friend and mistress?

Enter WINCOTT, [*his*] WIFE, RICOTT, *the two* LIONELS, [*the*] Owner, DALAVILL, PRUDENTILLA, REIGNALD *and* RIOTER.

Wincott. You've entertained me with a strange discourse
Of your man's knavish wit, but I rejoice
That in your safe return all ends so well.
Most welcome you, and you, and indeed all,
To whom I am bound that at so short a warning
Thus friendly you will deign to visit me.

Old Lionel. It seems my absence hath begot some sport,
Thank my kind servant here.

Reignald. Not so much worth, sir.

Old Lionel. But though their riots tripped at my estate
They have not quite o'erthrown it.

Wincott. But see, gentlemen,
These whom we most expected come at length.
This I proclaim the master of the feast,
In which, to express the bounty of my love,
I'll show myself no niggard.

Young Geraldine. Your choice favours
I still taste in abundance.

Wife. Methinks it would not misbecome me, sir,
To chide your absence, that have made yourself
To us so long a stranger.

He turns away sad, as not being minded.

Young Geraldine. Pardon me, sir,
That have not yet, since your return from sea,
Voted the least fit opportunity
To entertain you with a kind salute.

62. Voted] Q; Noted *conj. Da.*

40. *Where . . . from whence*] The terms are redundant; if deliberate, they may indicate Young Geraldine's distraction; or Heywood may have intended 'from whom' in the second instance.

41. *viperous*] Young Geraldine portrays himself as Adam, cast out of Eden by the serpent (cf. l. 125) and Eve (l. 122).

51–2. *tripped at . . . overthrown*] (the metaphors are from wrestling).

59.1. minded] well-disposed, friendly.

62. *Voted*] devoted.

Old Lionel. Most kindly, sir, I thank you.
Dalavill. Methinks, friend,
You should expect green rushes to be strowed
After such discontinuance.
Young Geraldine. Mistress Pru,
I have not seen you long, but greet you thus:
May you be lady of a better husband
Than I expect a wife.
Wincott. I like that greeting.
Nay, enter, gentlemen. Dinner perhaps
Is not yet ready, but the time we stay
We'll find some fresh discourse to spend away.
Exeunt. Manet DALAVILL.
Dalavill. Not speak to me, nor once vouchsafe an answer,
But slight me with a poor and base neglect?
No, nor so much as cast an eye on her,
Or least regard, though in a seeming show
She courted a reply? 'Twixt him and her,
Nay, him and me, this was not wont to be.
If she have brain to apprehend as much
As I have done, she'll quickly find it out.

Enter YOUNG GERALDINE *and* WIFE.

Now, as I live, as our affections meet,
So our conceits, and she hath singled him
To some such purpose. I'll retire myself,
Not interrupt their conference. *Exit.*
Wife. You are sad, sir.
Young Geraldine. I know no cause.
Wife. Then can I show you some:
Who could be otherways, to leave a father
So careful, and each way so provident?
To leave so many and such worthy friends?
To abandon your own country? These are some,
Nor do I think you can be much the merrier
For my sake.
Young Geraldine. Now your tongue speaks oracles,
For all the rest are nothing; 'tis for you,
Only for you, I cannot.
Wife. So I thought.
Why, then, have you been all this while so strange?
Why will you travel, suing a divorce
Betwixt us of a love inseparable?

---

65. *green rushes*] fresh floor covering, especially to welcome newcomers; proverbial (R213).

73. *not speak ... answer*] cf. *How a Man* 230: 'Not speak to me, nor once looke towards me?'

92. *tongue ... oracles*] proverbial (O74) for speaking ambiguously, but with truth.

94. *cannot*] (i.e., be merrier).

For here shall I be left as desolate
Unto a frozen, almost widowed bed,
Warmed only in that future stored in you,
For who can in your absence comfort me?

Young Geraldine. [*Aside*] Shall my oppressèd sufferance yet break forth
Into impatience, or endure her more?

Wife. But since by no persuasion, no entreats,
Your settled obstinacy can be swayed,
Though you seem desperate of your own dear life,
Have care of mine, for it exists in you.
O sir, should you miscarry I were lost,
Lost and forsaken. Then, by our past vows
And by this hand once given me, by these tears
Which are but springs begetting greater floods,
I do beseech thee, my dear Geraldine,
Look to thy safety and preserve thy health;
Have care into what company you fall;
Travel not late, and cross no dangerous seas;
For till heavens bless me in thy safe return
How will this poor heart suffer!

Young Geraldine. [*Aside*] I had thought
Long since the Sirens had been all destroyed;
But one of them I find survives in her;
She almost makes me question what I know,
An heretic unto my own belief.
O, thou mankind's seducer.

Wife. What, no answer?

Young Geraldine. Yes, thou hast spoke to me in showers; I will
Reply in thunder: thou adulteress,
That hast more poison in thee than the serpent
Who was the first that did corrupt thy sex,
The devil!

Wife. To whom speaks the man?

Young Geraldine. To thee,
Falsest of all that ever man termed fair.
Hath impudence so steeled thy smooth soft skin
It cannot blush? Or sin so obdured thy heart
It doth not quake and tremble? Search thy conscience;
There thou shalt find a thousand clamorous tongues
To speak as loud as mine doth.

Wife. Save from yours,
I hear no noise at all.

Young Geraldine. I'll play the doctor
To open thy deaf ears: Monday the ninth
Of the last month; canst thou remember that?

---

118. *Sirens*] The 'dangerous seas' of l. 115 give rise to this image of the charmers who tempted Odysseus with their song.

123–4. *showers . . . thunder*] Cf. the proverb T275: 'After thunder comes rain.'

That night, more black in thy abhorrèd sin
Than in the gloomy darkness. That the time.
Wife. Monday?
Young Geraldine. Wouldst thou the place know? Thy polluted
chamber,
So often witness of my sinless vows.
Wouldst thou the person? One not worthy name,
Yet to torment thy guilty soul the more
I'll tell him thee: that monster Dalavill.
Wouldst thou your bawd know? Midnight; that the hour.
The very words thou spake? 'Now what would Geraldine
Say if he saw us here?' To which was answered,
'Tush, he's a coxcomb, fit to be so fooled.'
No blush? What, no faint fever on thee yet?
How hath thy black sins changed thee! Thou Medusa.
Those hairs that late appeared like golden wires
Now crawl with snakes and adders. Thou art ugly.
Wife. And yet my glass till now ne'er told me so.
Who gave you this intelligence?
Young Geraldine. Only he
That, pitying such an innocency as mine
Should by two such delinquents be betrayed,
He brought me to that place by miracle
And made me an ear-witness of all this.
Wife. I am undone.
Young Geraldine. But think what thou hast lost
To forfeit me. Ay, notwithstanding these
(So fixed was my love and unalterable)
I kept this from thy husband, nay, all ears,
With thy transgressions smothering mine own wrongs
In hope of thy repentance.
Wife. Which begins
Thus low upon my knees.
Young Geraldine. Tush, bow to heaven,
Which thou hast most offended. I, alas,
Save in such scarce unheard-of treachery,
Most sinful like thyself. Wherein, O wherein,
Hath my unspotted and unbounded love deserved
The least of these? Sworn to be made a stale
For term of life, and all this for my goodness?
Die, and die soon; acquit me of my oath,
But prithee, die repentant. Farewell ever;

161. unalterable)] *V*; vnutterable) *Q*.

145. *bawd . . . Midnight*] proverbial (O70); cf. Shakespeare's 'night, desire's foul nurse' (*Venus & Adonis* 773), and 'Mother Midnight', *WWH* V.vi.214 note.

150. *Medusa*] One of the Gorgons, whose beautiful hair was changed by the jealous Athene into serpents.

170. *stale*] decoy, or laughing-stock.

'Tis thou, and only thou, hast banished me
Both from my friends and country.
Wife. O, I am lost. *Sinks down.*

Enter DALAVILL *meeting* YOUNG GERALDINE *going out.*

Dalavill. Why, how now, what's the business?
Young Geraldine. Go take her up whom thou hast oft thrown down,
Villain! [*Exit.*]
Dalavill. [*Aside*] That was no language from a friend,
It had too harsh an accent. But how's this,
My mistress thus low cast upon the earth,
Gravelling and breathless? Mistress, Lady, sweet—
Wife. O tell me if thy name be Geraldine;
Thy very looks will kill me!
Dalavill. View me well,
I am no such man; see, I am Dalavill.
Wife. Th'art then a devil, that presents before me
My horrid sins, persuades me to despair,
When he, like a good angel sent from heaven,
Besought me of repentance. Swell, sick heart,
Even till thou burst the ribs that bound thee in.
So, there's one string cracked. Flow, and flow high,
Even till thy blood distil out of mine eyes
To witness my great sorrow.
Dalavill. Faint again!
[*Calls*] Some help within there! No attendant near?
Thus to expire! In this I am more wretched
Than all the sweet fruition of her love
Before could make me happy.

Enter WINCOTT, OLD GERALDINE, YOUNG GERALDINE, *the two* LIONELS, RICOTT, [*the*] Owner, PRUDENTILLA, REIGNALD [*and the*] CLOWN.

Wincott. What was he
Clamoured so loud, to mingle with our mirth
This terror and affright?
Dalavill. See, sir, your wife
In these my arms expiring.
Wincott. How?
Prudentilla. My sister!
Wincott. Support her, and by all means possible
Provide for her dear safety.
Old Geraldine. See, she recovers.
Wincott. Woman, look up.
Wife. O sir, your pardon.
Convey me to my chamber; I am sick,

---

181. *Gravelling*] choked, stifled.
190. *string*] heart-string (but with a hint of the Fates' thread of life).

Sick even to death. [*To Dalavill*] Away, thou sycophant,
Out of my sight! I have, besides thyself,
Too many sins about me.
Clown. My sweet mistress.
[PRUDENTILLA *and* CLOWN *take* WIFE *away*.]
Dalavill. The storm's coming, I must provide for harbour. *Exit.*
Old Lionel. What strange and sudden alteration's this?
How quickly is this clear day overcast.
But such and so uncertain are all things
That dwell beneath the moon.
Young Lionel. A woman's qualm,
Frailties that are inherent to her sex,
Soon sick, and soon recovered.
Wincott. If she misfare
I am a man more wretched in her loss
Than had I forfeited life and estate,
She was so good a creature.
Old Geraldine. I the like
Suffered when I my wife brought unto her grave.
So you, when you were first a widower;
Come, arm yourself with patience.
Ricott. These are casualties
That are not new, but common.
Reignald. [*Aside*] Burying of wives—
As stale as shifting shirts—or for some servants
To flout and gull their masters.
Owner. Best to send
And see how her fit holds her.

Enter PRUDENTILLA *and* CLOWN [*with a letter*].

Prudentilla. Sir, my sister
In these few lines commends her last to you,
For she is now no more. What's therein writ
Save heaven and you, none knows. This she desired
You would take view of, and with these words expired.
Wincott. Dead?
Young Geraldine. [*Aside*] She hath made me then a free release
Of all the debts I owed her.
Wincott. [*Aside, reading*] 'My fear is, beyond pardon Dalavill
Hath played the villain, but for Geraldine,
He hath been each way noble. Love him still.
My peace already I have made with heaven;
O, be not you at war with me; my honour

210–11. *uncertain . . . moon*] proverbial (M111).
221. *shifting*] changing.
222. *gull*] deceive.
230. *beyond pardon*] Mistress Wincott clears her conscience by her confession in this letter (see ll. 234, 237–40, confirmed in l. 244). She still fears for Dalavill's unconfessed soul.

Is in your hands, to punish or preserve.
I am now confessed, and only Geraldine
Hath wrought on me this unexpected good.
The ink I write with, I wish had been my blood
To witness my repentance.' Dalavill!
Where's he? Go, seek him out.
Clown. I shall, I shall, sir. *Exit.*
Wincott. [*Aside*] The wills of dead folk should be still obeyed;
However false to me, I'll not reveal't.
Where heaven forgives, I pardon. [*To them*] Gentlemen,
I know you all commiserate my loss;
I little thought this feast should have been turned
Into a funeral.

Enter CLOWN.

What's the news of him?

Clown. He went presently to the stable, put the saddle upon his horse, put his foot into the stirrup, clapped his spurs into his sides, and away he's galloped as if he were to ride a race for a wager.

Wincott. All our ill lucks go with him. Farewell he,
But all my best of wishes wait on you
As my chief friend. This meeting that was made
Only to take of you a parting leave
Shall now be made a marriage of our love
Which none save only death shall separate.
Young Geraldine. It calls me from all travel, and from henceforth
With my country I am friends.
Wincott. The lands that I have left
You lend me for the short space of my life;
As soon as heaven calls me, they call you lord.
First feast, and after mourn; we'll, like some gallants
That bury thrifty fathers, think't no sin
To wear blacks without, but other thoughts within.
Exeunt omnes.

FINIS

---

242. *wills . . . obeyed*] proverbial (cf. M514).
250. *as . . . wager*] See Introduction for echo of *WKK*.
261–3. *gallants . . . within*] Cf. the proverbs F84, 'The father to the bough, the son to the plough' and F91, 'A sparing father and a spending son'.

Actus primus. Scena pra.

Enter wth Raphael a younge marchant mr Treadway his companion and a factor.

Raphael. You talke to one thats deafe I am resolvd

Treadway. I knowe you are but off that strange [illegible]

[illegible] but you will list to reason

Raphael. Alls but reason.

Treadway. [illegible]

Raphael. And [illegible] to [illegible]

Treadway. no consequent. ~~[illegible]~~

to thinke to follow [illegible]

[illegible]

[illegible]

that vanish in smoke. [illegible]

with all the ~~[illegible]~~ Oceans water cannot wash

the blacknes [illegible]

[illegible]

and the blackest [illegible]

and women [illegible]

[illegible] his destroyer,

[illegible]

Raphael. [illegible]

[illegible]

[illegible]

[illegible]

[illegible]

[illegible]

[illegible]

[illegible]

[illegible]

[illegible]

[illegible]

Tread. [illegible]

[illegible]

Raphael. I knewe it [illegible]

Treadway. [illegible]

[illegible]

and [illegible]

Raphael. [illegible] could not [illegible]

but that [illegible]

[illegible]

[illegible]

[illegible]

[illegible]

[illegible]

[illegible]

[illegible]

Treadway. [illegible]

Raphael. [illegible]

[illegible]

[illegible]

[illegible]

[illegible]

[illegible]

Treadway. [illegible]

Raphael. [illegible]

[illegible]

[illegible]

[illegible]

[illegible]

Treadway. Call itt so

and to dispose [illegible]

provided still that [illegible]

Raphael. I cannott but commende your charity

and to [illegible]

[illegible]

Enter the Clowne

[illegible]

THE CAPTIVES
OR
THE LOST RECOVERED

[DRAMATIS PERSONAE

Master RAPHAEL, *a young merchant.*
Master TREADWAY, *his companion.*
The CLOWN, *named Jaques, servant to Raphael.*
MILDEW, *a bawd.*
SARLABOIS, *his guest and friend.*
An ABBOT.
FRIAR JOHN.
FRIAR RICHARD.
Master John ASHBURN, *an English merchant.*
GODFREY, *his man.*
PALESTRA, *the lost daughter, Mirabel, of John Ashburn.*
SCRIBONIA, *the lost daughter, Winifred, of Thomas Ashburn.*
LORD D'AVERNE.
LADY D'AVERNE.
DENNIS, *Lord D'Averne's servant.*
Millicent, *Lady D'Averne's waiting maid.*
Two Fishermen, *one of them named* Gripus.

DRAMATIS PERSONAE] Based on *J* and *Br*; not in *MS*.

---

11. *Palestra*] name of the same character (Palaestra) in *Rudens*. Meaning 'wrestling-school', its humour may have appealed to Heywood.

14. *D'Averne*] In Masuccio, 'd'Angiaja'. To find a southern French equivalent for this Castilian nobleman, Heywood perhaps went no further than his 'witch of Averne' (Auvergne) in *Gun.*, p. 416.

17. *Gripus*] name of the same character in *Rudens*. (The other names in *Rud.* correspond as follows: Sceparnio/Godfrey; Plesidippus/Raphael; Daemones/John Ashburn; Ampelisca/Scribonia; Ptolemocratia/the Abbot; Trachalio/the Clown; Labrax/Mildew; Charmides/Sarlabois. Heywood's additions to Plautus are Treadway, Isabel, Thomas Ashburn and his Factor. These new characters develop the theme of family connexions, and double the recognitions and marriages in Acts IV and V.)

ISABEL, *John Ashburn's wife.*
THOMAS ASHBURN, *a merchant, younger brother to John Ashburn.*
A Factor *to Thomas Ashburn.*
A Baker.
A Shrieve.
Friars, Servants, Country Fellows, Officers.]

In this collation angle brackets indicate the loss of letters, and sometimes words, as a result of damage to the MS.

ACT I

SCENE i

Enter Master RAPHAEL, *a young merchant,* Master TREADWAY,
his companion and friend [*and others*].

Raphael. You talk to one that's deaf; I am resolved.
Treadway. I know you are not of that stupid sense
But you will list to reason.
Raphael. All's but vain.
Treadway. You say she's fair.
Raphael. And therefore to be loved.
Treadway. No consequent.
Although her person may perhaps content,
Consider but the place.
Raphael. I know it bad,
Nay, worst of ills.
Treadway. A house of prostitution
And common brothelry.
Raphael. Which could not stand
But that her virtue guards it and protects it
From blastings and heaven's thunder. There she lives
Like to a rich and precious jewel lost
Found shining on a dunghill, yet the gem
No way disparaged of his former worth
Nor bated of his glory. Out of this fire
Of lust and black temptation she's returned
Like gold repured and tried.
Treadway. Of what birth is she?
Raphael. Unknown to me or any, she protests—
Nay, to herself. What need I question that?
Sure, such sweet feature, goodness, modesty,
Such gentleness, such virtue, cannot be
Derived from base and obscure parentage.

0.2. *friend, and others.*] *this ed.*; ffrend. Etc. *MS.* 11. lives] *Bu*; lyv< *MS.*

An expansion of ll. 41–56 of the Prologue spoken by Arcturus (the storm-constellation Bootes) in *Rud.*

1. *talk . . . deaf*] proverbial (T51) for failing to convince another.

5. *consequent*] consequence. (See *App.* for text cut in *MS.*)

12. *jewel . . . dunghill*] ?proverbial (cf. 'turn up a pearl out of a dunghill', in Nashe, *Terrors of the Night*, from *The Unfortunate Traveller*, ed. J. B. Steane, Harmondsworth, 1972, p. 215).

15. *bated of*] reduced in.

17. *repured and tried*] much refined.

Treadway. What's then your end and purpose?
Raphael. To redeem her
Out of this jail of sin and leprosy,
This mart of all diseases, where she lives
Still under the command and tyranny
Of a most base he-bawd; about which business
We have already trafficked.
Treadway. Well, if so,
And to dispose her elsewhere to her good,
Provided still that virtue be your aim,
I cannot but commend your charity,
And, to my power, I'll seek to further it.
Raphael. You so entire me to you. [*Calls*] Within there!

Enter the CLOWN.

Clown. 'Within there' is now without here. Your worship's pleasure?
Raphael. Hie to the next quay and enquire for one
Called Signor Mildew, and resolve him from me
That I have kept appointment, the sum's ready,
And present to be tendered.
Clown. Who? The Neapolitan Signor, the man-mackerel and merchant of maidens' flesh, that deals altogether in flawed ware and cracked commodities? The bawdy broker, I means, where a man for his dollars may have choice of diseases, and sometimes the pox too, if he will leave behind him a good pawn for it?
Raphael. How thou demurst.
Clown. Myrrh, quoth he? So I may happen to bring it away in my nose. Well, I smell some bawdy business or other in hand. They call this place Marseilles Road, the chief haven town in France; but he keeps a road in his own house, wherein have rid, and been rid, more leaking vessels, more panderly pinks, pimps and punks, more rotten bottoms balanced, more fly-boats laden and unladen

34. 'Within there'] *this ed.*; Within their *Bu;* w< > theire *MS.* 35. the] *Bu*; th< *MS.* 36. Signor] *MS2*; Mounsier *MS1.* 39. Neapolitan Signor] *MS2b*; ffrenshe monsier meane you, *MS1;* Italian Seignor *MS2a.* man-mackerel] *Bu*; man makere< *MS.*

---

33. *entire*] attach (only in Heywood as a verb (*OED*)).

39. *Neapolitan*] (in the first draft, 'French'). *man-mackerel*] pimp.

42. *dollars*] money, from German *thaler*, with a pun on 'dolours', griefs. *OED* notes the same pun in a 1618 citation. *I means*] Heywood characterises the Clown as a colloquial speaker. Cf. another Clown's 'teeths' at *ET* II.i.56.

47. *Road*] sheltered anchorage; also in Shakespeare, a cant term for a prostitute (this usage not in *OED*).

49. *pinks*] fishing boats (?with pun on 'pink', pretty girl).
punks] prostitutes.

50. *bottoms*] ship's hulls (?with a bawdy pun).
balanced] ballasted.
fly-boats] small cargo vessels.

every morning and evening tide, than were able to fill the huge great bay of Portugal. This all, sir? [*Exit.*]

Treadway. And yet, methinks, ere fully you conclude,
You should a little stagger.
Raphael. Speak wherein?
Treadway. For many reasons; I'll allege some few.
Who knows, but this your fair and seeming saint,
Though disposed well, and in her own condition
Of promising goodness, yet living in the seminar
Of all libidinous actions, spectres, sights,
Even in the open market where sin's sold,
Where lust and all uncleanness are commerced
As freely as commodities are vended
Amongst the noblest merchants, who, I say,
So confident that dare presume a virgin
Of such a soft and maiden temperature,
Daily and hourly still solicited
By gallants of all nations, all degrees,
Almost all ages, even from upright youth
To the stooping and decrepit—
Raphael. Hear me now.
Treadway. Two words, and I have done. The place considered,
The baseness of the person under whom
She lives oppressed, a slave of sordid life,
Conditioned with the devil, tempting still,
Sometimes by fair means, then again by force,
To prostitute her for his servile gain,
And next, the dissolute crew with which she's housed,
Each night, each day, persuading both with tongue
And lewd example—all these circumstances
Duly considered, I should doubt at least,
If not presume the worst.
Raphael. O, you have pleased me,
And, in proposing all these difficulties,
Given of her graces ample testimony.
She is that miracle, that only one,
That can do these. Were't common in the sex,
'Twould not appear to me so admirable.

52. This] *MS2;* Is this *MS1.* 58. seminar] *MS;* seminar< *Br*; seminary *Bu, J.* 68. from upright] *MS2*; from the beard (*sc.* beardless) *MS1.* 76. housed] *Bu*; hows< *MS.*

52.] (See *App.* for text cut in *MS.*)
54. *stagger*] hesitate.
58. *seminar*] seminary, training-ground.
59. *spectres*] apparitions.
65. *temperature*] character, temperament.
68. *upright*] erect (bawdy).
73. *conditioned with*] contracted to.

It is for these I love her.
Treadway. You're resolved,
And I'll not stay your purpose.

Enter the CLOWN *with* MILDEW *and* SARLABOIS, *his guest and friend.*

Clown. I have brought this flesh-fly, whom as soon as the butchers' wives saw coming through the shambles, they all of 'em stood with their flaps in their hands, like fans. I demanding the reason, it was answered me again, it was to keep away his infectious breath, lest it should fill their meat with fly-blows.

Raphael. Well met, good Signor Mildew.
Mildew. My return
Of your salutes I cast below your feet.
Sir, I am yours to tread on.
Raphael. You will then
Stand to your former bargain?
Mildew. I were else
Not worthy to be styled what I am termed,
A true venereal broker.
Clown. That's in Italian, a damnable he-bawd.
Mildew. You've such a bargain.
Marseilles nor all France shall yield the like.
'Tis such a dainty piece of purity,
Such a coy thing. For our trade,
She's out at that. Neither promises, rewards,
Example or entreaty, fair, foul means,
Gain present, or the hope of future good,
Can force from her a presence, then much less
A friendly prostitution.
Raphael. Hearst thou this?
Sarlabois. This two years I have guested to his house
And know all this most certain.
Raphael. Witness, too.
Mildew. I do protest she spoils my family,
And rather grown a hindrance to my trade
Than benefit, so that, if not to loss,
I wish that I were cleanly rid of her.
For she hath got a trick to steal my whores,

92. lest *Bu*; leas (*possibly* least) *MS*. 93. Signor] *MS2*; Mr *MS1*. 99. Italian,] *MS2*; ffrenshe *MS1*. 109. *Sarlabois.*] *MS3 subst.*; Mildewe. *MS1*.

86. *stay*] hinder.
90. *flaps*] fly-swatters.
92. *fly-blows*] fly's eggs, maggots.
103.] (See *App.* for text cut in *MS.*)
107. *a presence*] a moment of her company.
108.] (See *App.* for text cut in *MS.*)
111. *family*] household (but cf. 'whores', 115, 'daughter', 121, and *WWH* II.i.104 note).
113. *to loss*] at a loss.

And such as of themselves are impudent
When she but comes in presence she makes blush
As if ashamed of what they late had done
Or are about to do.
Clown. Well said, old sinner.
Raphael. See, here's the sum: three hundred crowns.
Mildew. O, the sum!
Raphael. All current and full weight.
Mildew. I'll fetch my daughter,
That hath no lightness in her; current, too,
As any lass i'the city.
Raphael. Mildew, stay!
Clown. Stay, O thou father of fornication and merchant of nothing but miseries and mischief! Wheel about, thou dungcart of diseases! Sail this way, thou galley-foist of galls and garbage! Dost not hear my master? Stay!
Mildew. Why, did his worship call?
Clown. Didst thou not hear him call, and me cry out upon thee?
Mildew. His pleasure, then?
Raphael. I have bethought me better now, to keep
This business secret, lest it chance to arrive
To th'ears of some of my most noble friends,
And not to make it public, and this honest
Purpose of mine by that means misrated.
Here let her stay till night, beacause I am loath
In th'eye of day to man her through the streets.
Mildew. Good, sir.
Raphael. Now, in the village by, that fronts the sea,
Some half league off, where stands the monastery,
I have bespoke a place to sojourn her.
There I this evening do intend a feast
Where only we and some few private friends
Have purposed to be jovial. To that place
I prithee, with what privacy thou canst,
Conduct her, and so add unto our guests.
Mildew. The place I know, the time is perfect with me.
And for the feast you say you have prepared
I shall provide a stomach.
Raphael. Her casket, and such other necessaries
Included in our bargain, bring along,
Or let her maid do't for thee.
Mildew. I'll not bate her
A ruff, a rag; no pin that's useful to her

---

122. *lightness*] unchastity, with pun on debasement (of coinage); cf. 'current', in the same line.

126. *galley-foist*] ceremonial barge.
galls] poisonous sores.

135. *misrated*] misjudged (first used by Heywood, *OED*).

152. *bate*] remove from.

Will I keep back.
Raphael. To this you are witness, friend.
Treadway. I am, sir.
Mildew. So's my guest.
Raphael. Supper time
You will remember, Mildew?
Mildew. Possible
I should forget to eat of others' cost?
It never was my custom.
Clown. Choke you for't!
Raphael. Come, friend. Methinks I have done a deed this day
Crowns all my better actions, for I have raised
An innocent from the hands of an infidel.
Exeunt [RAPHAEL *and* TREADWAY].

Clown. Farewell, rot. Farewell, murrain. Adieu, Mildew. Farewell till soon. [*Exit.*]

Sarlabois. And do you mean to keep your promise, then,
And do as you have said?
Mildew. Why not, I prithee?
What else canst thou advise me?
Sarlabois. Are not we
Both of a rotten conscience, men deboshed,
Secluded from the company of such
As either are, or else would strive to be,
Reputed honest? Wherefore, then, should we
Keep touch with any that profess themselves
Not to be of our rank?
Mildew. Proceed, good friend;
Thou hast put project in my brain already,
Small time would better fashion.
Sarlabois. What if I
Lay such a plot that you shall gain those crowns,
Those full three hundred, to your proper use,
And of these peevish harlotries at home
Make a much greater market?
Mildew. Marry, sir,
That were a tale worth listening.
Sarlabois. Those crowns
Are all your own, in your possession.
So are the maids. I know you rich besides
In coin and jewels. Here you live despised,
And what's this clime to us of more esteem
Than any foreign region? Whores and bawds
May live in every corner of the world—
We know 'tis full of sinners. This, this day

186. This, this day] *MS1b*; Instantly *MS1a*.

154.] (See *App.* for text cut in *MS.*)
162. *murrain*] pestilence.
176. *proper*] personal.

Let's hire a barque—we dwell upon the haven,
And instantly 'tis done—ship all your goods,
With these she-chattels, put this night to sea.
England, they say, is full of whoremasters;
There will be vent for such commodities.
There strumpet them where they, you say, were born.
Else you in Spain may sell them to the stews.
Venice, or any place of Italy,
They're everywhere good chaffer. If not these,
What say you to Morocco, Fez, Algiers?
Tush, these are wares in all parts vendible,
No matter though to Turk and infidel
So it bring gain and profit.

Mildew. Let me hug thee
For this, dear friend. Hereafter I will style thee
My better genius. Thou hast moneyed me in this,
Nay, landed me, made me thy brain's executor,
And put me in a large possession.
Go, hire a barque.

Sarlabois. I shall.

Mildew. And instantly.

Sarlabois. I shall.

Mildew. Ere night we'll put into a sea
No larger than our full-stretched consciences.
Let me once more embrace thee. *Exeunt.*

ACT I SCENE ii

Enter an ABBOT *with his covent of friars, amongst them* FRIAR JOHN *and* FRIAR RICHARD. [*A chair set for the* ABBOT.]

Abbot. As I have here priority of place,
Both by our patron's favour and your voice,
So give me leave to arbitrate amongst you
Without respect of person.

Friar John. We acknowledge you
Our prince and chief.

Friar Richard. And to your fatherly
And grave advice humbly submit ourselves.

190. whoremasters;] *Bu, MS1b subst.*; marchandyse, *MS1a.* 0.2. *chair*] *indicated MS3, with* Iack: Gibsen *added.*

191. *vent*] a market.
193. *stews*] brothel.
195. *good chaffer*] easily sold.
202. *landed*] bestowed land upon (only in Heywood, *OED*).
205–6. *sea . . . consciences*] Cf. the proverb C599, 'a conscience as large as a shipman's hose'.
0.1. covent] early form of 'convent' (cf. 'coven' and Covent Garden).

Abbot. Know, then, in this small covent, which consists
Only of twelve in number, friars I mean,
And us the abbot, I have found amongst you
Many and gross abuses; yet for the present
I will insist on few. Quarrels, debates,
Whispering, supplantings, private calumnies—
These ought not be in such a brotherhood.
Of these, Friar John, and you, Friar Richard, are
Accused to be most guilty, ever jarring
And opposite to peace.
Friar John. The fault's in him.
Friar Richard. As in all other things, so even in this,
He still is apt to wrong me.
Friar John. He that first gives th'occasion first complains—
It ever was his fashion.
Friar Richard. Never mine—
I appeal to the whole covent.
Abbot. Malice rooted,
I find, is wondrous hard to be suppressed.
But know, where counsel and advice prevail not
(The fairest means that I can work your peace)
I'll take upon me my authority,
And where I find in you the least contempt
I shall severely punish.
Friar John. I submit.
Friar Richard. I yield myself to your grave fatherhood.
Abbot. Consider, sons, this cloistered place of ours
Is but new reared. The founder he still lives—
A soldier once, and eminent in the field,
And after many battles now retired
In peace to live a life contemplative.
'Mongst many other charitable deeds,
Unto religion he hath vowed this house
Next to his own fair mansion, that adjoins,
And parted only by a slender wall.
Who knows but that he, neighbouring us so near,
And having done this unto pious ends,
May carry over us and our behaviours
An austere eye of censure?
Friar John. Fit, therefore,
We should be in our actions cautelous.
Friar Richard. And careful lest we may incur displeasure
Of such a noble patron.
Abbot. Well observed.

31. soldier] *MS1b*; noble *MS1a*.

---

16. *opposite*] contrary.
18. *apt*] quick.
42. *cautelous*] circumspect.

His beauteous lady—
Friar John. A sweet soul indeed—
Friar Richard. [*Aside*] On whom Friar John casts many a leering eye—
I have observed that, too—
Abbot. Both for her outward feature
And for her inward graces excellent
Beyond compare, she likewise is to us
A worthy benefactor.
Friar Richard. 'Tis confessed.
Friar John. Would I might come to be her confessor—
It is a fair sweet lady.
Abbot. Morning and evening
They daily come to matins and to evensong.
Such and so great is their devotion,
That if not crazed or failing in their health
They do not miss us any hour of prayer,
And therefore it behoves us all in general
To set a careful watch upon our deeds,
Lest we, that are professed religious,
Be in the least defective. [FRIAR JOHN *makes faces.*]
Friar Richard. Note Friar John,
How he makes antic-faces, and in scorn
Of this your reverend counsel.
Friar John. I? Alas,
A weakness from my childhood I confess
I ever had and cannot help it now,
To have a troubled countenance. I, make mouths?
This, most observed father, but approves
My innocence and his envy. [FRIAR RICHARD *shakes his fist.*]
Marked you that?
Friar Richard bent his fist and threatened me.
I call all these to witness.
Friar Richard. No such thing.
I have a cramp oft takes me in this hand
And makes me wear clutched fingers, and that passion
Now came upon me. But for menacing him,
It ever was far from me. This but shows
His old inveterate malice, which in charity
I wish might here lie buried. [*Aside*] Sirrah, anon
I'll have you by the ears.
Friar John. [*Aside*] Do, if thou dar'st.
We'll tug't out by the teeth.
Friar Richard. [*Aside*] Meet me in th'orchard
Just after evensong.
Friar John. [*Aside*] I will make short prayers,
Because I'll keep appointment.
Abbot. I am plain

52.] (See *App.* for text cut in *MS.*)
55. *crazed*) infirm.

And brief withal: either betwixt you two
Make friendly reconcilement, and in presence
Of this your brotherhood (for what is 'friar'
But 'frater', and that's 'brother'?) or myself
Out of my power will put you to a penance
Shall make you in one week five fasting days.
Friar John. O, terrible!
Abbot. Or if that will not tame you,
I will complain to the founder of your looseness,
Your riots and disorders, and petition
That you, as sowers of seditions here
And sole disturbers of our common peace,
May be excluded this society,
Banished as common barrators and shut out
To public shame and beggary.
Friar Richard. Horrible!
Friar John. First, then, to show my submiss willingness
And forwardness withal: with as much charity
As any new-reformèd man may do,
I with a zeal and heart new reconciled
Thus humbly beg his love. [*Aside*] You're a rogue, Richard!
Friar Richard. To meet his true
And most unfeigned affection, here in face
And view of this our holy brotherhood,
As if in open court, with this embrace
I here confine all hatred. [*Aside*] John, you're a jacksauce,
I mean a saucy jack.
Friar John. [*Aside*] The orchard?
Friar Richard. [*Aside*] There.
Abbot. Why, this is as it should be, and becomes
A true religious order. Such as are sequestered
And vowed unto a strict monastic life
Ought to put off these gross and profane sins
Most frequent amongst laymen. Unity,
Due conformation and fraternal love,
Devotion, hot zeal and obedience, these
Are virtues that become a cloister best.
Now let's retire unto our orisons,
And pray for our good founders. May they still
Grow to our wish and thrive to their own will.
[*Exeunt all except* FRIAR JOHN.]

97. zeal and heart] *Ms1b subst.*; hart and zeale *MS1a*. 103. jacksauce] *Bu*; Iackstue *MS*.

---

92. *barrators*] rioters.
94. *submiss*] submissive.
103. *jacksauce*] saucy fellow. Bullen's emendation is surely correct, demanded by 'saucy jack' in the next line, and supported by *H5* IV.vii.138 and elsewhere (J23.1). The *MS* reading 'Iackstue', presumably Heywood's copying error, represents either 'jackstave' (= jackstaff; not in *OED* before 1692) or 'jackstew' (unrecorded).

Friar John. More than I would to have my wish on thee,
Richard—though I have a good stomach to't,
Ay, and to baste thee soundly!—I would now
To have my will on her. 'Tis a sweet creature.
Our patron old, she young—some hope in that.
Besides, she's wondrous kind and affable,
And when we duck or congee, smiles as if
She took some pleasure in our shaven crowns.
I am the first that every morning, when
She passes through the cloister to her prayers,
Attend her with 'Good morrow', pray for her health,
For her content and pleasure, such as cannot be
Hoped or expected from her husband's age,
And these my friendly wishes she returns
Not only in kind language, but sweet smiles,
The least of which breed some encouragement.
I will, if she persist to prove thus kind,
If not to speak my thoughts, to write my mind. [*Exit.*]

ACT I SCENE iii

Enter after a great tempestuous storm Master [John] ASHBURN, *an English merchant, and his man* GODFREY.

Ashburn. Was ever known such a tempestuous night
Of thunder, hail, wind, lightning? 'Twas as if
The four seditious brothers threatened war,
And were but now at battle.
Godfrey. The four winds,
You mean. Blustering fellows, they are. Pray God
All be well at sea, for I am sure the roofs'
Tiles and ridges have paid for it ashore.
Ashburn. The very rafters of the houses bend.
Some break, and are demolished, barns blown down.
The very chimneys rattle o'er our heads,
The strongest buildings tremble, just as if [*Thunder*]
There is above a tempest, so below
There were a fearful earthquake.
Godfrey. All our houses
Are nothing now but windows, broad bay windows
So spacious that carts laden may drive through

3. brothers threatened] *MS1b subst.*; brother weare at *MS1a*. 7. ashore] *Bu subst.*; a shower *MS* (*?copying* a shore. *Cf. MS ll. 1026 & 1071*). 11. *Thunder.*] MS3.

122. *duck or congee*] nod or bow.
124–7] a detail suggested by Masuccio, p. 17.
The first twenty-four lines of the scene are an expansion of *Rud.* 83–8, the remainder a loose version of 89–184. The three passages closest to the Latin are noted below.

And neither brush o'the top or either side.
Lights everywhere; we shall have lights enough.
Here's simple work for daubers.
Ashburn. We are forced
All to forsake the village, and to fly
Unto the fields for succour.
Godfrey. Sir, it put me
In mind of the great king Agathocles,
Who was, as I have heard you oft relate,
Brained with a tile. Why may not meaner men
Then fear the fall of brick-bats?

Enter RAPHAEL, TREADWAY *and the* CLOWN.

Treadway. A strange night,
And full of terror; yet, thanks heaven, well past.
Raphael. O, but I fear the greater storm's to come,
A gust that will more shake me.
Clown. [*Aside*] More, quoth he? I can scarce see how that well can be, for I can assure you, the garret that I lay in put me in mind of mine infancy, for I lay all the night long as if I had been rocked in a cradle.
Raphael. O friend, I fear this false and perjured slave
That hath not kept appointment hath deceived me
Both of my coin and precious merchandise.
Clown. [*Aside*] Did you ever look for better from a Judas of his hair?
Raphael. Which if he have—
Clown. [*Aside*] Why then he hath, and the mends is in your own hands, that's all that I can say to't.
Raphael. He hath undone me doubly.
Treadway. Hope the best.
Perhaps the threatening weather kept him back.
It was a troubled sky, the sun set blushing,
The rack ran swiftly rushing from the west,
And these, presages of a future storm.
Unwilling, too, to trust her tenderness
Unto such fears might make him fail his hour,
And yet with purpose, what he slacked last night

16. either.] *Bu*; eathers *MS.* 35. hair?] *Bu*; hey< *MS.* 44. Unwilling, too, to] *MS1b subst*; uwilling too *MS1a.* 45. fears might make him] *MS1b;* hazards. hee might *MS1a.*

---

18. *daubers*] plasterers.

21. *Agathocles*] tyrant of Syracuse. *J* notes that Heywood is probably recalling the death of Pyrrhus, king of Epirus; Agathocles died by poison.

35. *of his hair*] of the same quality; perhaps with a reference also to the traditional red hair of Judas, but, as *Bu* notes, Mildew is later described as 'grey and hoary' (*App.* 40) and also as 'bald' (II.ii.32).

42. *rack*] clouds.

Now to make good this morning.
Raphael. O, you tent
My wounds too gently, dally with my doubts,
And flatter my true fears. The even was calm,
The sky untroubled, and the sun went down
Without disturbance in a temperate air.
No, not the least conjecture could be made
Of such a sudden storm, of which the world
Till after midnight was not sensible.
His hour was supper, and in failing that—
Clown. Ay, now begin I to fear too, for if he break his word, if it be to come to dinner or supper, I'll never trust his bond for the value of a threepenny ordinary after.
Raphael. Post you back to the city. Make enquiry
And most strict search to find that Mildew out.
Whom if you meet, first, rate his last neglect,
Then hasten his repair. Here you shall find me,
Or in the way home, for in all this village
I will not leave a house, a place, unsearched.
If where he dwells you miss him, then demand
At every quay what shipping late went out.
If any vowed love still remain betwixt us,
Make it appear now in your present care
And expedition.
Treadway. I'll be your Mercury,
Not fail you in the least.
Raphael. And so betwixt us
Increase a friendship that was never flawed.
[*Exit* TREADWAY.]
Ashburn. This gentleman, it seems, hath in this tempest
Sustained some loss, he appears so much disturbed.
Clown. See, sir, here are some, it may be, belong to this village. You had best ask of them.
Raphael. And well advised. Hail, father.
Godfrey. No more hail,
If you love me; we had too much of that last night.
Ashburn. Of what sex are you, that you call me so?
I have been father, of a daughter, once,
Though not these many years blest with her sight,
But of a son yet never.
Raphael. What you have lost
May you in some most fair and fortunate hour

47. *tent*] prove.
58. *ordinary*] tavern meal.
61. *rate*] chide, berate.
62. *repair*] return.
69. *expedition*] promptness.
69–70. *Mercury*] cf. *ET* II.ii.97 and note.
76–81.] cf. *Rud.* 103–6.

Again find to your comfort.
Ashburn. You wish well.
Raphael. Saw you not 'bout this village, late last night
Or early now i'the morning, a short fellow,
Thin-haired, flat-nosed, sand-bearded and squint-eyed?
Clown. The map of misfortune and very picture of ill-luck.
Raphael. Gross-waisted, gouty-legged.
Clown. Whose face is puffed up like a bladder, and whose belly like a tun.
Ashburn. By such I have much suffered in my state,
Oppressed almost to utmost penury
In my once better fortune, but so late
I saw not any such.
Raphael. He was expected
To be attended by two handsome girls,
Both young, both fair, but th'one unparalleled,
Neither of which by computation
Hath told so high as twenty.
Ashburn. If such I chance to meet by accident,
I'll send you notice, please you leave your name
And place of your abode.
Raphael. Raphael I am called,
A merchant in Marseilles, and my lodging
Is at the Parrot in the market-place;
There you shall find me known.
Ashburn. And, by that name,
Presume I'll not forget you.
Raphael. Fare you well, sir.
[*Exeunt* RAPHAEL *and* CLOWN.]
Ashburn. Come, let us mount ourselves upon these rocks,
And having feeling of our hurts at land,
Let's see what ships have been distressed at sea,
If any shaken in this storm, or wracked,
And though we cannot help the miserable,
Yet let them taste our pity.
Godfrey. Sir, content.
But I hope your fishermen have not put to sea
This night. If they have, I swear they have showed themselves
Much madder than the tempest.
Ashburn. I hope they have been more discreet and wise

83. find] *MS1b*; recover *MS1a*. 105. Fare you well, sir.] *MS2*; ffor wch curtesy *MS1*.

84–91.] an extended translation of *Rud.* 124–6.
90. *tun*] barrel.
90.] [See *App.* for text cut in *MS.*)
102. *Marseilles*] a trisyllable (*MS* 'Marcellis'), as at I.I.101.
105.] (See *App.* for text cut in *MS.*)

Than with the hazard of my boats and nets
To endanger their own lives.
Godfrey. See! Do you see, sir!
Ashburn. What?
Godfrey. Why, yonder.
Ashburn. Where?
Godfrey. There, towards yon shore.
Ashburn. A ship labouring for life,
Now cast upon the rocks, now split, now sinking,
Now dashed to pieces.
Godfrey. I see all mischiefs do not come by land;
Some's done upon the water.
Ashburn. Though their goods perish,
Yet in thy mercy, heaven, protect their lives!
Some sit upon the planks, some on the masts,
Some hang upon the cables, and some few
Have only got the cock-boat. Others swim.
O, that we should behold their misery
And want power to assist them!
Godfrey. Sure, sir, it was some ship of passengers,
For see you not two women? Dainty ducks!
Would they could swim as ducks can! Look how they sprawl
And cast their legs abroad like naked frogs!
See how they spread their arms and strive for life!
Still their coats bear them up, keep them aloft,
The modest air not willing to discover
That which the bawdy waves shame not below
Rudely to kiss and handle.
Ashburn. Bless them, heaven!
The wind and tide still beat them towards the shore,
But O, that cursèd billow hath divided
And parted them asunder! Yet all's well,
They still bear up. If they but scape the next,
There may be hope of safety.
Godfrey. One's driven this way,
The t'other that. The men shift for themselves.
How shall we save this woman?
Ashburn. No means, unless we leap down from the rocks,
And that's mere desperation. Yet to show
Our charities to wretches thus extremed,

119. shore.] *MS1b*; rocke *MS1a*. 126. cables, and some few] *MS1c*; cables, one *MS1a*; cables, and one or two *MS1b*.

---

127. *cock-boat*] dinghy.
134.] [See *App.* for text cut in *MS.*)
146.] an inversion of *Rud.* 179–80 ('If she falls off that cliff, she'll get lost more quickly') but see II.i.24.
148. *extremed*] taken to extremity (not in *OED*).

Let's see if we can find the least descent
And hasten to their succour.
Godfrey. By your favour,
I had rather they with brine should break their bellies
Than I my neck with clambering. [*Exeunt. Storm continued.*]

ACT II

SCENE i

Enter PALESTRA *all wet, as newly shipwrack and escaped the fury of the seas.*

Palestra. Is this, then, the reward of innocence,
Of goodness to ourselves, namely chaste life,
Piety to our parents, love to all,
And above all, our Christian zeal towards heaven?
But why should we poor wretches thus contest
Against the powers above us, when even they
That are the best amongst us are starred bad?
Alas, I never yet wronged man or child,
Woman or babe, never supplanted friend
Or sought revenge upon an enemy.
You see yet how we suffer. How shall they, then,
That false their faiths, that are of uncleansed life,
And then not only sin unto themselves
But tempt and persuade others? What shall I think
Becomes of my base guardian? Though the waves
Have spared the guiltless, sure his putrid soul

152. *Storm continued.*] *MS3*; *Explicit Actus Pr^{s}: MS1.* 8–23.] *cancelled, MS3.* 12. uncleansed] *this ed.*; vnclene *MS1a*; vnclende *MS1b*, *presumably copying* vnclensde. 16. soul] *Bu*; so< *MS.* 18. punished] *J*; punishe *MS.*

The first twenty-three lines closely follow *Rud.* 185–219, with the addition of the casket, borrowed from *Rud.* 388–91. Lines 24–62 paralled *Rud.* 220–58, but the affection between the girls is more marked in Heywood. The echo scene (ll. 76–100) is an addition. The remainder of the scene replaces *Rud.* 259–89, where the girls are met by Ptolemocratia, priestess of Venus, a quite different effect from the friars and their Abbot.

0.1. shipwrack] Apparently a past participle, for 'shipwrecked', as in II.ii.101. But cf. II.ii.113, with the standard usage.

7. *starred bad*] born unfortunate.

12. *false*] violate.

Cannot escape heaven's justice. We, poor wretches,
Are punished for his gross impieties.
They moved the heavens' wrath, who stirred the winds and waves,
Striving whose fury should destroy us first.
These both conspiring in our ruin, th'one
Beat us below the billows whilst the other
Swallowed both ship and goods.

Enter SCRIBONIA.

Scribonia. With peril of oft falling, and the danger
Of second death, having new scaped the first,
I have with fear and terror climbed these rocks.
And these two past, I fear to meet a third.
I spy no house, no harbour, meet no creature
To point me to some shelter, therefore here
Must starve by famine, or expire by cold.
O'the sea the whistling winds still threaten wrack,
And flying now for refuge to the land
Find naught save desolation, though these three,
Three dreadful deaths all spare me, yet a fourth
I cannot shun, in my Palestra's loss,
For the best blood of mine ran in her veins,
This life breathed in her bosom. O, my Palestra!
Palestra. Numbness and fear, hunger and solitude,
Besides my casket, my Scribonia's loss,
All these at once afflict me.
Scribonia. Ha! Who's that spake?
Sure, 'twas some woman's voice. If my Palestra,
Only for her sake I could wish to live.
Palestra. Then live, my dear Scribonia, since I am only
Spared to partake with thee new miseries.
Scribonia. Scarce can I be persuaded you are she,
But be it but her shadow, give me leave
For her remembrance to embrace it thus. [*They embrace.*]
Palestra. These arms at once lock all my living hopes
In my reserved Scribonia.
Scribonia. Now I perceive
My comfort is not mere imaginary,
But real and essential. Live you, then?
Palestra. To triumph in your safety.
Scribonia. Possible
That 'mongst these desert, unfrequented rocks
You can imagine such a thing can be

41. woman's] *Bu*; woman *MS*.

16–40] (See *App.* for text cut in *MS*, following l. 16, and at 23, 35 and 40.)
49. *reserved*] preserved.
53. *desert*] deserted.

As that which you called safety?
Palestra. Yes, Scribonia,
And comfort, too. For see, I spy a village,
A manor and a fair-built monastery,
Just at the foot of this descending hill,
And where if not amongst religious men
Should we find that's called charity?
Scribonia. Then there, then.
Fire, at the least, I hope it will afford,
Besides relief and harbour.
Palestra. Can you beg?
Scribonia. What will not rude necessity compel
Distressèd folk to do? We'll not do't basely,
For being brought up to music and to song,
Demanding in that kind their charity,
And they perceiving us much better bred
Than these our present fortunes might deserve,
'T may move in them compassions.
Palestra. Let's retire
To the back gate, then. There complain our wants,
And that which others do with impudence
Let us in shame and blushes.
Scribonia. Some sweet echo
Speak from these walls, and answer to our wants,
And either lend some comfort to our griefs
Or send us hence despairing and ashamed.
[*They approach the monastery. A song follows.*]
Palestra. O Charity, where art thou fled?
And now how long hast thou been dead?
Answer within. O many, many, many hundred years.
Scribonia. In village, borough, town or city
Remains there yet no grace, no pity?
Answer. Not in sighs, not in want, not in tears.
Palestra. [*Aside*] Cold comfort in this answer. But proceed.
[*Sings.*] Above we see a threatening sky,
Below, the winds and gusts blow high.

57. fair-built] *Bu*; ffayre build *MS*. 75.1] *This ed.*; They go in *MS*.

60.] (See *App.* for text cut in *MS.*)

75.1. s.d.] The *MS* reads 'They go in', but it seems clear that they are answered from within the monastery. They may be half-hidden at 'the back gate' (ll. 70, 112).

76–100.] The echo scene has no parallel in *Rud.* It is a burlesque in song of such effective echo scenes as Webster's in *The Duchess of Malfi* (ed. J. R. Brown, 1964, who compares, p. xxv, scenes in Dekker's *Old Fortunatus*, Jonson's *Cynthia's Revels* and the anonymous 2 *Return from Parnassus*). Unlike his predecessors, who play ingeniously on the final words of the previous speech, Heywood suggests echo-effects by repetition and end-rhyme. The verse-form raises the possibility that the girls' couplets are sung to a repeated melody, while the Friar's prosaic replies may be in a parody of plainchant.

78. Answer within] (given by Friar John).

Answer. And all, all to fright hence this same jewel.
Scribonia. The lightnings blast, the thunders crack,
The billows menace naught save wrack.
Answer. And yet man is than these much more cruel.
Palestra. Unless my judgement quite miscarry
She may live in some monastery.
Answer. 'Tis a place too that was first assigned her.
Scribonia. If not amongst religious men
Yet where, where shall we seek her, then?
Answer. Yet even there, there you scarce, scarce can find her.
Palestra. If chastity and innocence tried
Have both escapèd wind and tide—
Answer. Yet O, why should the land, land these cherish?
Scribonia. Of whom even billows have a care,
Whom seas preserve, whom tempests spare—
Answer. Yet these, these amongst men may perish.
Palestra. Uncharitable echo, from a place
Of pure devotion canst thou answer thus?
If not in these religious monasteries,
In what place can we find cold charity?
Scribonia. Where'er we meet her, she is like ourselves,
Bare, without harbour, weak and comfortless.

Enter FRIAR JOHN.

Friar John. What singing beggars were these at the gate
That would so early rouse our charity
Before it was half stirring or awake?
I think I answered them in such a key
As I believe scarce pleased them.

Enter FRIAR RICHARD.

Friar Richard. What sweet music
Was that at the back gate? 'T'ath called me up
Somewhat before my hour.
Friar John. 'Morrow, Friar Richard.
How did you like our last night's buffeting?
Whilst all the rest of our fraternity
In fear of that great tempest were at prayers,
We two picked out that time of least suspicion
And in the orchard hand to hand were at it.
Friar Richard. 'Tis true, for bloody noses. And, Friar John,
As you like that which is already past,
So challenge me hereafter. But whence came

93. where, where shall] *MS1c, MS1a*; where where oh where shall *MS1b*. 94. scarce, scarce] *MS1b*; scarce scarce scarce *MS1a*. 98. billows] *MS2*; tempests *MS1*.

106. *harbour*] shelter.

These sweet and delicate voices?
Friar John. I bore part
In their sad choir, though none of these yet know't.
But peace: our father abbot!

Enter the ABBOT *with other friars.*

Abbot. 'Morrow, sons,
And early blessing on you, if, as the lark
Riseth betimes still to salute the sun,
So your devotion plucks you from your beds
Before your hour unto your orisons.
Did you not hear a musical complaint
Of women that in sad and mournful tones
Bewailed their late disasters, harshly answered
By a churlish echo?
Friar John. Some such thing we heard.
Friar Richard. The note's still perfect with me.
Palestra. [*To Scribonia*] There appears
In his grave looks both zeal and charity.
Let's to his sight boldly expose ourselves. [*They come forward.*]
Hail, reverend father.
Abbot. What are you, poor souls,
Thus wet and weather-beat?
Scribonia. Ere you demand
Further from us, let's taste your Christian charity.
Some fire, some harbour, lest ere our sad tale
Be fully told, we perish.
Abbot. Why, whence came you?
Palestra. From sea, our ship last night in the great storm
Cast on these rocks and split, this the first place
Exposed unto our eyes to beg relief.
But O, I faint!
Abbot. Whom the high powers miraculously preserve,
Whom even the merciless waves have borne ashore,
Shall we see sink aland? Even we ourselves,
That live and eat by others' charity,
To others shall not we be charitable?
All succour, all supply that can be given,
They from our hands shall taste.
Friar John. Shall we remove them
Into the cloister?
Friar Richard. 'Tis against our oath
On any though the great'st extremity

123. *Friar John.*] *MS3*; ffryar *MS1*. 126. And] *Br. conj. from MS*; An *MS as transcribed*. 134. note's] *this ed.*; noates (?*plural*) *MS*.

145.] (See *App.* for text cut in *MS.*)
148. *aland*] on land.

To admit women thither.
Abbot. That I know,
And yet in some out-office see them cheered,
Want nothing that the cloister can afford.
Their beauties (though my eye be blind at them)
Deserve no less. I look on their distress,
And that I pity. Each one lend a hand
To take off from their present misery
And ease their tender shoulders. When they're cheered
And better comforted, I'll find occasion
To enquire further from them.
Palestra. Heaven be as kind
To you as you to us.
Abbot. Fear not, fair damsels,
This place, though not within the monastery,
Yet stands within the cloister's privilege,
And shall be unto you a sanctuary.
Scribonia. No other we expect it.
Abbot. Guide them in.
Beauty and youth to pity, 'tis no sin.

The bell rings to matins. Enter the LORD D'AVERNE *and his* LADY, [*his servant*] DENNIS *and others.*

Friar John. Hark, the bell rings to matins!
Friar Richard. See withal
Our noble patron, with his lovely lady
Prepared for their devotion. Now, Friar John,
Your lecherous eye is conning.
Friar John. I know my place.
Abbot. Way, for our noble founder!
Lord d'Averne. 'Morrow, father.
So to the rest of all the brotherhood.

The choir and music. The friars make a lane with ducks and obeisance.

Music and voices. Te tuosque semper O semper beamus
Et salvos vos venisse, O venisse gaudeamus.
Friar John. Good day to our fair foundress.
Lady d'Averne. Mercy, Friar John,
Above the rest you are still dutiful,
For which we kindly thank you. *Exeunt* [*all except* FRIAR JOHN].
Friar John. 'Kindly thank you'!
Nay, smiled withal. Although that I have more

177. *Music and voices.*] *MS1*; Musicke and *deleted, MS3*.

---

174. *conning*] scanning.

176.1 The choir] Some or all of the monks who entered at l. 125; music from offstage.

177–8.] (Lat.) You and yours for ever, O for ever do we bless, / And at your safe arrival, O arrival we rejoice.

Than a month's mind to these young harlotries,
Yet here's the ground on which I first must build
And raise my fortunes many storeys high.
Nay, I perhaps, ere they can dry their smocks,
Will put th'affair in motion. While these are
At solemn matins I'll take pen and write,
And set my mind down in so quaint a strain
Shall make her laugh and tickle, whilst I laugh
And tickle with the thought on't, still presuming
These looks, these smiles, these favours, this sweet language
Could never breathe, but have their birth from love.
But how to have't delivered? There's the doubt.
Tush, I have plot for that, too. He, no question,
That set me on to compass this my will,
May, when the upshoot comes, assist me still.
[*Exit. The tempest continues.*]

ACT II SCENE ii

Thunder. Enter two Fishermen.

First Fisherman. The troubled sea is yet scarce navigable
Since the last tempest, yet we that only live
By our own sweat and labour, nor can eat
Before we fetch our food out of the sea,
Must venture, though with danger, or, be sure,
With empty stomachs go unsupped to bed.
Second Fisherman. And so it often happens.
First Fisherman. See the cordage
Be strong and tight, the nets with all their strings,
Plummets and corks well placed for hooks and baits.
This day we shall have little use of them.
The wind's still high; bear but a gentle sail,
And hazard not the channel. Keep along
Close by the shore. The rocks will shelter us,
And may perhaps afford us lobsters, prawns,
Shrimps, crabs and such-like shellfish. Here we may
Hunt the sea-urchin, and with safety, too.
There's many hold him for a dainty fish—
He sells well in the market. Thus poor men
Are forcèd, with a slender competence,

191–7. still . . . still.] *cancelled*, MS3. 197. *tempest.*] *MS3*. 0.1. *Thunder.*] *MS3*. 13. shelter us,] *Bu*; shelter's vs: *MS*. 15–20. Here . . . life.] *cancelled, MS3*. 19. forcèd, with] *this ed. (sugg. Smallwood)*; fforct too, ffor *MS1a*; fforct too, wth *MS1b*.

183. *month's mind*] strong liking (originally, a commemorative mass).
195. *He*] (i.e., the devil; cf. IV.ii.56).
An adaptation of *Rud.* 290–484.

A little to prolong a wretched life.
Second Fisherman. Come, then, let us weigh anchor and aboard.
The sun is up already.

Enter the CLOWN.

Clown. If ever man were mad, then sure my master is not well in his wits, and all about this wench. Here's such sending and seeking, hurrying and posting, and all to no purpose. I have now some thirty errands to deliver, and know not to whom, nor where, to what, nor to which place first. He's gone on to the city and sent me back to the village. Another travels. But what are these? These should be fishermen. Good morrow, you sea-thieves.
First Fisherman. You call us thieves that may prove honester
Than many go for true men on the shore.
Clown. Saw you not pass this way an old bald fellow, hunch-shouldered, crooked-nosed, beetle-browed, with a visage louring and a look scowling, one that heaven hates and every good man abhors, a cheating rascal and an ugly slave? Did none such pass you?
First Fisherman. If such a one as you describe you enquire for,
Methinks, my friend, thou hast mistook thy way.
Thou shouldst have sought him at the gallows, rather—
There such are soonest found.
Clown. By'r Lady, were't answered of a plain fellow! But, that you may know him the better, he had two handsome, sweet, smug-faced lasses in his company.
Second Fisherman. And for such creatures you'd best search the stews
I' the city; this our village yields none such.
This fellow doth but flout us—let's aboard.
First Fisherman. Enquire of us for wenches? Tush, we fish
For no such periwinkles! Farewell, fleshmonger.

[*Exeunt* Fishermen.]

Clown. No wonder these fellows pretend to be witty, for understanding so many have lost their wits (as my master hath) they have fished for it and in some draw-net or other have caught it. But where might these lost shrews be? I suspect this pestiferous *je vous prie* hath put some slovenly trick or other to cheat my master both of his ware and money.

47. of us for] *this ed.*; ffor vs off *MS*. 48.1.] *MS3*. 50. (as my master hath)] *this ed.*; (as my m< >ste< *MS*.

28.] (See *App*. for text cut in *MS*.)
31. *true*] honest.
42–3. *smug-faced*] smooth-faced.
48. *periwinkles*] shellfish; the other meaning of the word (the little blue flower) was a playful term for a young woman (*OED*, from 1633).
50. *as . . . hath*] the manuscript is badly worn at this place, but the meaning is clear, and there is space for the proposed reading.
52. *shrews*] playfully abusive term for young women.
52–3. je vous prie] (Fr.) beggar.

Enter SCRIBONIA *with an empty pail.*

Scribonia. Thus being cheered with warmth and change of clothes,
With all such comforts as the cloister yields,
I am directed to a neighbour's by
For water to refresh and wash ourselves,
And this should be the house.

Clown. [*Aside*] What, not Scribonia, one of the flock that's missing?

Scribonia. O, sweet Jaques, where is your noble master?

Clown. Nay, sweet rogue, where is his beauteous mistress?

Scribonia. Here within,
In this place joining to the monastery.

Clown. And Mildew, too?

Scribonia. Rot on that villain, no!

Clown. He promised to bring you two along and meet with my master and some other of his friends at supper.

Scribonia. Can such men, ever false unto their god,
Keep faith with men at any time?

Clown. But stay, stay, there's one riddle I cannot expound: how come you so suddenly to leap out of a house of roguery into a house of religion, from a stews to a cloister, from beastliness to blessedness, and from a sacrilegious place to a sanctuary?

Scribonia. Such was the grace heaven lent us, who from peril,
Danger of life, the extremest of all extremes,
Hath brought us to the happy patronage
Of this most reverend abbot.

Clown. What dangers, what extremes?

Scribonia. From the sea's fury, drowning, for last night
Our ship was split, we cast upon these rocks.

Clown. Heyday, a jest indeed, shipwrack by land! I perceive you took the wooden wagon for a ship, the violent rain for the sea, and because some one of the wheels broke, and you cast into some water-plash, you thought the ship had split and you had been in danger of drowning.

Scribonia. Are you then ignorant how, late in the even,
With purpose to make better sale of us
And to defraud thy master, he shipped us
With all the gold and jewels that he had,
All which, save we, are perished?

Clown. But that caterpillar, that old catamiting canker-worm, what's become of him?

Scribonia. Dead, I hope, with drinking of salt-water.

Clown. I would all of his profession had pledged him the same health. But how doth Palestra take this?

---

61. *sweet Jaques*] an oxymoron (jakes: privy).

81. *shipwrack . . . land*] Cf. the more elaborate comic tale of a supposed shipwreck by land in *ET* II.i.

84. *water-plash*] puddle.

91. *catamiting*] sodomising.

Scribonia. Glad to be rid of such a slavery,
Yet sadly weeping, for her casket's lost,
That which included ample testimony
Both of her name and parents.

Clown. All her ill luck go with it. [*Aside*] Here will be simple news to bring to my master. When he hears she hath been shipwrack, I'll make him believe I went a-fishing for her to sea, and either drew her ashore in my net, or baiting my hook, struck her, and drew her up by the gills with mine angle.

Scribonia. Make you haste, for I'll stay till you come back.
[*Exit* CLOWN.]
But this delay had almost put me from
What I was sent about. Yes, this the place. *Knock.*

Enter GODFREY.

Godfrey. Who's that that offers violence to these gates
That never yet offended? What want you?
Scribonia. That which the earth
Doth forbid none, but freely yields to all—
A little fair spring water.
Godfrey. [*Aside*] One of those girls,
Belike this morning shipwracked, and now scaped—
A dainty piece of maid's flesh—such sweet bits
Are not here often swallowed, and my mouth
Waters at this fine morsel.
Scribonia. Water, friend,
'Tis that I crave, for God's sake.
Godfrey. We have none
Of gift, unless you buy't.
Scribonia. Will you sell that
The earth affords you gratis, and set price
Of what a foe would yield an enemy?
Godfrey. Not, pretty lass, so thou'lt afford me that,
Freely and without bargain, which not only
One friend will to another, but oft-times
A stranger to a stranger.
Scribonia. What's that, prithee?
Godfrey. Only a kiss, sweet wench.
Scribonia. Ye are too familiar.
I'll buy none at that price. Or fill my pail,
Or I'll return back empty.
Godfrey. Well, for once,
I will not greatly stand out. Yet, in hope
That what at our first meeting you'll not grant

117. God's] *MS1*; heaven– *MS3*. 138–53] *cancelled, MS3*.

100.] (See *App.* for text cut in *MS.*)
108–9.] Cf. *ET* IV.i.3–4.

You'll not deny at parting, reach thy pail.
Scribonia. Quick, as you love me. [*Hands him the pail.*]
Godfrey. 'As you love me', right!
'Who ever loved, that loved not at first sight'—
The poet's excellent saying? [*Exit* GODFREY.]
Scribonia. What shall I say, or how shall I excuse
This my long stay? But now I cast mine eyes
Back on the rough, yet unappeasèd, seas,
I quake to think upon our dangers past.
[*She sees Mildew and Sarlabois in the distance.*]
But see, the fearful object of a death
More menacing and frightful, a sea-monster
Cast from the deeps, to swallow us ashore!
Malevolent fate and black disaster still
Pursues us to all places, but of all
This, this the greatest, and to this one compared
All that are past, but trifles. O, that grand master
Of mechal lusts, that bulk of brothelry,
That stillery of all infectious sins,
Hath scaped the wrack, and with his fellow guest
And partner in corruption makes this way,
And with no tardy pace. Where shall I hide me?
Whither shall I fly? I'll to Palestra back,
And with this sad relation kill her quite
That's scarce recovered. Rather you, high powers,
Than to prolong our griefs, shorten our hours. [*Exit* SCRIBONIA.]

ACT II SCENE iii

Enter the bawd MILDEW *and* SARLABOIS.

Mildew. He that would study to be miserable,
Let him forsake the land and put to sea.
What widgeon that hath any brain at all
Would trust his safety to a rotten plank
That hath on earth sound footing?
Sarlabois. None but madmen.
Mildew. Why, then, of one thrifty and well advised
Striv'st thou to make me such? Where's now the gain

4. plank] *MS1b*; barke *MS1a*.

132.] Marlowe, *Hero and Leander* I, 176; quoted *AYL* III.v.81.
139. *sea-monster*] Scribonia may be comparing herself with Andromeda or Hesione.
145. *mechal*] adulterous (only in Heywood, *OED*).
146. *stillery*] distillery.
153.] (See *App.* for text cut in *MS.*)
A free version of *Rud.* 485–583; ll. 584–592, a pointless short soliloquy by Charmides, are ignored by Heywood.
3. *widgeon*] simpleton.

And profit promised, the rich merchandise
Of lust and whoring, the great usury
Got by the sale of wantons? These, cursed wretch,
With all the wealth and treasure that I had,
All perished in one bottom, and all, all,
Through thy malicious counsel.
Sarlabois. Curse thyself!
The trusty barque, o'erladen with thy sins,
Bawdries, gross lies, thy thefts and perjuries,
Besides the burden of thy ill-got goods,
Not able to endure so great a weight,
Was forced to sink beneath them.
Mildew. Out, dog!
Sarlabois. Out, devil!
Mildew. By thee, I am made nothing! O, my girls,
You sweet and never-failing merchandise,
Commodities in all coasts worthy coin
Christian or heathen, by whom in distresses
I could have raised a fortune! Man undone,
That I should lose you thus!
Sarlabois. [*Aside*] I knew he had rather
See half a hundred of them burnt aland
Than one destroyed by water! But O, Neptune!
I fear I have supped so much of thy salt broth
'Twill bring me to a fever.
Mildew. O, my Palestra
And fair Scribonia, were but you two safe,
Yet some hope were reserved me.
Sarlabois. I pray, Mildew,
When you so early to the bottom dived
For whom were you a-fishing?
Mildew. Marry, for maids—
Would I knew how to catch them! But my guts,
How they are swelled with sea-brine!
Sarlabois. 'Tis good physic
To cure thee of the mangy.
Mildew. Wretched man,
That have no more left of a magazine
Than these wet clothes upon me—nay, the worst
Of all I had, and purposely put on
Only to lie a-shipboard.
Sarlabois. Once today

21. girls,] *MS1b*; whoores *MS1a*.

11.] (See *App.* for text cut in *MS.*)
18.] (See *App.* for text cut in *MS.*)
24. *in distresses*] under compulsion.
27. *burnt*] (i.e., with syphilis).
37. *mangy*] mange.
38. *magazine*] stock of clothes, possessions.

Thou wert in wealth above me. Now the seas have
Left us an equal portion.
Mildew. In all the world
I vow I am not worth a lighted faggot
Or a poor pan of charcoal.
Sarlabois. Justly punished,
Thou that hast all thy lifetime dealt in fireworks,
Stoves, and hot baths to sweat in, now to have
Thy teeth to chatter in thy head for cold
Nimbler than virginal jacks!
Mildew. Now, what shark
Or wide-mouthed whale shall swallow up my budget,
May it at th'instant choke him!
Sarlabois. Cursedly 'twas got,
And now thy curse goes with it.
Mildew. But those girls!
Naught so much grieves me as to part with them
Before they lost their maidenheads. Had they lived
Till I had seen them women, and o' the trade,
My cost and care bestowed to bring them up
I should have thought well spent, which now with them
Is merely cast away.

Enter GODFREY.

Sarlabois. Peace now your prating, and hear another speak.
Godfrey. The pail religious, which was the pledge
Of a kiss lascivious, I have given back,
Ay, and to boot, the water, but within
There's such a coil betwixt the two young girls
That I was afraid they were haunted with sprites
And therefore ran and left them. 'Las, poor girls,
They are in piteous fear!
Mildew. [*To Sarlabois*] He talked of girls. Why may not these be they,
Escaped as we? [*To Godfrey*] Stay, young man! Good friend, stay!
Godfrey. [*Aside*] Two old drowned rats! I'll have some sport with them,
And though I pity those, I'll play with these.
Mildew. What girls were these thou spakest of?
Sarlabois. Tell us first,
Where we might find some comfort.

64. sprites] *Bu subst.*; springht *MS.* 72. comfort.] *MS1b*; shelter *MS1a.*

46. *fireworks*] venereal diseases, or their treatment, as with the 'sweats' and 'baths' of l. 47. (Not in *OED.*)
49. *virginal jacks*] uprights that pluck the strings of a virginals (early harpsichord).
49.] (See *App.* for text cut in *MS.*)
50. *budget*] wallet.
63. *coil*] tumult.
63.] (See *App.* for text cut in *MS.*)

Godfrey. Let us, O let us be advised and loving still to all men,
So, though we be but middle-sized, we shall be held no small men.
Mildew. Concerning these fair damsels—
Sarlabois. Speak of that
Which now concerns us most: where may we meet
With warmth, with food and shelter?
Godfrey. O, thou that dost demand of me some fire, some meat and harbour,
I see thou lately hast been washed. Hath Neptune been thy barber?
Sarlabois. This fellow merely flouts our misery,
And laughs at our distresses.
Mildew. But, kind friend,
Concerning these young women: are they fair?
Godfrey. Fair, fresh and clean they both appear, and not like gipsy umbered.
Mildew. How many?
Godfrey. Just as thou and I when we but once are numbered.

Mildew. O, Sarlabois, there's comfort in these words;
They have already warmed my heart within.
Why may not these be they?
Sarlabois. Be they, or not,
I had rather see one caudle down my throat
To wash down this salt water than be master
Of all the wenches living.
Mildew. O, where, where,
Where might I see two such?
Godfrey. Thou that goest sideways like a crab, gap'st on me like an oyster,
Follow thy flat nose and smell them there, in th'out part of this cloister.
Mildew. O, may this piece of earth prove happy to me
As hath the sea been fatal! [*Exit*.]
Sarlabois. I'll follow, and could wish
Both cloister and whole village were a fire,
Only to dry my clothes by! [*Exit*.]
Godfrey. Marry, hang you,
You that so late scaped drowning, for I take you
For two pestiferous rascals. [*Exit*.]

84. but once are] *this ed.*; are once but *MS*. 93. flat] *Bu*; fflot *MS*. 99.1] *Explict Actus* 2^{S}. *MS1*.

83. *like . . . umbered*] dark-skinned.
84. *but once are*] The *MS* reading, 'are once but', appears to be a copying error.
88. *caudle*] a warm, spicy alcoholic drink.

ACT III

SCENE i

Enter the LADY D'AVERNE *with a letter in her hand, reading, and with her,* [Millicent *her*] MAID.

Lady d'Averne. And how came you by this?
Maid. Following you to the chapel,
And, I protest, not thinking anything,
Friar John o'the sudden plucked me by the sleeve
And whispered in mine ear to give that to you,
But privately, because it was a thing
Only concerned your person.
Lady d'Averne. 'Twas well done,
But prithee, do no more so. For this time,
Take't for a warning.
Maid. Madam, I am schooled.
Lady d'Averne. Do so, or ever lose me.
Can this be in a vowed monastic life,
Or to be found in churchmen? 'Tis a question
Whether to smile or vex, to laugh or storm,
Because in this I find the cause of both.
What might this saucy fellow spy in me
To encourage such a boldness? Yes, this letter
Instructs me what: he saith my affability
And modest smiles still gracing his salutes
Moved him to write. O, what a chary care, then,
Had women need have, both of lips and eyes,
When every fair word's censured liberty,
And every kind look mere licentiousness.
I have been hitherto so great a stranger
To these unused temptations that in troth
I know not how to take this. Silly friar,
Madness or folly, one of these 't must be.
If th'one, I pity, at the other laugh,
And so no more regard it.
Maid. Madam, if aught be in that letter ill,
Methinks 'tis good that you can take't so well.

0.2. MAID. *MS2*; mayde or page, *MS1*. 9–10. me. / can] *MS2*; mee. heares sweet stuffe, / can *MS1*. 28. *Maid.*] *Bu*; Madam, *MS*.

11]. (See *App.* for text cut in *MS.*)
20. *censured*] adjudged as.
24. *Silly*] simple-minded.

Lady d'Averne. Peace, you. A brainless, weak, besotted fellow!
But let me better recollect myself.
Madness nor folly, and add lust to them,
Durst not in fury, heat or ignorance
Have tempted my unquestioned chastity
Without a fourth abetter, jealousy.
The more I ponder that, I more suspect.
Say that my lord should have a hand in this,
And knowing there's such difference in our years,
To prove my faith might put this trial on me?
Else how durst such a poor penurious friar
Oppose such an unheard-of impudence
'Gainst my incensèd fury and revenge?
My best is, therefore, as I am innocent
To study mine own safety, show this letter
Which once my charity would have concealed
And rather give him up a sacrifice
To my lord's just incensement than endanger
Mine own unblemished truth and loyalty
By incurring his displeasure. Here he comes.

Enter the LORD D'AVERNE *with some followers,* [*among them*] *his man* DENNIS.

Lord d'Averne. Now lady, reading?
Lady d'Averne. Yes, a letter, sir.
Lord d'Averne. Imports it any news?
Lady d'Averne. Yes sir, strange news,
And scarce to be believed.
Lord d'Averne. Foreign?
Lady d'Averne. Domestic,
'Tis household business all.
Lord d'Averne. May I impart it?
Lady d'Averne. O sir, in any case, as one it most concerns.
But I intreat you, read it with patience—the simplicity
Of him that writ it will afford you mirth,
Or else his malice, spleen. [*Aside*] Now, by his temper
And change of countenance, I shall easily find
Whose hand was chief in this.
Lord d'Averne. All leave the place.
Dennis. We shall, sir.
[*Exeunt all except* LORD *and* LADY D'AVERNE.]
Lord d'Averne. Possible
That this should be in man, nay in man vowed
Unto a strict abstemious chastity?
From my own creature, and from one I feed!

38.] *deleted, MS3.*

---

53. *impart*] share.
63. *creature*] dependent.

Nay, from a place built in my holiest vows,
Established in my purpose, in my life
Maintained from my revenue, after death
Firmed and assured to all posterities,
That that should breed such vipers!
Lady d'Averne. Patience, sir.
The fellow sure is mad.
Lord d'Averne. I can be mad as he, too, and I will.
Thus to abuse my goodness in a deed
Some would hold meritorious, at the least
Intended for an act of piety!
To suffer in my zeal, nay, to be mocked
In my devotion, by those empty drones
That feed upon the honey of my hive!
To invert my good intendments, turn this nest
I built for prayer unto a bed of sins!
Which thus I'll punish: this religious place,
Once vowed to sanctity, I'll undermine
And in one instant blow the structure up
With all th'unhallowed covent.
Lady d'Averne. You're in extremes.
Where one offends, shall for his heinous fact
So many suffer? There's no justice in't.
Lord d'Averne. Some justice I will show them here on earth
Before they find it multiplied elsewhere.
Lady d'Averne. For my sake, sir, do not for one man's error
Destroy a work of perpetuity
By which your name shall live. One man offends—
Let the delinquent suffer.
Lord d'Averne. So't shall be,
And thou hast well advised. Some pen and ink, there!
Lady d'Averne. What purpose you?
Lord d'Averne. That's solely to myself,
And in my fixed thoughts stands irreprovable.

Enter DENNIS [*with pen, ink and paper*].

Dennis. Sir, here's pen, ink and paper.
Lord d'Averne. To his letter myself will give an answer. [*He*] *writes.*
Dennis. [*Aside*] Sure all's not well, that on the sudden thus
My lord is so distempered.
Lady d'Averne. [*Aside*] I have, I fear,
Stirred such a heat that naught save blood will quench,
But wish my tears might do't. He's full of storm,
And that in him will not be easily calmed.

86. elsewhere.] *MS2*; in heaven. *MS1*. 93.1. *with pen, ink and paper.*] *MS3*.

77. *intendments*] purposes.
83. *fact*] crime.
93. *irreprovable*] irreproachable.

His rage and trouble both pronounce him guiltless
Of this attempt, which makes me rather doubt
He may prove too severe in his revenge,
Which I with all endeavour will prevent.
Yet to the most censorious I appeal,
What could I less have done to save mine honour
From suffering beneath scandal?

Lord d'Averne. See, here's all—
'Tis short and sweet—write this in your own hand
Without exchange of the least syllable,
Insert in copying no suspicious dash
Or doubtful comma. Then subscribe your name,
Seal't then with your own signet, and dispatch it
As I will ha't directed. Do't, I charge you,
Without the least demur or fallacy—
By doing this you shall prevent distrust
Or future breach betwixt us. You shall further
Express a just obedience.

Lady d'Averne. Sir, I shall, [*She writes.*]
Whate'er your concealed purpose be, I shall.

Lord d'Averne. [*To Dennis*] Provide me horses; I will ride.

Dennis. When, sir?

Lord d'Averne. Instantly after dinner. And giv't out
I am not to return till three days hence—
So spread it through the house.

Dennis. What followers, sir,
Mean you to take along?

Lord d'Averne. Thyself, no more,
For 'tis a private business. And withal
Provide me—hark, thine ear. [*He whispers.*]

Dennis. A strong one, sir?

Lord d'Averne. One that will hold. Withal give private order
At night the garden gate may be left ope,
By which we may return unknown to any.
What I intend lies here.

Dennis. All we servants
Are bound to do, but not examine what—
That's out of our commission.

Lord d'Averne. 'Twixt us two
I shall resolve thee further.

Dennis. I am gone, sir. [*Exit.*]

Lord d'Averne. Now, sweet lady, have you done?

---

101. *trouble*] agitation.
106. *less have done*] have done with more restraint.
114. *fallacy*] deception.
119–28] *J* notes that the husband's pretended absence (here taken from the Masuccio source) brings about the denouement also in *WKK*, and (though the parallel is not close in the case of Chartley) also in *WWH*. To these should be added *ET*, where Wincott feigns sickness to allow a meeting between his wife and Geraldine.

Lady d'Averne. As you commanded.
Lord d'Averne. It wants nothing now
But seal and superscription—I'll see't done—
And mark me now: at evensong, passing through
The cloister to the chapel, when the friar
Amongst the rest bows with his wonted ducks,
Add, rather than diminish from, your smiles
And wonted favours. Let this she-post then
Convey this letter to the friar's close fist
Who no doubt gapes for answer.
Lady d'Averne. All shall be
As you instruct, but punish, sir, with pity.
Put him to pain or shame, but death, alas,
Is too severe example.
Lord d'Averne. Tush, wife, fear not.
Thinkst thou I'll geld a churchman? [*Exeunt.*]

ACT III SCENE ii

Enter after a great noise within, the CLOWN, *meeting with* [John] ASHBURN *and* GODFREY.

Clown. If this village be inhabited with men, as this place within is with monsters, if with men that have eyes and can distinguish beauty, or that have hearts, and therefore sense of pity, if you be fathers and know what belongs to children, or Christians, and therefore what is meant by charity, if husbandmen, and have hope of your harvest, or merchants, of your trade's increase, if fishermen, that would thrive by your labours, or any of all these that would be known by your honesty—

Ashburn. Many of these thou namest have place in us,
The greatest part, if not all.
Clown. Then lend your helping hands, to succour, relieve, defend, deliver, save, secure, patronage, abet and maintain.
Ashburn. Whom? What?

146. *Exeunt.*] *MS3*.

---

140. *she-post*] woman messenger.

The first forty lines of the scene are loosely based on *Rud.* 615–63. Heywood makes no use of lines 593–614, Daemones' prophetic dream of the monkey attempting to steal from the swallow's nest, despite their effectiveness as an unconscious premonition of the pimp's threat to the girls. Perhaps Heywood's Ashburn is not a dreamer of this kind, though he anticipates the truth in l. 26. Palestra and Mildew's duet (*App.* 124–39) is a version of *Rud.* 644–76, and the remainder of the scene an extremely free rendering of 677–891. The final lines (III.ii.196–201) are borrowed from the following act, *Rud.* 892–905.

12. *patronage*] protect.

Clown. Beauty, virtue, purity, sincerity, softness, sweetness, innocence and chastity.

Ashburn. 'Gainst what? 'Gainst whom?

Clown. Oppression, fraud, rudeness, reproach, sin, shame, debate, disease, theft, rapine, contempt of religion and breach of sanctuary, against a magazine of misdemeanors and a whole monopoly of mischiefs.

Godfrey. I know the business, sir, if in that place
These are the two distressèd wracks at sea
We saw this morning floating. Sweeter girls
I never yet set eye on, and oppressed
By two ill-looking rascals, that to warm them
Wished all the town a bonfire.

Ashburn. Miscreant slaves!
For one young damsel's sake I once called daughter,
And in the absence of their greater friends,
I'll stand betwixt them and these injuries.

Clown. These are they after whom I have been seeking, and my master was enquiring. If you will but secure them here in the village whilst I carry word to my master in the city, you shall do me a courtesy and him a most noble office.

Ashburn. It was no more than promise, and I should
Fail in my goodness not to see that done.
Post to thy master, bid him meet us here,
Meantime my man shall raise the villagers
Both in the rescue of these innocent maids
And in defence of holy privilege.

Clown. I fly like the winds.

Godfrey. And I'll go call the peasants
To raise another tempest.

Ashburn. Hasten, both.

[*Exeunt Clown and* GODFREY.]

A tumult within and sudden noise. Enter at one door GODFREY *with country fellows for their rescue, at the other* MILDEW, SARLABOIS, PALESTRA, SCRIBONIA.

Palestra. Where, in what place, shall we bestow ourselves
From this unjust man's fury?

Scribonia. If compelled
And dragged from sanctuary with profane hands,
Where shall we fly to safety?

Ashburn. Whither, if

20. mischiefs.] *this ed.*; mischeiff< *MS.* 27. sake] *this ed.*; sakes *MS.* 41.1.] Gib: Stage: Taylor: Cont: fellows *added, MS3.*

25–6. *that . . . bonfire*] cf. 2 *IAge* II.i: '*Synon* I hope shall warme his hands annon, / At a bright goodly bone-fire.'

36. *Post*] hurry.

41.] (See *App.* for text cut in *MS.*)

Not unto us? We often see the gods
Give and bequeath their justice unto men
Which we as faithfully will see performed.
All. Down with these saucy companions!
Godfrey. Down with these sacrilegious sarsaparilles,
These unsanctified Sarlaboises, that would make
A very seraglia of the sanctuary
And are mere renegadoes to all religion!
Mildew. Stay, hold! Are you banditti, rovers, thieves,
And wait you here to rob and pillage us
The sea so late hath rifled? These are mine,
My chattels and my goods, nor can you seize them
As wracks. I appeal unto the admiral.
Ashburn. His power I in his absence will supply,
And seize you all as forfeit, these as goods,
You as superfluous lading, till that court
Shall compromise betwixt us.
Mildew. I' the meantime
Let me possess mine own. These are my slaves,
My utensils, my movables, and bought
With mine own private coin.
Sarlabois. To which I am witness.
Mildew. And by the hair I'll drag tham as mine own,
Were't from the holy altar.
Palestra. Succour!
Scribonia. Help!
Ashburn. Are they not Christians?
Mildew. Yes.
Ashburn. What nation?
Mildew. English.
Ashburn. In mine own country born, and shall not I
Stand as their champion then? I tell thee, peasant,
England's no brood for slaves.
Palestra. O sir, to you
We fly, as to a father.
Ashburn. And I'll guard you
As were you mine own children.
Mildew. 'Gainst their lord,
Owner and master.
Ashburn. None is bred with us
But such as are free-born, and Christian laws
Do not allow such to be bought or sold,
For any bawd or pandar to hire such
To common prostitution. Here they stand—
Touch but a garment, nay, a hair of theirs
With thy least finger, thy bald head I'll sink

---

50. *sarsaparilles*] medicinal root (used in treatment of syphilis).
52. *seraglia*] harem.

Below thy gouty feet.
Mildew. I am oppressed.
Is there no law in France?
Ashburn. Yes, sir, to punish
These chastity's seducers.
Mildew. Give me fire,
I will not leave of all this monastery,
Of you or these, of what's combustible,
Nay, of myself, one moiety unconsumed.
Godfrey. His friend before him wished the town afire,
Now he would burn the cloister to arch-pillars.
Ashburn. And like such
Our purpose is to use them. Dare not, miscreant,
Once to give these a name whom thou callst thine,
No, not a beck or nod. If thou but stirst
To do unto this house of sanctity
Damage or outrage, I will lay thee prostrate
Beneath these staves and halberds.
Mildew. Is this law?
Godfrey. Yes, Stafford's Law.
Ashburn. Nay, fear not, pretty girls.
The friars themselves, were they not at their prayers,
Would have done more than this in just defence
Of their immunities, but in their absence
I stand for them. [*To Mildew*] Nor shall you part from hence,
Or dare to squetch, till they themselves be judges
Of injury done to this sacred place,
Or such as I have sent for make appearance
To claim what thou unjustly callst thine own.
Godfrey. Nay, thou shalt find we have two strings to our bow.
Ashburn. If he but stir, then strike.
Mildew. This Stafford Law,
Which I till now heard never named in France,
Is for the present a more fearful court
Than Chancery or Star Chamber. I want motion—
You have made a statue, a mere image.

Enter Master RAPHAEL, Master TREADWAY *and the* CLOWN.

Raphael. Durst then the slave use my Palestra thus,

86. one moiety] *MS1b*; dispeyring *MS1a*. 97. themselves,] *Bu. subst.*; them selff, *MS*. prayers,] *Bu*; pry< *MS*. 105. bow.] *Bu*; bo< *MS*. 110. made] *MS*; made me *Bu*.

---

86. *moiety*] half.
92. *beck*] signal.
95. *halberds*] weapons combining spear and battle-axe.
96. *Stafford's Law*] a beating (S808).
101. *squetch*] move.
105. *two . . . bow*] proverbial (S937) for being well prepared.
110.] (See *App.* for text cut in *MS*.)

And drag her by the hair from sanctuary?
Clown. Most true, sir.
Raphael. Why didst not kill him?
Clown. If I had had but a sword, I had done't, but I sought the village through, and could find ne'er a cutter.
Raphael. Were there no scattered stones lay in the street,
To have beat his brains out?
Clown. Not a stone to throw at a dog.
Raphael. Hadst thou not heels?
Clown. Yes, to have kicked him like a dog, but I reserved them to run the more nimbly about your business.
Palestra. I now spy a new sanctuary, his arms,
In which I may presume security.
My Raphael!
Raphael. My Palestra, are you safe?
Before I give due thanks to this good man,
Which time shall pay in all pluralities,
O, show me but that monster of mankind
And shame of men, on whom to be revenged!
Mildew. The storm at sea was not more terrible
Than this the land now threatens. Again undone,
Over and over wretched!
Clown. See the limb
Of his old sire the devil!
Raphael. Perjured slave!
Perfidious, but that I abhor to take
The hangman's office from him, this should open
A door by which thy black soul should fly out
Unto assured damnation!
Treadway. Be more patient,
Proceed with him after a legal course,
And be not swayed by fury.
Raphael. Well advised.
What can thy false tongue plead in thy excuse,
Thou volume of all vices?
Mildew. Why, what not?
Raphael. Is thy heart seared, thy brow made impudent,
And all thy malefactions armed with lies
Against just testates and apparent truths?
When I had paid full ransom for this prize,
Why didst thou bear her hence?
Mildew. I did not do't.
These be my witness. Have I borne her hence,
When I have brought her to thee?
Raphael. Thy bawd's rhetoric
Shall not excuse thee thus. Friends, guard him safe.

115. sought] *Bu*; sough< *MS*.

---

144. *testates*] testimony.

Clown. We will see his fool's coat guarded, ay, and regarded too, from slipping out of our fingers.

Treadway. [*Aside*] Believe me now, I do not blame my friend
To fish in troubled streams for such a pearl
Or dig in black mould for so rich a mine,
But to redeem a chaste and innocent soul
Forth from the fiery jaws of lust and hell
Expressed a most commended charity.
[*To Raphael*] What second beauty's that, I entreat you, friend,
That trembling flies from his infectious ills,
To patronise her youth and innocence
Beneath that grave man's goodness?

Raphael. A like sufferer
With her in all distresses, like in years,
In virtue no way differing, of our nation.
Who knows but near allied, too.

Treadway. I feel something
Growing on me, I know not how to style,
Pity or love, since it hath taste of both.
And since it were shame such parity in all things,
Age, minds, wracks, bondage, pursuits, injuries,
Should now be separate—the one be freed,
The t'other left in durance, for the want
And pious tender of so small a sum—
I somewhat have in purpose.

Raphael. Drag them both
Before the magistrate.

Sarlabois. Me? Wherefore? Why?

Godfrey. As his abetter and ill counsellor—
One would have burnt the village, and the other
Threatened to fire the cloister.

Raphael. Both acts capital,
And worthy severe censure.

Mildew. Though thou pleadst interest
In way of earnest in Palestra, yet
Rob me not quite, give me the t'other back,
My only portion left me by the sea,
And stock to set up trade by.

Scribonia. Rather torture me

167. were shame] *this ed.*; were *MS.* 168. Age,] *MS1b*; years *MS1a.*

---

150. *fool's ... regarded*] his motley uniform ornamented and carefully watched.
151.] (See *App.* for text cut in *MS.*)
153. *fish ... streams*] proverbial (F334): 'best fishing in troubled waters'.
160. *patronise*] protect.
167. *shame*] *MS* reads 'and since it were such ...', with clearly a word missing after 'were', with the sense 'wrong' or 'pity'. I propose 'shame', explainable as an example of copyist's eye-skip to 'such', immediately following.

With any violent death.
Treadway. Leave them in trust
And charge of this grave, reverend gentleman
Until you hear the sentence of the court.
Ashburn. I willingly accept their patronage.
Here at my house they shall have meat and harbour
With all supplies convenient.
Raphael. Nobly spoke.
Meantime hale these to the court.
Mildew. My Palestra,
What, not one word of pity?
Raphael. Stop his mouth.
Mildew. My Scribonia,
Not thou entreat them, neither?
Treadway. Time's but trifled.
Away with them to justice.
Mildew. Take my skin, then,
Since nothing else is left me.
Clown. That's rotten already, and will neither make good leather nor parchment. The town, there.
Exeunt [CLOWN, MILDEW *and* SARLABOIS, RAPHAEL *and* TREADWAY].
Ashburn. Come, damsels, follow me where I shall lead.
I have a curst wife at home, I tell you that,
But one that I presume will not be jealous
Of two such harmless souls.
Palestra. You are to us
A patron and defender.
Scribonia. Bound unto you
Not as an host, but father. *Exeunt.*

ACT III SCENE iii

Enter the LORD D'AVERNE, *his* LADY, [DENNIS] *and the waiting maid.*

Lord d'Averne. Are all things ready, as I gave in charge?
Dennis. Ready, sir.
Lord d'Averne. Enough. [*To Maid*] And you delivered it
To his own hands?
Maid. I did.
Lord d'Averne. How did he take't?
Maid. With smiles and seeming joy.
Lord d'Averne. Sorrow and shame

188. to the court.] *MS1b*; to Iustyce. *MS1a*. 0.1. DENNIS] *added, MS3*. 0.1. DENNIS] *added, MS3*.

185. *patronage*] custody.
197. *curst*] bad-tempered.

I fear will be the sad end on't.
Lady d'Averne. Sir, you're troubled.
Lord d'Averne. I would not have you so. Pray, to your rest;
You shall remove me from all jealousies
If you betake you to your soundest sleeps,
And without more enquiry.
Lady d'Averne. Sir, remember
That all offences are not worthy death.
Felony, murder, treason, and such like
Of that gross nature, may be capital,
Not folly, error, trespass.
Lord d'Averne. You advise well.
Let me advise you likewise: instantly
Retire in to your chamber without noise,
Reply or question, lest part of that rage
Is bent against him you turn upon yourself,
Which is not for your safety.
Lady d'Averne. Sir, goodnight.
[*Exit* LADY D'AVERNE.]
Lord d'Averne. Thy watch: how goes the hour?
Dennis. 'Tis almost ten.
Lord d'Averne. [*Aside*] The time of our appointment. [*To Maid*]. You attend
Upon his knock, and give him free admittance.
Being entered, usher him into this place.
That done, return then to your lady's chamber,
There lock yourself fast in.
Maid. My lord, I shall.
Poor friar, I fear they'll put thee to thy penance
Before they have confessed thee.
Lord d'Averne. Come, withdraw,
The watchword's not yet given.
[LORD D'AVERNE *and* DENNIS *withdraw.*]

Enter the FRIAR [JOHN] *with a letter.*

Friar John. 'Tis her own pen, I know it, since she set
Her hand to establish our foundation,
And—sweet soul—she hath writ a second time
To build me up anew: [*Reads*] 'My lord is rid
A three days' journey; lose not this advantage,
But take Time by the foretop.' Yes, I will,
By the foretop, and topgallant! [*Reads*] 'At the postern

11. worthy] *MS1b*; payde *MS1a*. 20. Thy watch:] *deleted, MS3*. 29. pen] *MS1b*; hand *MS1a*.

34. *take ... foretop*] proverbial (T311); Opportunity had a graspable forelock, but none at the back of her head.
35. *foretop ... topgallant*] proverbial (T437); the foremost mast and its sail.

She to whose hand you gave your letter first
Attends for your dispatch.' My business,
I hope, shall be dispatched, then! [*Reads*] 'Fare you well,
Fail me this night, and ever.' I'll sooner forfeit
All pleasures, hopes, preferments, with th'assurance
Of a long life, blest with most happy hours,
Than this one night's contentment!

Maid. Ha, who's there?
Friar John?

Friar John. The same, you mistress Millicent,
My lady's gentlewoman.

Maid. I am the closet
That treasures all her counsels.

Friar John. Is all clear?

Maid. As such a dark night can be—[*Aside*] to one, I fear,
That scarce will look on day more.

Friar John. Where's my lady?

Maid. Attends you in her chamber.

Friar John. Guide me to't,
Nay, quickly, girl. [*Aside*] How I already surfeit
In this night's expectation!

Maid. Stay you here
In this withdrawing-room, I'll fetch a light
For safeguard of your shins.

Dennis. [*Aside*] She might have said
For safeguard of his neck.

Maid. My scene's done—
The next act lies amongst them. [*Exit* MAID.]

Friar John. My part doth but begin now, and I'll act it
In exquisite clean linen, and this cap
Perfumed of purpose, lest I should smell friar.
What differ we i' the dark, save our shaven crowns,
From gentlemen, nay lords? Nature hath arrayed us
As well as the best laymen; why should law
Restrain from us what is allowed to them?
Let it curb fools and idiots, such as through folly
Will not, or niceness dare not, taste what's sweet,
Alike made for all palates!

Lord d'Averne. [*Aside*] How the slave
Insults in his damnation! Cease thee, wretch,

36. She] *MS1b*; my maide *MS1a*.

---

37. *business*] (bawdy).

44. *closet . . . counsels*] cf. *ET*. III.iii.150, but here with no humorous edge.

47–52.] *J* notes that the Maid as guide is a detail from Masuccio.

54. *act*] (with a bawdy second meaning).

57.] *J*, following Koeppel, quotes this as the most detailed parallel to Masuccio: 'lui molto bene perfumatosi, che non desse del fratino.'

63. *niceness*] fastidiousness.

I can endure no longer.
Friar John. Such as ban
Proffered delights may if they please refuse.
What's born with me I will make bold to use.
Lord d'Averne. [*Aside*] And I, what thou wert born to, that's the halter.
[*To Dennis*] Pull without fear or mercy, strangle him
With all his sins about him, 'twere not else
A revenge worth my fury. [*The friar is strangled.*]
Dennis. I dare now
Lodge him a whole night by my sister's side,
He's now past strumpeting.
Lord d'Averne. 'Tis night with him,
A long and lasting night.
Dennis. He lies as quiet.
You did well, friar, to put on your clean linen;
'Twill serve you as a shroud for a new grave.
Whither shall we lift his body?
Lord d'Averne. I am on the sudden
Grown full of thoughts, the horror of the fact
Breeds strange seditions in me.
Dennis. He, perhaps,
But counterfeits dead sleep. I'll holloa to him
To see if I can wake him.
Lord d'Averne. Trifle not—
The sin will prove more serious. What a terror
Is in the deed being done, which bred before
Both a delight and longing. This sad spectacle,
How it affrights me!
Dennis. Let's remove it, then.
Lord d'Averne. The sin itself, the church's malediction
As done to one of a sequestered life
And holy order, the law's penalty
Being double forfeiture, of life and state,
Reproach, shame, infamy, all these incurred
Through my inconsiderate rashness!
Dennis. My life, too!

72. *The friar is strangled.*] *MS3 subst.* 83. serious. What] *MS1b*; serious: to a consciens / startled with bloodd and murder. What *Ms1a.* 86. Let's remove it, then.] *Bu., perhaps before damage to MS*;< >t then *MS.*

---

71. *With ... about him*] an echo of *Ham.* I.v.79/III.iii.73ff? Certainly for a moment we enter the world of revenge tragedy.

72. s.d.] The friar is strangled either by Dennis alone, or with his master's help. In Marlowe's *Jew of Malta* IV.i. (a direct parallel; see Introduction) two men use one noose. In Webster's *Duchess of Malfi* IV.ii the executioners use two cords to kill the duchess.

74–5. *'Tis ... night*] a parody of the famous line of Catullus (poem 5.6, an invitation to love): 'nox est perpetua una dormienda'. The parody is especially bitter in this context.

79. *fact*] crime.

How to prevent the danger of all these?
Lord d'Averne. Ay, that will ask much brain, much project.
Dennis. Sir,
Shall we pop him in some privy?
Lord d'Averne. Double injury,
To prey upon the soul, and after death
Do to the body such discourtesy,
It neither savours of a generous spirit
Nor that which we call manly.
Dennis. Anything
For a quiet life, but this same wry-necked death,
That which still spoils all drinking, 'tis a thing
I never could endure. As you are noble,
Keep still my windpipe open.
Lord d'Averne. Out of many,
Musing for both our safeties, I have found
One that's above the rest most probable.
Dennis. What, what, I pray, sir?
Lord d'Averne. Interrupt me not.
Say I should now beget a stratagem
To save mine own life, mine estate and goods,
Ay, and secure thee, too?
Dennis. 'Twere excellent, sir.
Lord d'Averne. I have project for all these, as willingly
To lengthen both our lives, and limit us
Time to repent his death.
Dennis. But how, I pray, sir?
Lord d'Averne. Ay, there's the difficulty. But now I have't:
Betwixt us and the cloister's but one wall,
And that of no great height. Could we in private
Convey this friar into the monastery,
It might be then imagined some of them
Might be his death's-man, which might seem more probable
Because as I had late intelligence
There hath been strife amongst them.
Dennis. Better still.
Lord d'Averne. Now, how can we incur the least suspect,
For what should he do from the friary,
Or what make here, at this unseasoned hour?
Dennis. I apprehend you, and to further this
In the back yard there is a ladder, sir.

122. from the friary,] *MS1b*; out off the monastery *MS1a*.

---

94. *project*] planning.

99–100. *Anything . . . life*] This possibly proverbial phrase is first recorded as the title of a Middleton play, *c.* 1621.

103. *out of many*] (solutions).

111. *limit*] allow.

121. *suspect*] suspicion.

Mount him upon my back, and I'll convey him
Where some, not we, shall answer for his death.

Lord d'Averne. As desperate wounds still must have desperate cures,
So all rash mischiefs should have sudden shifts.
We'll put it to the venture.

Dennis. Mount him, then,
I'll once try if the venture of a ladder
Can keep me from the halter.

[*Exeunt* LORD D'AVERNE *and* DENNIS *with* FRIAR JOHN'S *body.*]

ACT IV

SCENE i

Enter the CLOWN.

Clown. I have left a full court behind me, Mildew pleading of the one side, my master on the other, and the lawyers fending and proving on both. There's such yelling and bawling, I know not whether it made any deaf to hear it, but I am sure I was almost sick to see't. While they are brabbling in the city, I am sent back to the village to cheer up the two young mermaids, for since their throats have been rinsed with salt water they sing with no less sweetness. But stay, I spy a fisherman drawing his net up to the shore. I'll slack some of my speed, to see how he hath sped since the last tempest.

132.1.] *Explicit Actus* $3^{S.}$ *MS.*

---

128. *desperate . . . cures*] proverbial (D357): 'extreme diseases call for extreme remedies'.

The first nine lines have no equivalent in Plautus. Lines 10–153 correspond to *Rud.* 906–1051. The discoveries (154–327) are a modernisation of *Rud.* 1052–1190: the contents of Palaestra's casket (a chain with a little gold sword inscribed 'Daemones', a two-headed axe inscribed 'Daedalis', a small silver sickle, a pair of clasped hands and a windlass) become a pair of handkerchiefs (with embroidered inscriptions in gold and silver thread) and a diamond brooch. Heywood sacrifices the individuality of the items in Plautus for a more domestic effect, and for the connexion of the handkerchiefs with tears later, with the entrance of Ashburn's wife. The scene between Mirabel/Palestra and the wife is merely described in *Rud.*, ll. 1205–7. The Gripus soliloquy and song (363–7 and *App.* 193–223) parallel *Rud.* 1184–90, but with quite different effect: in *Rud.*, Gripus plans to hang himself; Heywood's fisherman praises poverty, and his freedom, like that of Palestra and Scribonia, becomes a reward for virtue.

2. *fending and proving*] defending and probing; arguing.

5. *brabbling*] wrangling.

9.] (See *App.* for text cut in *MS.*)

Enter [Gripus,] *the* FISHERMAN.

Fisherman. Let me better
Survey my prize. 'Tis of good weight, I feel.
Now, should it be some treasure, I were made.

Clown. [*Aside*] Which if it prove, I'll half mar you or be half made with you.

Fisherman. It must be gold, by the weight.

Clown. [*Aside*] If it be so heavy, 'tis ten to one but I'll do you the courtesy to ease you of part of your burden.

Fisherman. None save myself is guilty of this prize.
'Tis all mine own, and I'll bethink me best
How to bestow of this rich magazine.

Clown. [*Aside*] And I am studying too, with what line, what angle, what fizgig, what casting net, I can share with you in this sea-booty.

Fisherman. I will dissemble, as most rich men do,
Plead poverty, and speak my master fair,
Buy out my freedom for some little sum,
And being mine own man, buy lands and house.
That done, to sea I'll rig ships of mine own,
And since the sea hath made me up a stock,
I'll venture it to sea. Who knows, but I in time
May prove a noble merchant.

Clown. [*Aside*] Yes, of eel-skins. [*To Fisherman*] Stay you, sirrah!

Fisherman. I know no fish of that name. Limpet, mullet, conger, dolphin, shark I know, and plaice—I would somebody else had thine! For herring, I would thou hadst none, nor cod, for smelt, thou art too hot in my nose already. But such a fish called 'sirrah' never came within the compass of my net. What art thou, a shrimp, a dog-fish or a poor-John?

Clown. I only come to desire thy judgement and counsel.

Fisherman. Go to the bench for judgement, and to the law-courts for counsel—I am free of neither, only one of Neptune's poor bastards, a spawn of the sea, and now gladly desires to be rid of thee aland.

Clown. Only one question resolve me, and I have done.

17. part] *MS1b*; half *MS1a*. 37. net.] *MS1b*; draught. *MS1a*.

---

18. *guilty*] An odd adjective, suggesting an uneasy conscience. Or it it a simple malapropism? In either case, it may derive from association with the gold: 'gilt'.

20. *magazine*] store, treasure.

22. *fizgig*] harpoon.

31–2. *merchant . . . eel-skins*] rag and bone man; proverbial (M882) for a salesman with no stock.

35. *herring*] (with pun on 'hearing').
cod] (bawdy).
smelt] a fish, but with pun on 'being smelled'.

38. *poor-John*] salted fish.

38.] (See *App.* for text cut in *MS.*)

Fisherman. To be well rid of thee, I care not if I lose so much time.

Clown. But faithfully.

Fisherman. As I am honest peterman.

Clown. Observe me, then:
I saw a thief committing felony,
I know the master of the thing was stolen,
I come unto this thief (as't might be, thee)
And make this covenant: either give me half
And make me sharer, or thou forfeitst all!—
I'll peach thee to the owner. In this case
What may I justly claim?

Fisherman. Rather than forfeit all, I should yield half.

Clown. Know, then, 'tis thy case and my case, a most plain case, and concerns the booty in that cap-case. I know the lord that wants it, and the master that owes it, both how it was lost and where it was lost. Then come, unloose, unbuckle, unclasp, uncase, let's see what fortune hath sent us, and so part it equally betwixt us.

Fisherman. Stay, stay, my friend, this my case must not be opened till your case be better looked into. Thou knowest who lost it, I who found it; thou the lord of it that was, I the owner that now is; thou who did possess it, I who doth enjoy it; he had it, I have it; he might have kept it, I will keep it. I ventured for all, I will inherit all, and there's thy pitiful case laid ope.

Clown. First prove this to be thine.

Fisherman. I can, and by the fisherman's rhetoric.

Clown. Proceed, sea-gull.

Fisherman. Thus, land-spaniel: no man can say 'this is my fish', till he find it in his net.

Clown. Good.

Fisherman. What I catch is mine own: my lands, my goods, my copyhold, my fee-simple. Mine to sell, mine to give, mine to lend and mine to cast away. No man claim part, no man share, since fishing is free and the sea common.

Clown. How canst thou prove that to be a fish that was not bred in the water, that could never swim, that hath neither roe nor milt, scale nor fin, life nor motion? Did ever man hear of a fish called a budget? What shape? What colour?

Fisherman. This shape, this colour. There's roe within better than the spawn of sturgeon. I must confess indeed they are rarely seen and seldom found, for this is the first I ever catched in all the time of my fishing.

Clown. All this sea-sophistry will not serve your turn, for where my

49. stolen,] *MS1b*; lost *MS1a*.

---

47. *peterman*] fisherman (after St Peter).
53. *peach*] inform against.
57. *cap-case*] portmanteau.
58. *owes*] owns.
74. *copyhold . . . fee-simple*] types of property ownership.
76.] (See *App.* for text cut in *MS.*)

right is detained me by fair means, I will have it by force.

Fisherman. Of what I caught in the sea?

Clown. Yes, and what I catch hold on ashore. With what conscience canst thou deny me part of the gain, when the owner, hearing it is in thy custody and within my knowledge, must either find me a principal in the theft or at least accessory to the felony?

Fisherman. I'll show thee a ready way to prevent both.

Clown. How that?

Fisherman. Marry, thus: go thou quietly thy way, I'll go peaceably mine; betray thou me to nobody, as I mean to impart to thee nothing; seek thy preferment by land, as I have done mine by sea; be thou mute, I'll be dumb; thou silent, I mumbudget; thou dismiss me, I'll acquit thee, so thou art neither thief nor accessory.

Clown. Sirrah, though you be owner of the boat,
I'll steer my course at helm. *Noise within.*

Fisherman. Hands off, I say. But hark, a noise within, let's cease our controversy till we see an end of that.

Clown. True, and be judged by the next quiet man we meet.

Fisherman. Content.

Enter after a noise or tumult [John] ASHBURN, *his* WIFE, PALESTRA, SCRIBONIA *and* GODFREY.

Wife. I'll not believe a syllable thou speakst.
False hearts and false tongues go together still—
They both are quick in thee.

Ashburn. Have patience, woman.

Wife. I've been too long a grizel. Not content
To have thy haunts abroad, where there are marts
And places of lewd brothelry enough
Where thou mayst waste thy body, purse and credit,
But thou wouldst make thy private house a stews!

Ashburn. But hear me, wife!

Wife. I'll hear none but myself.
Are your legs grown so feeble on the sudden
They fail when you should travel to your whores,
But you must bring them home and keep them here
Under my nose? I'm not so past my senses,
But at this age can smell your knavery.

Palestra. Good woman, here's none such!

Wife. Bold baggage, peace!
'Tis not your turn to prate yet. Lust and impudence
I know still go together.

88. ashore.] *MS1b*; a land *MS1a*.

---

97. *mumbudget*] quiet (from a children's game); proverbial (M1311).
107. *quick*] alive.
108. *grizel*] patient wife (cf. Chaucer's Griselda in *The Clerk's Tale*); see Introduction.
121.] (See *App.* for text cut in *MS.*)

Godfrey. [*Aside*] Why, this storm's worse than that untiled the house.
Ashburn. But understand me.
It is mere pity, and no bad intent,
No unchaste thought, but my mere charity,
In the remembrance of our long-lost child,
To show some love to these distressèd maids.
Wife. Sweet charity? Nay, usury withal
For one child lost, whose goodness might have blessed
And been an honour to our family,
To bring me home a couple of loose things—
I know not what to term them. But for thee,
Old fornicator, that jad'st me at home,
And yet can find a young colt's tooth abroad.
Old as I am, mine eyes are not so dim
But can discern this without spectacles.
Hence from my gate, you sirens come from sea,
Or as I live, I'll wash your paintings off,
And with hot scalding water, instantly. *Exit.*
Godfrey. Nay, then, sweethearts, you cannot say you have
Had cold entertainment.
Palestra. The land's to us as dreadful as the seas,
For we are here, as by the billows, tossed
From one fear to another.
Ashburn. Pretty souls,
Despair not you of comfort. I'll not leave you
To the least danger till some news return
From him that undertakes your patronage.
[*To Godfrey*] You, sirrah, usher them unto the friary
Whence none dares force them. I have a curst wife, you see,
And better you than I take sanctuary.
Scribonia. We will be swayed by you, as one in whom
We yet have found all goodness.
Ashburn. Leave them there
To safety, then return.
Exeunt [GODFREY, PALESTRA *and* SCRIBONIA].
Clown. What sayst thou to this gentleman?
Fisherman. No man better. [*Aside*] Now it will go on my side. This is my own master; sure he cannot be so unnatural to give sentence against his own natural servant. [*To Ashburn*] Sir, good day.
Ashburn. Gramercies. I in troth much suffered for thee,
Knowing how rashly thou exposed thyself
To such a turbulent sea.
Clown. I likewise, sir, salute you.
Ashburn. Thanks, good friend.
Clown. But sir, is this your servant?

---

133. *jad'st*] Pretending to be tired is the trick of a lazy horse, a jade.
134. *colt's tooth*] wantonness; proverbial (C525).
136. *discern . . . spectacles*] proverbial (S733.1) for something unambiguous.
162.] (See *App.* for text cut in MS.)

Ashburn. Yes, I acknowledge him,
And thou I think belongst to Master Raphael,
Employed about these women.

Clown. Yes, I acknowledge it. But you are sure he's yours?

Ashburn. Once again I do confess him mine.

Clown. Then hear me speak.

Fisherman. Hear me your servant.

Ashburn. Whate'er the strife be, I'll hear the stranger first.

Clown. In this you do but justice. I pray, tell me, you venture on the sea, is this a fish or no? Or if a fish, what fish do you call it? [*To Fisherman*] Peace, you.

Ashburn. It is nor fish nor flesh.

Clown. Nor good red herring. Fisherman, you're gone.

Fisherman. Thou art deceived, I am here still, and may have here, for aught I know, to buy all the red herring in Marseilles.

Clown. Did you ever hear of a fish called a budget?

Ashburn. I protest never since I knew the sea.

Clown. You are gone again, fisherman.

Fisherman. I am here still, and now master, hear me.

Clown. Let me proceed. This bag, this knapsack, or this portmantua he would make a fish, because took in his net. Now sir, I come to you with this old proverb, All's not fish that comes to net. There you are gone again.

Fisherman. But—

Clown. No but nor turbot. I suspect this budget to be the bawd's, in which are the discoveries of this young woman's country and parents. Now sir, for their sakes, for my master's sake, for all our sakes, use the authority of a master to search, and show the power you have over a servant to command.

Ashburn. Will he or not, he shall assent to that.

Fisherman. A mere trick to undo me ere I know what I am worth.

[*Enter* GODFREY.]

Ashburn. [*To Godfrey*] Call in the damsels,
Entreat them fairly hither. Say we hope
We shall have good news for them. [*Exit* GODFREY.]

Fisherman. I will part with it only on this condition: that if there be nothing in it which concerns them, the rest may return to me unrifled and untouched.

Ashburn. Did it contain the value of a mine,

171. you venture on / the] *J*; >ou vente< *MS*. 193. *Fisherman*.] *J*; Clowne *MS*.

169.] (See *App*. for text cut in *MS*.)
174–5. *fish . . . herring*] proverbial (F319).
177. *to buy*] enough to buy.
184. *All's . . . net*] as the Clown notes, proverbial (A136).
198. *nothing*] This would more logically read 'anything', and may be a copying error.

I claim no part in it.
Fishberman. Nor you.
Clown. Nor I.
Fisherman. By the contents of this budget.
Clown. I swear.
Ashburn. I vow.
Fisherman. Then there, tak't to you, master, and once more good luck on my side.

Enter GODFREY, *ushering in* PALESTRA *and* SCRIBONIA.

Palestra. You sent to speak with us.
Ashburn. I did, indeed.
Say, know you this? You've leave, survey it well.
Palestra. This? Know I this? O, my Scribonia, see!
Yes, and by this alone may know myself.
Look well upon't, dear sister. Ecstasy
May dim mine eyes, it cannot purblind thine.
Scribonia. It is the same, Palestra.
Fisherman. Then sure I shall not be the same man in the afternoon that I was in the morning.
Scribonia. In this is a great mass of wealth included,
All that the bawd hath by corruption got
In many a thrifty year.
Fisherman. Comfort for me.
Ashburn. But tell me, is there aught of yours included
Which you may justly challenge?
Palestra. Of that gold?
No, not the value of one poor denier.
'Tis all base brokage both of sin and shame
Of which we ne'er were guilty. Yet enclosed
There shall you find a cabinet of mine
Where both my natural parents you may see
In a small room intruded.
Fisherman. An unnatural child thou art, to thrust thy natural parents into a leathern bag and leave them in the bottom of the sea.
Palestra. Show me the casket. If before you ope it
I do not name you every parcel in't,
Let it no more be mine, make't your own prize.
But such small trifles as I justly challenge
And cannot yield you the least benefit,
Of them let me be mistress, since they are
The sum and crown of all my future hopes,
But from my tender infancy detained.

---

212. *shall not*] Gripus was happy in the morning, and now sad. If 'not' is a copying error, Heywood may have intended the meaning 'I shall be the same slave this afternoon as I was this morning', for which cf. *WWH* III.iii.l.
219. *denier*] small copper coin.
229. *cabinet*] jewel-case.

As for the gold and jewels, make't your spoil—
Of that I claim no portion.
Fisherman. I accept of the condition.
Ashburn. It is both just and honest. I' the meantime
Virgin, stand you aloof—we'll have no juggling.
And Gripus, since the business concerns you,
Have you a curious eye to't.
Fisherman. Fear not me, for both at sea and land I was ever a good markman.
[*The casket is opened.*]
Ashburn. The casket is now opened. What comes first?
Palestra. Above, the clothes in which I first was swathed,
The linen first worn in mine infancy.
Ashburn. These are child's swathings, whether thine or no
It is to me uncertain. To the rest.
Palestra. And next to these is a rich handkercher
Where you shall find in golden letters wrought
My place of birth, mine and my father's name.
Ashburn. Here's such a handkercher, such letters writ.
Speak them as I shall read them.
Palestra. 'Mirabel'—
Ashburn. Right, 'Mirabel'—
Palestra. 'Daughter of John Ashburn, merchant'—
Ashburn. True, 'of John Ashburn, merchant' (O, my soul!)—
Proceed, prithee, proceed.
Palestra. 'And born in Christ Church, London, *Anno* 1600.'
Ashburn. O, you immortal powers, I stagger yet
Between despair and hope, and cannot guess
Which way my fate will sway me. O, speak, speak
Thy mother's name!
Palestra. Read it in silver letters plainly wrought
In the next embroidered linen.
Ashburn. If that fail not,
I then have a firm rock to build upon.
'The gift of Isabel to her daughter Mirabel.'
O, friend, O, servant!
Clown. How is't, sir?
Fisherman. How now, master?
Ashburn. I, that so many years have been despoiled,
Neglected, scattered, am made up again,
Repaired and new created!
Palestra. Search but further,
And there's a golden brooch, in it a diamond,
Upon my birthday given me by my father.
Ashburn. I have long sought, and now at length have found,

257. 1600.'] *MS1*; 1530 *MS3*.

239. *juggling*] cheating.
247. *swathings*] swaddling-bands.

That diamond, thee, my daughter?
Palestra. How, sir?
Ashburn. She that so late excluded thee my house
And shut these gates against thee, Isabel
Thy mother, these were her own handiwork,
Bestowed upon thee in thine infancy
To make us now both happy in thy growth.
I am John Ashburn, merchant. London, Christ Church,
The year, place, time, agree thee to be mine,
O mirror of thy sex, my Mirabel!
Palestra. This surplusage of joy should not be feigned.
Ashburn. No more than these notes are infallible.
Palestra. Thus, then, in all humility I kneel
To you, my acknowledged father.
Ashburn. Rise, my girl.
Fisherman. Had I not drawn this kindred out of the sea, where had it been? All drowned, by this.
Ashburn. No trifling now. Post, Godfrey, to my wife,
Tell her no more than thou hast heard and seen—
She's hard of faith, relate it punctually.
Bear her—[*To Palestra*] O, let me borrow them so long—
These, better to confirm her. Bid her haste,
And for the truth add these as testimony.
Nay, art thou here still?
Godfrey. Like a shadow vanished,
But to return a substance. [*Exit.*]
Ashburn. O, my dear daughter! Where's young Raphael's man?
Bear him of all what thou hast seen a perfect
And true relation.
Clown. Ay, sir.
Ashburn. Bid him, too,
All business set apart, make hither.
Clown. Ay, sir.
Ashburn. Tell him that his Palestra is my Mirabel.
Clown. Ay, sir.
Ashburn. And that she is my daughter, my lost child.
Clown. Ay, sir.
Ashburn. And that of all this I am most assured.
Clown. Ay sir.
Ashburn. Thou wilt not do all this.
Clown. I will, you lie, sir.
Ashburn. How, sir?
Clown. Ay, sir.
Ashburn. Say that this day she shall be made his wife.
Clown. Ay, sir.

---

282. *agree*] grant.
292. *punctually*] accurately.
296–7. *shadow . . . substance*] cf. *ET* III.iii.71–2 and note.

Ashburn. Why, then, add wings unto your heels and fly, sir.
Clown. Ay, sir. But ere I take my flight for this good service,
You'll mediate with him for my freedom?
Ashburn. So.
Clown. And woo your daughter to do so, too?
Ashburn. So.
Clown. And say to him I shall be thankful?
Ashburn. So.
Clown. Your daughter's and your servant ever?
Ashburn. So.
Clown. To go, run, ride of all your errands?
Ashburn. So.
Clown. In all this you'll be slack in nothing?
Ashburn. So.
Clown. And you'll hereafter love me still?
Ashburn. So, so.
Clown. How? But 'so-so'?
Ashburn. Yes, so, and so, and so. [*Beats him.*]
Clown. Why, then, I go, go, go. [*Exit.*]
Ashburn. But one thing, I entreat you, Mirabel:
This thirteen years, since by rude creditors
Tossed and oppressed, nay, rent out of mine own,
I have been forced to seek my fate abroad—
How were you ravished thence, or since that time
What strange adventures passed?

Enter GODFREY *and the* WIFE, *with the handkerchief.*

Palestra. My mother's presence
Must now prevent my answer.
Wife. Where is she? O, where, where? For by these tokens,
These of her childhood most unfallid signs,
I know her for my daughter.
Palestra. I have been
The long and wretched owner of that cabinet,
With all therein contained.
Wife. Into thy bosom
O, let me rain a shower of joyful tears
To welcome thee, my Mirabel.
Godfrey. You threatened her but now with scalding water.
Methinks you had more need to comfort her
With hot waters, for sure she cannot be
Warm, since she came so late out of the cold bath.

313. your *MS1b*; thye *MS1a*. 318. your servant] *Bu*; your your servant *MS*. 325. years, since] *Bu*; yeares since *MS*. 329. *Palestra.*] *this ed.*; Mirable *MS* (*and for remainder of scene*).

332. *unfallid*] infallible (used only here, *OED*).
340. *hot waters*] alcoholic spirits (*OED* 1643); cf. *ET* I.ii.250.

Wife. Make fires, bid them make ready wholesome broths,
Make warm the bed and see the sheets well aired.
At length, then, have I found thee?
Ashburn. But what's she
That's in thy fellowship?
Palestra. My fellow sharer
In all misfortunes, and for many years
So dear to me, I cannot taste a blessedness
Of which she's not partaker.
Wife. For thy sake,
She shall be mine, too. And, in her, I'll think
The powers above have for my single loss
Given me at length a double recompense.
Scribonia. For which he that protects all innocence
Will in good time reward you.
Wife. Nay, in, in,
This cold is prejudicial to your healths.
I'll count you both my twins.
Exeunt [WIFE *and* CLOWN].
Ashburn. Strange alteration:
Scolding is turned to pity; spleen and malice
To mercy and compassion.
Fisherman. But your promise,
Touching my budget.
Ashburn. Godfrey, bear it in
And lodge it safe. There's now no time for that.
We'll talk of it hereafter.
Godfrey. Fellow Gripus, I am made for this time porter.
Ladies, your trusty treasurer.
Exeunt [*all except* FISHERMAN].
Fisherman. These are the fishermen, and I the fish catched in the net. Well, my comfort is, though my booty have made me no richer than I was, poorer than I am I cannot be. And yet for all this I have one crochet left in my pate to bait a new hook for the gold in the portmantua. [*Exit.*]

361. *I... porter*] cf. *WKK* xii, 20, Heywood's *Escapes of Jupiter* 1677, and *Err.* III.i.42.
365.] (See *App.* for text cut in *MS.*)
366. *crochet*] whimsy, device; but with a play on 'hook'.

ACT IV SCENE ii

Enter [from above] DENNIS, *with the [body of]* FRIAR [JOHN] *upon his back.*

Dennis. Whether a knavish or a sinful load,
Or one, or both, I know not. Massy it is,
And if no friend will for me, I'll be sorry
For mine own heaviness. And here's a place,
Though neither of the secretest nor the best,
To unlade myself of this iniquity.
[*Sets down the body against one of the stage posts.*]
When I sat late astride upon the wall
To lift the ladder this way for descent,
Methought the friar looked like Saint George a-horseback,
And I his trusty steed. But now's no trifling,
He's where he is in commons, we discharged
Both of suspect and murder, which let the covent
Tomorrow morning answer how they can.
I'll back the way we came. What's done, none saw
I'th' house nor here. They answer then the law. *Exit.*

Enter FRIAR RICHARD.

Friar Richard. Of all th'infirmities belonging to us
I hold those worst that will not let a man
Rest in his bed a-nights, and I of that
(By reason of a late cold I have got)
Am at this instant guilty. Which this rising
From a warm bed in these cold frosty nights
Rather augments than helps, but all necessities
Must be obeyed. But soft, there's one before me!

Scene heading] this ed.; Actus 4^s^. Scena 3^a^. *MS.* 0.1. *from above*] *MS3*. 3. if no friend will] *MS1b*; (iff no ffrend,) at this tyme, will *MS1a*. 6 s.d.] *Based on* Post *MS3* (*altered from MS3* Arras), *marginal note at l. 31.* 11. He's where he is] *MS1b*; hee's nwe where hee's *MS1a*. 13. how they can] *MS1b*; ffor my part *MS1a*. 16. us] *MS1b*; man, *MS1a*.

The remainder of Act IV follows the story, and some of the wording, of Masuccio. This scene, the 'murder' of an already dead man, has parallels in *The Jew of Malta* and *The Revenger's Tragedy* (see Introduction). Both Heywood and the Cockpit prompter had difficulty with the staging, Heywood allowing a choice of staff or stone as weapon, and the prompter placing the body first in front of the arras, and then further downstage against one of the posts supporting the 'heavens'. This allows Friar Richard to face the audience while addressing the dead friar, placed by Dennis on the friary's privy.

6.1. posts) The staging is indicated by the prompter's note at l. 31.

9. *Saint . . . a-horseback*] proverbial (S42).

11. *in commons*] in the privy. (See *App.* for text cut in *MS.*)

22–3. *necessities . . . obeyed*] proverbial (N62.11).

By this small glimpse of moonlight I perceive him
To be Friar John, my ancient adversary.
Why, John! Why, brother! What, not speak? Nay, then
I see 'tis done of malice, and of purpose
Only to shame me, since he knows the rest
Take notice what a loose man I am grown.
Nay, prithee, sweet Friar John, I am in haste,
Horrible haste! Do but release me now,
I am thy friend for ever. What, not hear?
Feign to be deaf, of purpose and of spite?
Then here is that shall rouse you.
Either strikes him with a staff or casts a stone.
Are you fall'n?
What, and still mute and silent, nay, not stir?
I'll rouse you, with a vengeance! [*Strikes again.*] Not one limb
To do his wonted office, foot nor hand?
Not a pulse beating? No breath? What, no motion?
O me, of all men living most accursed!
I have done a fearful murder, which our former
Inveterate hate will be a thousand testates
That I for that insidiated his life.
The deed's apparent, and the offence past pardon,
There's now no way, but fly. But fly which way?
The cloister gates are all barred and fast locked.
These sudden mischiefs should have sudden shifts.
About it, brain! And in good time I have't:
Suspicious rumours have been lately spread,
And more than whispered, of the incontinent love
Friar John bore the knight's lady. Had I means
How to convey his body o'er the wall,
To any, or the least part, of the house,
It might be thought the knight in jealousy
Had done this murder in a just revenge.
Let me survey th'ascent. Happy occasion—
To see how ready still the devil is
To help his servants—here's a ladder left!
Up, friar, my purpose is to admit you now
Of a new cloister. I will set his body
Upright in the knight's porch, and leave my patron
To answer for the fault, that hath more strength
Than I to tug with benches. *Exit* [*carrying up the body*].

29. Take notice] *MS1b*; knwe off *MS1a*. 62. s.d.] *indicated MS3*.

34.1. staff or . . . stone] See V.v.299: stone.
42. *insidiated*] plotted against (first used by Heywood, *OED*).
46. *sudden . . . shifts*] ?proverbial (cf. III.iii.128 and note).
62. *benches*] magistrates. (See *App*. for text cut in *MS*.)

[ACT IV SCENE iii]

Enter the knight, [LORD D'AVERNE,] *half unready, his* LADY *after him.*

Lord d'Averne. Ho, Dennis!
Lady d'Averne. Give me reason, I entreat,
Of these unquiet sleeps.
Lord d'Averne. You dog me, lady,
Like an ill genius.
Lady d'Averne. You were wont to call me
Your better angel.
Lord d'Averne. So I shall do still,
Would you betake you to your quiet sleeps
And leave me to my wakings.
Lady d'Averne. There belongs
Unto our bed so sweet a sympathy
I cannot rest without you.
Lord d'Averne. To your chamber.
There may grow else a worse antipathy
Betwixt your love and mine. I tell you, lady,
Mine is no woman's business. No reply!
Your least enforcèd presence at this time
Will but beget what you would loathe to bear,
Quarrel and harsh unkindness.
Lady d'Averne. Ever your lips
Have been to me a law. I suspect more
Than I would apprehend with willingness,
But though prevention cannot help what's past,
Conjugal faith may express itself at last. [*Exit.*]
Lord d'Averne. Why Dennis, ho! Awake, and rise in haste!
Dennis. [*Within*] What, is your lordship mad?
Lord d'Averne. Knowst thou what's passed,
And canst thou scape this danger?
Dennis. [*Within*] Did I not tell you
That all was safe, the body, too, disposed,
Better than in his grave?
Lord d'Averne. Strange thoughts solicit me.
Up, and enquire about the cloister wall
What noise thou hearst, if any private whispering
Or louder uproar 'bout the murder rise.
Dennis. [*Within*] I shall, I shall, sir.
Lord d'Averne. Guilt, though it wear a smooth and peaceful face,
Yet is within full of seditious thoughts
That makes continual faction. *Exit.*

Scene division] *indicated MS3.* 20. s.d.] *indicated MS3.* 30. faction.] *MS1b*; vprore *MS1a.*

0.1. half unready] not fully dressed; Dessen (p. 43) notes that this costuming can be emblematic of an uneasy conscience. For a discussion of the significance of this scene in the marriage relationship, see Introduction.

23. *solicit*] disquiet.

[ACT IV SCENE iv]

Enter FRIAR RICHARD *with* [*the body of*] FRIAR JOHN *upon his back.*

Friar Richard. This is the porch that leads into the hall.
Here rest for thine and mine own better ease.
This having done, to prevent death and shame
By the same steps I'll back the way I came.
[*Friar set up and left.*] *Exit* [FRIAR RICHARD].

[ACT IV SCENE v]

Enter DENNIS, *half unready.*

Dennis. This is the penalty belongs to service.
Masters still plot to their own private ends,
And we, that are their slaves and ministers,
Are chief still in the trouble. They engross
The pleasure and the profit, and we only
The sweat and pain. My lord hath done a mischief,
And now I must not sleep for't.
[*He sees Friar John's body.*]
What art thou?
None of the house, sure I should know thy face then.
Besides, my lord gives no such livery.
Now, in the name of heaven, what art thou? Speak?
Speak, if thou be'st a man, or if a ghost,
Then glide hence like a shadow. 'Tis the—O,
The friar hath nimbly skipped back o'er the wall,
Hath like a surly justice benched himself,
And sits here to accuse us. Where's my lord?
Help, help! His murdered ghost is come from hell,
On earth to cry *Vindicta*.

Enter LORD D'AVERNE.

Lord d'Averne. What clamour's this?
Dennis. O, sir!
Lord d'Averne. Why, how is't, Dennis?
Dennis. Never worse. The friar, sir—
Lord d'Averne. What of him?
Dennis. The slave, that would not leave the place but carried,
Is of himself come back.
Lord d'Averne. Whither?
Dennis. Look there!

4.1. s.d.] *indicated MS3.* Scene division] *indicated MS3.*

17. Vindicta] (Lat.) revenge; cf. *WWH* IV.i.238 and note.
20. *but*] unless.

Lord d'Averne. That which I took to be mere fantasy
I find now to be real. Murder is
A crying sin, and cannot be concealed.
Yet his return is strange.
Dennis. 'Tis most prodigious.
The very thought of it hath put a crick
Into my neck already.
Lord d'Averne. One further desperate trial I will make,
And put it to adventure.
Dennis. Pray, how that, sir?
Lord d'Averne. There's in my stable an old stallion, once
A lusty horse, but now past service.
Dennis. Good, sir.
Lord d'Averne. Him I'll have saddled and caparisoned—
Here in the hall a rusty armour hangs,
Pistols in rotten cases, an old sword,
And a cast lance, to all these suitable—
I'll have them instantly took down.
Dennis. And then?
Lord d'Averne. In these I'll arm the friar from head to knee,
Mount him into his saddle, with strong cords
There bind him fast, and to his gauntlet hand
Fasten his lance. For bases, 'tis no matter,
These his grey skirts will serve. Thus armed, thus mounted
And thus accoutred, with his beaver up
Turn him out of the gates, neither attended
With squire or page, like a strong knight adventures
To seek a desperate fortune.
Dennis. He may so, if he please,
Ride post unto the devil.
Lord d'Averne. This I'll see done,
'Tis a decree determined.
Dennis. Cap-à-pie
I'll see him armed and mounted.
[*Exeunt with* FRIAR JOHN'S *body.*]

48. s.d.] *indicated MS3.*

23–4. *Murder ... sin*] proverbial (M1315).
25. *prodigious*] ominous.
26. *crick*] (from imagining a noose).
32. *caparisoned*] harnessed.
35. *cast*] discarded.
40. *bases*] skirts of a knight's costume.
42. *beaver*] visor.
44. *adventures*] who travels.
46. *ride post*] go rapidly.
47. *Cap-à-pie*] (Fr.) armed head to toe.

[ACT IV SCENE vi]

Enter FRIAR RICHARD.

Friar Richard. This murder cannot be so smothered up
But I in th'end shall pay for't. But fear still
Is witty in prevention. Now, for instance,
There's but one refuge left me, that's to fly.
The gates are shut up on me, and myself
Am a bad footman, yet these difficulties
I can thus help: there to this place belongs
A mare, that every second day's employed
To carry corn and fetch meal from the mill
Distant some half league off. I, by this beast,
Will fashion mine escape. [*Calls*] What, baker, ho!
Baker. [*Within*] What's he that calls so early?
Friar Richard. I, Friar Richard.
Baker. [*Within*] What would you have, that you are stirring thus
An hour before the dawn?
Friar Richard. I cannot sleep,
And, understanding there's meal ready ground
Which thou must fetch this morning from the mill,
I'll save thee so much pains. Lend me the beast,
And let me forth the gate, I'll bring both back
Ere the bell ring to matins.
Baker. [*Within*] Marry, Friar Richard,
With all my heart and thank ye. I'll but rise
And halter her, then let you forth the gate.
You'll save me so much labour.
Friar Richard. This falls out
As I could wish, and in a fortunate hour.
Far better than to two legs, trust to four. [*Exit.*]

Scene division] *indicated MS3*. 12. s.d.] *indicated MS3*. 24.1.] *Explicit Actus 4^{s}: MS.*

2–3. *fear . . . prevention*] ?proverbial; cf. F133, 'fear gives wings'.
19. *Marry*] To be sure.

ACT V

SCENE i

Enter THOMAS ASHBURN, *the younger brother to* JOHN,
a merchant, with one of his factors.

Thomas Ashburn. Are all things safe aboard?
Factor. As you can wish, sir,
And, notwithstanding this combustious strife
Betwixt the winds and seas, our ship still tight,
No anchor, cable, tackle, sail or mast
Lost, though much dangered. All our damage is,
That where our purpose was for Italy
We are driven into Marseilles.
Thomas Ashburn. That's mine unhappiness,
That being bound upon a brother's quest,
Long absent from his country, who of late,
After confinement, penury, distress,
Hath gained a hopeful fortune, and I, travelling
To bear him tidings of a blest estate,
Am in my voyage thwarted.
Factor. In what province
Resides he at this present?
Thomas Ashburn. His last letters
That I received were dated from Leghorn,
Now we by this infortunate storm are driven
Into Marseilles roads.
Factor. For the small time
Of our abode here, what intend you, sir?
Thomas Ashburn. To take in victual and refresh our men,
Provide us of things needful, then once more
With all the expeditious haste we can
Set sail for Florence.
Factor. Please you, sir,
I'll steward all that business.
Thomas Ashburn. I' the meantime
I shall find leisure to survey the town,

0.1.] Fact: Gibson *added, MS3.* 1. sir,] *MS1b*; hem, *MS1a.* 23. I' the] *Bu*; I'l *MS.*

This scene has no Latin equivalent, except for 29–44 (*Rud.* 1265–80).
0.1. factors] agents.
2. *combustious*] turbulent.
15. *Leghorn*] Italian port (Livorno).

The quays, the temples, forts and monuments,
For what's the end of travel but to better us
In judgement and experience? What are these?
Withdraw, and give them street-room.

Enter RAPHAEL, TREADWAY *and the* CLOWN.

Raphael. Hath my Palestra found her parents, then?
Clown. As sure as I had lost you.
Raphael. And free born?
Clown. As any in Marseilles.
Raphael. English, sayst thou?
Clown. Or British, which you please.
Raphael. Her true name Mirabel,
And Ashburn's daughter?
Clown. Sure as yours is Raphael,
And Treadway's his.
Thomas Ashburn. Mirabel and Ashburn!
Factor. Names that concern you, sir.
Thomas Ashburn. Peace, listen further.
Raphael. Thou with these words hast ecstasied my soul
And I am all in rapture. Then he's pleased
We two shall be contracted?
Clown. 'Tis his mind, sir.
Raphael. The mother, too, consents?
Clown. So you shall find, sir.
Raphael. And Mirabel pleased, too?
Clown. She's so inclined, sir.
Raphael. And this the very day?
Clown. The time assigned, sir.
Raphael. She shall be surely mine?
Clown. As vows can bind, sir.
Raphael. Thou sawest all this?
Clown. I am sure I was not blind, sir.
Raphael. And all this shall be done?
Clown. Before you have dined, sir.
Raphael. O friend, either partake with me in joy
And bear part of this surplus, I shall else
Die in a pleasing surfeit.
Treadway. Friend, I do.
Withal entreat you intercede for me
To your fair love's companion, for if all
Th'estate I have in France can buy her freedom,
She shall no longer faint beneath the yoke
Of lewdness and temptation.
Raphael. The extent

33. *Raphael,*] *J*; Raphaels *MS*.

36. *ecstasied*] (first used by Heywood, *OED*).

Of that fixed love I ever vowed to thee
Thou in this act shall find.
Treadway. And it shall seal it,
Beyond all date or limit.
Raphael. Come, hasten, friend, methinks at length I spy
After rough tempests a more open sky.
[*Exeunt* RAPHAEL *and* TREADWAY.]
Clown. And I will after you, kind sir,
Since so merrily blows the wind, sir.
Thomas Ashburn. Stay, friend. I am a stranger in these parts,
And would in one thing gladly be resolved.
Clown. I am in haste.
Thomas Ashburn. That little leisure thou bestowest on me
I shall be glad to pay for. Nay, I will. [*Gives him money.*]
Drink that for my sake.

Clown. Not this, sir, as it is, for I can make a shift to dissolve hard metal into a more liquid substance. A cardecu? O, sir, I can distil this into a quintessence called *argentum potabile.*

Thomas Ashburn. I heard you name one Ashburn. Can you bring me
To the sight of such a man?

Clown. Easily I can, sir. But for another piece of the same stamp I can bring you to hear him, to feel him, to smell, to taste him, and to feed upon him your whole five senses.

Thomas Ashburn. [*Giving more money*] There's for thee, though I have no hope at all
To find in France what I in Florence seek.
And though my brother have no child alive,
As long since lost, when I was robbed of mine,
Yet for the name sake, to my other travels
I'll add this little toil, though purposeless.
I have about me letters of import
Directed to a merchant of that name,
For whose sake, being one to me entired,
I only crave to see the gentleman.

Clown. Believe me, sir, I never love to jest with those that beforehand deal with me in earnest. Will you follow me?

Thomas Ashburn. [*Aside*] Prove he my brother and his daughter found,
Lost by my want of care—which cannot be,

85. that] *Bu*; that that *MS.*

---

66. *make a shift*] manage.
67. *cardecu*] French silver quarter-crown (*quart d'écu*).
68. *quintessence*] final refinement (alchemy). argentum potabile] drinkable silver; cf. *aurum potabile.*
79. *name sake*] Dropping the possessive before 'sake' is not uncommon (eleven examples in Shakespeare); here there may also be a pun on 'namesake'.
83. *entired*] united.
86. *in earnest*] (with pun on 'earnest', instalment).

All reasons well considered—and I so happy
To bring him news of a recovered state,
Who to his foes so long hath been a prey,
I'd count my months and years but from this day! *Exeunt.*

ACT V SCENE ii

Enter at one door LORD D'AVERNE *and* DENNIS *with the* [*dead*] *friar armed, at the other* FRIAR RICHARD *and the* Baker.

Lord d'Averne. So, now all's fit, the daylight's not yet broke.
Mount him and lock him in the saddle fast,
Then turn him forth the gates.
Dennis. Pray, sir, your hand to raise him.
Lord d'Averne. Now let him post whither his fate shall guide him.
[*Exeunt with* FRIAR JOHN'S *body.*]
Baker. The mare's ready.
Friar Richard. Only the key to ope the cloister gate,
Then all is as it should be.
Baker. Take't, there 'tis.
But make haste, good Friar Richard, you will else
Have no new bread to dinner.
Friar Richard. Fear not, baker,
I'll prove her mettle. Thus I back one mare,
Lest I should ride another. *Exit.*
Baker. It is the kindest novice, of my conscience,
That e'er wore hood or cowl.
A noise within, trampling of horses.
What noise is that? Now, by the abbot's leave,
I will look out and see. [*Exit.*]

[ACT V SCENE iii]

Enter [LORD] D'AVERNE *and* DENNIS.

Lord d'Averne. How now, the news? The cause of that strange uproar?
Dennis. Strange indeed. But what th'event will be, I cannot guess.
Lord d'Averne. How is it? Speak.
Dennis. I had no sooner, as your Lordship bade,
Put him upon his voyage, turned him out,
But the old resty stallion snuffed and neighed,
And smelt, I think, some mare, backed—I perceived

14. abbot's] *Bu*; abbot *MS*. Scene division] *indicated MS3*.

11. *another*] (i.e., the gallows).
6. *resty*] restive.

By the moonlight—by a friar, in whose pursuit
Our new-made horseman with his threatening lance,
Pistols and rotten armour made such noise
That th'other, frighted, clamours through the streets
Nothing but 'Death and murder!'

Noise.

Lord d'Averne. But the sequel. The clamour still increaseth.

Enter the BAKER *running.*

Baker. O, never, never was seen such open malice!
Dennis. What's the business?
Baker. Give me but leave to breathe.
O, especially in a cloister!
Dennis. Out wi't, man!
Baker. The novice Richard, to save me a labour,
Borrowed my mare to fetch meal from the mill.
I know not how the devil Friar John knew't,
But all in armour watched him going out,
And after spurs to charge him, being unarmed,
And sure, if he cannot reach him with his lance,
He'll speed him with his pistols.
Dennis. [*Aside*] All's well yet.
Baker. This noise hath called much people from their beds
And troubled the whole village.

Noise.

Friar Richard. (*Within*) Hold, hold, I do confess the murder!
Baker. Sure, he hath slain him, for murder is confessed.
Lord d'Averne. [*Aside*] 'Tis better still.

Enter [John] ASHBURN, GODFREY, [*and others.*]

Godfrey. Was never known the like!
Baker. Is Richard slain?
I saw Friar John armed dreadfully with weapons
Not to be worn in peace, pursue his life,
All which I'll tell the abbot. [*Exit.*]
John Ashburn. Most strange it is, that the pursued is found
To be the murderer, the pursuer slain.
How was it, Godfrey? Thou wast up before me,
And canst discourse it best.
Godfrey. Thus, sir. At noise of murder, with the trampling
Of horse and rattling armour in the streets,
The villagers were woken from their sleeps.
Some gaped out of their windows, others ventured
Out of their doors, amongst which I was one

28.1. GODFREY, *and others*] *this ed.*; godffrey etc. *MS.* 39. woken] *Greg, from MS*; waken *Br. from MS.*

23. *speed*] murder.

That was the foremost, and saw Richard stopped
At a turning lane, then overtook by John,
Who not himself alone, but even his horse
Backing the t'other's beast, seemed with his feet
To paw him from his saddle. At this assault
Friar Richard cries 'Hold, hold, and haunt me not,
For I confess the murder!' Folk came in,
Found John i'the saddle, dead, the t'other sprawling
Upon the earth, alive, still crying out
That he had done the murder.
Lord d'Averne. [*Aside*] Excellent still. Withdraw, for we are safe.
[*Exeunt.*]

[ACT V SCENE iv]

Enter the ABBOT, *the* Baker, FRIAR RICHARD *prisoner and guarded.*
[*Stage-keepers as a guard.*]

Abbot. These mischiefs I foretold. What's malice else
Than murder half committed, though th'event
Be almost above apprehension strange?
Yet, since thine own confession pleads thee guilty,
Thou shalt have legal trial.
Friar Richard. I confess
I was the malefactor, and deserve
Th'extremity of law, but wonder much
How he, in such a short time after death,
Should purchase horse and weapons.
Abbot. Murder's a sin
Which often is miraculously revealed.
Let justice question that. Bear him to prison,
The t'other to his grave.
Baker. Being so valiant after death, methinks
He deserves the honour to be buried
Like a knight in his complete arms.
Abbot. These things should not be trifled. Honest friends,
Retire you to your homes. These are our charge.
We will acquaint our patron with this sad
And dire disaster, first his counsel use,
Next, as we may, our innocence excuse. [*Exeunt.*]

0.2. *Stagekeepers as a guard.*] *MS3*; guarded, etc. *MS1*. 14. deserves] *Bu*; deserve< *MS*. 15. armes.] *this ed*; arm< *MS*; armor *Bu*.

0.1. Stage-keepers] stagehands, specified by the prompter, Heywood's call for eighteen speakers in this final act having already stretched the company's resources; see Introduction.

20. *innocence*] ignorance.

[ACT V SCENE V]

Enter MILDEW *and* SARLABOIS.

Mildew. May the disease of Naples, now turned French,
Take both the judge and jurors! They have doomed
The fair Palestra from me.
Sarlabois. So they had
Scribonia, too, and mulcted us besides,
But that in part they did commiserate
Our so great loss by sea.
Mildew. This is the curse
Belongs to all us bawds, gentle and noble:
Even th'oldest fornicator will in private
Make happy use of us with hugs and bribes,
But let them take us at the public bench,
'Gainst conscience they will spit at us and doom us
Unto the post and cart. O, the corruptness
Of these dissembling lechers!
Sarlabois. 'Tis well, yet
You have reserved one virgin left for sale.
Of her make your best profit.
Mildew. A small stock
To raise a second fortune, yet come, friend,
We will go seek her out.

Enter Gripus *the* FISHERMAN.

Fisherman. No budget to be come by. My old master,
He stands on conscience to deliver it
To the true owner, but I think, in conscience,
To cheat me, and to keep it to himself,
Which he shall never do. To prevent which,
I'll openly proclaim it. Oyez!
If any usurer or base exacter
Any noble merchant, or merchant's factor,
Be't merchant-venturer or merchant-tailor,
Be he master pilot, boatswain, or sailor—
Godfrey. Hist! Gripus, hist!
Fisherman. Peace, fellow Godfrey! I'll now play the blabber:
If either passenger, owner, or swabber,

Scene heading] Actus 5[s.] Scena 3[s.] et vltima *MS1*. 3–6. *Sarlabois . . .* sea.] *cancelled, MS3*. 13–15. *Sarlabois . . .* profit.] *cancelled, MS3*.

Lines 1–125 are a version of *Rud.* 1281–end. The haggling and oath-taking (46–70) follow Plautus closely in tone, if not verbally.

1. *disease*] (venereal).
4. *mulcted*] fined.
12. *post and cart*] places of public whippings.
23. *Oyez!*] A town-crier's call for attention.
30. *swabber*] deck-hand.

That in the sea hath lost a leather budget,
And to the dolphins, whales, or sharks doth grudge it—
Godfrey. Wilt thou betray all? I'll go tell my master.
Fisherman. Yes, Godfrey, go, and tell him all and spare not.
I am grown desperate. If thou dost, I care not.
[*Exit* GODFREY.]
Mildew. [*Aside*] He talked of a leathern budget lost at sea.
More of that news would please me.
Fisherman. Be he a Christian, or believe in Mahomet,
I such a one this night took in my draw-net.
Mildew. My son, my child, nay rather, thou young man,
I'll take thee for my father, for in this,
Sure, thou hast new begot me.
Fisherman. Blessing on thee,
But should I have a thousand children more,
I almost durst presume I never should have
Another more hard-favoured.
Mildew. Thou art anything?
But hast thou such a budget?
Fisherman. Sir, I have,
And new took from the sea. What wouldst thou give
And have it safe?
Mildew. I'll give a hundred crowns.
Fisherman. Tush, offer me a souse—but not on the ear,
I will bar that aforehand.
Mildew. And all safe?
I'll give thee then two hundred.
Fisherman. Offer me a cardecu.
Mildew. Three hundred. Four. Nay, five,
So nothing be diminished.
Fisherman. I will have
A thousand crowns or nothing.
Mildew. That grows deep.
Fisherman. Not so deep as the sea was.
Mildew. Make all safe,
And I will give a thousand.
Fisherman. 'Tis a match,
But thou wilt swear to this?
Mildew. Give me mine oath.
Fisherman. If, when first I shall behold
My leathern bag that's stuffed with gold,
At sight thereof I pay not down
To Gripus every promised crown—
Now say after me:
May Mildew I in my best age—
Mildew. May Mildew I in my best age—

---

45. *hard-favoured*] ugly.
49. *souse*] halfpenny (Fr. sou), or a blow.

Fisherman. Die in some spital, stocks or cage—
Mildew. Die in some spital, stocks or cage.
Fisherman. I'll keep my promise, fail not thou thine oath.
So in, and tell my master. [*Exit.*]
Mildew. Yes, bawds keep oaths? 'Tmust be in leap-year, then,
Not now. What we swear we'll forswear again.

Enter [John] ASHBURN, *and* Gripus [*the* FISHERMAN].

John Ashburn. And he in that did well, for heaven defend
I should enrich me with what's none of mine.
Where is the man that claims it?
Fisherman. Here's my sworn son, that but even now
Acknowledged me to be his father.
John Ashburn. Knowest thou this?
[*Shows him the leather bag.*]
Mildew. Yes, for mine own. I had thought, like one forlorn,
All fortune had forsook me. But I see
My best days are to come. [*Takes the bag.*]
Welcome, my life.
Nay, if there be in any bawd a soul,
This now hath met the body.
John Ashburn. All's there safe,
Unrifled, nay, untouched, save a small casket
With some few trifles, of no value in't,
Yet to me precious, since by them I have found
My one and only daughter.
Mildew. How's that, pray?
John Ashburn. Thus: thy Palestra is my Mirabel.
Mildew. Now may you to your comfort keep the girl.
Since of my wealth I'm once again possessed,
I here acquit you of all charges past
Due for her education.
John Ashburn. You speak well.
Fisherman. It seems you are possessed, and this your own.
Mildew. Which I'll know how I part with.
Fisherman. Come quickly, and untruss.
Mildew. Untruss, sir, what?
Fisherman. Nay, if you stand on points, my crowns, my crowns.
Come, tell them out, a thousand.
Mildew. Thousand deaths
I will endure first, since I neither owe thee,
Nor will I pay thee anything.
Fisherman. Didst thou not swear?
Mildew. I did, and will again,
If it be to my profit, but oaths made

65. *spital*] hospital, especially for lepers.
92. *untruss*] unfasten.
93. *stand . . . points*] be meticulous (with pun on 'points', laces of a doublet).
98–9. *oaths . . . keep*] proverbial (O7): 'a sin to keep a sinful oath'.

And I but late for new disasters cursed,
Have with their light wings mounted me aloft
And for a haven in heaven new harboured me.
Yet they but feed upon their known delights.
Anon I'll make them surfeit.
Scribonia. If to this friendly, fair society
I, a poor destitute virgin, so much bound,
Should put you off with dilatory trifles
When you importune answer, 'twould appear
In me strange incivility. I am yours,
And being so, therefore consequently his.
John Ashburn. A match, then. But ere further you proceed,
Resolve me one thing, Mildew, not as thou art
Thyself, but as thou once wert made a Christian,
Knowest thou this maid's descent and parentage?
Mildew. I will resolve you like a convertite,
Not as the man I was: I knew their births,
But for mine own gain kept them still concealed.
John Ashburn. Now, as thou hop'st of grace—
Mildew. The nurse late dead
That had these two in charge, betrayed a-shipboard
And ravished from her country ere she expired,
Named her, the daughter of John Ashburn, merchant.
Her I Palestra called, she Mirabel,
That Winifred, daughter to Thomas Ashburn,
Brother to the said John, I called Scribonia,
They two are cousin germans.
Wife. This our niece!
Thomas Ashburn. [*Aside*] My daughter!
Palestra. Partners in sorrow, and so near allied,
And we till now ne'er knew it!
Scribonia. My dear cousin!
John Ashburn. Nay, I'll be my words' master. Reach your hands,
And though no nearer than an uncle, once
I'll play the father's part.
Thomas Ashburn. Pray, hold your hand, sir,
Here's one that will do't for you.
John Ashburn. Brother Thomas!
Thomas Ashburn. Peruse that letter, whilst I breathe these joys,
Imparting those a most unlimited love
In equal distribution: daughter, niece,
Sister and friends, let me divide amongst you
A father's, brother's and a kinsman's zeal,
With all th'unmeasured pleasures and delights

166. new] *MS1b*; strange *MS1a*. 191. *Wife.*] *MS1*; Ashb: *MS3*. 199. joys,] *Bu*; Ioy *MS*. 202. Sister] *MS1*; Brother *MS3*.

191. *cousin germans*] first cousins.

That thought of man can wish you.
John Ashburn. Spare reply.
These tell me that these bloodhounds who pursued
My fall, my oppressing creditors, I mean,
Are gone before to answer for my wrongs,
And in their deaths with due acknowledgement
Of all their violence done me—peace with them.
That likewise, by the death of a rich alderman,
My uncle, I am left a fair estate
In land eight hundred by the year, in coin
Twenty-five thousand pound. Make me, O heavens,
For this great blessing grateful, and not least
To you, my endeared brother.
Thomas Ashburn. One thing wonders me,
That I should find you near Marseilles here
When I was aimed for Florence, where your letters
Informed me you were planted.
John Ashburn. But even thither
Those cruel men dogged me with such pursuit
That there I found no safety, but was forced
To fly thence with that little I had left,
And to retire me to this obscure place
Where by the trade of fishing I have lived
Till now of a contented competence.
Those baits, hooks, lines and nets, for thy good service,
Gripus, I now make thine.
Fisherman. You are my noble master, and would I could have found more tricks than these in my budget—they had been all at your service.
John Ashburn. I purpose now for England, whither, so please,
These gentlemen consort us with their brides.
Both. Most willingly.
John Ashburn. There you shall see what welcome
Our London, so much spoke of here in France,
Can give to worthy strangers.
Thomas Ashburn. At my charge
Your shipping is provided, and at anchor
Lies ready in the road.
John Ashburn. O, happy storm
That ends in such a calm!

Enter GODFREY *in haste.*

Godfrey. Stay, gentlemen, and see a doleful sight,
One led to execution for a murder

238.1. *Enter* GODFREY *in haste.*] *MS1b*; Enter godffrye in hast / Actus 5[s]. Scena prima, memorandum *MS1a*.

---

216. *wonders*] amazes.
229. *tricks*] knicknacks.
232. *consort*] accompany.

The like hath scarce been heard of.
John Ashburn. Of the friar—
In part we were eye-witness of the fact,
Nor is our haste so great but we may stay
To view his tragic end, whom the strict law
Hath made a just example.

Enter the ABBOT, FRIAR RICHARD, Shrieve *and officers* [,with others].

Abbot. Upon thy true confession I have given thee
Such absolution as the church allows.
What hast thou else to say, ere thou art made
To all men here a woeful spectacle?
Friar Richard. This only: that betwixt Friar John and me
Was ever hate and malice and, although
With no intent of murder, this my hand,
This most unfortunate hand, bereft his life.
For which vile deed I mercy beg of heaven,
Next of the world, whom I offended too,
Pardon and pity. More to say I have not.
Heaven of my soul take charge, and of my body
Dispose, thou honest hangman.
Clown. 'Las, poor friar, and yet there's great hope of his soul, for I cannot spy one hair betwixt him and heaven.
Fisherman. And yet I doubt he will make but a bald reckoning of it.

Enter the LORD D'AVERNE *and his man* DENNIS.

Lord d'Averne. Stay the execution.
Abbot. Our noble founder, out of his great charity
And wonted goodness, begged him a reprieve.
Lord d'Averne. Brought a reprieve I have. Let go the friar
And take from me your warrant. I discharge him.
Shrieve. And yet, my lord, 'tis fit for our discharge
That the king's hand be seen.
Lord d'Averne. If not my word
Will pass for current, take my person, then,
Or if you think unequal the exchange,
I tender my man's too, to value his.
Meantime, dismiss him, as one innocent
Of what he is condemned.
Abbot. By his own mouth he stands accused.
Lord d'Averne. And witness, all of you, as freely I acquit him.

245.1.] officers E (*sc.* Etc.) *MS1a.* 271. value *MS1b*; equall *MS1a.* 274. accused] *MS1b*; condemd MS1a.

245.1. *Shrieve*] Sheriff.
260. *cannot ... betwixt*] proverbial (H24) for seeing no difference; the Clown's joke plays on the friar's baldness.
261. *bald reckoning*] plain confession.
269. *current*] genuine.

Shrieve. Honoured sir, be more plain, we understand you not.
Lord d'Averne. I'll make it plain, then.
Clown [*To Friar Richard*] Now, if thou be'st wise, draw thy neck out of the collar. Do, slip-string, do.
Friar Richard. Marry, with all my heart, and thank him, too.
Lord d'Averne. Attend me, reverend father, and you all
Of this assembly: for some spleen conceived
Against the friar deceased, I strangled him—
The cause why, no man here importune me,
For many reasons to myself best known
I hold fit to conceal it—but I murdered him
In mine own house.
Abbot. But, by your honour's favour,
How can that be, when Richard here confessed
He slew him in our cloister?
Lord d'Averne. Hear me out.
At first untouched with horror of the fact,
My purpose was to lay the guilt elsewhere,
And for that purpose caused my man to mount him
Over the cloister wall.
Dennis. Which soon I did,
By th'help of a short ladder, set him there
In a close place, and though not of the sweetest,
Yet, as I thought, the safest, left him then.
Friar Richard. Just in that place I found him, and imagining
He sat of purpose there, to despite me,
I hit him with a stone, he fell withal,
And I thought I had slain him.
Dennis. But how the devil
Got he into our porch? That wonders me.
Friar Richard. I found a ladder there—
Dennis. The same I left.
Friar Richard. Got him upon my shoulders, and by that
Conveyed him back, and left him in that porch
Where, as it seems, you found him.
Lord d'Averne. This troubling us, it drove us to new plots,
We armed the friar, accoutred as you saw,
Mounted him on a stallion, locked him fast
Into the saddle, turned him forth the gates
To try a second fortune.
Friar Richard. Just at the time
When I, being mounted on the baker's mare,
The gates were set wide ope for me to fly.
Abbot. So that it seems one beast pursued the t'other,

276. be] *MS1b*; praye bee *MS1a*. 277. plain,] *Bu*; plye *MS*.

278–9. *draw . . . collar*] escape the noose; proverbial (N69).
279. *slip-string*] rogue who deserves hanging.
295. *close*] secret; also with meaning of 'close-stool', privy.

And not the dead friar, Richard.
Lord d'Averne. Howsoever,
As one repentant for my rashness past,
And loath to imbrue me in more innocent blood,
I first confess my servant's guilt and mine,
Acquit the friar, and yield our persons up
To the full satisfaction of the law.

Enter the LADY D'AVERNE *and her* MAID, Millicent.

Lady d'Averne. Which, noble sir, the king thus mitigates.
See, I have here your pardon. In the time
That you were seized with this deep melancholy
And inward sorrow for a sin so foul,
Myself in person posted to the king,
In progress not far off, to him related
The passage of your business, neither rose I
From off my knees, till he had signed to this.
Lord d'Averne. Thou'st done the office of a noble wife.
His grace I'll not despise, nor thy great love
Ever forget, and if way may be found
To make least satisfaction to the dead,
I'll do't in vowed repentance.
Abbot. Which our prayers
In all our best devotions shall assist.
John Ashburn and [*the*] *rest.* All ours, great sir, to boot.
Lord d'Averne. We know you well, and thank you.
John Ashburn. But must now
Forsake this place, which we shall ever bless
For the great good that we have found therein,
And hence remove for England.
Lord d'Averne. Not before
All your successful joys we hear related
To comfort our late sorrows. To which purpose
We invite you and your friends to feast with us.
That granted, we will see you safe aboard,
And as we here rejoice in your affairs,
Forget not us in England in your prayers. [*Exeunt.*]

FINIS

325. *progress*] state visit.

APPENDIX

Text of passages of one line or more of *The Captives* cancelled by the author:

I.i.5

Treadway. No consequent. For instance, who so fond
To trust to colour? Are not the beauteous lilies,
The garden's pride and glory of the fields,
Though to the eye fair and delectable,
Yet rank in smell? The stainless swan
With all the ocean's water cannot wash
The blackness from her feet, 'tis born with her.
Oft painted vessels bring in poisoned cates
And the blackest serpents wear the golden'st scales;
And woman, made man's helper at the first,
Doth oft prove his destroyer.
Raphael. Say perhaps
Some friend of yours miscarried in his choice,
Will you condemn all women for that one?
Because we read one Lais was unchaste,
Are all Corinthian ladies courtesans?
Shall I, because my neighbour's house was burnt,
Condemn the necessary use of fire?
One surfeits, and shall I refuse to eat?
That merchantman by shipwrack lost his goods;
Shall I, because he perished in the sea,
Abjure the gainful trade of merchandise,
Despoil my ships and unbecome the deeps

5–9.] The series of proverbs (L297, W323, V35) illustrates the 'fair face, foul heart' theory of female beauty. It is not surprising that Heywood, generally an admirer of women, should decide against giving these sentiments to Treadway.

8. *cates*] delicacies.

14. *Lais*] celebrated Corinthian courtesan.

16–23. *Shall . . . tackles?*] An expansion of *Apology*, p. 50: 'Because such a man had his house burnt, we shall quite condemne the use of fire, because one man quaft poyson, we must forbeare to drinke, because some have beene shipwrack't, no man shall hereafter trafficke by sea.' See Arthur Brown, *MLR* 50 (1955), 497–8.

22. *unbecome*] deprive (this example only in *OED*).

Of their fair sails and tackles?
Treadway. Not so, friend,
Yet although her person . . .

I.i.52

. . . Portugal. Is this all, sir?
Raphael. Yes, all, and here's the sum.
Clown. [*Aside*] A small sum of that is worth all the business that I am sent about, for the all in all on't is, I am afraid that 'all' will prove worth nothing. [*Exit.*]

I.i.103

Such a coy thing, that he unto whose lot
She shall hereafter fall may boast himself
To be a happy husband. For our trade,

FOLLOWING I.i.108

Treadway. Yes and commend it in her, if that tongue,
Even from his first of speaking trained to lies,
Can now at length speak truth.
Clown. Ay, there's the doubt.

I.i.155

Treadway. I am, sir.
Mildew. So's my guest.
Clown. [*Aside*] And looks as if with me
He only could write 'witless'.
Raphael. Supper time

I.ii.52

It is a fair sweet lady.
Friar Richard. [*Aside*] How the lecher
Hugs at the very name!
Abbot. Morning and evening

FOLLOWING I.iii.90

Raphael. Old, grey and hoary.
Clown. And withal, cheating, cozening and crafty, a remarkable rascal, a damnable deceiver and a most substantial sinner.

I.iii.105

Presume I'll not forget you.
Raphael. For which courtesy
You shall oblige me to you. If not here,
We'll seek her further. France shall not contain this,
But I will find their start-holes.
Ashburn. Good speed with you.
Clown. If I were a dog now, and could hunt dry-foot, I could smell them out presently.

(The above passage, 'For . . . presently', replaced with Raphael's 'Fare you well, sir'.)

FOLLOWING I.iii.134

I would I were some dolphin, or some whale,
That they might sit astride upon my back
To bear them safe ashore, but I as yet
Could ne'er endure salt water. See, yet still,

FOLLOWING II.i.16

Is, if there be left any mercy for him,
Now in these briny waves made clean for heaven.

II.i.23

Amongst the rest
A budget or portmantua, which included
All the bawd's wealth; but that were nothing to me,
Though he had vowed and sworn to make me his heir;
The loss I so lament is a small casket
Kept by him from my childhood and packed up
Amongst his treasure, and that perishing,
I forfeit the long expectation
Ever to know my parents, therefore wish
With it I had i' the sea been buried.

FOLLOWING II.i.35

More dear to me than all the world besides,

46. *start-holes*] burrows (only citation in *OED* in this form; but see entry 'starting hole').
47. *hunt dry-foot*] track by scent.

II.i.40

All these at once afflict me.
Scribonia. Nothing me
More than Palestra's death.
Palestra. Ha! Who's that spake?

FOLLOWING II.i.60

Let us make haste with all the speed we can.

II.i.145

But O, I faint!
Abbot. Some faggots, instantly,
Hot broths, hot waters for them, and warm clothes!

II.ii.28

... Village. His friend's gone one way, he another, and I a third, contrary from them both. He cannot believe his enquiry to be well done, but he must send me to do't over again. I have asked all I met, and demanded of all I have seen, but for aught I can perceive, all to no purpose, I can understand of no such people. But what are these? Though they have slipped us, no creature shall slip me. These should be fishermen. Good...

II.ii.100

Clown. ... it. [*Aside*] I'll first in and see her, because I will be sure 'tis she. O Mercury, that I had thy wings tied to my heels! Here...

FOLLOWING II.ii.153

Enter GODFREY *with water.*

Godfrey. Where is my dainty damosella? Where?
Methought the water met me the half way
And leapt up full three steps to meet my pail.
'Tis thus whenas a man goes willingly
About his business. How fresh a kiss will taste
From her whose lips and every part besides
From head to toe have been so lately ducked

70. *clothes!*] *this ed*; cloath< *MS.* 82. meet] *Ms1b*; fill *MS1a.*

And rinsèd in salt water. Where's my sweet?
Not here? Nowhere. Why ho, my whiting mop
Late scaped from feeding haddocks! Ha, what, gone?
Nay, then, go thou too that she sent me for
To him that next shall find thee. Yet not so,
This learnèd pail instructs me by these letters
That it belongs unto this monastery,
And if it should be lost by my default
I may be charged with theft or sacrilege.
No, I'll deliver't to the owners, sure
(And this the place)
And not detain't, for fear't be to my cost,
Though both my kiss and all my pains be lost. [*Exit.*]

FOLLOWING II.iii.11

A magazine of riches, nay even those
By whom I meant to raise a fortune by,

FOLLOWING II.iii.18

Had not thy greater fraught been shipped with mine,
She had ne'er been overset.
Sarlabois. I rather think
Had we, when first the ship began to dance,
Hurled thee with thy cursed lading overboard,
We had sailed light and tight.

II.iii.49

Nimbler than virginal jacks!
Mildew. Thou'rt a sweet guest.
Sarlabois. Too good for such a host. Better to have been
Lodged in some spital, or if possible
To be imprisoned in some surgeon's box
That smells of salves and plasters.
Mildew. Now, what shark

FOLLOWING II.iii.63

Such quaking, shaking, quivering, shivering,
Such crying and such talk of flying, then of hiding

95. may] *MS1b*; should *MS1a*. 96–7.] *one line, MS.*

89. *whiting mop*] young fish; playful term for a girl.
102. *fraught*] freight.

And that there's no abiding. One cries out, and calls
The others ready to break down the walls,
Then weeping they whisper together
And say they would run if they knew whither,
And are indeed put to such strange affrights

III.i.11

Or to be found in churchmen? Nothing but love,
And all sir-reverence-like! 'Tis a question

FOLLOWING III.ii.41

And till aid come I'll lay mine ear and listen
To hear what further coil is kept within.
All's silent on the sudden.
Music. [*A song from within, sung by Palestra and Mildew.*]
[*Palestra.*] Help, help, O aid a wretched maid,
Or else we are undone, then.
[*Mildew.*] And have I caught, and have I caught you?
In vain it is to run, then.
[*Palestra.*] Some rescue, when? From gods or men?
Redeem us from these crosses.
[*Mildew.*] 'Tis all in vain, since now I gain
Part of my former losses.
[*Palestra.*] O heaven, defend! What, yet no end
Of these our strange disasters?
[*Mildew.*] No favour's known, no pity's shown,
To them that fly their masters.
[*Palestra.*] Why to defame, reproach and shame
Poor innocents thus drag ye?
[*Mildew.*] With your offence there's no dispense.
Away then. Wherefore lag ye?

FOLLOWING III.ii.110

Godfrey. Stir, and thou diest; we'll maul you.
Mildew. If there I can have none, let me depart
To seek elsewhere for justice.
Sarlabois. Keep him prisoner,
And set me free to find some advocate

---

120. *sir-reverence-like*] foul (sir-reverence: excrement).
124–39.] in *Rud.* (664–76) , a solo song by Palaestra.
129. *crosses*] adversities.
138. *dispense*] pardon.

To plead in his just cause.
Godfrey. Neither stir,
In pain of two French crowns, and they so cracked
Ne'er more to pass for current.
Ashburn. That presume.
Mildew. Misery of miseries, I am bound hand and foot,
And yet both legs and arms at liberty.
Godfrey. Yes, by the law called Stafford.

FOLLOWING III.ii.151

Godfrey. We'll find amongst us more than to make him
Four elbows. Elbow him of all sides, gentlemen.
It shall appear, before he parts with us,
That he hath showed himself no better than
A coxcomb.

FOLLOWING IV.i.9

Fisherman. I see, he that naught ventures nothing gains.
He that will be awake when others sleep
May sometimes purchase what may give him rest
When other loiterers shall be forced to rise
Or perish through mere want, as for example
Although the tempest frighted hence the fish
I have dragged something without fin or scale
May make me a good market. Let me better

FOLLOWING IV.i.38

Clown. I am one that watched the tide to know what thou hast caught, and have money in my pocket to buy thy draught.
Fisherman. And I am one, thou seest, that have only an empty wet net, but not so much as the tail of a sprat at this time to sell, for love or money.

145. cracked] *Bu*; crack< *MS.* 166. sprat] *Bu*; sprotte, *MS.* 167. or] this ed; off *MS.*

---

145. *French crowns*] heads bald from venereal disease.
cracked] damaged (of coins, the other meaning of 'crowns').

151. *Elbow him*] ?Take him by the arms (this usage not in *OED*); possibly 'jostle him'. There may be a joke here, and in 'Four elbows', that is now lost, or the play may simply be a development of 'fingers' (III.ii.150). Perhaps the obscurity of the jest is the reason for this cut.

155. *naught . . . gains*] proverbial (N319, 320): 'nothing venture, nothing win'.

164. *draught*] catch (of fish).

Clown. I grant this is no Friday, and I at this time no cater for the fish-market.

FOLLOWING IV.i.76

Clown. If all be common that the sea yields, why then is not that as much mine as thine?

Fisherman. By that law, when we bring our fish to the market, if everyone may freely choose where he likes and take where he list, we should have quickly empty dorsers and clean stalls, but light purses.

IV.i.121

I know still go together. [*To Ashburn*] Shows it well
In one that's of thy years and gravity,
That ought to be in life and government
To others an example, now to dote;
So near the grave, to walk before his door
With a young pair of strumpets at his tail,
Nay, make his honest and chaste wife no better
Than a madam mackerel!

FOLLOWING IV.i.162

Fisherman. Yes, sirrah, and this my master.
Clown. Then I have nothing at this time to do with thee.
Fisherman. Marry, a good motion. Farewell, and be hanged.
Clown. We are not so easily parted. [*To Ashburn*] Is this your man?

FOLLOWING IV.i.169

[*Ashburn.*] Say, what's the strife?
Clown. Marry, who first shall speak?
Fisherman. That's I.
Clown. I appeal, then, to the courtesy due to a stranger.
Fisherman. And I to the right belonging to a household servant.

179. an] *Bu*; and *MS.* 188. sp. pref.] *Bu; not in MS.* 192. household] *J*; howshou< *MS.*

---

168. *cater*] purchaser.
174. *dorsers*] baskets (carried on the back).
183. *madam mackerel*] bawd.

IV.i.365

. . . I cannot be. Now wherein is the rich more happy than the poor? I think, rather, less blessed, and that shall appear by this excellent good ballad, though set to a scurvy tune:

Let each man speak as he's possessed,
I hold the poor man's state most blessed,
For if long life contentment breeds,
In that the poor the rich exceeds.
The rich man's days are short, as spent
In pleasures and supposed content,
Whilst to us poor men, care and trouble
Makes every hour we waste seem double.
He that hath each day to his back
Change of gay suits, whilst we, alack,
Have but one coat, that coarse and old,
Yet it defends us from the cold
As warm, too, in an equal eye,
As they in all their purple dye.
'Mongst all their store they wear, we see,
But one at once, and so do we.
The rich that at his table feasts
With choice of dainties sundry guests
In all his plenty can but fill
One belly; so the poor can still
With cheese and onions; and disgest
As well with them as th' other's feast.
The peasant with his homespun lass
As many merry hours may pass
As courtiers with their satin girls
Though richly decked in gold and pearls,
And, though but plain, to purpose woo,
Nay, oft-times with less damage, too.

And yet for all this . . .

IV.ii.11

He's now where he's in commons. We have our parts
Here on this seat—nay, hold your head up, John,
Like a good boy—freely discharged ourselves
Both of suspect . . .

206. old,] *MS1b*; bare *MS1a*.

208. *equal*] impartial.
216. *disgest*] digest.
218. *homespun*] unsophisticated, as can be seen from her plain clothes.

IV.ii.62

. . . . . . benches. That done, to secure
A guilty life and prevent death with shame,
By the same steps return the way I came.

230. prevent] *MS1b possibly*; present *MS1a possibly, Br.*

229. *secure*] protect.

230. *prevent*] The line is heavily scored through in the manuscript, but it appears that Heywood first wrote 'present' in error, and then altered the long 's' to a 'v', before cancelling the whole line. Cf. IV.iv.3–4.

LINEATION
in *Q The Wise-woman of Hogsdon*, *Q The English Traveller* and *MS The Captives*

The Wise-woman of Hogsdon

(*a*) Verse lines printed as prose in Q (with source of first printing as verse, in Verity's Mermaid edition (*V*) or Leonard (*L*); otherwise this edition): I.i.1–4 (*V*); I.i.22–3; I.i.40–1; II.i.167–8; II.ii.44–51 (*V*); II.ii.55–6 (*V*); II.ii.145–48; II.ii.149–54 (*V*); III.i.148–9 (*V*); III.ii.21–3; III.II.29–33; III.III.7–9 (*V*); III.iii.169–70 (*V*); III.iii.174–5 (*V*); IV.i.1–4 (*V*); IV.i.16–22 (*V*); IV.i.29–30; IV.i.31–38 (*V*); IV.i.40–1; IV.i.49–50 (*V*); IV.i.97–8; IV.i.115–8; IV.i.121–2 (*L*); IV.i.136–7; IV.i.141–2; IV.i.197–9; IV.i.210–12 (*V*); IV.ii.9–10 (*V*); IV.ii.67–71; IV.ii.80–1; IV.ii.88–9; IV.iv.43–4; IV.iv.47–8; IV.v.7–8 (*V*); IV.v.81–2; IV.v.108–11; IV.v.123–6 (*V*); V.i.1–3 (*V*); V.i.6–9; V.i.11–20 (*V*); V.i.61–2 (*V*); V.i.72–3 (*V*); V.ii.5–6 (*V*); V.iii.4–8; V.v.1–2 (*V*); V.v.5–6 (*V*); V.vi.10–12; V.vi.22–5 (*V*); V.vi.38–9 (*V*); V.vi.60–1; V.vi.87–9; V.vi.96–9; V.vi.126–8; V.vi.130–1 (*V*); V.vi.145–7; V.vi.151–5; V.vi.163–4 (*V*); V.vi.174–6; V.vi.184–97; V.vi.199–201; V.vi.205–13.

(*b*) Prose lines printed as verse in Q;
II.ii.134–6 (*V*); II.ii.164–6 (*V*); IV.iv.13–14 (*V*); IV.iv.16–18 (*V*).

(*c*) Mislined verse in Q:
I.i.5–6 (pound, / And); I.i.23–7 (losers. / Have . . . finger, / Must . . . purse? / A); I.i.33–4 (dice. / I); I.i.50–1 (Trayes. / With . . . that? / Oh); I.i.74–5 (temper. / But); IV.i.209–11 (Lady / In . . . Chayne, / These); IV.ii.39–40 (friend / so); IV.ii.102–3 (him; / Hee's . . . too. / *Ioseph* . . . Sword. / This); IV.v.3–4 (say / Grace,); IV.v.100 (spurres. / Why); V.i.23–4 (ile / Warrant); V.i.54–5 (*Grace.* / Is . . . pray. / Of); V.ii.1–2 (come. / Presume . . . too. / Ile); V.iii.1–2 (ever / Since); V.vi.1–2 (looke / Into . . . company. / Harke,); V.vi.65–7 (for / I . . . whether / I . . . time, / More); V.vi.74–5 (would / Iustifie); V.vi.171–2 (become / A).

(*d*) Rhymed verse printed as long lines or as prose in Q and relineated in this edition:
III.i.64–5; III.i.67–8; III.i.121–2; IV.I.23–8; IV.i.51–72; IV.i.74–5; IV.i.94–5; IV.i.104–12; IV.i.122–3; IV.i.165–74; IV.v.21–4.

The English Traveller

(*a*) Verse lines printed as prose in *Q* (with source of first printing as verse):
I.ii.240–1 (*This ed.*); II.i.82–3 (*V*); II.i.246–7 (*Di*); II.i.265–6 (*Di*); II.ii.6–7 (*Di*); IV.vi.212–15 (*V*); IV.vi.218–20 (*This ed.*); IV.vi.247–9 (*This ed.*).

(*b*) Prose lines printed as verse in *Q*:
I.i.191–4 (*Di*); I.ii.131–3 (*Di*); II.i.103–5 (*Di*); II.i.172–3 (*V*); III.iii.147–8 (*V*); III.iii.156 (*V*); IV.ii.13–14 (*Di*); IV.ii.25–6 (*Di*); IV.iii.16 (*Di*); IV.vi.37–8 (*V*); IV.vi.208–9 (*Di*); IV.vi.301–3 (*Di*).

(*c*) Mislined verse in *Q*:
I.i.2–3 (the / Theoricke, . . . Practicke. / I); I.i.195–196 (clocke, / Hee); I.ii.48–9 (contented. / But . . . questioned. / Looke); I.ii.61–2 (Secrets. / Let . . . is. / So); I.ii.78–9 (Table. / Where . . . absent. / Nor); I.ii.80–2 (plenty. / Caviare, . . . Yes, / And); I.ii.90–2 (sir. / Yes, . . . going. / To); I.ii.217–20 (servants. / Shall . . . you? / Come . . . quarells. / 'Tis . . . possible. / Those); I.ii.226–8 (quaking. / Now . . . how? / Her); I.ii.256–7 (eare. / And . . . eye. / Ha.); II.i.92–7 (patience; / Wife, . . . one, / Graces . . . cold, / The . . . gaine / Some); II.i.100–1 (Harbour. / Tis . . . weaknesse / Incident); II.i.111–13 (it. / Master . . . Eare, / With); II.i.115–17 (one. / Wee . . . novell, / Speake, . . . Sir. / I); II.i.222–6 (Husband. / You . . . young; / And . . . renew'd; / So . . . pleas'd / I); II.i.283–85 (happens, / It . . . this. / By); II.ii.36–42 (Sir/ Why, . . . breath. / Where? . . . hand. / Upon . . . him? / I . . . eyes. / Oh . . . then? / Aske . . . yet / Had); II.ii.50–4 (Sea. / If . . . againe / Can . . . Inventions, / Braines, . . . all / Should); II.ii.70–1 (doo't, / That . . . fury. / I); II.ii.80–2 (them? / No . . . company, / And); II.ii.95–7 (else? / Onely . . . durance, / To); II.ii.121–4 (store. / See . . . Sir. / Then . . . things, / And); II.ii.151–2 (it? / How . . . noise? / You); II.ii.208–14 (me? / I . . . flie . . . too? / What . . . friends. / But Reignald. / Tush, . . . deserved, / Nor . . . gate. / To . . . spakest? / Was't); III.i.32–4 (Master. / Sir . . . walke. / What . . . Dalavill, / Will); III.i.86–8 (honest. / Howsoever . . . So. / Some . . . devis'd, / To); III.i.41–3 (promise. / Not . . . self: / If . . . false / To); III.i.175–7 (contenting. / I . . . further; / Say); III.i.193–5 (true. / For . . . can. / Yet . . . may; / And); III.i.214–18 (innocency, / Which . . . low, / Shall . . . you. / Well . . . on. / There's); III.i.230–40 (eye, Look . . . Further—/ / Enough; . . . perform'd / Assures . . . protestations. / Name it then. / Take . . . fame; Which . . . farre, / To . . . forward, / To . . . blessing. / As . . . charge. / I am satisfied.); III.ii.18–21 (murder? / No . . . it. / Impudent . . . Officer / Bring); III.ii.79–81 (morrow. / least . . . bestowed? / Safe); III.ii.83–5 (rest, / Your . . . Houses. / Land, . . . say? / A . . . Gardens. / Now); III.ii.99–101 (defraid. / It . . . word. / Now . . . Reignald, / For); III.ii.132–4 (purchase. / Councell'd . . . hence. / This . . . past, / All); III.iii.12–15 (Money. / That's . . . day. / 'Tis . . . vented: / What . . . Friend, / You); III.iii.43–5 (Girle? / Faith . . . so / Great); III.iii.51–60 (friend. / Come . . . prooue. / And . . . home? / Nay, . . . wine, / And . . . Boy, / Anon, Sir. / A . . . quickly. / Nay, . . . thee, / I . . . of / Thy . . . too. / Euer . . . too / In); III.iii.63–5 (wench? / Nay, . . . know. / Introath . . . Sir, / And); III.iii.89–94 (buried. / I . . . you, / But . . . Chamber-maid. / Play . . . Market-maid, /

And . . . businesse. / Well, . . . fool'd. / She . . . Prostitute? / Nay); IV.i.45–7 (example. / Willingly; . . . within, / And); IV.i.60–4 (could. / And . . . hau't. / 'Tis . . . it / Both . . . Maineprize? / Nay, . . . power. / Then . . . him; / I); IV.i.109–12 (about? / Euery . . . betternesse. / Tarrast . . . You? / All); IV.i.114–17 (cost me. / If . . . the / Money . . . ground, / That); IV.ii.37–9 (reputation. / How . . . questioned? / Oh . . . Sir, / Bad); IV.v.25–7 (Shoulder. / No . . . protest / Thy . . . all. / I); IV.vi.68 (cleere? / Murder); IV.vi.78–80 (havocke. / My . . . busines, / Resolve); IV.vi.98–9 (Reignald. / And . . . haunted? / Saue); IV.vi.101–3 (my / Neighbour . . . sure / More); IV.vi.112–15 (words / I . . . you, / And . . . tender, / I . . . willing, / As); IV.vi.147–53 (him; / Furnish . . . Fetters, / I . . . Prison. / Weele . . . you. / And I. / And all; / But . . . Reignald. / His); IV.vi.180–5 (is: / Nor . . . Him / on . . . conditions. / I . . . pleasant, / Knowing . . . euer / Were); IV.vi. 188–9 (was. / Now . . . too. / I); IV.vi.194–8 (him. / I . . . me. / Come . . . Reignald. / First . . . Merchandize / Bought); IV.vi.245–6 (Ladders. / Yes, . . . Ropes. / I'le); IV.vi.250 (Reignald, / This); IV.vi.283–7 (pardon. / All . . . soundly, / Yet . . . wanton, / Her, . . . quite; / So); V.i.52–5 (it. / But . . . expected, / come . . . Feast, / In); V.i.123 (showers, / I); V.i.127–9 (man? / To . . . faire; / Hath); V.i.164–6 (repentance. / Which . . . knees. / Tush, . . . Heaven, / Which); V.i.168–71 (selfe; / Wherein, . . . Love / deseru'd . . . stale / For); V.i.196–200 (happy. / What . . . lowd, / To . . . terrour / And affright? / See . . . expiring. / How? . . . sister? / Support).

(*d*) Stage directions placed between one and three lines early in *Q*: I.ii.129.1; I.ii.204.1; II.i.30.1; II.ii.63.1; II.ii.139.1; III.i.147.1; III.iii.14.1; III.iii.61.1; III.iii.114.1; IV.i.4.1; IV.i.59.1; IV.i.77.1; IV.ii.8.1; IV.iii.6.1; IV.iii.89.1; IV.vi.69.1; IV.vi.100.1; IV.vi.155.1; V.i.42.1; V.i.80.1.

The Captives

(*a*) Verse lines copied as prose in MS:
(1) I.iii.4–7, (2) 76–7, (3) 112–14, (4) III.ii.50–3, (5) 108–9, (6) IV.i.48–9, (7) 338–41, (8) 361–62, (9) V.iv.14–15, (10) V.v.74–5, (11) 333–4. Of these examples, numbers 1–4, 7 and 8 are the speeches of Godfrey discussed in the Note on the Texts. No. 6 is a rare case of the Clown speaking verse. The other four cases (5, 9–11) are simple copying errors.

(*b*) Mislined verse in MS:
I.i.178–9 (market, / marry syr / that . . . listninge. / those); III.i.68–9 (vipers, / patiens); IV.i.357–8 (compassion, / but . . . budgett, / godffreye).

PRESS-CORRECTIONS
in Q *The Wise-woman of Hogsdon* and Q *The English Traveller*

I have collated the copies belonging to the following libraries; those copies consulted on microfilm or in photocopy are marked with an asterisk.

WWH: British Library (4 copies), Bodleian (3), Dyce Library (V & A Museum), National Library of Scotland (2), Eton College Library, Folger (3), Library of Congress, Huntington (2), Illinois (Urbana)*, Newberry*, Pennsylvania*, Pforzheimer*, Texas*, Yale (3)*
ET: British Library (2), Bodleian (3), Dyce (2), National Library of Scotland (2), Abbotsford (Scott collection), Folger (2), Library of Congress (2), Huntington, Clark (Los Angeles), Chicago*, Illinois (Urbana)*, Newberry*, New York Public Library*, Pennsylvania*, Texas (2)*, Yale*

The following list is of undoubted press-corrections, and does not include the loosening of type following upon correction. Uncorrected readings are given first.

The Wise-woman of Hogsdon

Sheet A

A1 (t-p)	7.	*Delectare.*	*Delectare—*
	11.	*The Bible*	the *Bible*
A1v		Incomplete ornament	Fully impressed
A2	title	HOGSDEN.	HOGSDON.
A2v	I.i.47.	To thee,	To tho,
A3v,	A4 r.t.	*Hogsden.*	*Hogsdon.*
A4v	I.ii.12.	Save, thee.	Save thee.
	I.ii.13.	you are	y'are
	catchword on two lines		c.w. on one line

(A(o) is in four states: t.p. and A2v corrected first, then A4v in two stages of correction; A(i) is in two states.)

Sheet B

B2	I.ii.117.	yonr	your
B4	II.i.26.	weaknesse on	weaknesse of
	II.i.27.	Matron of	Matron on
	II.i.40.	*Faber.*	*Taber.*

B4v	II.i.68.	I shoule	I should

(Leonard's apparent variant on B3 is paper damage.)

Sheet C

C1v	II.i.128.	my	one
C2	II.i.161.	Bride; betimes	Bride betimes
C3v	II.ii.68.	Watch, hit	Watch, went and hit
	II.ii.69.	mee of	me of
C4	II.ii.95.	neither, Gentlemen:	neither: Gentlemen,

Sheet D

The only press variant is in the catchword on D4v (correct alignment of hyphen).

Sheet E

E2v	III.iii.93.	had done	have done
E3	III.iii.131.	Moneth, 'tis	Moneth, 'tis
	catchword	stop correct	c.w. stop out of alignment
E3v	III.iii.159.	me o lay	me to lay
	catchword	gua	c.w. guage
E4	III.iii.184.	Thisis	This is
	III.iii.197.	Mo rrow.	Morrow.
E4v	catchword lacking		c.w. Actus

(E(o) received two stages of correction: E4v first, then E2, allowing type to loosen on E3. The press was also stopped twice for E(i), first for corrections to text, then for the E3 catchword.)

Sheet F

F1	IV.i.0.1.	*Harrin gs field*	*Harringsfield*
	IV.i.i.	*Harrings fi eld*	*Harringsfield*
	IV.i.18.	wee tho ght	wee though
	IV.i.22.1	*Sencer disguised*	*Sencer, disguised*
F2v	IV.i.108.	treue	true
	IV.i.109.	madgick	magick
	IV.i.110.	him made	made him
	IV.i.118.	animus.	animus—
	IV.i.122.	*Sir Boniface.*	*Sir Bonif.*
	IV.i.122–3.	syr *Harry*you	syr *Harry* you
	IV.i.129.	ebrius;	ebrius.
	IV.i.131.	saith I	saith, I
	IV.i.131.	Hebrewe.	Hebrewe
	IV.i.133.	Hel, speake	He'l, speake
	IV.i.135.	but with, an	but with an
	IV.i.142.	victor.	victor:
	catchword	*Si*	c.w. *Sir*
F3	IV.i.147.	Ile make	I'le make
	IV.i.160.	daughter,	daughter
	IV.i.161.	tongue in	tongue, in
F4	IV.ii.4.	pacified, (last two letters misplaced)	pacified,

F4v	IV.ii.6.	*Lnce*	*Luce*
	IV.ii.10.	absence,	absence.
	IV.ii.18.	Gentleman:	Gentleman.

Sheet G

G1	IV.ii.41.	Whylookst	Why lookst
	IV.ii.43.	grace of *Gratious streete.*	*Grace* of *Gratious* street.
	IV.ii.45.	*Beshrowe*	Beshrow
	IV.ii.49.	*within*	within,
	IV.ii.50.	*echoing*	ecchoing
	IV.ii.53.	*untruth.*	untruth,
	IV.ii.55.2.	*aud attendants.*	*and attendants.*
	IV.ii.59.	you: *Luce*?	you: *Luce*?
	IV.ii.60.	*Grace* come	*Grace*, come

(The spacing at IV.ii.59 may have been intended in MS to represent a pause, so that the press correction here may obscure Heywood's intentions.)

G2v	IV.ii.127.	Gold.	Gold,
	IV.ii.128.	yet.	yet
	IV.iii.4.	looming womans, the fortune	Looming womans, the Fortune
	IV.iii.8.	be like	belike
	IV.iii.18.	in ile . . . Mistresse,	in, ile . . . Mistresse.
G3	IV.iv.15.	O mee	O mee!
	IV.iv.17.	his, make	his, make
G4v	IV.v.26.	Gr amercy	Gramercy
G4v	IV.v.27.	off, I	off I
	IV.v.36.	O Mr	O, Mr
	IV.v.45.	deere most	deere, most
	IV.v.46.	*these*	these
	IV.v.47.	contente.	contents.
	catchword	*Sence.*	c.w. *Sencer.*

Sheet I

I3	V.vi.150.	disguisd	disguis'd

(Sig. I1 has corrections of displaced type in lines 2 and 5, and I2 a similar correction in line 1; most copies with the corrected state of I(o) have I(i) uncorrected.)

The English Traveller

Sheet C

C1v	I.ii.161.		
	I.ii.163.	Fencer?	Fencer,
C4	II.i.66.	Well;	Well?
		Heeles; Tthen	Heeles; Then

Sheet F

F3	no catchword	c.w. Use

Sheet G

G2v	IV.i.12.	Gould	Gold

Sheet H

H2	IV.iii.120.	And and this	And this
H3	IV.v.21.	varlots	varlets

Sheet I

I3	IV.vi.240.	Stranger, Oh	Stranger; Oh